INTERMEDIATE BIBLICAL HEBREW GRAMMAR

RESOURCES FOR BIBLICAL STUDY

Editor
Marvin A. Sweeney, Old Testament/Hebrew Bible

Number 89

SBL PRESS

INTERMEDIATE BIBLICAL HEBREW GRAMMAR

A Student's Guide to Phonology and Morphology

Eric D. Reymond

SBL PRESS

SBL PRESS

Atlanta

Library of Congress Cataloging-in-Publication Data

Names: Reymond, Eric D., author.
Title: Intermediate biblical Hebrew grammar : a student's guide to phonology and morphology / by Eric D. Reymond.
Description: Atlanta : SBL Press, [2017] | Series: Resources for biblical study ; number 89 | Includes bibliographical references and index.
Identifiers: LCCN 2017037103 (print) | LCCN 2017037346 (ebook) | ISBN 9780884142492 (ebook) | ISBN 9781628371895 (pbk. : alk. paper) | ISBN 9780884142508 (hardcover : alk. paper)
Subjects: Hebrew language—Phonology. | Hebrew language—Morphology.
Classification: LCC PJ4576 (ebook) | LCC PJ4576 .R49 2017 (print) | DDC 492.45/9—dc23
LC record available at https://lccn.loc.gov/2017037103

Printed on acid-free paper.

To Robin, Lucy, and Oliver

ἀρχὴ γὰρ αὐτῆς ἡ ἀληθεστάτη παιδείας ἐπιθυμία
"The beginning of wisdom is open yearning for instruction" (Wis 6:17).

Contents

Acknowledgments

The initial draft of this book was written during a professional development leave that I was granted in the spring of 2015. It is in large part due to this leave that I have been able to complete this project in a relatively short time. The present book has its roots in handouts prepared for different classes I have taught here at Yale Divinity School, including a class in historical Hebrew grammar. I would like to thank the students in my classes for their help in spotting errors of different kinds and in suggesting alternative ways of presenting the material. Their suggestions have helped me make the information in the book easier to read and understand. The numerous symbols that I have used and my idiosyncratic transliteration of Hebrew has, no doubt, added to the burden of producing the book. Therefore, I wish also to thank the team at SBL for putting the book into a form that will make its material accessible, if not also easy to use. My colleagues here at YDS and beyond have also been of assistance in ways they perhaps did not perceive. I have learned much about Hebrew and its texts from my conversations with them, including with Joel Baden, Hindy Najman, Jean-Sébastien Rey, Jan Joosten, and Samuel Adams. My parents have been a constant source of encouragement for this work, as well as for all my other projects; they seemed sometimes more anxious than I to see the book completed. My wife and children deserve the ultimate thanks. Their contribution to this work was not only in their patient acceptance at my periodic absence but also in the genuine interest they expressed in the topic of the work itself and in its steady progress.

Abbreviations

Grammatical Abbreviations

1cp	first common plural
1cs	first common singular
2fp	second feminine plural
2fs	second feminine singular
2mp	second masculine plural
2ms	second masculine singular
3fp	third feminine plural
3fs	third feminine singular
3mp	third masculine plural
3ms	third masculine singular
abs.	absolute
acc.	accusative
adj(s).	adjective(s)
Aram.	Aramaic
cohort.	cohortative
const.	construct state
du.	dual
esp.	especially
fem.	feminine
fp	feminine plural
fs	feminine singular
gen.	genitive
impv.	imperative
inf(s).	infinitive(s)
intrans.	intransitive
l(l).	line(s)
masc.	masculine
mp	masculine plural

ms	masculine singular
nom.	nominative
pl.	plural
ptc(s).	participle(s)
sg.	singular
spec.	specifically
suf.	suffix
trans.	transitive

Other Abbreviations

AfAsL	*Afroasiatic Linguistics*
AfO	*Archive für Orientforschung*
AKM	Abhandlungen für die Kunde des Morgenlandes
ANEM	Ancient Near Eastern Monographs
ANESSupp	Ancient Near Eastern Studies Supplement Series
AOAT	Alter Orient und Altes Testament
AOS	American Oriental Series
BA	Biblical Aramaic
BDB	Brown, F., S. R. Driver, and C. A. Briggs. *Hebrew Lexicon of the Old Testament*. Oxford: Oxford University Press, 1906.
BH	Biblical Hebrew
BHS3	*Biblia Hebraica Stuttgartensia*. Edited by Elliger, K. and W. Rudolph. 3rd edition. Stuttgart: Deutsche Bibelgesellschaft, 1987.
BHT	Babylonian Hebrew (Pronunciation) Tradition
BibOr	Biblica et Orientalia
BSOAS	*Bulletin of the School of Oriental and African Studies*
BZAW	Beihefte zur Zeitschrift für die alttestamentliche Wissenschaft
C. Ap.	Josephus *Contra Apionem*
CEWAL	*Cambridge Encyclopedia of the World's Ancient Languages*. Edited by Roger D. Woodard. Cambridge: Cambridge University Press, 2004.
DCH	*The Dictionary of Classical Hebrew*. Edited by David J. A. Clines. 8 vols. Sheffield: Sheffield Academic, 1993–2007.

DJBA	Sokoloff, Michael. *A Dictionary of Jewish Babylonian Aramaic of the Talmudic and Geonic Periods*. Ramat Gan: Bar Ilan University Press, 2002.
DJD	Discoveries in the Judaean Desert
DJPA	Sokoloff, Michael. *A Dictionary of Jewish Palestinian Aramaic of the Byzantine Period*. 2nd ed. Ramat-Gan: Bar Ilan University Press, 2002.
DSS	Dead Sea Scrolls
EHLL	*Encyclopedia of Hebrew Language and Linguistics*. Edited by Geoffrey Khan. 4 vols. Leiden: Brill, 2013.
Ges^{18}	*Hebräisches und Aramäisches Handwörterbuch über das Alte Testament*. Edited by Wilhelm Gesenius et al. 18th ed. Berlin: Springer, 2012.
GKC	*Gesenius' Hebrew Grammar*. Edited by E. Kautzsch. Translated by A. E. Cowley. 2nd ed. Oxford: Oxford University Press, 1910.
HALOT	Koehler, Ludwig and Walter Baumgartner. *The Hebrew and Aramaic Lexicon of the Old Testament*. Translated by M. E. J. Richardson. 5 vols. Leiden: Brill, 1994–2000.
HAR	*Hebrew Annual Review*
HBH	*A Handbook of Biblical Hebrew*. Edited by W. Randall Garr and Steven E. Fassberg. 2 vols. Winona Lake, IN: Eisenbrauns, 2016.
HdO	Handbuch der Orientalistik
HGhS	Bauer, Hans and Pontus Leander. *Historische Grammatik der hebräischen Sprache des Alten Testamentes*. 2 vols. Halle: Niemeyer, 1922.
HSK	Handbücher zur Sprach- und Kommunikationswissenschaft
HSM	Harvard Semitic Monographs
HSS	Harvard Semitic Studies
IPA	International Phonetic Alphabet
JAOS	*Journal of the American Oriental Society*
JBL	*Journal of Biblical Literature*
JBS	Jerusalem Biblical Studies
JHS	*Journal of Hebrew Scriptures*
JNES	*Journal of Near Eastern Studies*
JNSL	*Journal of Northwest Semitic Languages*

Joüon	Joüon, Paul. *A Grammar of Biblical Hebrew*. Translated and revised by T. Muraoka. 2 vols. Rome: Pontifical Biblical Institute, 1993.
JPS	*Tanakh: The Holy Scriptures: The JPS Translation according to the Traditional Hebrew Text*
JSJ	*Journal for the Study of Judaism*
JSJSup	Journal for the Study of Judaism Supplement
JSPSup	Journal for the Study of the Pseudepigrapha Supplement Series
LBH	Late Biblical Hebrew
LSAWS	Linguistic Studies in Ancient West Semitic
LSJ	Liddell, H. G., R. Scott, and H. S. Jones. *A Greek-English Lexicon*. Revised edition. Oxford: Clarendon, 1968.
LXX	Septuagint
MT	Masoretic Text, specifically the Leningrad Codex, as represented in *BHS3*
NJB	New Jerusalem Bible
NRSV	New Revised Standard Version
NWS	Northwest Semitic
OED	*Oxford English Dictionary*. 2nd ed. Oxford: Oxford University Press, 1992.
Or	*Orientalia* NS
OrGand	Orientalia Gandensia
Orientalia	Orientalia: Papers of the Oriental Institute (Moscow)
OTWSA	*Oud Testamentiese Werkgemeenskap van Suid-Afrika, Pretoria*
pers. comm.	personal communication
PIASH	Proceedings of the Israel Academy of Sciences and Humanities
PLO	Porta Linguarum Orientalium
PNWS	Proto-Northwest Semitic
PS	Proto-Semitic
RBS	Resources for Biblical Study
RH	Rabbinic Hebrew
SLIH	*The Semitic Languages: An International Handbook*. Edited by Stefan Weninger, Geoffrey Khan, Michael P. Streck, and Janet C. E. Watson. HSK 36. Berlin: de Gruyter Mouton, 2011.
SP	Samaritan Pentateuch

SSLL	Studies in Semitic Languages and Linguistics
STDJ	Studies on the Texts of the Desert of Judah
TDOT	*Theological Dictionary of the Old Testament*. Edited by G. Johannes Botterweck and Helmer Ringgren. Translated by John T. Willis et al. 15 vols. Grand Rapids: Eerdmans, 1974–2006.
THT	Tiberian Hebrew (Pronunciation) Tradition
ThWQ	*Theologisches Wörterbuch zu den Qumrantexten*. Edited by H.-J. Fabry and U. Dahmen. Stuttgart: Kohlhammer, 2011–.
UF	*Ugarit-Forschungen*
VT	*Vetus Testamentum*
VTSup	Vetus Testamentum Supplement Series
WS	West Semitic
ZA	*Zeitschrift für Assyriologie*
ZAH	*Zeitschrift für die Althebraistik*
ZDMG	*Zeitschrift der Deutschen Morgenländischen Gesellschaft*

List of Tables

Preface
Transliteration, Etymological Bases, and Basic Terms

In the course of describing Biblical Hebrew (BH), I will often transliterate the relevant Hebrew word or phrase. In relation to the Tiberian Hebrew pronunciation tradition (THT), I will attempt to represent the word(s) according to their phonemes. A phoneme is a "unit of sound in a language … that can distinguish one word from another" (*OED*). The pair of sounds represented by the letters /l/ and /r/ are examples of two phonemes in English. The two sounds are similar (both are called liquid consonants), but English speakers hear them as meaningfully discrete sounds. This means that we can create and use individual words that differ in only this one feature. For example, we immediately recognize that "lace" and "race" are different words. Even if we did not understand the words already, we would assume that two words which differed only in this one consonant were distinct words with different meanings, as with the imaginary words "lupish" and "rupish." Some languages, by contrast, do not distinguish these liquid consonants as distinct phonemes. Japanese, for example, has a single liquid consonant phoneme, which is commonly realized somewhat like our /r/.[1] For this reason, pairs of distinct words like "lace" and "race" (or "lupish" and "rupish") would not typically appear in Japanese.

Each phoneme, however, can be articulated in a number of different ways, depending on various factors such as where it occurs in a word and the character of surrounding letters. In English, for instance, the exact pronunciation of the /l/ phoneme is different depending on the preceding vowel. To pronounce the /l/ in the word "fall," the tongue is low, toward the base of the mouth, whereas in the word "fell," it is considerably higher, in the middle of the mouth. Such distinct pronunciations of a single pho-

1. See, e.g., Laurence Labrune, *The Phonology of Japanese*, Phonology of the World's Languages (Oxford: Oxford University Press, 2012), 92–94.

neme are called allophones. The allophones are different realizations of a single phoneme.

Since in my transliteration of THT, I will indicate only phonemes, I will not distinguish between allophones in Hebrew, like spirantized and nonspirantized *begadkepat* letters. A *bet* with a *dagesh* will be transliterated exactly like a single *bet* without a *dagesh*: *b*. Nor will I attempt to discriminate between vowels accompanied by *matres* and those without *matres*. A *qamets* in the interior of a word will be represented in the same way as a word-final *qamets* with *mater he*: שָׁמְרָה *šåmrå* (< **šāmərā*) "she guarded." Furthermore, as this example indicates, when transliterating a word in the Masoretic Text (MT; i.e., Leningrad Codex B19a), I will make a distinction where relevant between the phonemes as they would have been perceived by the Tiberian Masoretes and the vowels and consonants of pre-Masoretic times. The transliteration of words from the era(s) preceding that of the Tiberian Masoretes will also avoid any indication of obvious allophones (like the *begadkepat* distinctions) or *matres*, though, it should be admitted, the knowledge of what specifically constituted a phoneme in this period is harder to determine. Because this earlier pre-Masoretic pronunciation is not explicitly indicated by the vowel symbols in the texts that we possess, such transliterations are preceded by an asterisk. An asterisk does not imply that a form is from Proto-Semitic (PS) or Proto-Northwest Semitic (PNWS), but simply that it is not explicitly reflected in the orthography of the Tiberian Masoretes. Moreover, not every word or example is reconstructed back to its PS/PNWS form. Such reconstruction is done only where relevant. Usually, where a given word's development is fully traced, the starting point is the hypothetical form of the word after PNWS and before the Canaanite evidenced in the Amarna correspondences (ca. 1350 BCE). In these cases, I will usually present the nouns/adjectives with the nominative case vowel (**-u*).

When I transliterate words as preserved in the MT, I will generally use the following system of transliteration: *hireq* and *hireq yod* = *i*, *sere* and *sere yod* = *e*, *segol* = *ɛ*, *patakh* = *a*, *qamets* = *å*, *holem* = *o*, *qibbuts* and *shureq* = *u*. *Shewa* is not transliterated because it was not recognized as a phoneme; also, I will not transliterate epenthetic vowels, like the furtive *patakh* or the short vowel (e.g., /ɛ/ or /a/) in the second syllable of absolute singular nouns like מֶלֶךְ (= *mɛlk*) "king."[2] One will also notice that I do not dis-

2. See Geoffrey Khan, "Syllable Structure: Biblical Hebrew," *EHLL* 3:670–73.

tinguish between long and short vowels.[3] In addition, I will represent the letter *śin* (שׂ) as /s/ in transliterations of THT. This system of transliteration, it should be noted, does not exactly correspond to the pronunciation of THT, which was a good deal more complex.

Overall, the description of the language that follows in this book pertains to a version of Hebrew that precedes the time of the Tiberian Masoretes. This is the era (very roughly the Second Temple era) when many of the features we are familiar with as "Biblical Hebrew" (e.g., the spirantization of *begadkepat* consonants; merging of /ś/ and /s/; compensatory lengthening) likely developed. Usually, but not always, a word in transliteration that precedes the same word in Hebrew letters (often in parentheses) is indicating the form from the Second Temple era. The version of Hebrew described here is an ancestor of the Tiberian Masoretic pronunciation and vocalization, but not identical with it. Due to this lineage, there is often a correlation between the symbols of the Tiberian vocalization system and the vowels of this pre-Masoretic version of Hebrew, such that one will frequently observe the following correspondences: *hireq* = *i*, *hireq yod* = *ī*, *sere* = *e* or *ē*, *shewa* = *ə* or zero (i.e., no vowel), *segol* = *ɛ* or *e*, *patakh* = *a*, *qamets* = *ā* or *o*, *holem* = *o* or *ō*, *qibbuts* = *u* or *ū*, and *shuruq* = *ū*. Although it is counterintuitive, it is only the latter set of correspondences that coincide with the typical transliteration of BH. That is, the Hebrew of the Bible is typically transliterated (and pronounced) in a way that does not explicitly reflect the pronunciation implied by the vowel symbols. For this pre-Masoretic version of Hebrew (from the Second Temple era), I will still transliterate *śin* (שׂ) as /s/ since already by the middle of the first millennium BCE the phoneme /ś/ had begun to be pronounced as /s/. Nevertheless, when indicating forms of a given word from before 500 BCE I will indicate the phoneme as /ś/.

Since the vocalization of the Masoretes so regularly and neatly corresponds to the Hebrew of this era (i.e., the Second Temple era), it is not necessary to transliterate every word from the Masoretic Hebrew spelling into a romanized version. Only in the discussion of the vowels (in ch. 3) is it necessary to transliterate all the words, in order to clearly distinguish Masoretic from pre-Masoretic pronunciations. Thus, in that chapter the

---

3. Vowel length was not regularly used to distinguish words in THT. See Geoffrey Khan, "Tiberian Pronunciation Tradition of Biblical Hebrew," *ZAH* 9 (1996): 14–15; he writes: "Meaningful contrasts between words were not usually made by differences in vowel length alone" (14).

features discussed are always illustrated with transliterated versions of the words, with the Masoretic Hebrew spellings in parentheses. If nothing else, this should reinforce the idea that the Masoretic pointing/vocalization represents only one stage in a very long linguistic development.

The reconstruction of the history of any dead language is fraught with uncertainties. The reconstructions of particular Hebrew words in the various stages before they reached their form in the MT are quite hypothetical. I have tried to adhere to generally accepted ideas, but, due to the nature of the evidence, much remains uncertain. This is particularly true in relation to the history of the vowels and their development.

In addition, because the present work seeks to introduce students to the historical study of Biblical Hebrew, especially as a means of providing greater access to ancient Hebrew literature, I have generally avoided documenting all previous scholarship on the various phenomena described (including all competing interpretations). Instead, I have usually opted to follow the most recent conclusions by scholars as presented especially in the *Encyclopedia of the Hebrew Language and Linguistics*, where readers can find further discussion as well as references to more in-depth and detailed studies. The chronological sequence of linguistic developments presented especially in chapter 3 should be viewed as particularly tentative.

In cases where I am entirely unsure what vowel to reconstruct for a given word in a pre-Masoretic era, I use *V* to represent simply "vowel." The symbols < and > indicate linguistic developments and derivations, respectively. They function, in essence, like arrows. The notation "x > y" indicates that x became y; conversely, "y < x" indicates that y derives from x.

In describing the morphology of BH, I will use the standard transliteration of the root **qtl* in its earliest form. The root is realized in BH with a *tet*, קטל "to kill"; this *tet* is a later development of the root. The earlier (nonemphatic) /t/ was pronounced as *tet* (/*ṭ*/) due to the influence of the preceding emphatic *q*. This root, **qtl*, will be used to indicate the etymological bases of nouns and verbs, which reflect the early forms of nouns and verbs. In these cases, the form will be preceded by an asterisk (e.g., **qatl*).

When I refer to a word's "stem," I refer to that part of a word that remains consistent throughout its inflection. For example, the word דָּבָר "word, matter" is inflected with many suffixal components, including suffixal morphemes like *-*īm* (to make the plural form דְּבָרִים) and the set of possessive pronouns like *-*ō* (to make the expression דְּבָרוֹ "his word"). The stem of דְּבָרִים and דְּבָרוֹ is דבר. The stem vowels of both the plural form and the singular form with the third-person masculine singular suffix are *ə-ā (represented with the symbols *shewa-qamets* in THT). For the verbal form יִכְתְּבוּ "they will write," the stem is כתב and the vowel of the stem is simply *ə, while for הִגַּדְתָּ "you told," the stem is הגד and the vowels of the stem are *i-a*. The verbal categories *qal*, *piel*, *hiphil*, and so on are referred to as conjugations.

It is assumed that students know what the construct state is. This is not the only state for a noun, however. A noun that is not in the construct state and is not accompanied by a suffixed pronoun is said to be in the absolute state. This is essentially the form of the word found in a dictionary entry.

The word "pause" refers to a place in a verse where a person reading or reciting would extend the pronunciation of a word. This typically results in a longer form of the word, one in which the vowels are often not reduced or elided and sometimes where the vowels are lengthened. A word that appears in such a place is said to be "in pause" or to be a "pausal form." Pause usually is marked by the *atnach* symbol, ֑ (in the middle of the verse), the *silluq* symbol, ֽ (at the end of a verse) and sometimes by the *zaqef* symbol, ֔ (at the quarter point and three-quarter point of the verse). A word that is not in pause, that is most of the words of a verse, is said to be "in context" or to be a "contextual form." These forms often reflect vowel reduction and/or elision of vowels. All words are either pausal or contextual.

We will refer to open and closed syllables. An open syllable has the sequence consonant + vowel; a closed syllable has the sequence consonant + vowel + consonant. We will also refer to the tonic syllable, that is, the syllable that bears the tone, accent, or stress.[4] This will also be called the accented syllable or the stressed syllable. The syllable that precedes the tonic syllable is the pretonic syllable. The syllable that precedes the pretonic is the propretonic syllable. In פָּרָשִׁים "horse riders," the last syllable, -שִׁים, is the tonic syllable; it is also a closed syllable. The preceding consonant and vowel, -רָ-, is the pretonic syllable; it is an open syllable. The initial -פָּ is the propretonic syllable; it is also an open syllable.

It is also helpful to identify here four types of irregular nouns and their salient characteristics: geminate nouns (e.g., עַם "people"), segolate nouns

4. Although tone, accent, stress can refer to different linguistic phenomena, they are used here synonymously.

(e.g., מֶ֫לֶךְ "king"), a subcategory of which are middle-weak nouns with a diphthong (e.g., זַ֫יִת "olive"), and etymological III-*vav/yod* nouns, also commonly called III-*he* nouns (e.g., חֹזֶה "seer"). Geminate nouns are those that have a doubled consonant as part of their base, something revealed whenever a pronominal suffix or suffixal morpheme is attached to their stem: עַם "people" and עַמִּים "peoples"; חֵץ "arrow" and חִצִּים "arrows"; חֹק "statute" and חֻקִּים "statutes." The gemination is explicit in the nouns with the feminine morpheme: חֻקָּה "statute." Segolate nouns are those that have three different root consonants (i.e., no geminated root consonants) and that, in their historical singular form, had a single vowel (**qatl*, **qitl*, **qutl*). With the exception of some III-*vav/yod* segolates, the masculine segolate nouns are all accented on their first syllables in the absolute (e.g., מֶ֫לֶךְ "king," סֵ֫פֶר "book," and קֹ֫דֶשׁ "holy thing"), thus distinguishing them from most other nouns, which are accented on their last syllable (e.g., דָּבָר "word"). The etymological base vowel of the segolates (**qatl*, **qitl*, **qutl*) is typically revealed in forms bearing a pronominal suffix: מַלְכִּי "my king," סִפְרִי "my book," קָדְשִׁי "my holy thing." Feminine segolate nouns can be identified by their initial syllable, which is a closed syllable that begins with a root consonant (e.g., מַלְכָּה "queen," where the initial *mem* is a root consonant and the first syllable is *mal-*). Almost universally, the plural forms of the absolute segolate nouns exhibit the sequence of **ə-ā* in their stem (realized in THT spelling as *shewa-qamets*): מְלָכִים "kings" and מְלָכוֹת "queens." Middle-weak nouns with a diphthong lose the diphthong in construct or with a pronominal suffix or suffixal morpheme: זַ֫יִת "olive" and זֵיתִים "olives"; מָ֫וֶת "death" and מוֹתִי "my death." Etymological III-*vav/yod* nouns exhibit an */e/ (> *segol* in THT) as a final vowel in the masculine absolute, קָצֶה "end," but an */ā/ (> *qamets* in THT) in the feminine absolute, קָצָה "end." The final */e/ and *he mater* (in the masculine) are absent with a pronominal suffix or suffixal morpheme: קָצֵ֫הוּ "his end."

As for verbal forms, the label *qåṭal* refers to what is often referred to as the suffix-conjugation or perfect; *yiqṭol* refers to the prefix-conjugation or imperfect; *wayyiqṭol* to the *vav*-consecutive imperfect and *wəqåṭal* to the *vav*-consecutive perfect. The jussive/preterite verb form is referred to as the short-*yiqṭol*. Other verbal forms are referred to by their traditional labels (imperative, cohortative, infinitive construct, infinitive absolute, participle, and passive participle).

The following book presumes a certain familiarity with Biblical Hebrew. In particular, it presumes some knowledge of how the Hebrew noun and verb inflect. Since students coming into an intermediate or advanced Hebrew class often have different backgrounds, it will be useful for some students to review the basics of Hebrew morphology. In the appendix, I have gathered a number of different guidelines that aid in producing the basic nominal and verbal forms.

1
Introduction

1.1. What Is Biblical Hebrew?

When we speak about Biblical Hebrew what do we mean? Of course, we refer to the language of the Hebrew Bible/Old Testament (HB/OT). But behind this common label hides an often unacknowledged fact: the language we learn in "Biblical Hebrew" class is not really the language known to the Bible's writers and early readers.[1] In relation to phonology, we often learn the pronunciation of the consonants and vowels that is current in modern Israel today. When we learn the forms of certain words, we learn how some speakers and readers in the first millennium CE read and spoke Hebrew.

For example, when we speak of the pronunciation of *ḥet* as equivalent to the *ch* in the North American English pronunciation of "Chanukkah" or in the Scottish pronunciation of "loch," we reflect of course a pronunciation for the letter typical of modern, Israeli Hebrew. This pronunciation, contrary to what one might assume, developed at the earliest in Europe in the early second millennium CE.[2] Needless to say, this is well after the HB/OT had been written. In a similar manner, when we learn that the word for "king" was pronounced *mɛlɛk* (IPA [ˈmɛlɛχ]), with the accent on the first of two syllables, we are learning the form of the word that perhaps became part of the literary register of "Biblical Hebrew" only in the first

1. This, of course, is not a new observation; Alexander Sperber made this point many years ago in his *A Historical Grammar of Biblical Hebrew: A Presentation of Problems with Suggestions to Their Solutions* (Leiden: Brill, 1966), 17, though his analysis of how the contemporary articulation of the language differs from that of antiquity is not followed in the present work.

2. See Ilan Eldar, "Ashkenazi Pronunciation Tradition: Medieval," *EHLL* 1:188; Nimrod Shatil, "Guttural Consonants: Modern Hebrew," *EHLL* 2:169, 171.

millennium CE. Even then, speakers likely did not conceive of such words as having two syllables, in the same way that modern students do not consider a word with furtive *patakh* (e.g., רוּחַ "spirit") to have two syllables.[3]

Curiously and perhaps counterintuitively, we do not even learn precisely the pronunciation of the vowels known to the scribes and scholars who innovated the vowel marks that lie beneath (and sometimes above) the consonants. For example, when we speak of the twofold pronunciation of *qamets* as either "long /ā/" or "short /o/" we reflect the modern pronunciation, which derives from Sephardic tradition.[4] Although this basically reflects a pronunciation of BH current at the turn of the eras, it does not reflect the manner in which the Masoretic scribes pronounced Hebrew.[5] When the Masoretic scribes used the *qamets* symbol, it marked what was for them, in their oral tradition, not two vowels, but a single vowel: /å/, the "aw" in North American English "paw" (i.e., IPA [ɔ]).[6]

As I hope will be obvious, learning about the language in the time that it was used to write and copy the Bible (and also about the language's development) has many benefits for the student of the Hebrew scriptures. In the first place, it allows one to get closer to the text, allowing readers to perceive more clearly the sound and rhythm of the biblical language (both in its ancient and medieval realizations). This can be both inspirational as well as instructive. In some cases, perceiving the earlier pronunciation(s) of the language can help explain apparent ambiguities in the lexicon. For example, the word חָפַר in the *qal* means "to dig, search for" and the word חָפֵר in the *qal* means "to be ashamed." Although the verbs appear identical in many of their forms (e.g., חָפְרוּ "they dug" Gen 26:18 and חָפְרוּ "they were ashamed" Ps 71:24; יַחְפְּרוּ "they will search" Deut 1:22 and יַחְפְּרוּ "they will be ashamed" Ps 40:15), it is likely that the two words were distinguished in their pronunciation during most of the first millennium BCE. The first root ("to dig, search") may have been real-

---

3. See, e.g., Choon-Leong Seow, *A Grammar for Biblical Hebrew*, rev. ed. (Nashville: Abingdon, 1995), 13.

4. Joshua Blau, *Phonology and Morphology of Biblical Hebrew*, LSAWS 2 (Winona Lake, IN: Eisenbrauns, 2010), 108–9.

5. See "*Qamets* in the Tiberian Hebrew Tradition" in ch. 3 §16.

6. The shift in quality from what was previously /ā/ to /å/ (= [ɔ]) was simultaneous with the shift of short /o/ or /u/ to /å/ (= [ɔ]). The exact pronunciation of the vowel in terms of its length is much more complicated; see Khan, "Tiberian Pronunciation Tradition," 4.

ized with a lighter, less guttural sound than the second ("to be ashamed"): **ḥāpərū* versus **ḫāpərū*.[7]

In addition, knowledge of the history of Hebrew helps explain certain pairs of Hebrew roots, like נטר/נצר both of which seem to derive from a PS/PNWS root *nṭr* "to guard." At the least, knowing the link between such roots can aid in the acquisition of vocabulary. For example, it seems helpful to link in one's mind the more common (and hopefully therefore more easily remembered) verb נצר "to guard" with the rarer נטר "to guard" (which appears with this simple sense at least three times in the Song of Songs, and with the nuance "to preserve anger" in another five passages).[8] Knowing the link between the two roots also helps explain the etymology of the noun מַטָּרָה "guard, target" (which often occurs in the expression חֲצַר הַמַּטָּרָה "courtyard of the guard," i.e., prison).

Pairs of antonyms with similar sounds can also be explained by means of historical phonological developments in the language, as with סֶ֫כֶל = *sɛkl* < **sakl* "folly" (Qoh 10:6) versus שֶׂ֫כֶל = *sɛkl* < **śikl* "prudence" (1 Sam 25:3) and the pair סוֹרֵר < **sōrēr* "who are stubborn" (Isa 65:2) versus שֹׂרֵר < **sōrēr* < **śōrēr* "one who rules" (Esth 1:22). Although sharing a common pronunciation in THT, these pairs of words were earlier distinguished. Such an explanation may also help the student to remember the sense of such pairs. Even if one already knows the vocabulary items individually, it is useful to set them side-by-side and consider them together.

Recognizing commonly occurring variations among roots can help explain other incongruities in the lexicon as well as facilitate sight reading. For example, being alert to the fact that sometimes the same basic root or verb will appear with different sibilants (e.g., *tsade* and *zayin*) makes reading Ps 68:4–5 all the easier (יַעַלְצוּ "they will rejoice" [v. 4] ... וְעִלְזוּ "rejoice!" [v. 5]). Being aware of the possibility of byforms between certain weak root classes (e.g., II-*vav*/*yod* and I-*vav*/*yod*) can also sometimes

---

7. See below for an explanation of the difference between /ḥ/ and /ḫ/. Similarly, for the first half of the first millennium BCE (if not for a period after), the absence of spirantized allophones for the *begadkepat* letters would mean that words like *nimšaḥ* "he is anointed" (1 Chr 14:8) would be distinct from **nimšak* "he is postponed" (cf. תִּמָּשֵׁךְ Ezek 12:25).

8. Although נטר in the sense "to preserve anger" can be explained as derived from another root entirely, it seems likelier that this is simply a nuance of the verb נטר; one can compare, e.g., the use of שמר "to guard" in a similar sense, parallel with נטר, in Jer 3:5, as well as alone in Amos 1:11.

help one quickly identify a possible meaning of a word, such as for וַתְּנִיקֵהוּ (from נוק or ניק; Exod 2:9), especially where the context is clear (as in Exod 2:9, which contains the phrase וְהֵינִקִהוּ "and nurse it!" from the more common ינק). The phrase וַתְּנִיקֵהוּ is translated "she nursed it."

Cognizance of the phonology of ancient Hebrew can help explain certain translations, if not provide the grounds for new interpretations. Note, for instance, the translation of עָרֶךָ (in 1 Sam 28:16) "your adversary" in JPS and "your enemy" in NJB, NRSV. The word, however, looks like a defective spelling of the phrase "your cities," that is, a spelling without the *yod mater* (עָרֶיךָ*). The dictionaries (like *HALOT*, Ges[18]) suggest that עָרֶךָ is derived from the Aramaic equivalent to Hebrew צַר. Evaluating this suggestion depends (at least partially) on understanding the relationship between Aramaic ע and Hebrew צ. Do other words exhibit this correspondence? If so, how frequently do such correspondences occur in the lexicon of Biblical Hebrew?

Learning more about the morphology of Hebrew in the era of the Bible's authors is also helpful. Such knowledge makes the inflection of words more comprehensible and, thus, easier to remember. If a student learns that through the first millennium BCE the word for "king" was most likely pronounced something like **malk* and not "*mɛlɛk*," the forms of the word with pronominal suffix are more comprehensible: מַלְכִּי < **malkī* "my king," מַלְכָּהּ < **malkāh* "her king," מַלְכֵּנוּ < **malkēnū* "our king." In addition, understanding that nouns as seemingly disparate as קֹדֶשׁ "holiness," בְּאֹשׁ "stench," and עֳנִי "poverty" all derive from the **qutl* base helps us predict, for example, their consistent form with suffixes: for example, קָדְשׁוֹ < **qodšō* < **qudšahu* (Isa 52:10), בָּאְשׁוֹ < **boʾšō* < **buʾšahu* (Joel 2:20), עָנְיוֹ < **ʿonyō* < **ʿunyahu* (Job 36:15).

The following book is intended for the intermediate or advanced student who wishes to learn more about the history of the Hebrew language, specifically its phonology and morphology. But, not all historical aspects of the language are treated. I concentrate most on those aspects that will encourage a student to better remember the words and their inflection. Students should not expect to learn every detail in the book; it is most important to learn the general principles. The specific examples that can be memorized are outlined at the end of each chapter.

In addition, this book intends to provide students with a "full" picture of the language's morphology by providing tables of the inflection of individual words for most classes of nouns/adjectives as well as tables that set similar verbal inflections side by side. The nouns/adjectives are classified primarily according to their historical bases which usually reflect common manners of inflection. These tables can also be used by the student as an easy resource in vocalizing unpointed Hebrew texts. Ultimately, it is hoped that the study of the book will provide the student greater access to the texts of the Bible and to other early Hebrew writings.

1.2. Varieties of Ancient Hebrew

Before moving on to studying the sounds and forms of Biblical Hebrew, we should pause and consider the varieties of the Hebrew language in antiquity. In the first half of the first millennium BCE (1000–500 BCE), one can imagine a variety of dialects and subdialects of Hebrew spread across the southern Levant. Ultimately, these dialects, in contact with Phoenician to the north and Aramaic to the east, would have exhibited different traits, partially dependent on their proximity to these other languages.[9] The northern varieties of Hebrew, as attested in inscriptional material, do, in fact, seem to attest certain features common to Phoenician, but distinct from the Hebrew of the southern region, that is, Judah. For example, the word "wine" is found in ostraca from Samaria written *yn* in the absolute state, reflecting presumably a resolved diphthong, *yēn*, while the same word is found in Judean texts spelled with a medial *yod*, presuming the preservation of the diphthong, *yyn* = **yayn*.[10] Scholars, especially Gary A. Rendsburg, have found traces of similar features in portions of the Bible.[11] The dialect of the Balaam or Deir ʿAlla inscription, on the other hand, evidences traits that are similar to Hebrew, though it mainly contains Aramaic-like features, reflecting in one way or another its presumed place of composition (and discovery): Transjordan (i.e., just east of the Jordan River, close to Aram-Damascus).[12] It is no wonder, therefore, that

9. On the dialect continuum of Syria-Palestine, see W. Randall Garr, *Dialect Geography of Syria-Palestine, 1000–586 B.C.E.* (Philadelphia: University of Pennsylvania, 1985), 205–40.

10. See ibid., 38–39, and below "Triphthongs and Diphthongs," §3.12.

11. See Gary A. Rendsburg, "A Comprehensive Guide to Israelian Hebrew," *Or* 38 (2003): 5–35 and the references cited there.

12. See Holger Gzella, "Deir ʿAllā," *EHLL* 1:691–93. The inscription's mixture of traits may reflect an archaic, rural dialect; the dialect geography between the Canaanite west and Aramaic east; the shift in political dominance from Israel to Damascus. Note also Garr, *Dialect Geography*, 223–24; John Huehnergard, "Remarks on the Classification of the Northwest Semitic Languages," in *The Balaam Text from Deir ʿAlla Re-*

within the Bible itself we find numerous small differences between books, sources, and authors that are commonly dated to the first half of the first millennium BCE.

In addition to the different dialects reflective of geographic location, different varieties of the literary language are perceptible within the Bible. The Hebrew of the biblical corpus itself is typically divided into four different epochs: Archaic Biblical Hebrew, Standard Biblical Hebrew, Transitional Biblical Hebrew, and Late Biblical Hebrew.[13] The first three of these are commonly located between the years 1200–500 BCE. Standard Biblical Hebrew represents the language of most books of the Bible. Archaic Biblical Hebrew is exemplified in the the Song of Deborah (Judg 5), which contains much material that is typically considered both extremely old as well as reflective of northern Hebrew (e.g., some *qåṭal* 2fs [suffix-conjugation] verb forms end with *-*tī* [as in Aramaic]: קַ֫מְתִּי "you [Deborah] arose" Judg 5:7).[14] Transitional Biblical Hebrew is found in works that were composed close to or during the exile, such as Jeremiah.[15] Late Biblical Hebrew is found in books such as Daniel and Ezra, and is exemplified by numerous linguistic shifts that have parallels in the Dead Sea Scrolls and in rabbinic literature.[16]

Still, the vocalization of the text as we have it in the MT has likely been made uniform to a degree that largely masks most dialectical and many chronological differences.[17] So, for example, the archaic/northern/

---

evaluated: Proceedings of the International Symposium Held at Leiden, 21–24 August 1989, ed. J. Hoftijzer and G. van der Kooij (Leiden: Brill, 1991), 282–93; and Naʿama Pat-El and Aren Wilson-Wright, "Deir ʿAllā as a Canaanite Dialect: A Vindication of Hackett," in *Epigraphy, Philology, and the Hebrew Bible: Methodological Perspectives on Philological and Comparative Study of the Hebrew Bible in Honor of Jo Ann Hackett*, ed. Jeremy M. Hutton and Aaron D. Rubin, ANEM 12 (Atlanta: SBL Press, 2015), 13–23.

13. On the periodization of Biblical Hebrew and the difficulty of diachronic analysis, see Aaron Hornkohl, "Biblical Hebrew: Periodization," *EHLL* 1:315–25. Specific articles pertain to each of these varieties of the literary language.

14. Instead of קַמְתְּ. See Hornkohl, "Biblical Hebrew: Periodization," 1:318. See also Agustinus Gianto, "Archaic Biblical Hebrew," *HBH* 1:19–29; Alice Mandell, "Biblical Hebrew, Archaic," *EHLL* 1:325–29.

15. Aaron D. Hornkohl, "Transitional Biblical Hebrew," *HBH* 1:31–42; Hornkohl, *Ancient Hebrew Periodization and the Language of the Book of Jeremiah*, SSLL 74 (Leiden: Brill, 2014).

16. See, e.g., Avi Hurvitz, "Biblical Hebrew, Late," *EHLL* 1:329–38; Matthew Morgenstern, "Late Biblical Hebrew," *HBH* 1:43–54.

17. See Hornkohl, *Ancient Hebrew Periodization*, 19–20.

Aramaic-like *qåṭal* second feminine singular ending *-*tī* found vocalized in Judg 5:7 seems also to be reflected in the consonantal text of other parts of the Bible, but frequently not in the vocalization (e.g., וְיָרַדְתִּי "go down!" Ruth 3:3 and הָלָכְתִּי "you went" Jer 31:21).[18] In addition, even the consonantal text seems not to have been immune from alteration. It is likely that the spelling of words was also made uniform at a certain time, perhaps in the exilic era or just after.[19] Notice, for example, that the third masculine singular suffix on most nouns is almost uniformly marked with a *vav mater* in the MT, though in epigraphic sources from preexilic times, the same suffix is almost uniformly written with a *heh mater*. The *heh mater* as marker of the third masculine singular suffix becomes regular in epigraphic sources only in the postexilic era. This implies, of course, an updating of the orthography of biblical texts in the exilic or postexilic era.

In the second half of the first millennium BCE (ca. 500–1 BCE), in addition to LBH, one finds evidence of still other varieties of the language.[20] The Hebrew of the DSS evidences (in certain texts) traits that are distinct from any other dialect of Hebrew, while still maintaining a close proximity in other ways to earlier (Biblical) Hebrew.[21] Many of these texts were presumably written and certainly were copied in circa 200–1 BCE. Other loosely contemporary dialects were also written. The Hebrew evidenced in early rabbinic writings such as the Mishnah is foreshadowed in a few DSS (e.g., 4QMMT and 3Q15 [the Copper Scroll]). Later Judean Desert texts (e.g., the Bar Kochba texts from the 100s CE) exhibit a slightly different version of Hebrew.[22] In addition, Samaritan Hebrew was likely a distinct dialect (based on various textual, social, and political factors),

18. See GKC §44h.

19. See ibid., 72–73.

20. See Gary A. Rendsburg, "Biblical Hebrew: Dialects and Linguistic Variation," *EHLL* 1:338–41; Geoffrey Khan, "Biblical Hebrew: Linguistic Background of the Masoretic Text," *EHLL* 1:304–15; Khan, "Biblical Hebrew: Pronunciation Traditions," *EHLL* 1:341–52.

21. See, e.g., Elisha Qimron, *Hebrew of the Dead Sea Scrolls*, HSS 29 (Atlanta: Scholars Press, 1986); Eric D. Reymond, *Qumran Hebrew: An Overview of Orthography, Phonology, and Morphology*, RBS 76 (Atlanta: Society of Biblical Literature, 2014); Steven E. Fassberg, "Dead Sea Scrolls: Linguistic Features," *EHLL* 1:663–69; Jan Joosten, "The Hebrew of the Dead Sea Scrolls," *HBH* 1:83–97.

22. See Uri Mor, *Judean Hebrew: The Language of the Hebrew Documents from Judea between the First and Second Revolts* (Jerusalem: Academy of the Hebrew Language, 2016) (in Hebrew); also Mor, "Bar Kokhba Documents," *EHLL* 1:254–58.

though its details only become clear from evidence recorded in the early twentieth century CE (specifically the oral reading tradition of the Samaritan Pentateuch).[23] Nevertheless, this version of Biblical Hebrew seems to reflect traits from a much earlier era, as demonstrated by the second feminine singular *qåṭal* (suffix-conjugation) verb forms regularly ending with *-*ti*, as in the paradigmatic verb פקדת *fåqadti*.[24]

During the first millennium CE, in addition to the varieties of Rabbinic Hebrew, there were preserved different pronunciation traditions of Biblical Hebrew, including ones from the regions of Tiberias, Palestine, and Babylon.[25] The latter two are primarily known to us through their unique pointing and vocalization systems (the Palestinian and Babylonian) which reveal a different articulation of the vowels from that known to us from the Tiberian Masoretic system.[26]

Furthermore, for all times and places, we must recognize that the manner in which individuals read and spoke varied by context. An individual in a ritual context would speak in a manner very different from how he or she would speak in the context of discussing the weather with a friend. Similarly, that same individual would speak of the weather in one way, but probably write about it in yet another. Due to such variables, words were likely articulated in subtly different ways and sometimes these were reflected in the orthography while in other cases they were not.

---

23. Moshe Florentin, "Samaritan Hebrew: Biblical," *EHLL* 3:445–52; Florentin, "Samaritan Tradition," *HBH* 1:117–32.

24. Ze'ev Ben-Ḥayyim, *A Grammar of Samaritan Hebrew: Based on the Recitation of the Law in Comparison with the Tiberian and Other Jewish Traditions* (Jerusalem: Magnes; Winona Lake, IN: Eisenbrauns, 2000), 108. Ben-Ḥayyim notes that, although this trait might have been preserved due to Aramaic influence, it likely originates in Hebrew (103–4).

25. See Khan, "Biblical Hebrew: Pronunciation Traditions," 1:341–52; Khan, "Tiberian Reading Tradition," *EHLL* 3:769–78; Yosef Ofer, "The Tiberian Tradition of Reading the Bible and the Masoretic System," *HBH* 1:187–202; Shai Heijmans, "Babylonian Tradition," *HBH* 1:133–45; Joseph Yahalom, "Palestinian Tradition," *HBH* 1:161–73.

26. Note too the Tiberian-Palestinian tradition (see Holger Gzella, "Tiberian-Palestinian Tradition," *HBH* 1:175–85).

2
Phonology of Ancient Hebrew: Consonants

In this chapter I first describe the values for the graphic symbols familiar to us from an elementary study of Biblical Hebrew. The inventory of phonemes that these letters represent is slightly more complex than is often presented in an elementary Hebrew course. Next I describe the consonantal phonemes common to PS and PNWS before describing various relationships between roots and words based on correspondences between these phonemes. The vowels will be addressed in the next chapter.

2.1. Classical and Tiberian Biblical Hebrew Consonants

The number of Hebrew consonantal phonemes thought to exist for the majority of the first millennium BCE is probably the following, together with the Hebrew/Aramaic letters used to represent them. Also included in a separate column to the right, for comparison, are the phonemes of Tiberian Hebrew (ca. 800 CE); the spirantized allophones of the *begadkepat* letters are in parentheses. It should be recognized at the outset that we do not know precisely the articulation of the various phonemes; the values presented below are merely approximations.

Table 2.1. Consonantal Phonemes of Biblical Hebrew

Phonemes of Classical Biblical Hebrew, ca. 800 BCE	letter	Phonemes of (Tiberian) Biblical Hebrew, ca. 800 CE
ʾ	א	ʾ
b	ב	b (v)
g	ג	g (ʁ)
d	ד	d (ḏ)

h	ה	h
w	ו	w
z	ז	z
ḥ	ח	ḥ
ḫ	ח	ḥ
ṭ	ט	ṭ
y	י	y
k	כ	k (χ)
l	ל	l
m	מ	m
n	נ	n
s	ס	s
ʿ	ע	ʿ
ġ	ע	ʿ
p	פ	p (f)
ṣ	צ	ṣ
ḳ	ק	q
r	ר	r
ś	שׂ	s
š	שׁ	š
t	ת	t (ṯ)

Most of the transliteration symbols for the phonemes are recognizable from a basic knowledge of our modern languages. In some cases, however, a brief explanation is helpful. The /ʾ/ (IPA [ʔ]) is the glottal stop, the momentary halting of the air flow that goes through the glottis (the opening between the vocal chords), expressed, for example, in the Cockney English pronunciation of "better," *beʾuh*, as well as in some varieties of North American English as in the pronunciation of "Bat Man" *baʾman*, "atmosphere" *aʾməsfeer*, "delightful" *dəlieʾful*.[1] Spirantized *gimel* in Tiberian Biblical Hebrew was pronounced like the Parisian French *ar* (i.e., a

1. See David Eddington and Michael Taylor, "T-Glottalization in American Eng-

voiced uvular fricative; see the IPA audio example ʁ).[2] The spirantized *dalet* (/ḏ/ = IPA [ð]) in THT would have been realized as the "th" in North American English "this." The /ḫ/ (IPA [x]), the voiceless velar fricative, represents the sound found in the North American English pronunciation of "Chanukkah" (IPA [xɑnəkə]) and "chutzpah" (IPA [xʊtspə]).[3] This sound is very close to the voiceless uvular fricative IPA [χ], though the [χ] is its own sound; it is the pronunciation of spirantized *kaph* in THT.[4] The degree to which ancient Hebrew speakers could distinguish the two sounds (i.e., IPA [x] and [χ]) is an open question. The sound of /ḥ/ (IPA [ħ]) is a "lighter" sound than /ḫ/, but more forceful (and easier to hear) than simple /h/ (IPA [h]). The *ayin* (IPA [ʕ]) has been likened to "the guttural noise made by a camel being loaded with its pack saddle."[5] For /ġ/, the voiced velar fricative, see the IPA audio example for [ɣ]. It sounds like a combination of a /g/ and an /ʿ/. The /q/ represents the sound of a uvular stop; see the IPA audio example under [q]. It is pronounced deeper in the throat than /k/. In Classical Hebrew the *qoph* letter represented an

---

lish," *American Speech* 84 (2009): 298; and John Goldsmith, "Two Kinds of Phonology," http://tinyurl.com/SBL0395b.

2. See Khan, "Tiberian Pronunciation Tradition," 4. Audio examples are available from the University of Victoria website: https://web.uvic.ca/ling/resources/ipa/charts/IPAlab/IPAlab.htm.

3. For the phonetic transliterations, see *OED*, s.v. That the /ḫ/ phoneme was realized as [x] is suggested by Gary A. Rendsburg, "Ancient Hebrew Phonology," in *Phonologies of Asia and Africa*, ed. Alan S. Kaye (Winona Lake, IN: Eisenbrauns, 1997), 1:71 and Lutz Edzard, "Biblical Hebrew," *SLIH*, 482–83. This seems to have been the articulation of the equivalent consonant in Ugaritic (Josef Tropper, *Ugaritische Grammatik*, AOAT 273 [Münster: Ugarit-Verlag, 2000], 121; Dennis Pardee, "Ugaritic," *CEWAL*, 292) and in Proto-Semitic (John Huehnergard, "Afro-Asiatic," *CEWAL*, 142).

4. See Khan "Tiberian Pronunciation Tradition," 8. Others, however, view spirantized *kaph* as a velar fricative, i.e., IPA [x]. Edzard lists two possibilities for spirantized *kaph* in Tiberian Hebrew: "[x or χ]" ("Biblical Hebrew," 482). If spirantized *kaph* represents [x], then the /ḫ/ phoneme might have been realized as a uvular fricative, i.e., [χ]. These are the explicit equivalences suggested by Aron Dolgopolsky, *From Proto-Semitic to Hebrew: Phonology, Etymological Approach in a Hamito-Semitic Perspective*, Studi Camito-Semitici 2 (Milan: Centro Studi Camito-Semitici, 1999), 67.

5. C. Huart, *Littérature arabe* (Paris: Colin, 1902), 139; cited and translated by Joüon §5l. Joüon also note the possibly onomatopoeic Arabic word *uʿuʿ* "vomiting" (citing W. Wright et al., *A Grammar of the Arabic Language*, 3rd ed. [Cambridge: Cambridge University Press, 1896–1898], 1:295).

emphatic /ḳ/.[6] (For a description of emphatics, see below.) The exact pronunciation of *resh* in the first millennium BCE is unknown. In THT it may have been articulated back in the throat, as a voiced uvular roll/trill (IPA [R]), but near alveolars (/d/, /z/, /ṣ/, /t/, /ṭ/, /s/, /l/, /n/) or *shewa* as a voiced alveolar roll/trill (IPA [r]), essentially the same as the Spanish pronunciation in the word *perro* ("dog"); consult the audio examples online.[7] The /ś/ represents a lateral fricative (IPA [ɬ]). It is a sound between an /s/ and an /l/. Imagine holding a piece of candy to the roof of your mouth with your tongue and saying the word "slow"; the sound you produce in pronouncing the /sl-/ is close to /ś/. The phoneme is thus distinct from the /s/-sound which was represented by *samek* (IPA [s]). The spirantized *tav* in THT, /ṯ/, would have been realized as in North American English "thin" (cf. /ḏ/ in "this").

The emphatics were, in PS, pronounced with a following glottal stop (ṭ = IPA [tˀ]; ṣ = [sˀ]; ḳ = [kˀ] as in Ethiopic and Modern South Arabian).[8] In PNWS and later Hebrew, they were perhaps pharyngealized (i.e., pronounced with a following *ayin* sound: *ṭ* = IPA [tˁ]), or perhaps they remained glottalized, that is, pronounced with a following glottal stop, or even velarized (pronounced with a following /ġ/ sound: *ṭ* = IPA [tˠ]).[9]

2.2. *Begadkepat*

The spirantized versions of the *begadkepat* consonants were allophones, that is alternative pronunciations, of the relevant phonemes. These generally appear in THT after a syllable that ends with a vowel. They do not imply a different meaning for a word. The word "house" would have been pronounced *bayit* when preceded by a consonant but as *vayit* when imme-

---

6. It can be pointed out here for the sake of clarity that the prototypical root *qtl* might be more accurately transliterated *ḳtl* for this reason. The spelling with "q" is used instead out of convention.

7. See Khan "Tiberian Pronunciation Tradition," 11–12.

8. See Rendsburg, "Ancient Hebrew Phonology," 73.

9. John Huehnergard ("Features of Central Semitic," in *Biblical and Oriental Essays in Memory of William L. Moran*, ed. Agustinus Gianto, BibOr 48 [Rome: Pontifical Biblical Institute, 2005], 167–68) specifies that pharyngealization may have been a feature of the even earlier Central Semitic. See also Joüon §5i; Rendsburg "Ancient Hebrew Phonology," 75–76; P. Kyle McCarter, "Hebrew," *CEWAL*, 324; Blau, *Phonology and Morphology*, 68; Leonid Kogan, "Proto-Semitic Phonetics and Phonology," *SLIH*, 60–65.

diately preceded by a prefixed particle like ב "in" (e.g., בְּבַ֫יִת *bəvayit* "in a house" Exod 12:46). When a word ending in a vowel (e.g., וַיַּֽעֲלוּ < **wayyaʿlū* "they went up (to)" or תַּעֲלוּ < **taʿlū* "you will go up (to)") precedes such a *begadkepat* phoneme, the letter could be pronounced in either way; thus, the word "house" could be pronounced *bayit* (see, e.g., Hos 4:15) or *vayit* (see, e.g., Judg 1:22). Whether pronounced *bayit* or *vayit*, the word denoted "house."

Since spirantization of consonants is triggered due to an immediately preceding vowel, it is assumed that where the spirantized consonant comes after a consonant an immediately preceding vowel has been lost or elided. For example, in the construct singular form בִּרְכַּת "blessing of," the spirantized *kaph* reflects the earlier presence of a vowel before the *kaph*: **barakatu* > **barakat* > **barkat* (> בִּרְכַת). This, of course, presupposes that the *begadkepat* letters spirantized before vowel reduction became widespread (and then continued to be pronounced as spirantized consonants even when they were no longer preceded by a vowel). This sequence of developments also helps explain why the *kaph* in the expression מַלְכִּי "my king" is not spirantized (it developed from **malkiyya*), but the *kaph* in מַלְכֵי "kings of" is (it developed from **malakay*).

The spirantized pronunciation of the six *begadkepat* phonemes appeared probably sometime in the second half of the first millennium BCE.[10] When exactly this took place is, however, unclear. Many scholars suggest that it took place approximately in 400 BCE.[11] By contrast, some, like P. Kyle McCarter, suggest it was later. McCarter writes that spirantization may have taken place "in the second half of the first century BC," though he cautions in relation to the *begadkepat* allophones that "their existence before the Common Era is not unambiguously documented."[12]

Part of the question relates to when /ḫ/ and /ġ/ disappeared from the language (for which see below).[13] The spirantized pronunciation of *gimel*

---

10. For evidence from Greek transliterations, see Gerard Janssens, *Studies in Hebrew Historical Linguistics Based on Origen's Secunda*, OrGand 9 (Leuven: Peeters, 1982), 45–50.

11. See Gotthelf Bergsträsser, *Hebräische Grammatik* (Leipzig: Hinrichs, 1918–1929), 1:§6m; Rendsburg "Ancient Hebrew Phonology," 75; Edzard, "Biblical Hebrew," 483.

12. McCarter, "Hebrew," 330.

13. Another related question is the time of spirantization in Aramaic since the spirantization in Hebrew is thought to derive from Aramaic. On Aramaic, see Klaus

(IPA [ʁ]) and *kaph* (IPA [χ]) was very close to the pronunciation of /ġ/ (IPA [ɣ]) and /ḫ/ (IPA [x]), respectively. Therefore, if spirantization took place before /ġ/ merged with /ʿ/ and before /ḫ/ merged with /ḥ/, then one would expect confusion between these sounds and frequent misspellings of *gimel* for *ayin* (= /ġ/) and *ayin* for spirantized *gimel* as well as *khet* (= /ḫ/) written for spirantized *kaph* and *kaph* for *khet*. Since this does not happen with any regularity, one might conclude with McCarter that spirantization did not take place before circa 50 BCE.[14]

Nevertheless, it remains likely that spirantization did at least begin earlier than the first century BCE. As Richard Steiner argues, speakers may have been able to distinguish between the relevant sounds (i.e., they distinguished [ʁ] from [ɣ] and [χ] from [x]) or spirantization took place in the following sequence: *bet*, *dalet*, *pe*, and *tav* spirantized initially, then /ḫ/ and /ġ/ merged with /ḥ/ and /ʿ/, and then the velars *gimel* and *kaph* spirantized.[15] The second possibility would imply that /b/, /d/, /p/, /t/ spirantized before circa 200 BCE and /g/ and /k/ after circa 100 BCE.[16] In addition, since spirantization took place before vowel reduction, and since vowel

---

Beyer, *Die aramäischen Texte vom Toten Meer* (Göttingen: Vandenhoeck & Ruprecht, 1984–1994), 1:126–28 and note Steiner's arguments described below, n. 15.

14. Although the DSS do evidence at least three cases of misspellings related to *khet* and *kaph* (יאחלו corrected to יאכלו "they will eat" 4Q514 1 I, 6; הכול corrected to החול "the sand" 4Q225 2 I, 6; ניחוחכם "your pleasing sacrifice-odor" 4Q270 7 I, 18), only the last involves an etymological /ḫ/. See Reymond, *Qumran Hebrew*, 70–71.

15. Richard C. Steiner, "Variation, Simplifying Assumptions, and the History of Spirantization in Aramaic and Hebrew," in *Shaʿarei Lashon: Studies in Hebrew, Aramaic, and Jewish Languages Presented to Moshe Bar-Asher; Vol I: Biblical Hebrew, Masorah, and Medieval Hebrew*, ed. A. Maman, S. E. Fassberg, and Y. Breuer (Jerusalem: Bialik Institute, 2007), *52–*65. Steiner notes (*55–*56) that some Caucasian languages distinguish [χ], [x], and [ħ]. Furthermore, he notes (*54) that in Samaritan Hebrew, one does not see the spirantization of *gimel* and *kaph*, which might imply that these consonants spirantized at a later time. He also cites similar possible evidence for Syriac. His article emphasizes that different consonants spirantized in different places at different times. He argues against Beyer's idea that spirantization occurred in Aramaic only very late.

16. The examples יאחלו and ניחוחכם from the DSS are compatible with this hypothesis. 4Q514 is dated to the mid-first century BCE and 4Q270 to the first half of the first century CE (see B. Webster, "Chronological Index of the Texts from the Judaean Desert," in *The Texts from the Judaean Desert: Indices and an Introduction to Discoveries in the Judaean Desert Series*, ed. E. Tov et al., DJD 39 [Oxford: Clarendon, 2002], 400 and 426).

reduction took place at the very latest in the first century BCE, spirantization must have taken place in an earlier era.

2.3. Classical Hebrew /ḫ/, /ġ/, /ś/

The inventory of Classical Biblical Hebrew phonemes listed above is three greater than the number of graphic letters used to represent these sounds. This resulted in some letters representing more than one phoneme. Specifically, three letters were used to represent two phonemes each. The *khet* represented the phonemes /ḥ/ (IPA [ħ]) and /ḫ/ (IPA [x]). The *ayin* represented /ʿ/ (IPA [ʕ]) and /ġ/ (IPA [ɣ]). The *sin/shin* letter represented /ś/ (IPA [ɬ]) and /š/ (IPA [ʃ]). (Recall that the dot that distinguishes *sin* from *shin* is a medieval invention.) The existence of the phonemes /ḫ/, /ġ/, and /ś/ is thought to have existed in the Late Bronze Age Canaanite, as implied by names and words in the El Amarna texts as compared to Egyptian transcriptions.[17] The evidence for these phonemes in the first millennium BCE as well as their approximate time of merger is explained below.

The existence of a lateral fricative sound (/ś/) is suggested by words appearing in Hebrew with a *sin* and in other languages with an /l/. Note, for example, Hebrew כַּשְׂדִּים "Chaldeans" versus Akkadian *kaldu* and Greek χαλδαιοι; Hebrew בֹּשֶׂם "balsam" versus Akkadian *baltammu* and Greek βαλσαμον.[18] The lateral fricative phoneme probably was lost and merged with the /s/ of *samek* some time in the mid-first millennium BCE, based on the relatively common misspellings of etymological /ś/ with *samek* in exilic and later writings (e.g., סֹכְרִים "hiring" Ezra 4:5 versus the expected spelling שֹׂכְרִים in 2 Chr 24:12)[19] and of /s/ with the *sin/shin* letter (e.g., שִׂכְלוּת "folly" Qoh 1:17 vs. the expected spelling סִכְלוּת in Qoh 2:3 and

17. Daniel Sivan, *Grammatical Analysis and Glossary of the Northwest Semitic Vocables in Akkadian Texts of the 15th–13th c.B.C. from Canaan and Syria*, AOAT 214 (Kevelaer: Butzon & Bercker; Neukirchen-Vluyn: Neukirchener Verlag, 1984), 50–52.

18. This and other evidence is described by Richard C. Steiner, *The Case for Fricative-Laterals in Proto-Semitic*, AOS 59 (New Haven: American Oriental Society, 1977) and Steiner, "Addenda to *The Case for Fricative-Laterals in Proto-Semitic*," in *Semitic Studies in Honor of Wolf Leslau on the Occasion of his Eighty-Fifth Birthday, November 14th, 1991*, ed. Alan S. Kaye (Wiesbaden: Harrassowitz, 1991), 1499–1513; and with more recent evidence by Kogan, "Proto-Semitic Phonetics and Phonology," 71–80.

19. Note also גָּרְסָה "is crushed" (Ps 119:20) and וַיַּגְרֵס (Lam 3:16) vs. גֶּרֶשׂ "grits" (Lev 2:16); הַחַרְסוּת "potsherds" (Jer 19:2) vs. חֶרֶשׂ "potsherd" (passim); מִכְמָס "Mikhmas" (Ezra 2:27 and Neh 7:31) vs. מִכְמָשׂ (passim); see Joshua Blau, *On Pseudo-*

passim).[20] Students should be aware that, due to the commonness of these misspellings, the dictionaries (BDB, *HALOT*) sometimes will list verbs according to their etymology. Thus, if one encounters a word spelled with *sin* and cannot find it in the dictionary under this letter, one should look the word up under *samek*.

The merger of /ġ/ and /ʿ/ is thought to have taken place, according to Blau, in the spoken language some time after the Septuagint (= LXX) translation of Genesis (slightly before ca. 200 BCE) and in the reading tradition some time later; Steiner suggests that the merger had taken place at least by the first century CE.[21] Note, for example, the following correspondences that suggest an etymological /ġ/ was still recognized by the LXX translators of the Pentateuch: γομορρα for עֲמֹרָה "Gomorrah"; γαζα for עַזָּה "Gaza"; γομορ for עֹמֶר (an "omer" measure).[22] By contrast, etymological /ʿ/ was not represented with a corresponding Greek letter, as seen in ιακωβ for יַעֲקֹב "Jacob."[23] It should be noted, however, that the evidence for the existence of /ġ/ in early Hebrew is not as strong as that for /ḫ/; some of the evidence is ambiguous and there is some contradicting evidence.[24] All the

---

Corrections in Some Semitic Languages (Jerusalem: Israel Academy of Sciences and Humanities, 1970), 114–20.

20. Note also נָשׂוֹג "turned back" (2 Sam 1:22) vs. נָסוֹג (passim); יִשְׂפֹּק "will clap" (Job 27:23) vs. יִסְפֹּק (Job 34:37 and passim); כַּעַשׂ (Job 17:7 and three other times in Job) vs. כַּעַס "anger" (passim). For more explanations, see Blau, *Pseudo-Corrections*, 120–25. Some cases are ambiguous, as with שׂוּךְ "to hedge" (Job 1:10, Hos 2:8) vs. סוּךְ "to hedge" (Job 3:23, 38:8); מְשׂוּכָה; "hedge" (Prov 15:19) vs. מְסוּכָה "hedge" (Mic 7:4); שַׂעַר "storm" (Isa 28:2) vs. סַעַר "storm" (passim); שְׂעָרָה "storm" (Nah 1:3, Job 9:17) vs. סְעָרָה "storm" (passim); see Blau, *Pseudo-Corrections*, 115–16.

21. Joshua Blau, *On Polyphony in Biblical Hebrew*, PIASH 6/2 (Jerusalem: Israel Academy of Sciences and Humanities, 1982), 39–40, 70; Richard C. Steiner "On the Dating of Hebrew Sound Changes (**Ḫ* > *Ḥ* and **Ġ* > ʿ) and Greek Translations (2 Esdras and Judith)," *JBL* 124 (2004): 247, 266; Steiner, "Variation, Simplifying Assumptions," *56 n. 15.

22. Blau, *Polyphony*, 33–35. Further evidence is provided by Steiner "On the Dating of Hebrew," 229–67.

23. Blau, *Polyphony*, 21.

24. See ibid., 19–20, 36, 39, 70; Dolgopolsky, *From Proto-Semitic to Hebrew*, 65–69, 154; Steiner, "On the Dating of Hebrew," 232; Kogan, "Proto-Semitic Phonetics and Phonology," 116. Geoffrey Khan ("Some Parallels in Linguistic Development between Biblical Hebrew and Neo-Aramaic," in *Semitic Studies in Honour of Edward Ullendorff*, ed. Geoffrey Khan, SSLL 47 [Leiden: Brill, 2005], 92–93) emphasizes three points: (1) the existence of the relevant phonemes in one dialect (e.g., that of the LXX)

same, it seems likely that /ġ/ was articulated in some registers and dialects of Biblical Hebrew in antiquity before the Common Era.

The merger of /ḫ/ and /ḥ/ began, according to Steiner, in circa 100 BCE in the spoken language and circa 100 CE in the reading tradition.[25] Note, for example, the following correspondences that suggest an etymological /ḫ/ was still recognized by the LXX translators of the Pentateuch: χορραι for חֹרִי "Horite," χαρραν for חָרָן "Harran," χετ/χεται for חֵת/חִתִּי "Heth"/"Hittite"; and ραχηλ for רָחֵל "Rachel."[26] By contrast, etymological /ḥ/ was not represented with a corresponding Greek letter, as seen in ἰσαακ for יִצְחָק "Isaac."[27]

The fact that the letter *khet* likely represented the phoneme /ḫ/ (along with /ḥ/) for most of the first millennium BCE means that the pronunciation for at least some words in the modern classroom, although not reflecting THT, may, in fact, be the same as an even earlier pronunciation. Thus, the pronunciation of רָחֵל "Rachel" in the contemporary classroom as [rɑxel] is closer in some ways to the earlier first millennium *rāḫēl* [ʀaːxeːl] than the medieval *råḥel* [ʀɔːħeːl].

Recognizing the existence of these three phonemes, /ḫ/, /ġ/, and /ś/, helps explain some of the paradoxes of the Biblical Hebrew lexicon, especially the existence of some antonymous words with similar spelling. Two distinct pronunciations /s/ and /ś/ suggest that early speakers could distinguish words like סֶ֫כֶל (= *sɛkl* < **sakl*) "folly" (Qoh 10:6) and שֶׂ֫כֶל (= *sɛkl* < **sikl* < **śikl*) "prudence" and similarly the *hiphil* forms of the two related verbs הִסְכַּ֫לְתִּי (< **hiskaltī*) "I have acted like a fool" (1 Sam 26:21) and הִשְׂכַּ֫לְתִּי (< **hiskaltī* < **hiśkaltī*) "I understand" (Ps 119:99).[28] Note also סרר "to be stubborn" (e.g., סוֹרֵר < **sōrēr* "who are stubborn" Isa 65:2) and שׂרר "to act as a prince" (e.g., שֹׂרֵר < **sōrēr* < **śōrēr* "one who rules"

---

does not necessitate the existence of the same phonemes in other dialects (e.g., that which led eventually to the Tiberian tradition); (2) conceivably the different pronunciations of Greek names reflect allophones in the underlying Hebrew dialect; (3) the articulation of Greek names may have retained a more antique pronunciation than other words in the language. In relation to this last point, however, note the pronunciation of the common noun עֹ֫מֶר.

25. Steiner, "On the Dating of Hebrew," 266.

26. Blau, *Polyphony*, 62. Blau lists many examples from the LXX. Further evidence is provided by Steiner "On the Dating of Hebrew," 229–67.

27. Blau, *Polyphony*, 52.

28. On the phonemic contours of segolate nouns, see the subsection "Segolate Nouns" in ch. 4 §18.

Esth 1:22); סתר *niphal* "to hide" (e.g., וַיִּסָּתֵר < **wayyissāter* < **wayyissatir* "he hid" 1 Sam 20:24) and שׂתר *niphal* "to break out" (e.g., וַיִּשָּׂתְרוּ < **wayyissātərū* < **wayyiśśatirū* "they broke out" 1 Sam 5:9).[29]

Similarly, two distinct pronunciations for *ayin* suggest why speakers for most of the first millennium BCE could distinguish ערב = *ʿrb* "to stand as surety, to barter" (e.g., לַעֲרֹב < **laʿrōb* "to barter" Ezek 27:9) and ערב = **ġrb* "to turn to evening" (e.g., לַעֲרֹב < **laġrōb* "to turn to evening" Judg 19:9); עדר = *ʿdr niphal* "to hoe" (e.g., יֵעָדֵר < **yēʿāder* "it will [not] be hoed" Isa 5:6) and עדר = **ġdr niphal* "to be lacking" (e.g., נֶעְדַּר < **niġdar* "[nothing] was lacking" 1 Sam 30:19).

Note as well חנן = *ḥnn* "to show favor" (e.g., וְחַנֹּתִי < **wəḥannōtī* "I will be gracious" Exod 33:19) and חנן = **ḫnn* "to be loathsome" (e.g., וְחַנֹּתִי < **wəḫannōtī* "I am loathsome" Job 19:17); חרשׁ = *ḥrš* "to plough" and in a metaphoric sense "to devise" in the *qal* and *hiphil* (e.g., מַחֲרִישׁ < **maḥrīš* "one devising" 1 Sam 23:9) and חרשׁ = **ḫrš* "to be silent, dumb" in *qal* and *hiphil* (e.g., מַחֲרִישׁ < **maḫrīš* "[a fool] who is silent" Prov 17:28).

The distinction between these phonemes should also inform any discussion of wordplay and double entendre. Although wordplay may be only approximate (i.e., between words that merely sound similar, not identical), it is still the case that at least some speakers would have been able to distinguish more words than might at first be obvious.

In the lists above, it is assumed that a distinct pronunciation would help scribes distinguish words that were graphically identical. This is not to deny, however, that ancient Hebrew, like other languages, contained what are sometimes called "contradictanyms" or "Janus words," that is, words with the same sounds but opposite meanings (as in English "to cleave," meaning "to divide" and "to cleave" meaning "to stick to").[30] Note,

---

29. It should be noted that many of the examples are cited from works that do (or, at least, might) date from the latter half of the first millennium BCE when /ś/ and /s/ had merged; therefore, the writers of Qohelet, Esther, etc., might not have been aware of the phonetic difference between these words. Nevertheless, presumably these words existed in the first half of the first millennium BCE and, if so, earlier writers would have been able to distinguish them. It goes without saying, of course, that there was a distinction in this early period not only between /s/ and /ś/, but also between these phonemes and /š/, facilitating distinctions between the above words and שׁכל "to be childless," שׁרר "to make abundant" (only once in Jer 15:11 *qere*).

30. This category of words has many unofficial labels. Dictionary.com lists "antilogy," "autoantonym," "contranym," "contronym," "enantiodrome," "Janus word." The label "contradictanym" is also sometimes found, as in Ben Schott, *Schott's Original*

for example, the two words חֶסֶד "shame" and חֶסֶד "loving-kindness" have nearly opposite meanings.[31] In other cases, the very same word or phrase expresses apparently contradictory senses (like in English "to dust," i.e., to clear of dust, as in "dusting" the shelf, or to introduce dust, as in "dusting" a cake with sugar). Note, for example, the Hebrew phrase נשׂא עון "to lift iniquity" can mean either to bear guilt (i.e., bear responsibility for) or to forgive an offense.[32]

It should also be kept in mind that the exact etymology of many words is uncertain. Steiner notices, for example, that the Hebrew name חֶבֶר "Heber" may derive potentially from *ḥbr* or *ḫbr*.[33] Finally, given the numerous variables in language, even with a clear etymology, it is not certain that in any given word a particular phoneme would be pronounced according to its historical pronunciation. One may note, for example, that in Akkadian etymological /ḥ/ is usually not realized as a consonant. Thus, the etymological root **bḥr* "to choose" is usually realized in Akkadian as a verb *bēru* "to choose." However, in cases where Akkadian has borrowed a word from Aramaic, the etymological /ḥ/ is articulated instead as /ḫ/, as in the alternative form for the same verb *beḫēru* "to select."[34] Similarly,

---

Miscellany (New York: Bloomsbury, 2002), 40. The two meanings of "cleave" correspond to two different roots, according to the *OED*.

31. Note also דמם "to be silent" and דמם "to wail" (following *HALOT*; cf. *Ges*[18]); and הוה "to fall" (+ הַוָּה "destruction") and הוה "to become." The mergers of the phonemes discussed above meant, of course, an increase in the number of contradictanyms, like סֶכֶל (*sɛkl* < **sakl*) "folly" and שֶׂכֶל (*sɛkl* < **sikl* < **śikl*) "prudence."

32. The verb חלץ means "to take off" and occurs with the word "sandal," but as a passive participle it has the sense "to be girded for battle" (perhaps the two sense reflecting two roots, though both would be expressed in the same way with /ḫ/); the verb חפשׂ means "to search, examine" in the *qal*, but in the *hithpael* means "to hide oneself"; רגע means "to stir up (sea)" in the *qal*, but in the *hiphil* "to make peace, linger" (the two senses here likely reflecting two different roots, though again the two roots in Hebrew would be pronounced the same). One often encounters such correspondences in etymologically related words that occur in different languages, as in שׁכח "to forget" in Hebrew but "to find" in Aramaic; similarly, קלס *piel*/D-stem "to mock" in Biblical Hebrew but "to praise" in Aramaic (which derives from Greek, according to *A Syriac Lexicon: A Translation from the Latin, Correction, Expansion, and Update of C. Brockelmann's Lexicon Syriacum*, trans. Michael Sokoloff (Winona Lake, IN.: Eisenbrauns; Piscataway, NJ: Gorgias, 2009], s.v.).

33. Steiner, *Fricative-Laterals*, 44, 74.

34. For the examples from Akkadian, see Kathleen Abraham and Michael Sokoloff, "Aramaic Loanwords in Akkadian—A Reassessment of the Proposals," *AfO* 52

ḫilb "milk" appears for etymological **ḥlb*. Tropper notes that a nearby sibilant or sonorant in an Akkadian root seems to effect a phonetic shift from etymological /ḥ/ to /ḫ/, as in *raḫāṣu* "to flood, wash" from PS **rḥṣ*.[35] All things considered, then, it is often difficult to be absolutely sure how the relevant consonants of a word were pronounced in Classical Hebrew. Therefore, when transliterating words I have marked with an asterisk words including the phonemes /ḫ/ and /ġ/. The articulation of /ś/, on the other hand, is clear from the consistent distinction in spelling in early Hebrew (i.e., words with /ś/ are usually spelled with a *sin*/*shin* and not a *samek*).

Students may get a better idea about the scholarly opinion about the etymology of words spelled with *khet* and *ayin* by consulting the dictionary *Ges*[18].[36] Generally speaking, one may get a picture of the etymological root consonants by consulting cognate words in the other Semitic languages. For /ḫ/ and /ġ/ the most helpful languages include Ugaritic, Akkadian, and Arabic.

(2011): 28, 33. Note the criticisms in Michael P. Streck, "Akkadian and Aramaic Language Contact," *SLIH*, 416–24. Similarly, note the appearance of /ḫ/ for Aramaic /ḥ/ in some dialects of Arabic (see Jan Retsö, "Aramaic/Syriac Loanwords," in *Encyclopedia of Arabic Language and Linguistics*, ed. K. Versteegh et al. [Leiden: Brill, 2005–2009], 1:181).

35. Josef Tropper, "Akkadisch *nuḫḫutu* und die Repräsentation des Phonems /ḥ/ im Akkadischen," *ZA* 85 (1995): 65. John Huehnergard ("Akkadian *ḫ* and West Semitic **ḥ*," in *Studia Semitica*, ed. Leonid Kogan, Orientalia 3 [Moscow: Russian State University Press, 2003], 102–19) criticizes Tropper's conclusions and suggests that the evidence points to an otherwise unknown PS phoneme IPA [x̣] that developed into /ḫ/ in Akkadian and /ḥ/ in West Semitic. See also Alexander Militarev and Leonid Kogan, *Semitic Etymological Dictionary*, 2 vols., AOAT 278 (Münster: Ugarit-Verlag, 2000–2005), 1:lxxiii–lxxv.

36. The etymological identifications in this dictionary are easy to read and comprehend. In many cases, one finds a "?" and no etymological root is suggested. *HALOT* also contains frequent references to etymological root consonants. More thorough treatments for some words are found in, e.g., Militarev and Kogan, *Semitic Etymological Dictionary*; Leonid Kogan, "Proto-Semitic Lexicon," *SLIH*, 179–258; and David Cohen, *Dictionnaire des racines sémitiques, ou attestées dans les langues sémitiques*, 10 vols. (Leuven: Peeters, 1994–).

2.4. Pronunciation of Gutturals

Although the guttural consonants seem to be weakened in their pronunciation in at least some spoken dialects of ancient Hebrew by the first century CE, the gutturals continue to be distinguished in most reading traditions of BH.[37] One gets a sense of the relative degree to which gutturals weakened in the first century BCE by considering how often words with gutturals are misspelled in the DSS. Since *aleph* is intrinsically the most difficult of the gutturals to articulate, especially in certain positions (e.g., at the end of a syllable or word), words containing *aleph* (as well as *resh*) are the most frequently misspelled. Next in frequency are words spelled with *he*, also a consonant inherently difficult to articulate at the end of words and syllables. Words containing *ayin* are less frequently misspelled and words with *khet* are usually spelled correctly. Furthermore, evidence from the LXX, the Secunda, and Jerome's transcriptions provides indirect evidence for the existence of gutturals.[38]

2.5. Proto-Semitic/Proto-Northwest Semitic */ṯ/, */ḏ/, */ṣ́/, */ṭ̱/

In addition to the phonemes listed above in the chart, PS and PNWS are thought to have contained four other phonemes.[39] These include the voiced and unvoiced dental fricatives (/ṯ/ and /ḏ/ respectively), the emphatic lateral fricative (/ṣ́/),[40] and the emphatic interdental (/ṭ̱/).[41] These phonemes

37. See the analysis in Reymond, *Qumran Hebrew*, 71–114.

38. Note, e.g., the spellings of /ḫ/ and /ġ/ with χ and γ in the LXX, described above, as well as spellings with two short vowels in sequence in the Secunda (e.g., νεεμαν corresponding to נֶאֱמָן "enduring" Ps 89:38) (see Alexey Yuditsky, "Transcription into Greek and Latin: Pre-Masoretic Period," *EHLL* 3:805).

39. Technically, the phonemes in the above chart do not always represent their presumed articulation in PS/PNWS. See below for another chart that illustrates the assumed phonemes in these earlier strata of the language.

40. The PS/PNWS emphatic lateral fricative is transliterated often according to the transliteration of the Arabic letter to which it corresponds etymologically (/ḍ/). This practice is problematic for several reasons. First, the Arabic letter is only in some dialects realized phonetically as an emphatic voiced dental stop/plosive (/ḍ/); the "classical pronunciation [of *dād*, i.e., /ḍ/ or ض] is as lateral emphatic spirant (thus a sound distantly related to l)" (Gotthelf Bergsträsser, *Introduction to the Semitic Languages: Text Specimens and Grammatical Sketches*, trans. Peter T. Daniels [Winona Lake, IN: Eisenbrauns, 1983], 162). Second, the symbol /ḍ/ does not clearly indicate

early on merged with other Hebrew/Canaanite phonemes in the following manner: */ṯ/ > /t/ (*tav*); */ḏ/ > /z/ (*zayin*); */ṣ́/ > /ṣ/ (*tsade*); */ṭ/ > /ṣ/ (*tsade*).[42] The dental fricatives (/ṯ/ and /ḏ/) are the same sounds as those realized in Tiberian Hebrew as the spirantized versions of the *tav* and *dalet*. Yet, unlike in Tiberian Hebrew, in PS/PNWS these were phonemes and, thus, meaningfully distinct from /t/ and /d/, respectively. A verb pronounced with a /d/ (e.g., **dky* [> דָּכָה] "to crush") would be recognized as a verb entirely distinct from another otherwise identical word with a /ḏ/ (e.g., **ḏky* [> זָכָה] "to be bright"). The emphatic lateral fricative and interdental (/ṣ́/ and /ṭ/) are simply emphatic versions of previously described phonemes (i.e., they were articulated like the previously described phonemes /ś/ and /ṯ/ followed by a glottal stop in PS/PNWS).

Since these phonemes (*/ṯ/, */ḏ/, */ṣ́/, */ṭ/) are reflected to varying degrees in Ugaritic, Aramaic, and Arabic, it is presupposed that they were part of the common ancestor to these languages, in other words, the hypothetical Central Semitic as well as Proto-Northwest Semitic. Nevertheless, it would seem, based largely on the El Amarna tablets, that by the middle of the second millennium BCE they had at least partially disappeared from the southern dialect of NWS spoken in Syria/Palestine.[43] Specifically, the El Amarna texts suggest that */ṣ́/ had shifted to /ṣ/; that */ṭ/ also had shifted to /ṣ/; that */ḏ/ had perhaps shifted to /z/ (the Sumero-Akkadian cuneiform leaving things ambiguous); that */ṯ/ remained in pronunciation, something revealed not through the cuneiform texts, but through Egyptian transcriptions of names and regular nouns/verbs.[44] Some scholars (e.g., Rendsburg), suggest that Classical Hebrew of Transjordan (that of the Gileadites) did contain etymological */ṯ/, though the evidence for

---

the lateral nature of the PS/PNWS phoneme. Due to such confusions, many contemporary scholars of Semitic languages prefer to render the PS emphatic lateral fricative phoneme as /ṣ́/. Alternatively, it could be represented as / ɬ̣/.

41. The transliteration of the PS/PNWS emphatic voiceless interdental (/ṭ/) is often transliterated /ẓ/, based on the transliteration of the corresponding Arabic letter. The Arabic letter, however, is only in some dialects realized as an emphatic /z/; in other dialects it is realized as an emphatic voiced interdental fricative (whose IPA symbol is [ðˤ]) (Huehnergard, "Afro-Asiatic," 144; Bergsträsser, *Introduction to the Semitic Languages*, 161–62). One can also transliterate the /ṭ/ phoneme as /θ̣/.

42. For a concise presentation and analysis of the evidence from the various dialects in Syria/Palestine, see Garr, *Dialect Geography*, 23–30.

43. Pardee, "Ugaritic," 389.

44. Sivan, *Grammatical Analysis*, 38, 41, 43.

this (even he admits) is slight, existing primarily in the Shibboleth incident in Judg 12:6.[45] In any case, even he agrees that there is no evidence for this phoneme for most Classical Hebrew dialects.

Cognizance of these phonemes is primarily useful for the student of Hebrew in learning and understanding the vocabulary of other related languages like Aramaic and Ugaritic (as well as Arabic and other Semitic languages). All the same, knowledge of these also helps make sense of the Biblical Hebrew lexicon. For example, knowing that Hebrew /ṣ/ can derive from PS/PNWS /ṣ/, */ṭ̱/, and */ṣ́/ helps to explain how dictionaries can distinguish between otherwise similar words, like צרר/צור "to bind" (related to Arabic *ṣarra* "to tie, bind" < PS/PNWS **ṣrr*) and צרר/צור "to attack" (related to Arabic *ḍarra* "to harm, injure" < PS/PNWS **ṣ́rr*).

Moreover, the fact that the PS/PNWS emphatic interdental, */ṭ̱/, corresponds to /ṣ/ (= צ) in Hebrew and to /ṭ/ (= ט) in Aramaic helps explain the existence of synonymous pairs of roots in Biblical Hebrew like נצר "to guard" (the expected realization of the PS/PNWS root **nṭ̱r* in Hebrew) and נטר "to guard" (the expected realization of the same root in Aramaic). The verb נטר and its associated noun מַטָּרָה "guard, target" must have been borrowed from Aramaic (or from another Canaanite dialect that experienced the same shift of */ṭ̱/ > /ṭ/ as in Aramaic).[46] Learning such correspondences can help the student build her vocabulary; this is particularly useful where one of the roots is relatively common (as with נצר).

In addition to explaining the lexicon and assisting in vocabulary learning, knowledge of these correspondences can sometimes assist in comprehending and evaluating various interpretive proposals. As noted above,

45. Rendsburg, "Ancient Hebrew Phonology," 69–70. He assumes that the story is based around the dual realization of the word "stream" as *sibbōlɛt* by the Ephraimites (according to Israelite pronunciation norms) and *ṯibbōlɛt* by the Gileadites (according to Transjordanian norms, which are etymologically more accurate, the word going back to a PNWS *ṯbl* root). Rendsburg's explanation is complicated due to the apparent Arabic cognates (*sabal* meaning "flowing rain" and *sublat* "wide spread rain," cited in *HALOT*), which suggest that the Proto-Hebrew root of the word "stream" is *šbl* and the PS/PNWS root is *sbl*. See Joshua Blau, "'Weak' Phonetic Change and the Hebrew *śîn*," *HAR* 1 (1977): 109.

46. As Holger Gzella remarks in relation to preexilic biblical material: "One cannot simply attribute an isolated word or form to Aramaic with any degree of certainty based on a single linguistic hallmark, because the true extent of dialect diversity in Iron-Age Syria-Palestine remains unknown" (A *Cultural History of Aramaic: From the Beginnings to the Advent of Islam*, HdO 111 [Leiden: Brill, 2015], 96).

contemporary dictionaries of Biblical Hebrew list the word עָר* as an Aramaic loanword "enemy," etymologically related to Hebrew צַר "enemy." The word is listed as occurring as עָרֶ֫ךָ (in 1 Sam 28:16) and עָרֶ֫יךָ (Ps 139:20).[47] In these passages, one can also find other explanations (e.g., עָרֶ֫ךָ may be a misspelling of צָרֶ֫ךָ; and עָרֶ֫יךָ may be a misspelling of עָלֶ֫יךָ).[48] In part, deciding on the likelihood that these letters are examples of an Aramaic loanword (or an Aramaic-like word) involves being familiar with similar lexical pairs.

Note the corresponding roots in Biblical Hebrew that relate to the following PS/PNWS phonemes:

emphatic interdental (*/ṯ̣/)

- נצר "to guard" (the expected realization in Hebrew) versus נטר "to guard, preserve anger" (the expected realization of the same root in Aramaic) (+ מַטָּרָה "guard, target")
- צלל *hiphil* "to shadow" (Ezek 31:3) versus טלל *piel* "to shadow" (Neh 3:15)
- צען "to travel" (Isa 33:20) versus טען "to load" (Gen 45:17)
- קוץ "to feel loathing" versus קוט "to feel loathing"[49]

47. See, e.g., BDB.

48. See, e.g., BDB and *HALOT*.

49. Note also the pair קמץ "to grasp" (Lev 2:2) vs. קמט "to grasp" (Job 16:8), though the etymological link is less clear. In the case of שֶׁטֶף "flood" and שֶׁצֶף "outpouring" (Isa 54:8), the words might reflect different realizations of a common PS/PNWS root (e.g., the *shaphel* conjugation of *ṯ̣wp* [= צוף in Hebrew and טוף in Aramaic]; for which see C. J. Labuschagne, "Original Shaphʿel Forms in Biblical Hebrew," *OTWSA* 13 [1971]: 51–64, as cited in *HALOT* s.v. "שֶׁטֶף"). In relation to שֶׁצֶף, note also the RH verb with the same consonants meaning "to cut, slash," which root with two initial sibilant consonants seems incongruous. Alternatively, BH שֶׁצֶף might simply be a mistake for שֶׁטֶף since in its one occurrence it appears adjacent to קֶצֶף "wrath." That two adjacent words might affect each other's pronunciation is suggested by the form of מָבוֹא "entrance" in the expression וּמוֹצָאָיו וּמוֹבָאָיו "its exits and entrances" (Ezek 43:11; similarly note the *qere* of 2 Sam 3:25: אֶת־מוֹצָאֲךָ וְאֶת־מְבוֹאֶךָ); also מחשבל בליעל for מחשבת בליעל* "thought of Belial" in 4Q177 12–13 I, 6. Some verbs that look like they are etymologically related might not be. The verbs נטל "to lift" and נצל *hiphil* "to tear, save, rescue" may be from distinct roots.

voiced dental fricative (*/ṯ/)

- חרשׁ "to engrave" (the expected realization in Hebrew) versus חרת "to engrave" (the expected realization in Aramaic; Exod 32:16 and in the DSS)
- פֵּשֶׁר "interpretation" (Qoh 8:1 and in the DSS) versus פתר "to interpret" and פִּתְרוֹן "interpretation"[50]
- שׁנה "to repeat, speak again" versus תנה *piel* "to recount" (Judg 5:11; 11:40)[51]

the unvoiced dental fricative (*/ḏ/)

- זלל "to be foolish, rash" *hiphil* "to treat disrespectfully" (the expected realization in Hebrew) versus דלל "to be insignificant" (the expected realization in Aramaic) (+ דַּל "weak, poor," דַּלָּה "weak, poor population")[52]
- נזר "to dedicate" versus נדר "to vow"[53]
- עזר "to help" versus עדר "to help" (1 Chr 12:34)

the emphatic lateral fricative (*/ṣ́/)

- נתץ "to pull down" (the expected realization in Hebrew) versus נתע *niphal* "to be broken" (the expected realization in Aramaic; Job 4:10)
- רבץ "to lie down, stretch out" versus רבע "to lie down"
- רעץ "to destroy" versus רעע "to smash"[54]
- רצה "to be pleased with" versus רעה in nouns like רְעוּת "longing."[55]

---

50. The etymology of these words is complex. See H. J. Fabry and U. Dahmen, "פשר," *TDOT* 12:152.

51. Note also עשׁר "to be rich" vs. עתר in עֲתֶרֶת "abundance of" (const.; Jer 33:6). In other cases, there is not necessarily any connection between semantically similar words with corresponding consonants, as with שׁור "to watch, lie in wait" and תור "to spy out, explore."

52. Conceivably these are etymologically different roots. See the brief discussion of similar roots in Kogan, "Proto-Semitic Phonetics and Phonology," 96–97, with references.

53. See the article by J. Boyd, "The Etymological Relationship between *ndr* and *nzr* Reconsidered," *UF* 17 (1986): 61–75.

54. Note also the possibly related רצץ "to oppress."

55. Note also מחק "to destroy" in Judg 5:26, which matches an early Aramaic orthography where /ṣ́/ was marked by ק, and the more common מחץ "to destroy," characteristic of Hebrew. See Holger Gzella, "מחה," *ThWQ* 2:638; Christian Stadel,

Table 2.2. PS/PNWS Consonantal Phonemes

	bilabial	labiodental	(inter)dental	alveolar	palatal	velar	uvular	pharyngeal	glottal
voiceless →		← voiced, for each column							
plosive	p b			t d		k g	(q)		ʾ
nasal	m			n					
trill							R		
affricate				^{t}s ^{d}z					
fricative		(f) (v)	ṯ ḏ	s [> š/h]	(š)	ḫ ġ	(χ) (ʁ)	ḥ ʿ	h
lateral fricative				ś					
approximant					y	w			
lateral approximant				l					
emphatic			ṯ̣	ṭ ^{t}ṣ ṣ́		ḳ			

Note: For this chart, the usual Semitic transliterations are used, with the exceptions of /^{t}ṣ/ for what is often /ṣ/, /ṣ́/ for /ḍ/ (or /δ̣/), /R/ for /r/, /^{t}s/ for /s/, /^{d}z/ for /z/, and /ṯ̣/ for /ẓ/. Letters in parentheses are phonemes or allophones attested in at least one stage of Hebrew; see Huehnergard, "Afro-Asiatic," 142–43.

It does not seem surprising that words exhibiting the typical Hebrew realization of these phonemes are often more common than their corresponding Aramaic-like counterparts (e.g., חרשׁ instead of חרת). On the other hand, it is not uncommon that the Aramaic-like word appears more often than the corresponding Hebrew realization (e.g., דלל [also דַּל and דַּלָּה] instead of זלל; and פִּתְרוֹן instead of פֵּשֶׁר; as well as רעע instead of רעץ). In still other cases, both realizations of a root appear frequently, one taking on a particular meaning distinct from the other (e.g., נזר "to dedicate" versus נדר "to vow").

It is important to note that the words and roots listed in the preceding section and following sections (I assume) are not examples of scribal errors or misspellings (e.g., due to a scribe's confusion between the graphic similarity of *ayin* and *tsade*).[56] Related languages attest similar kinds of plurality in their lexicons so it is a fair guess that Hebrew also contained such pairs of words.[57] Of course, it is entirely conceivable that some rare attestations of words are due to scribal lapse. The working assumption here, however, is that they are not.

The inventory of PS/PNWS consonantal phonemes is presented in the table on page 34. The correspondences of the various early phonemes to Hebrew, Ugaritic, and Aramaic phonemes and letters are presented in the following table.

"Aramaic Influences on Biblical Hebrew," *EHLL* 1:162. In addition, note the possible correspondence between צוק "to press" (+ מוּצָק "distress" Isa 8:23) vs. עוק "to press" (Amos 2:13) (+ מוּעָקָה "distress" Ps 66:11; עָקָה "pressure" Ps 55:4).

56. For a few examples of scribal errors, see §10 below, "Variation of Orthography and Pronunciation within Roots and Words."

57. Sometimes a particular root appears more often in one particular dialect or register and the parallel root appears in another dialect or register (e.g., the verb זעק "to cry out" occurs primarily in later books of the Bible, while the parallel root צעק "to cry out" occurs primarily in earlier books of the Bible).

Table 2.3. Correspondences of Phonemes[58]

PS/PNWS	Biblical Hebrew ca. 800 BCE	Biblical Hebrew ca. 400 CE	Ugaritic	Old Aramaic ca. 800 BCE
Phoneme →		← how it was written (for polyphonous letters)		
ʾ	ʾ	ʾ	ʾ	ʾ
b	b	b	b	b
g	g	g	g	g
d	d	d	d d	d ד
ḏ	z	z	ḏ/d ḏ/d/z	ḏ ד
h	h	h	h	h
w	w	w	w	w
^{d}z	z	z	z	z
ḥ	ḥ ח	ḥ	ḥ	ḥ ח
ḫ	ḫ ח	ḥ	ḫ	ḫ ח
ṭ	ṭ	ṭ	ṭ	ṭ ט
y	y	y	y	y
k	k	k	k	k
l	l	l	l	l
m	m	m	m	m
n	n	n	n	n
^{t}s	s	s	s	s
ʿ	ʿ ע	ʿ	ʿ	ʿ ע
ġ	ġ ע	ʿ	ġ ġ	ġ ע

58. Note the following references: Huehnergard, "Afro-Asiatic," 142–43; Kogan, "Proto-Semitic Phonetics and Phonology," 54–151; Pardee, "Ugaritic," 292; Stuart Creason, "Aramaic," *CEWAL*, 396–97; Frederick Mario Fales, "Old Aramaic," *SLIH*, 566; Holger Gzella, "Imperial Aramaic," *SLIH*, 575–76. In Imperial Aramaic, the interdentals (/ḏ/, /ṯ/, /ṯ̣/) merged with the dentals (/d/, /t/, /ṭ/); the Aramaic reflex of /ṣ́/ (perhaps an "emphatic lateral spirant" [so Fales] or "voiced velar or uvular affricate" [so Gzella]) became /ʿ/.

p	p	p	p	p
ᵗṣ	ṣ	ṣ	ṣ	ṣ
ḳ	ḳ	q	ḳ	ḳ ק
r	r	r	r	r
ś	ś ש	s ש	. š	ś ש
ṣ́	ṣ	ṣ	ṣ	ṣ́ ? ק
s[PS] > š/h [NWS]	š ש	š ש	š	š ש
t	t	t	t	t
ṯ	š ש	š ש	ṯ	ṯ ש
ṱ	ṣ	ṣ	ẓ/ġ ẓ/ġ	ṱ ט

In order to remember these unfamiliar PS/PNWS phonemes, one can associate them with the following Hebrew words:

- /ḏ/ as in **ḏaqanu*; Hebrew זָקָן "beard" versus Aramaic דְּקַן
- /ḫ/ as in **ḫarranu*; Hebrew חָרָן "Harran" versus Akkadian *ḫarrānu* and Greek LXX to Gen. *χαρραν*. Note also **ḫattiyyu*; Hebrew חִתִּי "Hittite" versus Ugaritic *ḫt* and *ḫty* and Akkadian *ḫattû* and LXX *χεται*
- /ġ/ as in **ġazzatu*; Hebrew עַזָּה "Gaza" versus Greek *γαζα* and Arabic *ġazzat*
- /ś/ as in **kaśdu*; Hebrew כַּשְׂדִּים "Chaldeans" versus Akkadian *kaldu* and Greek *χαλδαιοι*
- /ṣ́/ as in **ʾarṣ́u*; Hebrew אֶרֶץ "land" versus Aramaic אֲרַע
- /ṱ/ as in **ṱalmūtu*; should be in Hebrew *צַלְמוּת "shadow" but is reanalyzed as צַלְמָוֶת "shadow of death" versus Ugaritic *ẓlmt* and *ġlmt*
- /ṯ/ as in **ṯalgu*; Hebrew שֶׁלֶג "snow" versus Aramaic תְּלַג

2.6. Proto-Semitic/Proto-Northwest Semitic /w/

At some early stage in the history of Canaanite, what was /w/ in PS and PNWS shifted to /y/ at the beginning and end of roots. So, what was **waṯiba* "to dwell" became **yašaba* and then **yāšab* (> יָשַׁב); similarly **yišlawūna* became יִשְׁלָיוּ "they will be at ease" (Job 12:6), even though the /w/ is still attested in the *qåṭal* form שָׁלַוְתִּי "I am at rest" (Job 3:26). Medial

/w/, on the other hand, became */ū/ (e.g., קוּם "to arise").[59] The exceptions to this shift are relatively rare (e.g., וָלָד "child" vs. יֶ֫לֶד "child, boy"; and עָנָו "afflicted" vs. עָנִי "afflicted").

2.7. Correspondences between Weak Roots

In the lexicon of Biblical Hebrew, it is easy to see that certain combinations of consonants have the same or similar meanings. In fact, it is often the case that three classes of weak roots (i.e., II-*vav*/*yod*, III-*vav*/*yod*, and geminate roots), have semantically similar verbs.[60] In most cases, the verbs seem to be byforms of each other.[61] Note, for example, the following correspondences between root-types:

II-*vav*/*yod* and III-*vav*/*yod* roots

- בוז and בזה "to despise"[62]
- גור "to attack" and גרה *piel* "to stir up strife"[63]

II-*vav*/*yod* and geminate roots

- מוש and משש "to feel, grope"[64]
- צור "to bind" and צרר "to confine, besiege"
- צור and צרר "to attack"
- רום "to rise" and רמם "to exalt oneself"[65]

---

59. In the same way, medial /y/ became */ī/ (e.g., שִׂים "to set").

60. Many of the examples below are drawn from Jerzy Kuryłowicz, *Studies in Semitic Grammar and Metrics*, Prace Językoznawcze 67 (Wrocław: Zakład Narodowy imienia Ossolińskich, 1973), 10–12.

61. One can sometimes identify roots that have developed out of other roots, as with פוח "to breathe, blow" (Central Semitic *pwḫ*), which developed apparently from a reanalysis of the verb נפח "to breathe, blow" (Common Semitic *npḫ*) as a *niphal* or N-stem conjugation. See John Huehnergard and Saul Olyan, "The Etymology of Hebrew and Aramaic *ykl* 'To Be Able,'" *JSS* 58 (2013): 17.

62. Contrast בזז "to plunder" and the related noun בִּזָּה "plunder."

63. Contrast גור "to sojourn" and גור "to fear" as well as גרר "to drag away," *niphal* "to chew cud." Note also שׂוּט (Ps 40:5) and שׂטה "to turn aside" and the respective roots assumed for שׁוֹאָה "ruin" (< *šwy*) and שְׁאִיָּה "ruin" (< *šʾy*).

64. Contrast משה "to draw out (from water)."

65. Contrast רמה "to throw, shoot" and רמה *piel* "to betray." Note also דוך "to crush" (Num 11:8) and דכך as evidenced in דַּךְ "crushed" as well as דכא *piel* "to crush"; טוח "to plaster" and טחח "to be smeared" (Isa 44:18); מוך "to be poor" and מכך "to be low"; שׂוך "to fence in" and שׂכך "to cover" (Exod 33:22); and perhaps also שׁית and

III-*vav/yod* and geminate roots

- דמה "to cease," *niphal* "to be destroyed" and דמם "to be silent, dumb," *niphal* "to be destroyed"[66]
- זכה "to be clear" and זכך "to be clean, pure"
- חרה "to be hot, angry" and חרר "to burn"[67]
- ידה and ידד "to throw"
- מסה *hiphil* "to cause to melt" and מסס *niphal* "to melt"
- ערה *piel* "to uncover" and ערר "to strip"[68]
- קלה *niphal* and קלל *niphal* "to be contemptible"
- קצה and קצץ "to cut off"[69]
- רבה and רבב "to be numerous"
- רדה "to rule" and רדד "to subjugate, conquer"
- שׂגה and שׂגג "to go astray."[70]

There are also cases where these weak root-classes overlap with I-*vav/yod* and I-*nun* roots. Note also the correspondences between I-*vav/yod* roots and I-*nun* roots.[71]

I-*vav/yod* and II-*vav/yod* roots

- יגר and גור "to be afraid"[72]

שׁתת "to set" (though the latter might really be a mirage, שַׁתּוּ of Pss 49:15 and 73:9 being an alternative form for שָׁתוּ, influenced perhaps by the similarly spelled second- and first-person forms שַׁתָּ and שַׁתִּי).

66. Note also דום as suggested by דּוּמָה "silence."

67. Contrast חָוַר "to be white."

68. Contrast עור "to awake."

69. Note also the frequently occurring nouns: קְצָת/*קָצוּ/קֵצֶה/קָצָה/קָצֶה "end" (all from קצה) and קֵץ "end" (from קצץ). Contrast קוץ "to loathe," יקץ "to awake" (intrans.), and קיץ *hiphil* "to awake" (trans.).

70. Note also גזה "to cut off" (Ps 71:6) (+ גָּזִית "hewn") and גזז "to shear" (+ גֵּז "shearing"); כלה "to cease" and כלל "to complete, perfect" (+ כֹּל "all"); מצה "to slurp" and מצץ "to lap" (Isa 66:11).

71. The one correspondence between I-*vav/yod* and III-*vav/yod* roots may be due to reanalysis: יגה *hophal* (2 Sam 20:13) "to be expelled" and הגה "to remove." Examples of correspondences between I-*vav/yod* and geminate roots are also relatively rare: יחם *piel* "to conceive" (+ חֵמָה "heat") and חמם "to be hot" (חַמָּה "heat, sun"); יעז *niphal* "to be insolent" (perhaps Isa 33:19) and עזז "to be strong"; ימשׁ *hiphil* "cause to touch" (perhaps Judg 16:26) and משׁשׁ/מושׁ "to feel, grope"; ירק and רקק (Lev 15:8) "to spit."

72. Contrast גור "to sojourn" and גור "to attack" as well as גרר "to drag away," *niphal* "to chew cud."

- יטב and טוב "to be good"
- יעף and עיף "to be weary" (+ יָעֵף/עָיֵף "weary")
- יקץ "to awake" (intrans.) and קיץ *hiphil* "to awake" (trans.)[73]

I-*nun* and and II-*vav*/*yod* roots

- נסך "to pour" and סוך "to anoint oneself"[74]
- נפח and פוח "to breathe, blow" [75]
- נפץ and פוץ "to be scattered"[76]
- נצץ and צוץ "to shine, blossom"[77]

I-*nun* and III-*vav*/*yod* roots

- נבל "to languish, fall, be worn out" and בלה "to wither, crumble"
- נדח *niphal* "to be scattered," *hiphil* "to expel" and דחה "to drive off" (+ דחה *niphal* "to be expelled")

I-*nun* and geminate roots

- נדח *niphal* "to be scattered," *hiphil* "to expel" and דחח *niphal* "to be expelled"[78]
- נסך "to weave" and סכך "to weave"[79]
- נקב "to bore through, slander" and קבב "to curse"[80]

---

73. Contrast קצה and קצץ "to cut off," and קוץ "to loathe." Note also ימר *hiphil* "to exchange" (perhaps Jer 2:11) and מור "to change"; ימש *hiphil* "cause to touch" (perhaps Judg 16:26) and משש/מוש "to feel, grope"; ינק "to suck" and נוק or ניק "to suckle" (Exod 2:9); יעץ and עוץ "to advise"; יצת "to kindle" and צות *hiphil* "set on fire" (Isa 27:4); יקש "to trap with a snare" and קוש "to trap with a snare" (Isa 29:21) (+ נקש *niphal* "to be ensnared"). In addition, note that the verb בוש "to be ashamed" in the *hiphil* attests two forms, one clearly formed from the root בוש meaning "to make ashamed" (e.g., הֱבִישׁוֹתָ) and the other formed as though from יבש meaning "to be ashamed" (e.g., הֹבַשְׁתָּ).

74. Contrast נסך/סכך "to weave" and סכך "to cover."

75. Note also יפח (Jer 4:31).

76. Note also פצץ *poel* "to shatter" and contrast פצה "to open (the mouth)."

77. Note also נקר "to gouge (the eyes)"and קור "to bore, dig" (perhaps 2 Kgs 19:20, Isa 37:25); נקש *niphal* "to be ensnared" and קוש "to lay a snare" (Isa 29:21) (+ יקש "to trap with a snare").

78. Note also דחה "to drive off."

79. Contrast נסך "to pour" and סוך "to anoint oneself," סכך "to cover."

80. Note also the root יקב presumed in the word יֶקֶב "wine vat."

I-*vav/yod* roots and I-*nun* roots

- יצב *hithpael* and נצב "to take a stand"
- יקע and נקע "to turn away in disgust"
- יקשׁ "to trap with a snare" and נקשׁ *niphal* "to be ensared."[81]

Note especially that geminate roots often correspond to II-*vav/yod* and III-*vav/yod* roots, less often with the others. Also, I-*vav/yod* and I-*nun* roots correspond most often with II-*vav/yod* roots.

Another common variation between synonymous roots is evidenced in the pairs of III-*aleph* and III-*vav/yod* roots. In these cases, often a *lamed* or *resh* is the second root consonant. Note the pairs, listed in alphabetical order: ירא versus ירה "to shoot"; סלא versus סלה "to weigh"; פלא "to be wonderful" versus פלה "to be separate"; קרא versus קרה "to occur"; תלא versus תלה "to hang."[82] It may appear that the primary difference between the members of these pairs is only a *mater*, that is, an *aleph* used as a *mater* to mark a preceding */ā/ as in Aramaic versus a *he mater* (e.g., נִקְרָא "has been met" Exod 5:3 vs. נִקְרָה "has been met" Exod 3:18). Given the sparse attestation of some roots, this may be correct in certain instances. However, most ancient readers conceived of the roots (and associated verbs) as independent entitites, as revealed in certain unambiguous verbal forms like וַיִּ֫קֶר "it happened" (Ruth 2:3), which is unambiguously III-*vav/yod*, and קְרָאַ֫נִי "it befell me" (Job 4:14), which is unambiguously III-*aleph*.

Some examples of correspondences without a *lamed* or *resh* include: דכא and דכה both *piel* "to crush"; חבא and חבה *niphal* "to hide oneself"; נכא *niphal* "be wiped out" (+ נְכָאִים "stricken" Isa 16:7) and נכה "to strike," *niphal* "to be struck"; נשא and נשה "to lend on interest"; שׂגא and שׂגה "to grow, increase."[83]

A further set of correspondences is found between I-*aleph* and I-*vav/yod* roots. The clearest examples are relatively few: אֶחָד "one" and יחד "to be united" (+ יָחִיד "only one," יַ֫חַד "together"); אלה "to wail" (Joel 1:8; +

81. Note also קוֹשׁ "to lay a snare" (Isa 29:21). Note as well the following corresponding roots: יאה (Jer 10:7) and נאה "to be pretty, fitting"; יפח (Jer 4:31) and נפח/פוח "to breathe."

82. Not all such pairs seem synonymous or related, as with כלא "to restrain" and כלה "to finish." Another superficially similar example might be ירה/ירא "to fear," though the latter is also listed by BDB under the root רהה. It occurs once, as תִּרְהוּ (Isa 44:8).

83. Note also קיא and קיה "to vomit."

אַלְלַי "alas!") and ילל *hiphil* "to wail"; אשר "to go straight" and ישר "to go straight." In addition, note the correspondences in sense and form between אסף "to gather" (תֹּסֵף "you gather" Ps 104:29) and יסף "to add," *hiphil* "to add, do again" (תֹסֵף "do [not] add" Deut 13:1).[84] Finally, note how some I-*aleph* words appear to be I-*vav*/*yod*, like מוֹסֵר* "bond."

In some cases two roots form a suppletive paradigm. That is, one root supplies forms for one part of the verbal paradigm and another, related root supplies forms for other parts of the paradigm. Notice, for example, how the *niphal* of נצב supplies *qåṭal* and participial forms and the *hithpael* of יצב supplies *yiqṭol* forms such that we read in Num 22:22 that "the angel of the lord stood (וַיִּתְיַצֵּב) in the path" but in Num 22:23 that the ass saw "the angel of the lord standing (נִצָּב) in the path."[85] In a similar way, note how the root טוב supplies forms for the *qåṭal*, infinitives, and participle, while the root יטב supplies the *yiqṭol*.[86]

It should be quickly added, of course, that not all of the pairs of verbs listed above are necessarily related to each other etymologically (e.g., בלה/נבל). It will not be surprising that such historically unrelated pairs are often not exact synonyms of each other. However, even verb pairs that do seem to be related etymologically do not always express the exact same sense (e.g., חרה/חרר).

Cognizance of the above correspondences is useful to intermediate students in several ways. First, it is helpful to memorize certain verbs together, as with יצב and נצב described above, since they can appear together and form one paradigm.[87] Second, when sight-reading, one can

---

84. In addition, note אסר "to tie, bind (as prisoner)" and יסר "to discipline."

85. Although it is conceivable that the *niphal* forms like נִצָּב should really be derived from יצב (cf. נִצְּתָה from יצת), note the cognate evidence from other languages for נצב as well as the BH nouns/adjectives like נְצִיב "pillar, overseer" that attest to this root. Similarly, יקץ supplies *qal* forms and קיץ *hiphil* forms.

86. Note also יגר is used for the *qåṭal* but גור for the *yiqṭol* and imperative. The roots דחה and דחח in the *niphal* appear only in the *yiqṭol* (and perhaps in the participle), while the root נדח in the *niphal* appears only in the *qåṭal* and participle.

87. Notice that most vocabulary aids used by students to memorize Biblical Hebrew words list the verbs separately. Larry A. Mitchel (*A Student's Vocabulary for Biblical Hebrew and Aramaic* [Grand Rapids: Zondervan, 1984]) lists נצב on p. 16 but יצב on p. 23 without cross-reference; George M. Landes (*Building Your Biblical Hebrew Vocabulary: Learning Words by Frequency and Cognate*, RBS 41 [Atlanta: Society of Biblical Literature, 2001]) lists נצב on p. 73 but יצב on p. 84 without cross-reference; Miles V. Van Pelt and Gary D. Pratico (*The Vocabulary Guide to Biblical Hebrew*

sometimes make an educated guess about the meaning of a word based on knowledge of another word or root. For example, when one encounters unfamiliar verbal forms like וַתְּנִיקֵהוּ (Exod 2:9) in the context of "nursing" (וְהֵינִקֵהוּ "and nurse it!" Exod 2:9), one can make an educated guess that the unfamiliar verb (i.e., נוק or ניק) is a byform of ינק, with the same sense "she nursed it." It must be kept in mind, of course, that not all weak roots are related to each other. Although בוז and בזה both mean "to despise," the geminate root בזז means something different, "to plunder."

In addition, the correspondences between different types of weak roots listed above are also reflective of broader similarities between the same root classes, especially in the inflection of the verbal paradigms. For example, although there are relatively few semantic correspondences between I-*vav*/*yod* and I-*nun* roots, it is not uncommon for *yiqṭol* forms from I-*vav*/*yod* roots to exhibit assimilation of the first root consonant such that they look as though they derive from I-*nun* roots. Thus, we find אֶצֹּק "I will pour" (Isa 44:3) from יצק; also וַיִּצֶר "he formed" (Gen 2:19) from יצר.[88] Being familiar with the most common correspondences between weak roots helps a reader identify and quickly look up relevant verbs in the dictionary. These correspondences are addressed with greater detail in the chapters on morphology.

2.8. Correspondences between Roots with Similarly Articulated Consonants

In the above sections, I have listed pairs of words and roots that are not only semantically similar, but are also (for the most part) etymologically related, derived presumably from a single PS/PNWS root or word or from a biconsonantal "core."[89] In the following section, I also list semantically similar words and roots. These too are often related etymologically, but sometimes are not. Occasionally, an easy historical explanation is offered (as for the pair צָעִיר/זְעֵיר "little," where the former seems influenced from Aramaic). However, the historical links between many roots and words

---

[Grand Rapids: Zondervan, 2003]) list נצב on pp. 26, 116, 190, 208, 220 but יצב on pp. 34, 183, 215, 224 without cross-reference.

88. More regularly, the form of 3fp/2fp III-*vav*/*yod* roots (e.g., תִּרְאֶינָה "they will see" Isa 17:7) have informed the paradigms of II-*vav*/*yod* (תְּעוּפֶינָה "they will fly" Isa 60:8) and III-*aleph* roots (תִּמְצֶאןָ "they find" Deut 31:21).

89. For the term, "core," see Joüon §84.

(if they exist) are often rather complex and I have avoided explaining how each word or root in a pair might be related. In essence, it is most important for the intermediate student to recognize the possible interconnections between words/roots in order to facilitate the acquisition and retention of vocabulary and in order to better evaluate proposed translations and interpretations. Let me stress again that the listing of words together does not necessarily imply an etymological or historical link between them.

One of the most frequent correspondences between consonants is that between sibilants, especially when the sibilant is followed by *resh* or a guttural. Note the roots with correspondences between *zayin* and *tsade*: זעק "to cry out" and צעק "to cry out"; זְעֵיר "little" and צָעִיר "little"; זרב *pual* "be scorched" (Job 6:17) and צרב *niphal* "be scorched" (Ezek 21:3) (+ צָרֶ֫בֶת "burning" Prov 16:27 and צָרֶ֫בֶת "scar, inflammation" Lev 13:23, 28). Correspondences between *tsade* and *sin* are somewhat fewer: צחק "to laugh" and שׂחק "to laugh" (as with the different realizations of the name "Isaac" יִצְחָק vs. יִשְׂחָק); as are those between *tsade* and *samek*: חמס "to act violently toward" and חמץ "be ruthless" (Ps 71:4); נוץ (Lam 4:15) and נוס "to flee";[90] and between *tsade* and *shin*: פוץ "to be dispersed," *niphal* "to be scattered" and פוש "to scatter," *niphal* "to be scattered" (Nah 3:18). There are a few sets of roots that exhibit correspondences between several different sibilants: עלז, עלס, עלץ all mean "to rejoice"; שׂפן, צפן, ספן (Deut 33:19) all mean "to hide;"[91] נתס (Job 30:13), נתץ, נתשׁ all mean "to tear up" or "tear down."[92]

In some of these cases, a straightforward historical explanation may be possible (e.g., borrowing from Aramaic in the case of זְעֵיר), though in other cases such explanations become rather complex.[93] In rare cases, the

90. The parsing reflects that of *HALOT*. BDB parse נָצוּ of Lam 4:15 not as from נוץ but from נצה "to fly (?)." This makes sense of the accent on נָצוּ, which is not penultimate as we would expect if it were from נוץ. *HALOT* cites *HGhS* 398e, which lists other examples of irregular accenting for the sake of "rhythm."

91. See Steiner, *Fricative-Laterals*, 118 nn. 3, 6.

92. Note also the etymologically related נתע *niphal* "to be broken." Correspondences between *samek* and *sin*, if they occurred, would be obscured by the merger of originally distinct /s/ and /ś/ and their subsequent confusion in spelling (see above).

93. For Aramaic borrowing, see Max Wagner, *Die lexikalischen und grammatikalischen Aramaismen im alttestamentlichen Hebräisch*, BZAW 96 (Berlin: Töpelmann, 1966), 49–50. Note Steiner's description of how צחק and שׂחק are related to each other, and perhaps also to לעג "to mock" (*Fricative-Laterals*, 111–20, esp. 112) and cf. Blau, *Polyphony*, 4. Similar senses sometimes lead speakers to select similar-sounding

meaning of the two words is only remotely related and any connection between them seems likely to be purely accidental: צרף "to smelt" and שׂרף "to burn."[94] In still other cases, the similarity in sounds between two different words might have encouraged their use in similar contexts. The word אֱזוֹר "loincloth" is used naturally enough with the etymologically related אזר "to gird" in 2 Kgs 1:8, though in Job 12:18 the noun אֱזוֹר is instead the object of the verb אסר "to bind."

Sometimes one observes parallels between roots with an emphatic and corresponding nonemphatic consonant. Note, for example, the many correspondences between *tet* and *tav*: חטף and חתף (Job 9:12) "to catch, seize"; טעה (Ezek 13:10) and תעה "to wander, err"; טפל "to smear" and תפל in תָּפֵל "whitewash"; קשט in קֹשֶׁט "bow, archery" (Ps 60:6) and קשת in קֶשֶׁת "bow."[95] Note the correspondences between *kaph* and *qoph*: דכה/דכא *piel* "to crush" and דקק "to crush" and the associated nouns/adjectives: דַּכָּא "crushed" (of dust) (Ps 90:3); דַּךְ "crushed"; דַּק "thin, small, fine" (of dust in Isa 29:5).[96] Borrowing from Aramaic may explain some of these pairs of words (e.g., קֹשֶׁט and קֶשֶׁת). One can also find pairs of what appear to be etymologically unrelated words that exhibit vaguely similar meanings: זכך "to be pure" (+ זַךְ "pure" and זְכוֹכִית "glass" Job 28 :17) and זקק "to refine"; כהה "to be dim" (said of eyes) (+ כֵּהֶה "dim") and קהה "to be blunt" (said of teeth); מְכֹרָה "origin" and מָקוֹר "source, spring"; תכן *piel* "to measure" and תקן *piel* "to arrange"; שׁחט "to slaughter" and שׁחת *piel* "to annihilate, destroy."

Other correspondences include those of the gutturals. Correspondences involving *aleph* and *ayin* include גאל *niphal* "to be defiled" and געל "to loathe," *niphal* "to be defiled"; פִּתְאֹם "suddenly" and פֶּתַע "suddenly"; שׁאה *hithpael* (Gen 24:21) and שׁעה "to gaze"; תאב *piel* "to make repulsive"

---

roots to express these senses, and, conversely, similarly formed roots sometimes lead speakers to assume a common sense shared between them (Blau, *Phonology and Morphology*, 52–53).

94. The semantic correspondences between other roots and words is even more remote: צהב *hophal* "to gleam," said of bronze (Ezra 8:27), and זָהָב "gold"; also זהר *hiphil* "to shine" (+ זֹהַר "shining") and צָהֳרַיִם "noon."

95. Note also סכת *hiphil* "to keep silent" (Deut 27:9) and שׁקט "to be quiet," *hiphil* "to keep quiet," which also shows the variation in sibilants.

96. Note also דוך "to pound" (Num 11:8) and the related noun מְדֹכָה "mortar" (Num 11:8). Note also the semantically and phonetically similar רַק "thin" (said of cows) in Gen 41:19, 20, 27 (vs. דַּק in Gen 41:3, 4). The word רַק is phonetically similar to another word used in relation to cattle: רַךְ "tender" (said of a calf in Gen 18:7).

(Amos 6:8) and תעב "to loathe."[97] Those involving *aleph* and *he* include אדר *niphal*: "to be glorious" and הדר *niphal* " be honored"; אַוָּה "desire" and הַוָּה "desire; אוֹן "power, wealth" and הוֹן "wealth"; לאה and להה (Gen 47:13) "to languish."[98]

Sometimes roots with bilabial consonants evidence correspondences, as with *bet* and *pe*: בזר *piel* "to scatter" and פזר *piel* "to scatter"; כבשׁ "to subdue" and כפשׁ *hiphil* "to subdue" (Lam 3:16); נשׁב "to blow" and נשׁף "to blow."[99] The consonants *mem* and *pe* correspond in the pair מלט *niphal* "to escape," *piel* "to deliver" and פלט "to escape," *piel* "to deliver." Note also the apparent correspondences between *bet* and *vav* in גַּב "the back of a person" (Ps 129:3) and גֵּו/גַּו "the back of a person"; in דאב "to be faint" (+ דְּאָבָה "faint" Job 41:14) and דוה "to be sick" (Lev 12:2; + דָּוֶה "faint"; דְּוַי "illness; דַּוַּי "faint"; מַדְוֶה "illness"); and in תַּאֲבָה "longing" (Ps 119:20; also תאב "to desire" Ps 119:40, 174) and תַּאֲוָה "longing"; the correspondences between *pe* and *vav* in גְּוִיָּה "body" and גּוּפָה/גַּף "body."[100]

In other cases there are semantically similar words that differ in their velar consonants, as in סגר "to shut up," *niphal* "be shut up" and סכר *niphal* "be shut up."[101] Rarely they differ in their sonorants like *mem* and

---

97. Note also the correspondences between nonetymologically related אֵפֶר "ashes" and עָפָר "dust"; ירא "to fear" and ירע "to quiver."

98. Other correspondences between roots seem accidental: נַחֲרָה/נַחַר "snorting" vs. נער "to growl"; שׁוּחָה "pit" and שׁוֹאָה "destruction."

99. In relation to the last pair, note also נשׁם "to breathe, pant," and נפשׁ *niphal* "to breathe." Other words are more loosely related semantically: חבא *niphal*/חבה "to hide oneself" (Isa 26:20) and חפה "to cover"; צָרָב "burning" (modifying אֵשׁ "fire" in Prov 16:27) and צרף "to smelt, refine" (modifying אֵשׁ "fire" in Mal 3:2); קבץ "to gather (people)," קפץ "to draw together hand, mouth," and קמץ "to grasp" (+ קֹמֶץ "handful"); רמה as in רְמִיָּה "slackness (of hand)" and רפה "to relax" and in "sinking (of hands)" (Jer 47:3). Note also the pair זוב "to flow" and צוף "to flow over," *hiphil* "make flow," which exhibits not only different bilabial consonants, but also different sibilants.

100. Note also דוב *hiphil* "to make faint" (Lev 26:16; + דּוֹב "atrophy" Job 33:19). Note the use of גְּוִיָּה in 1 Sam 31:12 and גּוּפָה in the parallel account in 1 Chr 10:12. Another root pair might be עבת *piel* "to twist, pervert" (Mic 7:3; + עֲבֹת "rope") and עות *piel* "to twist, pervert" (which verb derives ultimately from עוה "to do wrong," *piel* "to twist").

101. Note also גָּבִיעַ "cup, bowl" and קֻבַּעַת "cup"; נגף "to strike" and נקף "to cut, tear"; סָגָן or סֶגֶן "official, attendant" and סֹכֵן "official"; פֶּלֶךְ "district" and פְּלֻגָּה/פְּלַגָּה (in 2 Chr 35:5) "subdivision (of family/tribe)."

nun, שׂטם "to have animosity toward" and שׂטן "to act as adversary"; and *lamed* and *resh*, אַלְמָן "palace" (Isa 13:22) and אַרְמוֹן "palace."[102]

Some words experience metathesis of root consonants. This results in two synonymous words with the same root consonants, but in different sequences: בֶּהָלָה "dismay, terror" and the metathesized version בַּלָּהָה "terror, calamity"; זַוָעָה "terror" and the metathesized version זַעֲוָה "terror"; כִּשְׂבָּה/כֶּשֶׂב "lamb" and the metathesized byforms כַּבְשָׂה/כִּבְשָׂה/כֶּבֶשׂ (Lev 5:6) "lamb"; נאק "to groan" (+ נְאָקָה "groan") and the metathesized version אנק "to groan" (+ אֲנָקָה "groan"); לעג "to mock, stammer" and עִלֵּג "stammerer" (Isa 32:4); פצר and פרץ, both meaning in the *qal* "to urge someone"; שִׂמְלָה "garment" and the metathesized form שַׂלְמָה "garment." In other cases, the apparent metathesis may really reflect two individual roots, as with כֶּסֶל/כֵּסֶל "stupidity" and סֶכֶל "folly" (Qoh 10:6); חפר "to be ashamed" and חרף "to reproach" (+ חֶרְפָּה "rebuke, shame"); and the pair פרשׂ "to declare distinctly" and פֵּשֶׁר "interpretation." Sometimes the etymology is unclear: ערף means "to drip" (+ עָרִיף and עֲרָפֶל "cloud") as does רעף. The correspondence of יעף and עיף "to be weary" may be due to the existence of byforms between root-classes, as suggested above.

Recognition of the preceding relationships is important not only in helping to build vocabulary (and to distinguish similar sounding but distinct words), as mentioned above in chapter 1, but also in helping to comprehend various proposed emendations to the biblical text, even if a definitive evaluation of these interpretations is difficult to make. For example, in 1 Sam 21:14, we read the verb form וַיְתָו; often this is understood as the *piel* form of תוה (a byform of תאה) and is translated "he marked" (see *HALOT*). On the other hand, the LXX rendering "he pounded" (ἐτυμπάνιζεν) has suggested the reconstruction *וַיָּתֹף "he knocked" (from תפף). Although a confusion between *vav* and *pe* is possible regardless of other evidence, its likelihood increases in the context of etymologically unrelated word pairs that seem to show a fluctuation between *vav* and other bilabial consonants. Similarly, one may better weigh different possi-

102. Note also בחן "to test" and בחר usually "to choose" but "to test" in Isa 48:10 (בְּחַרְתִּיךָ corresponds to בחנתיך in 1QIsa[a]). See Wagner, *Aramaismen*, 33–34; E. Y. Kutscher, *The Language and Linguistic Background of the Complete Isaiah Scroll*, STDJ 6 (Leiden: Brill, 1974), 223. For more possible examples, see Aloysius Fitzgerald, "The Interchange of L, N, and R in Biblical Hebrew," *JBL* 97 (1978): 481–88. See also David Testen, "The Significance of Aramaic r < *n," *JNES* 44 (1985): 143–46. Perhaps also the pair כמס "to gather" (Deut 32:34) and כנס "to gather, collect" belongs here.

bilities, for example, whether *HALOT* may be correct in suggesting a connection between יִתְאַבְּכוּ "they swirled" (Isa 9:17) and the *niphal* verb אבק "to wrestle" (Gen 35:24–25), or whether BDB may be correct in construing the same verb (i.e., אבך) as a byform of הפך, akin to the *hithpael* of this verb in Judg 7:13, where it seems to describe a rolling motion.[103]

2.9. Correspondences between Etymologically Unrelated Roots

In the examples that follow, there is often no specific etymological connection between the words, even when the meanings are very close. In many cases, the connection between words is likely due to "lexical contamination."[104] This is a phenomenon in which roots and words "similar in sound and form … tend to attract each other," even though the roots/words are otherwise unrelated.[105] It should also be recognized that the identification of common meanings is a subjective one and that another reader may organize the words in different ways.

The words listed here often have the same sequence of consonants at their beginning, as with the many words associated with spreading, dividing, tearing that begin with the sequence *pe-resh*: פרד, פרם, פרס, פרץ, פרק, פרר, פרשׂ (see below for specific definitions).[106] Sometimes a sequence of consonants occurs only at the end of a root, as with כנע *hiphil* "to make humble" and צנע *hiphil* "to make humble" (Mic 6:8).[107] Alternatively, the

103. It might be noted that further complicating the evaluation is the fact that in the DSS and in later Hebrew we find evidence for the root אפך as a byform of הפך (see Reymond, *Qumran Hebrew*, 189).

104. See Blau "Śîn," 68. The term is from Y. Malkiel, "Weak Phonetic Change, Spontaneous Sound Shift, Lexical Contamination," *Lingua* 11 (1962): 263–75. Blau also refers to it as "blending of synonymous or semantically related roots" (*Phonology and Morphology*, 52). Other explanations are also available; see Florin-Mihai Dat, "Métathèse et homonymie en hébreu biblique," *Suvremena lingvistika* 67 (2009): 1–21.

105. See Blau "*Śîn*," 68.

106. See ibid., 68 n. 3 and Kuryłowicz, *Studies*, 6. This list does not even exhaust the set of words having to do with spreading, dividing, and tearing that begin with *pe* and a liquid consonant: פלח *piel* "to pierce, cut in pieces"; פלג *niphal* "to be divided," *piel* "to split." In addition to these, note the semantically similar words that begin with *pe*: פאה *hiphil* "to wipe out" (Deut 32:26); פוץ "to disperse"; פושׂ "to scatter," *niphal* "to be scattered"; פשׂה "to spread."

107. Although the root צנע occurs only once in the Hebrew Bible, it occurs four times in Ben Sira and over ten times in the DSS.

first and last consonants correspond: פקח "to open (the eyes)" and פתח "to open."[108] In still other cases, the relevant consonants appear in different places and sequences, as with the words with *qoph* and *dalet* that describe burning: דלק "to burn"; יקד "to burn"; קדח "to set fire to." In some cases, it is partially due to nominal morphology that the words look and sound similar, as with פַּחַת and שַׁחַת "pit"; I have avoided listing most examples of this sort.

Note the following clusters of roots and words that seem semantically and phonetically close, only some of which are etymologically related:[109]

- *aleph-nun:* mourning, lamenting, groaning: אנה "to mourn" (+ תַּאֲנִיָּה, אֲנִיָּה, אֳנִי "mourning"); אנח *niphal* "to sigh, groan" (+ אֲנָחָה "groan"); אנן *hithpoel* "to murmur, complain"; אנק "to groan" (+ אֲנָקָה "groan"); נאק "to groan" (+ נְאָקָה "groan")[110]
- *gimel-bet:* convex, concave things: אַרְגָּב "heap"; גַּב "back of a person, brow"; גֵּב "pit"; גֶּבֶא "cistern"; גבה "to be high"; גָּבִיעַ "cup, bowl"; גִּבֵּן "hunchbacked"; גִּבְעָה "hill"; מִשְׂגָּב "high point"[111]
- *gimel-zayin:* cutting: גזה "to cut"; גזז "to shear"; גזר "to cut, divide," *niphal* "be destroyed"[112]
- *he:* exclamations: הֵא "lo"; הֶאָח "aha!" (joy); הָהּ "ah, alas"; הוֹ "ah, alas"; הוֹי "ah, alas"
- *he-mem*: being tumultuous and loud: הום "to confuse"; המה "to be upset, groan"; המם "to disturb"; נהם "to growl" (+ נְהָמָה "growl")[113]

---

108. Cf. also פצה "to open (the mouth)."

109. Some of the examples are drawn from Dat, "Métathèse et homonymie," 12–16. There is overlap in certain rare cases between sets of words (e.g., נהם appears in the set containing *he-mem* and *nun-he*).

110. Note also perhaps נוח "to sigh" (Hab 3:16). Furthermore, note the parallels to the roots listed below containing the letters *nun-he* that indicate groaning, lamenting, and other inarticulate sounds (נהג, נהה, נהם, נהק) and those containing the letters *he-mem* that indicate being tumultuous and loud (הום, המה, המם, נהם).

111. Note also גֵּו/גַּו "the back of a person." English has a similar set of words with overlapping senses and sounds: gibbous, convex.

112. Note also the possible case of the byform גרז (spec. נִגְרַזְתִּי "I am cut off" Ps 31:23), unless this is a simple scribal slip.

113. Note the parallels to the roots listed above containing the letters *aleph-nun* and those below containing *nun-he*, all of which indicate groaning, lamenting, and other inarticulate sounds: אנה, אנח, אנק, נאק and נהג, נהה, נהם, נהק.

- *zayin-resh*: scattering: בזר "to scatter," זרה "to scatter," and זרע "to sow, scatter seed," זרק "to scatter, sprinkle," פזר "to scatter"
- *khet-bet:* binding: חֶבֶל "cord"; חבק *piel* "to clasp, embrace"; חבר "to unite, be joined"; חבשׁ "to bind up, saddle"[114]
- *khet-tsade:* cutting, dividing: חצב "to divide, cleave"; חצה "to divide"; חצץ "to divide" (+ חֵץ "arrow"); חרץ "to cut, sharpen"[115]
- *lamed-lamed:* being insignificant, mocking: דלל "to be insignificant"; הלל *poel* "to mock"; זלל "to be foolish, rash" *hiphil* "to treat disrespectfully"; קלל "to be insignificant," *piel* "to curse"; *hiphil* "to mock"; תלל *hiphil* "to mock"
- *lamed-ayin:* mocking, stammering: לעב *hiphil* "to mock" (2 Chr 36:16); לעג "to mock, stammer"; לעז "to speak in an incomprehensible manner"; לעע "to talk wildly"; עִלֵּג "stammerer" (Isa 32:4)[116]
- *mem-khet:* destroying: מחה "to wipe out"; מחץ "to wound severely"; מחק "to annihilate"[117]
- *nun-dalet*: expelling, putting to flight: נדד "to flee," *hiphil* "to put to flight"; נדה *piel* "to drive away, postpone"; נדח *niphal* "to be scattered," *hiphil* "to expel"; נדף "to scatter, destroy"[118]
- *nun-he*: groaning, lamenting, and other inarticulate (nonhuman) sounds: נהג "to wail, lament"; נהה "to lament" (נְהִיָה, נְהִי, נִי "lamentation"); נהם "to growl" (+ נְהָמָה "growl"); נהק "to bray"[119]

---

114. The letter *khet* in these words likely represents /ḥ/ (based especially on the Ugaritic cognates), but for חֶבֶל and חבר there is limited contradictory evidence from Arabic and Akkadian. In relation to חבק, note דבק "to cling, keep close."

115. The cognate evidence for *khet* in these words is often contradictory. Nevertheless, it seems the *khet* in חצב represents /ḫ/, though the *khet* in חרץ and חצץ represents /ḥ/ (see *Ges*[18]). Note the parallels to roots with the letters *qoph-tsade* listed below that denote cutting: קצב, קצה, קצע, קצץ, קצר.

116. Arabic cognates (listed in *HALOT*) suggest /ʿ/ for *ayin* in לעב, לעג and /ġ/ for *ayin* in לעז and לעע.

117. Note also מחא "to clap hands." It is often assumed that most, if not all, of these roots are related to each other from the earlier root **mḫś* (see Gzella, "מחה," 2:638).

118. In relation to נדח, note דחה "to drive off"; דחח *niphal* "to be expelled" (all with /ḥ/), as well as נסח "to tear away," *niphal* "to be forcibly removed" (with /ḫ/). In relation to נדף, note also הדף "to push away."

119. Note also הגה "to growl, mutter" and the following words containing a *khet*: נבח "to bark" (Isa 56:10); נַחַר (Job 39:20)/נַחֲרָה (Jer 8:16) "snorting." Note the parallels to the roots listed above containing the sequence *aleph-nun* that indicate mourning,

- *nun-vav*: shaking, waving, wandering: נוד "to sway, shake (the head), be homeless"; נוט "to tremble" (Ps 99:1); נוע "to tremble, wander without home," *hiphil* "to shake (the head)"; נוף "to move back and forth"[120]
- *nun-qoph:* boring, digging, cutting: נקב "to bore"; נָקִיק "cleft"; נקף "to cut, tear"; נקר "to gouge out (eyes)"[121]
- *nun-tav*: tearing, breaking: נתח *piel* "to cut up" (+ נֵ֫תַח "piece of meat"); נתס "to tear"; נתע *niphal* "to be broken" (Job 4:10); נתץ "to pull, break down"; נתק "to pull down, tear"; נתשׁ "to pluck up, root out"[122]
- *samek-khet:* removing: נסח "to tear down" *niphal* "be removed"; סחב "to drag away"; סחה "to sweep away"
- *pe-resh:* spreading, dividing, tearing: פרד "to spread," *hiphil* "to separate"; פרם "to tear (a garment)"; פרס "to break (bread)"; פרץ "to break down, breach (a wall), spread out"; פרק "to tear apart"; פרר *hiphil* "to break (a covenant)"; פרשׂ "to spread out (a garment, scroll)"
- *pe-tsade*: smashing, destroying: נפץ "to smash"; פצח *piel* "to smash" (Mi 3:3); פצם "to split (the earth)" (Ps 60:4); פצע "to crush" (פֶּ֫צַע + "wound"); פצץ *poel* "to smash"[123]
- *qoph-dalet:* burning: דלק "to burn"; יקד "to burn"; קדח "to set fire to"
- *qoph-tsade:* cutting, extremity: קצב "to cut (wood), shear (sheep)" (+ קֶ֫צֶב "shape, extremity"); קצה "to cut off (days)" (also קָצֶה, קָצָה, קֵ֫צֶה, קָצוּ, קְצָת "end"); קצע *hiphil* "to scrape off" (Lev 14:41); קצץ "to cut off" (+ קֵץ "end"); קצר "to be short," *piel* "to shorten (days)"[124]

---

lamenting, groaning (נאק, אנק, אנח, אנה) and those containing *he-mem* that indicate being tumultuous and loud (נהם, המם, המה, הום).

120. In relation to נוד, note רוד "to roam, wander" (+ מָרוּד "homelessness"). In relation to נוט, note מוט "to totter" and שׁוט "to roam about."

121. Note the parallels to the roots below with *qoph-resh* that indicate boring, digging: קור, עקר, נקר, דקר.

122. Note also the similarities between these roots and the following: נסח "to tear down," *niphal* "to be forcibly removed" and נסע "to tear out (door, peg), journey on."

123. Cf. נפץ "to scatter" and פוץ "to scatter."

124. Note the parallels to the roots listed above containing the sequence *khet-tsade* that indicate cutting and dividing: חצב, חצה, חצץ, חרץ.

- *qoph-resh:* digging, boring: דקר "to pierce"; נקר "to gouge out (eyes)," *pual* "to be quarried"; עקר "to uproot"; קור "to dig" (+ מָקוֹר "source, spring")[125]
- *resh-gimel*: churning, being upset, creating strife: גור "to attack"; גרה "to stir up strife"; רגז "to shake" (with earth as subject), "to be distressed"; רגע "to stir up (sea)," *hiphil* "to make peace"; and רגשׁ "to be restless" (Ps 2:1; + רֶגֶשׁ Ps 55:15/רִגְשָׁה Ps 64:3 "unrest")[126]
- *resh-ayin*: trembling, shaking: ירע "to tremble, fear"; נער "to shake (e.g., leaves, garment)"; רעד "to tremble"; רעל "to quiver"; רעם "to thunder"; רעשׁ "to quake"[127]
- *shin-khet*: lowering: חוה *hishtaphel* "to bow down"; שׁוח "to sink" (+ שַׁחַת "pit"); שׁחה "to bow down"; שׁחח "to be bowed down"[128]
- *shin-lamed*: drawing off or out: נשׁל "to slip off (sandal)"; שׁלף "to slip off (sandal), draw (sword)"; שׁלל "draw out (sheaves) (+ שׁוֹלָל "barefoot")[129]

The above represents only a sampling of the most obvious examples; below are further examples. It is probably not possible to remember all such correspondences within the BH lexicon. The most essential thing to retain from these lists is the existence of such correspondences. Each word will usually have its own nuance and be used in a unique manner, but the general sense is sometimes easier to remember and can often be useful when sight-reading.

A few generalizations can be made about the above groupings. Roots connected with inarticulate sounds (frequently associated with mourning and lamenting) often include the letter *he* or *aleph* and either *mem* or *nun*. Presumably this is connected to the numerous interjections with the letter *he*, which are themselves presumably based in onomatopoeia. Roots

---

125. Note also the phonetically similar כרה "to dig." Note the parallels to the roots above with *nun-qoph* that indicate boring, digging: נקר, נקף, נָקִיק, נקב.

126. Note also גרשׁ "to toss up, churn (mud from sea)," listed as a root separate from גרשׁ "to drive away" in *HALOT*.

127. In relation to רעשׁ, note געשׁ "to shake." The words above are often associated with fear; note the semantically and phonetically close ערץ "to dread." In all the roots *ayin* may represent the /ʿ/ sound, though in רעם, it may instead represent /ġ/.

128. The *khet* in these roots represents different sounds, to judge from the comparative evidence: /ḥ/ in חוה and שׁחה but /ḫ/ in שׁוח and שׁחח.

129. Note perhaps also שׁלה "draw out (soul)" (Job 27:8). See Blau, "*Śîn*," 1 and Kuryłowicz, *Studies*, 6.

that indicate cutting often have *tsade* accompanied by either *khet* or *qoph*. The letter *qoph* with either a *nun* or *resh* often occurs in roots denoting boring and digging. *Lamed* and *ayin* often appear in roots connected with mockery.

Oftentimes only two roots with similar meanings correspond in their consonants. Those that correspond in their initial consonants include:

- בדד "to be separated" and בדל *hiphil* "to separate"
- בלל "to mix, confuse" and בלע "to confuse"
- שַׁלְהֶבֶת/לֶהָבָה/לַהַב "flame" and לַהַט "flame" (Gen 3:24) (+ להט "to blaze")
- נשׁך "to bite" and נשׁק "to kiss"
- עוה "to do wrong," *piel* "to twist" and עות *piel* "to bend"
- פגע "to meet, encounter" and פגשׁ "to meet, encounter" (cf. נגע *hiphil* "to touch, reach" and נגשׁ "to approach")
- קשׁה "to be hard," *hiphil* "to harden (heart)" (+ קְשִׁי "stubborn") and קשׁח *hiphil* "to harden (heart)" (Isa 63:17)
- שׁאג "to roar" (+ שְׁאָגָה "roaring") and שׁאה "to roar" (+ שָׁאוֹן "roar")
- שׁקד "to watch (over)" and שׁקף *niphal/hiphil* "to look down upon."[130]

Those that correspond in their final two consonants include:

- דבק "to cling to" and חבק "to embrace"
- זבח "to sacrifice" and טבח "to slaughter" (+ שׁחט "to slaughter for sacrifice")
- חתם "to seal" and סתם "to stop up"
- חתת "to shatter, be terrified" and כתת "to crush"
- כנע *hiphil* "to make humble" and צנע *hiphil* "to make humble" (Mic 6:8)
- יאב (Ps 119:131) and תאב "to long for" (+ אהב "to love")
- נפל "to fall" and שׁפל "to sink"
- סמך "to support" and תמך "to grasp, support"

---

130. Another pair of rarely occurring roots is עצה "to shut the eyes" (Prov 16:30) and עצם "to shut the eyes" (*qal* Isa 33:15 and *piel* Isa 29:10).

- פשע "to rebel" (+ פֶּ֫שַׁע "crime") and רשע "to be guilty, wrong" (+ רֶ֫שַׁע "offense")
- שלה "to be quiet, at rest" (+ שַׁלְוָה, שָׁלוּ, שָׁלֵו "quietness, ease") and שלם "to be healthy, complete," *hiphil* "to make peace" (+ שָׁלוֹם "welfare, peace")

Those that correspond in their first and last consonants include:

- ידה "to cast, throw" and ירה "to cast, throw"[131]
- ינה "to be violent," *hiphil* "to oppress" and יגה "to suffer," *hiphil* "to cause suffering"
- נהר "to light" (+ נְהָרָה "light" Job 3:4) and נור in נֵר "light" and מְנוֹרָה "lampstand"
- נסך "to pour out" and נתך "to pour forth" (+ מסך "to mix, pour")
- עלף and עטף "to wrap oneself, to faint"[132]
- פקח "to open (the eyes)" and פתח "to open."

Those words whose consonants appear in different places and sequences include:

- בלע "to swallow" and לעט "to swallow" (Gen 25:30)
- דֶּ֫גֶל "banners, division (of tribe)" and פְּלֻגָּה/פְּלַגָּה (in 2 Chr 35:5) "subdivision (of family/tribe)"
- עיף/יעף "to be faint" and עטף "to be faint"
- קוץ "to loathe" and שקץ *piel* "to detest" (+ שִׁקּוּץ "abhorrence," שֶׁ֫קֶץ "abomination").[133]

Sometimes semantically similar roots and words contain only approximately similar sounds, as with the words associated with baldness and shaving that begin with a voiced velar consonant (/g/ or /ḳ/) and end with a *khet* (presumably all representing /ḥ/): גִּבֵּחַ "bald head," גַּבַּ֫חַת "bald-

131. Note the possible confusion of ירה for ידה in 4Q169 (4QpNah) 3–4 IV, 2, listed by *HALOT*.

132. Note also עטה "to wrap oneself." The *ayin* in עטה and עלף may represent /ġ/, while the *ayin* in עטף may represent /ʿ/.

133. The verb קצף "to be furious" seems semantically and phonetically close to שקץ/קוץ (note also קוט "to loathe"). Note the antonymous relationships between כרה "to purchase" and מכר "to sell"; and נשת "to dry up" and שתה "to drink."

headed," קֵרֵחַ "bald" (+ קרח *niphal* "to shave one's head"), and גלח *piel* "to shave" (the head, beard, etc.), the two last roots (גלח/קרח) both containing a liquid as a second root consonant. In a similar way, note the sequence of *nun* followed by a bilabial consonant (/b/, /m/, /p/) in the verbs related to blowing and breathing: נפח "to breathe, blow"; נפש *niphal* "to breathe"; נשב "to blow"; נשם "to breathe, pant"; נשף "to blow."[134] Words associated with binding and restraining often contain a sibilant and *resh*, as in אזר "to gird on"; אסר "to bind"; עצר "to restrain, lock up"; צרר/צור "to bind, restrict." Verbs that indicate languishing, drying out, weakening often have a *lamed* accompanied by a bilabial and/or an *aleph*: אבל "to languish"; אמל "to languish" (אֻמְלַל *pulal*); בלה "to be worn out"; לאה "to languish"; נבל "to languish, wither."

As with the other roots and words listed above, the relevant letters can occur in any order. Note in particular the set of words connected to hiding: טמן "to hide" (+ מַטְמוֹן "treasure") and צפן "to hide" (+ שׂפן/ספן "to cover, hide"); and the words related to flowing: נגר *niphal* "to flow"; נהר "to flow, stream" (+ נָהָר "river"); נזל "to flow, drip"; נַחַל "wadi."[135] Certain relationships will no doubt already be familiar to the student, as with היה "to be"

---

134. Another word of the same semantic field is expressed with similar sounds: שׁאף "to gasp, pant."

135. Note also the initial-*nun* verbs נבע "to flow" and נזה "to spurt." Note the initial *khet* (the exact realization of which is often obscure) followed by a final *resh* in verbs denoting searching and digging: חפר "to dig, search for"; חקר "to search, examine"; חתר "to dig, row" (+ note the similarity with חפשׂ "to search for, examine"). Note too אַיִל "ram" and יָעֵל "mountain goat"; הפך "to turn, change" and חלף "to pass away," *hiphil* "to change"; צעק/זעק "to cry out" (+ צְעָקָה/זְעָקָה "cry") and שׁוע *piel* "to cry out" (+ שַׁוְעָה "cry"); חבק "to embrace" and חשק "to be attached to = to love" (cf. Aram. חשק "to saddle"); כרע "to bow down" and קרס "to bend"; כרת "to cut" and קרע "to tear"; מאס "to reject" and נאץ "to spurn"; מסך "to mix, pour," נסך "to pour out," נתך "to pour forth," סוך "to anoint oneself," and צוק "to melt, pour out" (+ מָצוּק "molten pillar"); נגע "reach, attain"; נגשׁ "to approach," נשׂג "to reach, attain"; סָגָן or סֶגֶן and סֹכֵן "official" and סֶרֶן "ruler, tyrant" (+ נָשִׂיא "prince"); סֶמֶל "image, statue" and פֶּסֶל "idol, image" and צֶלֶם "image"; צמת "to destroy," *niphal* "to be destroyed" and שׁמד *niphal* "to be destroyed," *hiphil* "to exterminate," as well as שׁחת *niphal* "to be destroyed," *hiphil* "to annihilate, ruin, destroy"; רוח *pual* "to be wide" (+ רֶוַח "width, space") and רחב "to be broad, wide" (+ רַחַב "wide space," רֹחַב "breadth"); רמשׂ "to creep" and שׁרץ "to swarm"; שׂבע "to be satiated" and שׂפק "to be sufficient (+ סֵפֶק/שֶׂפֶק "sufficiency"); שׁקט "to be quiet" and שׁתק "to be silent" (+ perhaps סכת *hiphil* "to be quiet" Deut 27:9).

and חיה "to live." Many correspondences have already been listed above in the footnotes (e.g., קבץ, קמץ [plus קֹמֶץ], and קפץ).[136]

In certain rare cases, correspondences between roots and words may be due to their origin through onomatopoeia, as with רקק/ירק (Lev 15:8) "to spit" and לקק/לעע "to lick up." Note also the verb לחך "to lick up" that is a separate root, but similar in sound to לקק.

The benefit to the intermediate student of being at least familiar with some of these sets of words should be obvious. Recognizing the meanings associated with a pair of consonants can help one learn and remember vocabulary, even if not every word of a set is remembered and even if the nuances of particular words are not thrown into relief. We must remember, however, that similarity in sound does not always mean a similarity in meaning.[137]

In addition, being sensitive to these groups of related words helps us understand the biblical text. The similarities between these words were not ignored by the ancient writers, who sometimes used these words together, as with כרע "to bow down" and קרס "to bend" in Isa 46:1, 2. In other passages, the similarities between the various roots seem to have led to confusion. In 2 Kgs 17:21, we find the form וַיַּדֵּא, which reflects a *ketiv/qere* distinction. The *ketiv* reflects the root נדא, an otherwise unknown byform of נדה (which appears in the *piel* "to drive away, postpone" only twice, Isa

136. Even more vague associations can be noticed. E.g., note the numerous verbs having to do with breaking or shattering that involve a *tsade* as a final root consonant: נפץ "to smash"; נתץ "to tear down"; פצץ "to break into pieces"; פרץ "to break"; רעץ "to destroy"; רצץ "to oppress, smash" or words connected to dripping that end with a *pe*: דלף "to leak, shed (tears)"; זַרְזִיף "drop" (Ps 72:6); נטף "to drip"; ערף "to drip"; רעף "to drip." Note the number of verbs denoting opening the lips or mouth that begin with a *pe*: פטר "to escape," *hiphil* "to open (lips)"; פער "to open (the mouth)"; פצה "to open (the mouth)"; פשׂק "to spread (the lips)." The examples are easily multiplied. Just among words beginning with *tsade*, note the numerous words having to do with dryness: צִיָּה "dryness"; צִחֶה "parched"; צמא "to be thirsty"; צמק "to dry up" (Hos 9:14; + צִמּוּק "raisins"); perhaps also צנם "to be dried out" (? Gen 41:23); and the numerous words having to do with screaming (with a guttural following the *tsade*): צהל "to cry out, rejoice"; צוח "to cry out" (Isa 42:11; + צְוָחָה "cry"); צחק "to laugh" [cf. שׂחק "to laugh"]; צרח "to shriek"; צעק "to cry out" (+ צְעָקָה "cry").

137. Sometimes it seems even lexicographers were influenced by the similarity in sound. So, e.g., BDB glosses נגן as "touch (strings), play a stringed instrument," just before the more common verb נגע "to touch," though *HALOT* glosses the former as simply "to play a stringed instrument." No evidence is presented in BDB to explain the gloss "touch."

66:5; Amos 6:3), while the *qere* (together with the ancient translations) reflects the more common verb נדח in the *hiphil* "to expel."

2.10. Variation of Orthography and Pronunciation within Roots and Words

Some of the examples from preceding sections may be due to a particular scribe's or author's personal predilections, the peculiar ways that one scribe or author wrote or pronounced Hebrew. In some cases these may reflect dialectal peculiarities. Although both זעק and צעק ("to cry out") occur throughout the Bible, זעק appears just once in the Pentateuch, but six times in Nehemiah and 1–2 Chronicles, as well as throughout the DSS; צעק occurs, on the other hand, over fifteen times in the Pentateuch, but just twice in Nehemiah and 1–2 Chronicles and never in the nonbiblical DSS; זעק can safely be considered characteristic of LBH.[138]

Some variations in spelling/pronunciation no doubt reflect simple scribal mistakes. These are clearest where a particular spelling does not make sense as with Hos 5:11: צָו "commandment (?)" for שָׁו* "something worthless"[139] and הָאֹהֶל in (1 Kgs 7:45), the *ketiv* reflecting "the tent" (= הָאֹהֶל*), which makes no sense, and the *qere* reflecting "these" (= הָאֵלֶּה*).[140] Often, the scribal mistakes mirror phenomena described above. Thus, צָו versus שָׁו* is similar to the variation between sibilants; the *ketiv* and *qere* alternatives in הָאֹהֶל reflects metathesis of the *he* and *lamed*. In some cases, determining what is a scribal mistake from what is a true trait of a dialect or register of the language can be hard. Note, for example, the single instance of the root זעך, thus: נִזְעָכוּ "they are extinguished" (Job 17:1). Is this root truly a byform of דעך "to extinguish" or is it a simple mistake?

In other cases, the evidence from the MT and DSS seems to suggest that variations in the orthography/pronunciation reflect developments in the language during the course of the first millennium BCE. A particularly clear example of this is the cases where *aleph* replaces an etymological *vav*

138. See Reymond, *Qumran Hebrew*, 188; Kutscher, *Isaiah Scroll*, 34. For a lengthy description of these byforms, see Hornkohl, *Ancient Hebrew Periodization*, 78–82.

139. Friedrich Delitzsch, *Die Lese- und Schreibfehler im Alten Testament* (Berlin: de Gruyter, 1920), 125. Note also לְהָשִׁיב "to return" in 2 Sam 8:3 for presumably לְהַצִּיב as found in 1 Chr 18:3 and with velar consonants וַיַּצִּקוּ "they poured" in 2 Sam 15:24 for וַיַּצִּגוּ* "they set" (ibid.).

140. Emanuel Tov, *Textual Criticism of the Hebrew Bible*, 3rd rev. ed. (Minneapolis: Fortress, 2012), 233.

or *yod*, as with פְּתִי "simple" in the plural: פְּתָאִים "simple" Ps 116:6 and passim (the *ketiv* presuming *ptåʾim* < **pətāʾīm* and the *qere* presuming *ptåyim* < **pətāyīm* [cf. פְּתָיִים in Ps 119:130]);[141] נְאוֹת "pasture of" (Ps 23:2) and passim instead of נְוֹת (Zeph 2:6). This kind of dissimilation may also appear in תְּתָאוּ "you will mark" (in Num 34:7, 8) (as though from תָּאָה) for תְּתַוּוּ* "you will mark" (from תוה).[142] In other words, etymological *vav* and *yod* were replaced by a glottal stop in certain positions within words. Words in which this took place were spelled with *aleph* in the Second Temple era and this was preserved in the consonantal text of the MT. On the other hand, the oral tradition known to the Masoretes either preserved the earlier articulation of these words with *vav*/*yod* or it revocalized these words according to their perceived etymology. The reverse phenomenon, of *vav* or *yod* appearing for etymological *aleph*, is rarer: דּוֹאֵג "Doeg" (in Ps 52:2) instead of דּוֹיֵג (in 1 Sam 22:18); and רִבֹּאוֹת "ten thousands" (in Dan 11:12 and Ezra 2:69) for רִבּוֹת* = **ribbowot*.[143] In all these cases, the spellings represent phonetic variations of a single root and, so, are usually listed under just one root. Sometimes, however, dictionaries do list the roots separately (as in תאה and תוה).

2.11. Chapter Summary

Historical Details

1. In Classical Hebrew, ח represented two phonemes /ḥ/ and /ḫ/; ע represented /ʿ/ and /ġ/; שׁ represented /š/ and /ś/.
2. Classical Hebrew contained byforms reflecting different PS/PNWS phonemes (e.g., נטר/נצר "to guard"), different root classes (e.g., בזה/בוז "to despise"), and different realizations of a basic sound (e.g., bilabials: נשׁף/נשׁב "to blow").

141. This dissimilation of /y/ > /ʾ/ likely helps preserve the syllable structure of the word (see Reymond, *Qumran Hebrew*, 127–31). Note also חֲלָאִים Song 7:2 for חֲלָיִים*; and עֳפָאִים Ps 104:12 for עֳפָיִים*. This phenomenon also occurs with final *yods* that are not part of the root, as with הַהַגְרִיאִים "the Hagarites" (1 Chr 5:19, 20) for הַהַגְרִיִּים*; and הָעַרְבִיאִים "the Arabians (2 Chr 17:11) for הָעַרְבִיִּים*.

142. Cf. וַיְתָו "he marked" 1 Sam 21:14 (for expected וַיְתַו*) and וְהִתְוִיתָ "you set a mark" Ezek 9:4.

143. See Reymond, *Qumran Hebrew*, 123–24. Note also דָּנִיֵּאל < **dāniyyēl*/**dānīyēl* "Daniel" Ezra 8:2 and passim vs. דָּנִאֵל < **dānīʾēl* in Ezek 14:14 and passim.

3. Classical Hebrew often expressed a common idea through similar sounding but etymologically distinct roots (e.g., the words having to do with spreading, dividing, tearing that begin with *pe-resh*).

Learning Tips

1. Memorize weak roots together in order to remember their similarities and disparities (e.g., בזה/בוז means "to despise," but בזז means "to plunder").
2. Memorize the most common examples of alternation between similarly articulated consonants (e.g., צעק/זעק "to cry out"; צָעִיר/ זְעֵיר "little"; דַּךְ "crushed," דַּק "thin, small, fine," and רַק "thin"; זכך "to be pure" and זקק "to refine"; הדר/אדר *niphal* "be glorious/ honored"; אוֹן "power, wealth" and הוֹן "wealth")
3. Memorize the most common examples of metathesis that result in new words (i.e., בַּלָּהָה/בֶּהָלָה "terror, calamity"; זַעֲוָה/זְוָעָה "terror"; כֶּבֶשׂ/כַּבְשָׂה and כֶּשֶׂב/כִּשְׂבָּה "lamb"; אנק/נאק "to groan" [+ אֲנָקָה/ נְאָקָה "groan"]; שַׂלְמָה/שִׂמְלָה "garment").
4. Use the similarities between the sounds of words to help remember rarer words one encounters while reading (e.g., פזר/בזר *piel* "to scatter"; קרח *niphal* "to shave one's head"; and גלח *piel* "to shave" [the head, beard, etc.]). This is particularly useful when you know one of the words already.
5. Memorize, when practical, the sequences of letters and their semantic associations (e.g., *pe-resh:* spreading, dividing, tearing).

3
Phonology of Ancient Hebrew: Vowels

As is the case with the consonants, the vowels of Biblical Hebrew differed in their articulation in different eras. However, the historical development of the vowels is more complex than that of the consonants. We begin with the vowels of the Tiberian tradition, then move backward in time to the vowels likely present at circa 200 BCE–100 CE and the correspondences between all these later vowels and the much earlier PS/PNWS set of vowels.

As stated in the preface, the central focus of this study is a form of Biblical Hebrew in Second Temple times that is an ancestor to THT. Although it may seem merely speculative to attempt to reconstruct the vocalic dimension of BH for a period in which vowels were not explicitly or consistently committed to writing, I believe it is useful. Tracing the possible development of vowels provokes us to think about the language's evolution at this crucial period of its history with more precision. Moreover, identifying common vocalic shifts allows us to perceive the underlying similarities between sets of words that we would otherwise not associate with each other. This, in turn, can make their memorization easier.

Several matters should be explained before going further. In relation to vowels, we will distinguish two general characteristics: quality and length. Quality refers to the character of the sound as determined by the manipulation of the tongue, lips, and mouth. The /i/, for example, is produced with the tongue pushed up, toward the roof of the mouth, while the /a/ is produced with the tongue low, where it usually rests. Length refers to the duration of the sound, that is, the length of time it is pronounced.[1] In other words, a long /ī/ has the same place of articulation in the mouth as

1. This is slightly different from how the term is used in primary and secondary education (in the USA), where a "short vowel" often has an entirely different manner of articulation than the same vowel when it is "long" (e.g., the "short a" in "bat" = IPA [bæt] tongue low vs. the "long a" in "ape" = IPA [eɪp] tongue slightly raised).

a short /i/, but the long /ī/ is pronounced for a longer time. Usually a long vowel is indicated with a macron (e.g., /ī/); another way of transliterating a long vowel is with the ":" symbol used with IPA symbols: /ī/ = [iː].

As just mentioned, the pronunciation of /a/ requires the tongue to lie flat, at the bottom of the mouth. The mouth is relatively open in the pronunciation of this vowel. Thus, the /a/ is often characterized as a low or open vowel. An /i/ or /u/ requires the tongue to be raised toward the roof of the mouth. Furthermore, the /i/ is produced with the tongue pressed toward the top front of the mouth and the /u/ with the tongue pressed toward the top back. The /i/ and /u/ are both high vowels, the /i/ being a high front vowel and the /u/ a high back vowel.[2] The common place of articulation of /i/ and /u/ means that they often will behave in a similar way, unlike the /a/ vowel. Vowels that are articulated with the tongue half-way between the bottom and roof of the mouth are called midvowels and can be described in relative terms to each other. For example, the sound of /e/ (IPA [e]; the "e" in "hey") is higher than /ɛ/ (IPA [ɛ]; the "e" in "pet"); similarly, /o/ is higher than /a/ and lower than /u/. In Hebrew, there is evidence not only of the lengthening of vowels (e.g., */a/ > */ā/), but also of the lowering of vowels (i.e., */i/ > /e/, */i/ > /ɛ/, and */u/ > /o/), as explained below.

The relative place of articulation for the vowels of BH is represented in the chart below.

Table 3.1. Place of Articulation for the Vowels of Biblical Hebrew

roof/palate

i u

lips e o uvula

ɛ å

a

tongue

2. In addition, it is common to see references to these vowels (/i/ and /u/) as "close" vowels, meaning that the tongue is pressed close to the roof of the mouth. This is a somewhat confusing term since, in relation to vowels, we often refer to closed syllables. In any case, "close" is the opposite of "open."

There are three /i/-class vowels: /i/, /e/, and /ɛ/; one /a/-class vowel: /a/; and three /u/-class vowels: /u/, /o/, and /å/.

It is also important to acknowledge here the place of the accent or tone in Hebrew words. As described below, the place of a syllable in relation to the accent or tone has a direct bearing on how the vowels of that syllable developed. The identification of the tonic syllable below will be based on the place of stress as implied in THT. Typically, the last syllable of an absolute noun is the tonic syllable in THT (e.g., **dābār* "word" [> דָּבָר]). One apparent exception is the segolate nouns (in the absolute singular) that appear penultimately stressed (e.g., מֶ֫לֶךְ "king").[3] But, this is misleading. The second *segol* in מֶ֫לֶךְ is an epenthetic vowel and, according to the Masoretic conception, it does not constitute its own syllable; thus, the word מֶ֫לֶךְ = *mɛlk* does not reflect an exception to the general rule.

The last syllable of many verbal forms is also accented in THT:

- the third-person forms of the *qåṭal* (e.g., **kātab* [> כָּתַב] "he wrote," **kātəbā* [> כָּתְבָה*] "she wrote," **kātəbū* [> כָּתְבוּ] "they wrote")
- all forms of the *yiqṭol* except the third- and second-person feminine plurals (e.g., **yiktob* [> יִכְתֹּב] "he will write," **yiktəbū* [> יִכְתְּבוּ] "they will write")
- all forms of the imperative except the feminine plural (e.g., **kətob* [> כְּתֹב] "write!," **kitbū* [> כִּתְבוּ] "write!")
- infinitives (e.g., **kətōb* [> כְּתֹב] "writing" and **kātōb* [> כָּתוֹב] "write")
- participles (e.g., **kōtēb* [> כֹּתֵב] "one writing").

On the other hand, most second- and first-person *qåṭal* verbs are penultimately stressed (e.g., **kātabtā* [> כָּתַ֫בְתָּ] "you wrote" and **kātabtī* [> כָּתַ֫בְתִּי] "I wrote").

As for construct forms, no syllable is considered tonic (though in THT construct forms are supplied with accent/cantillation marks). Nor is

3. Note that in singular nouns with pronominal suffixes the final syllable is usually accented (e.g., **dəbārī* [> דְּבָרִי], **dəbārō* [> דְּבָרוֹ], **dəbārāh* [> דְּבָרָהּ], versus **dəbārēnū* [> דְּבָרֵ֫נוּ]). In plural nouns with pronominal suffixes, the penultimate syllable is often accented, though not exclusively (e.g., **dəbārekā* [> דְּבָרֶ֫יךָ], **dəbārehā* [> דְּבָרֶ֫יהָ], **dəbārēnū* [> דְּבָרֵ֫ינוּ] versus **dəbāray* [> דְּבָרַי], **dəbārāw* [> דְּבָרָיו], **dibrēkɛm* [> דִּבְרֵיכֶם]).

any considered pretonic, even if the noun following the construct form is accented on its first syllable.

An important source of information on the vowels is that provided by the transcriptions of Hebrew words in the LXX and in the second column of Origen's Hexapla. The words transcribed in the LXX are generally names, but some common nouns are also transcribed. Since such transcriptions were not governed by standard rules of grammar, they were easily misspelled in the course of the LXX's transmission.[4] The second column of Origen's six-column Hexapla is conventionally referred to as the Secunda. It was a full transcription of the Hebrew Bible into Greek letters. The multi-volume Hexapla is now lost. The Secunda, itself, exists only in extremely small fragments and in a medieval palimpsest that preserves portions of only some transcriptions of a few psalms.[5]

Although the Secunda is commonly associated with Origen and although it formed the second column of his Hexapla, he is not necessarily its author. This is implied especially by the fact that the values of the Greek letters do not seem to match the pronunciation of Greek letters at the time of Origen, in the first half of the third century CE.[6] At this time, for example, the *ēta* (*η*) was pronounced as /ī/; this value for *ēta* is calculated to have become dominant in the literary register already by circa 150 CE.[7] This is clearly not what the Secunda presupposes. The Greek transcription of the Hebrew preserved in the Secunda seems to presuppose, in fact, a version of Greek pronunciation that dates no later than the first century CE.[8] In earlier Greek, including at the time of the LXX translation of Genesis, the

4. See Yuditsky, "Transcriptions into Greek and Latin Scripts," 3:803.

5. See G. Mercati, *Psalterii Hexapli Reliquiqae, pars, prima, Codex rescriptus Bybliothecae Ambrosianae O. 39 SVP: Phototypice expressus et transcriptus*. Rome: Pontifical Biblical Institute, 1958; and Alexey Yuditsky's new readings ("New Readings of MS O39 from the Ambrosian Library" [Heb.], *Leshonenu* 68 [2008]: 63–71). In addition, note the fragments, e.g., in C. Taylor, *Hebrew-Greek Cairo Genizah Palimpsests from the Taylor-Schechter Collections, Including a Fragment of the Twenty-Second Psalm according to Origen's Hexapla* (Cambridge: Cambridge University Press, 1900), 10–11.

6. See Janssens, *Studies in Hebrew Historical Linguistics*, 20.

7. See W. Sidney Allen, *Vox Graeca*, 3rd ed. (Cambridge: Cambridge University Press, 1987), 63–64, 70–71.

8. Allen (*Vox*, 74) notes that Dionysius of Halicarnassus distinguishes *ēta* from *iōta* in the first century BCE.

ēta represented a long /ɛ̄/.[9] But, presumably in the following centuries (up to ca. 100 CE), the *ēta* moved closer in articulation to /ē/, on its way to being pronounced as /ī/.[10] As for *epsilon*, we assume a pronunciation /e/ (IPA [e]), meaning that in the Secunda *ēta* and *epsilon* were distinct primarily in length.[11] This distinction, however, does not necessarily reflect the vowels of the Hebrew tradition that the Secunda seeks to transcribe.

In what follows I often assume that the underlying Hebrew midvowel to which the *ēta* corresponds is /ē/ and the underlying vowels to which the *epsilon* corresponds are /e/ and /ɛ/.[12] More generally, I assume that the Hebrew pronunciation that the Secunda attempts to render is contemporary with the pronunciation of Greek letters implied by it (i.e., ca. 100 BCE–100 CE). It should be admitted here that although we will rely on the Greek transcriptions to inform our understanding of the development of Hebrew, they do not represent the direct antecedent to THT; rather, each exists as an independent tradition.

3.1. Tiberian Biblical Hebrew Vowels

The vowel phonemes known from Tiberian Biblical Hebrew (dating to ca. 800 CE) are listed below in the chart.[13] Each vowel's approximate pronun-

9. Geoffrey Khan, "The Historical Background of the Vowel *ṣere* in Some Hebrew Verbal and Nominal Forms," *BSOAS* 57 (1994): 135–37, esp. 136 n. 14.

10. Ibid., 137.

11. Khan (ibid.) notes that in the Secunda *epsilon* "was pronounced [e]." Khan (141) cautions not to assume that the Secunda tradition is the "direct forbear of the medieval Tiberian pronunciation tradition" and notes that it is not clear whether the shift in quality that resulted in two /i/-class vowels, /ɛ/ and /e/, is evidenced in the Secunda. As stated above, I assume for this study that *ēta* and *epislon* were distinct in quantity, not quality.

12. The *epsilon* also occurs where I assume a sophisticated pronunciation of Second Temple Hebrew had /i/ (e.g., νεβαλ "one terrified" Ps 30:8, cf. נִבְהָל; βρεδεθι "in my descent" Ps 30:10, cf. בְּרִדְתִּי; ιεσμωρου "they will guard" Ps 89:32 cf. [pausal] יִשְׁמֹ֫רוּ); for the examples, see Alexy Eliyahu Yuditsky, "Hebrew in Greek and Latin Transcriptions," *HBH* 1:111 and Einar Brønno, *Studien über Hebräische Morphologie und Vokalismus auf Grundlage der mercatischen Fragmente der zweiten Kolumne der Hexapla des Origenes*, AKM 28 (Leipzig: Brockhaus, 1943), 35. As in the penultimate example, *epsilon* even appears where THT lacks a vowel.

13. See Khan, "Tiberian Pronunciation Tradition," 13–23.

ciation is made clear to us by the medieval Hebrew grammarians.[14] The phonemes are listed according to their place of articulation, beginning in the front of the mouth and working backward toward the throat.

Table 3.2. Vocalic Phonemes of Tiberian Biblical Hebrew

Name of Vowel Symbols	Phonemes of (Tiberian) Biblical Hebrew, ca. 800 CE	Common Transliteration	*matres* typical of the MT	Contemporary USA Classroom Pronunciation
hireq	i "ski"	i or ī	(י)	i and ɪ "ski/hit"
tsere	e "hey"	ē	(י)/(ה)	e
shewa	-	- and ə		- and ə
segol	ɛ "pet"	e	(ה)	ɛ and e
patakh	a	a		a or ɑ
qamets	å [IPA ɔ] "paw"	ā or o	(ה)	a or o
holem	o	ō	(ו)	o
shureq	u	ū	ו	u
qibbuts	u	u (and ū)		u

The symbols used to represent the sounds seem mostly self-explanatory, but this is somewhat deceiving. One should note the values described below. Of the symbols that might be unfamiliar, note that the "å" and "ɔ" symbols represent the "aw" sound in the North American pronunciation of the word "paw" (i.e., IPA [pɔ]). The two symbols "a" and "ɑ" represent two slightly distinct sounds, the first heard in the British pronunciation of "handle" and the second in the pronunciation of the word "car."[15] The "ɛ" symbol represents the "e" in "pet" (IPA [pɛt]), while the "e" represents the sound of "e" in "hey" (IPA [heɪ]). The *shewa* symbol, "ə", represents a muttered vowel; when pronounced by the Masoretes it was articulated as /a/.[16] The IPA [ɪ] symbol represents the sound of "i" in the word "hit." The symbol "i" in the chart, however, represents a different sound, the sound

14. Ibid. See also Geoffrey Khan, "Karaite Transcriptions of Biblical Hebrew," *HBH* 1:147–60.

15. See *OED*, s.v.

16. See Geoffrey Khan, "Shewa: Pre-Modern Hebrew," *EHLL* 3:544.

of "i" in the English word "ski" (IPA [ski]) and the sound of "ee" in "street" (IPA [strit]).[17]

In the above chart, one will notice that for the Tiberian Masoretes there was no significant distinction between long and short vowels. The *qamets* did not represent a long /ā/ sound, but rather the sound of /å/ (= the "aw" in "paw"). Thus, the distinction between *qamets* and *patakh* was not one between long and short /a/, but between /å/ and /a/, sounds that are made in different parts of the mouth.[18] This was even the case where *qamets* corresponds to a historical short /u/, as in the word חָכְמָה = *ḥåkmå* (< **ḥukmatu*) "wisdom."

Although it is true that depending on its place in a word, a vowel might have been pronounced for a longer or shorter time, vowel length was generally not used to distinguish different words.[19] This is one major distinction between the Hebrew of the Tiberian Masoretes and earlier Hebrew. In the earlier phases of Hebrew (including the dialect of Canaanite that became Hebrew), a word or form with a long vowel would mean something different from a word or form with a corresponding short vowel. For example, the base **qatil* would imply an adjectival form while the base **qātil* would imply a participle (often a substantivized verbal adjective). Thus, **ʾaminu* (> **ʾāmēn* > אָמֵן "truly") would have been distinct from **ʾāminu* (> **ʾōmēn* > אֹמֵן "foster-father"). Similarly, even in later, Second Temple times, the length of a vowel could imply a different sense for a word, as is presumed based on distinctions like **dām* (> דָּם) "blood" and **dam* (> דַּם) "blood

17. For audio examples, see the website https://web.uvic.ca/ling/resources/ipa/charts/IPAlab/IPAlab.htm from the University of Victoria (British Columbia).

18. Similarly, the difference between *segol* and *tsere* is not the difference between short and long /e/, but rather a difference in the quality of vowels.

19. Khan, "Tiberian Pronunciation Tradition," 14–15. Note one possible exception: אָכְלָה "food" and אָכְלָה "she ate" (see ibid., 20). In the Tiberian tradition, length was based, in part, on where the vowel occurred in a word. In a tonic syllable, the short vowels /i/, /ɛ/, /a/, and /u/ became long (i.e., IPA [iː], [ɛː], [aː], [uː]). A similar thing happened when the following letter was a guttural or a *yod*, *lamed*, or *nun*. It should be emphasized, however, that although the pronunciation was lengthened, the symbol associated with the vowel remained the same. That is, a lengthened /a/ was still written with a *patakh*. Although the length of vowels was not commonly used to differentiate meaning, Khan does note that to discern the underlying phonological system of THT, one must discriminate between long vowels that are "invariably long" and those only long due to where they occur in a word. See Khan, "Vowel Length: Biblical Hebrew," *EHLL* 3:981–85.

of."[20] For the Tiberian Masoretes, however, these words and forms were distinguished especially by the different qualities of vowel: *ʾåmen* versus *ʾomen* and *dåm* versus *dam*. The loss of vowel length as a meaningful characteristic seems to have taken place sometime near the middle of the first millennium CE, just prior to the time of the Masoretes, as implied by the fact that Jerome testifies to the existence of distinctions between vowel length.[21]

Several other details of the above chart deserve attention. Note the disparity between the phoneme marked by *segol* in Tiberian Hebrew and the manner in which it is commonly transliterated. The common transliteration of *segol*, as "e," partially masks the fact that the vowel for the Tiberian Masoretes (/ɛ/) was qualitatively different from *tsere* (/e/); at the time of the Masoretes, the two vowels were made in distincts parts of the mouth (/e/ is pronounced with the tongue more raised than in the pronunciation of /ɛ/). Despite their common transliteration by a single Roman letter, the two vowels (*segol* and *tsere*) are often distinguished in the classroom, corresponding with the basic phonemes of the Tiberian Masoretes.[22]

A similar disparity relates to the *qamets*. The vowel marked by the *qamets* in THT (/å/ = IPA [ɔ]) is distinct in its quality from the vowel implied by its common manner of transliteration (i.e., /ā/ or /o/), not to mention how it is usually pronounced in the classroom. The distinction between /a/ and /o/ in the modern classroom derives from contemporary Modern Israeli Hebrew, which descends ultimately from Sephardic tradition.[23] Although this differs from the tradition of the Tiberian Masoretes, the distinction between a *qamets* that sounds like /a/ and a *qamets* that sounds like /o/ does have a legitimate BH pedigree, as described below.

Finally, notice that for the Masoretes the absence of a vowel and the presence of a muttered vowel (i.e., a *shewa* vowel) were, according to their system, phonologically identical.[24] Although the Masoretes, according to their own descriptions, pronounced a muttered vowel (phonetically [a]),

20. The distinction in length may be reflected in the Secunda where יָדוֹ is transcribed ιαδω (Ps 89:26) and בְּיַד־ is transcribed βιεδ (Ps 31:9). The Greek letter *epsilon* in the Secunda sometimes corresponds to *patakh* in THT, but not to *qamets*.

21. See Tapani Harviainen, "Transcription into Latin Script: Jerome," *EHLL* 3:823.

22. Though etymological III-*vav*/*yod* roots that end in *segol* are routinely pronounced as if they contained *tsere*.

23. See Blau, *Phonology and Morphology*, 109.

24. Khan, "Shewa," 3:544.

they did not conceive of this vowel as part of a separate syllable. It represented essentially an epenthetic vowel, that is, a vowel secondarily inserted into the word, not unlike a furtive *patakh* (on which, see below).[25] Where the *shewa* would be pronounced after a guttural it had a specific quality (indicated through the *khatef*-vowels, also called composite vowels: *khatef-patakh*, *khatef-segol*, *khatef-qamets*). But, such a vowel was not part of its own syllable. For this reason, these vowels are not typically indicated in this book in the transliteration of words in THT.

If an /i/-class or /u/-class vowel precedes a guttural at the end of the word, often a *patakh* will appear between this vowel and the following guttural (e.g., גָּבִיעַ "bowl," and רוּחַ "spirit"). This is the furtive *patakh*. Here, again, the vowel did not initiate a new syllable (and is ignored in transliteration).[26]

The reason that we do not follow the Tiberian Masoretic pronunciation model more closely in our classrooms is not only due to the influence from the pronunciation of the living, modern language. It is also due to the complexity of the pronunciation tradition. The precise articulation of the Tiberian tradition was even difficult for near contemporaries of the Masoretes to master.[27]

Here, it should be remarked again that the Tiberian pronunciation represents only one tradition among many. As mentioned before, the Babylonian and Palestinian traditions both differ from the Tiberian in various ways.[28] For example, the Babylonian and Palestinian have no vowel symbol corresponding to THT *segol*.[29] Furthermore, the various transcriptions into Greek and Latin do not correspond exactly with the Tiberian tradition, each transcribed text exhibiting its own peculiarities.

---

25. Ibid.; Khan, "Syllable Structure," 3:666.

26. The furtive *patakh* is not attested in the Secunda, though it does seem to be reflected in transcriptions in the LXX (like νωε for נֹחַ "Noah" Gen 5:29) (Yuditsky, "Transcription into Greek and Latin Script," 3:805).

27. See Khan, "Tiberian Reading Tradition," 3:770, who writes: "It appears that the Tiberian pronunciation was not fully known even to the medieval grammarians of Spain … (eleventh century C.E.)."

28. See Khan, "Biblical Hebrew: Pronunciation Traditions," 1:341–52; Heijmans, "Babylonian Tradition," 1:133–45; Yahalom, "Palestinian Tradition," 1:161–73; Gzella, "Tiberian-Palestinian Tradition," 1:175–85.

29. The Palestinian tradition has a single symbol to mark what are in THT /ɛ/ and /e/, while the Babylonian has a single symbol to mark what are in THT /ɛ/ and /a/.

3.2. Classical Biblical Hebrew Vowels

The documentation of vowels for the early periods of Biblical Hebrew is complicated by the fact that the orthography did not typically indicate vowels in the interior of words. What we assume about these early eras (e.g., ca. 800 BCE) is in large measure based on historical reconstruction of the language. In the early part of the first millennium BCE, when many of the early biblical texts were first composed, it is assumed that Hebrew had the same vowels as in PNWS, in addition to a few others (e.g., /ē/, /ō/) which emerged due to various linguistic developments described below. Still, it is hard to say anything definite about the nature of vowels in this era due to the lack of evidence.

Toward the end of the first millennium BCE, the inventory would have been slightly larger.[30] The chart on page 71 contrasts the PS/PNWS vowels with the corresponding vowels presumed for Hebrew at circa 200 BCE–100 CE, when we have a slightly better guess as to their articulation. In this chart, the historical long vowels and their reflexes are listed first and then the short vowels.[31]

The vowels of PS/PNWS are assumed based on comparative evidence (e.g., Ugaritic and Arabic) and historical reconstruction.[32] The vowels of Hebrew from circa 200 BCE–100 CE are based on, among other things, historical considerations, spellings in the DSS, transcriptions in Greek, and later pronunciation traditions. Given the nature of this evidence (which is often contradictory), the isolation of individual phonemes is difficult. For example, it is unclear to what degree the various vowels were allophones of each other. Was /e/ simply an allophone of /ɛ/? Or, was /ɛ/ an allophone of /a/?[33] Was there, in addition to the short midvowel /ɛ/, perhaps also /ɛ̄/?

The sequence of vowels for the late Second Temple era listed in the table below is one less than the sequence sometimes assumed for pre-Masoretic Hebrew. The vowel /ɛ̄/ may have existed as a reflex of certain

30. We assume, e.g., that vowel reduction had not taken place in the earlier period.

31. Some ambiguity pertains to some of the vowels in the second column; see below. Column 3 is informed by but not identical to the chart in Yuditsky, "Hebrew in Greek and Latin Transcriptions," 1:103. For a summary of correspondences between the vowels of the Secunda and those of THT, see Brønno, *Studien*, 453–63.

32. See, e.g., Huehnergard, "Afro-Asiatic," 142–43; Kogan, "Proto-Semitic Phonetics and Phonology," 119.

33. See Blau, *Phonology and Morphology*, 113.

Table 3.3. Vowels of Biblical Hebrew

Phonemes of PS/PNWS	Vowels of Biblical Hebrew, ca. 200 BCE–100 CE	*Common Realization in the Secunda*	Phonemes of (Tiberian) Biblical Hebrew, ca. 800 CE	Name of Vowel Symbol	Contemporary USA Classroom Pronunciation
ī	ī	ι and ει	i	*hireq*	i
ā	ō	ω	o	*holem*	o
ū	ū	ου	u	*shureq, qibbuts*	u
i	- and ə	(ι and ε [?])	-	*shewa*	- and ə
	i	ι and ε	i	*hireq*	i and ɪ
	ε	ε	ε	*segol*	ε and e
	e		e	*tsere*	e
	ē	η			
a	- and ə	(ι and ε [?])	-	*shewa*	- and ə
	a	α and ε	a	*patakh*	a
	ā	α	å [IPA ɔ]	*qamets*	a or ɑ
u	- and ə	(ι and ε [?])	-	*shewa*	- and ə
	u	ο	u	*qibbuts*	u
	o		å [IPA ɔ]	*qamets*	o
	ō	ω	o	*holem*	o

triphthong contractions, especially at the ends of III-*vav*/*yod* words (e.g., **yabniyu* > *yibnē̜* "he will build").[34] Since the final vowel of such words is represented in the Secunda by a short vowel, *epsilon*, I assume that at some point in the first millennium, the vowel had shortened (i.e., **yibnē̜* > *yibnɛ* = יִבְנֶה).

The existence of *shewa* /ə/ (or a muttered vowel) in the Hebrew of the era of circa 200 BCE–100 CE is suggested by numerous pieces of evidence. For the evidence and arguments, see §3.6 below, "Vowel Reduction."

3.3. Developments of Individual Vowels[35]

The hypothetical transformations of the vowels are summarized initially, and then a more detailed presentation is given. Following this, more specific phenomena are described.[36] The goal of the illustrations here and below is not to give the student a comprehensive picture of the development of ancient Hebrew vowels (for which one may consult more in-depth treatments, such as Blau's *Phonology and Morphology of Biblical Hebrew*), but rather to introduce the student to the basic underlying developments and to give the student the rudimentary framework that will enable them to absorb the language's morphology and predict the inflection of nouns and verbs. Again, the hypothetical nature of the identification of vowels should be emphasized.

The historical long vowels remained long vowels; their length did not change. Their qualities were, for the most part, also stable over time. The

34. See, e.g., Joseph Lam and Dennis Pardee, "Standard/Classical Biblical Hebrew," *HBH* 1:8.

35. The earliest forms of nouns and adjectives (including participles and infinitives) reconstructed in this section are represented with word-final historical short vowels; these word-final vowels mark the nominative case in the hypothetical second millennium version of Canaanite (see ch. 4 §2, "Case and Number in Second Millennium Northwest Semitic").

36. Much of the following chapter, as well as material in chaps. 4–6 is informed by John Huehnergard, "Biblical Hebrew Nominal Patterns," in Hutton, *Epigraphy, Philology, and the Hebrew Bible*, 25–64; Joshua Fox, *Semitic Noun Patterns*, HSS 52 (Winona Lake, IN: Eisenbrauns, 2003); and *HGhS*. In addition, I have benefited from attending historical Hebrew lessons in my training under Dennis Pardee at the University of Chicago and from consulting the unpublished manuscript by Thomas O. Lambdin and John Huehnergard, "The Historical Grammar of Classical Hebrew: An Outline" (2000), as well as earlier realizations of the same manuscript.

vowels /ī/ and /ū/ continued to be articulated in the same way from earliest times to latest times in almost every environment (e.g., **yamīnu* > **yāmīn* [> יָמִין] "right hand" and **katūbu* > **kātūb* [> כָּתוּב] "written"). The PS/PNWS */ā/, however, shifted in quality to */ō/ (e.g., **šāpiṭu* > **šōpēṭ* [> שֹׁפֵט] "judge"). This is called the Canaanite Shift and is described in greater detail below. Even here, the */ō/ that is the result of the Canaanite Shift is very stable; it does not change in length or further alter in its quality (e.g., **šōpəṭīm* [> שֹׁפְטִים]).

The historical short vowels also evidence stability, but primarily in just one environment. In closed unaccented syllables, the short vowels generally did not change. Short */i/ remained */i/:

- **ḥiṯṯīma* > **ḥiṣṣīm* (> חִצִּים) "arrows"
- ***sip**riyya* > ***sip**rī* (> סִפְרִי) "my book"
- ***dim**ʿatu* > ***dim**ʿā* (> דִּמְעָה) "tears."

Short */a/ remained */a/:

- *ʿ***am**mīma* > *ʿ***am**mīm* (> עַמִּים) "peoples"
- ***mal**katu* > ***mal**kā* (> מַלְכָּה) "queen."

Short */u/ remained */u/ before geminated consonants:

- ***ḥuq**qīma* > ***ḥuq**qīm* (> חֻקִּים) "statutes"
- ***muṣ**ṣalu* > ***muṣ**ṣāl* (> מֻצָּל) "one torn out" (*hoph*. part. נצל).

But, in a closed nontonic syllable followed by two different consonants, */u/ lowered to */o/:

- ***ḥuk**mataha* > ***ḥok**mātāh* (> חָכְמָתָהּ) "her wisdom"
- ***kulu** haʾʾarṣi* > ***kol** hāʾārṣ* (> כָּל־הָאָרֶץ) "all the land."

In THT, this */o/ lowered further to /å/ (e.g., חָכְמָתָהּ = *ḥåkmåtåh*).[37] There are some exceptions, but the regularity of these correspondences in closed, unaccented syllables should be noted.

37. For more on this, see §16 below, "*Qamets* in Tiberian Hebrew Tradition." See also Joshua Blau, *A Grammar of Biblical Hebrew*, 2nd ed., PLO 12 (Wiesbaden: Harrassowitz, 1993), 37.

The historical short vowels evidence some consistency in their development based on the type of syllable in which they appear. Three types of syllable can be isolated: what are (in THT) the tonic syllable, the pretonic syllable, and those syllables that are both nontonic and nonpretonic.

1. In a tonic syllable, the historical short vowels usually lengthened and/or lowered in articulation, in both open and closed syllables:[38]
   1.1. */i/ vowel
      1.1.1. */i/ > */ē/
      - **zaqinu* > **zāqēn* (> זָקֵן) "elder"
      - **yiqqaḥinī* > **yiqqāḥēnī* (> יִקָּחֵנִי) "he will take me"

      1.1.2. */i/ > /e/
      - ***libbu* > ***lebb* > ***leb*** (= לֵב) "heart"
      - **kabida* > **kabid* > **kābed* (> כָּבֵד) "it is heavy"
      - **yudabbiru* > **yədabber* (> יְדַבֵּר) "he will speak"

      1.1.3. */i/ > /ɛ/
      - **qirbu* > **qɛrb* (= קֶרֶב) "midst"
      - **ṯibtu* > **šibt* > **šɛbt* (= שֶׁבֶת) "dwelling" (inf. const. ישׁב)
      - **yāṯibtu* > **yōšibt* > **yōšɛbt* (> יוֹשֶׁבֶת) "one dwelling"

   1.2. */a/ vowel: */a/ > */ā/
   - **dabaru* > **dābār* (> דָּבָר) "word"
   - **barakatu* > **bərākā* (> בְּרָכָה) "blessing"

   1.3. */u/ vowel
      1.3.1. */u/ > */ō/
      - **gadulu* > **gādōl* (> גָּדוֹל) "great"
      - **šumuru* > **šəmōr* (> שְׁמֹר) "guarding" (inf. const.)

      1.3.2. */u/ > */o/
      - **ʿuzzu* > **ʿozz* > *ʿoz* (> עֹז) "strength"
      - **qudšu* > **qodš* (> קֹדֶשׁ) "holiness"
      - **yašmuru* > **yišmur* > **yišmor* (> יִשְׁמֹר) "he will guard"
      - **š(u)mur* > **šəmor* > (> שְׁמֹר) "guard!" (impv.).[39]

38. Lowering occurs in the case of an */i/ that becomes */e/ and a */u/ that becomes */o/.

39. Note also the verbs of other conjugations: *piel* **baqqiša* > **biqqeš* (> בִּקֵּשׁ) "he sought"; **yubaqqišu* > **yəbaqqeš* (> יְבַקֵּשׁ) "he will seek"; *hiphil* **hapqida* > **hipqīd* (> הִפְקִיד) "he appointed"; **yapqidu* > **yapqīd* (> יַפְקִיד) "he will appoint"; **yapqid* > **yapqed* (> יַפְקֵד) "may he appoint."

One frequent exception is evident in the forms of *qåṭal* verbs where the /a/ vowel did not lengthen:

- **ša**ma**ra* > **šā**mar*** (> שָׁמַר) "he guarded"
- **ša**mar**ta* > **šā**mar**tā* (> שָׁמַ֫רְתָּ) "you guarded."

2. In an open pretonic syllable, short */i/ and */a/ lengthened to */ē/ and */ā/:

   2.1. */i/ > */ē/
   - ****li**babu* > ****lē**bāb* (> לֵבָב) "heart"
   - **ka**bi**dīma* > **kə**bē**dīm* (> כְּבֵדִים) "heavy"
   - ****hi**bīna* > ****hē**bīn* (> הֵבִין) "he understood" (*hiphil qåṭal* בין)

   2.2. */a/ > */ā/
   - ****da**baru* > ****dā**bār* (> דָּבָר) "word"
   - **da**ba**rīma* > **də**bā**rīm* (> דְּבָרִים) "words"
   - **da**ba**rahu* > **da**ba**rō* > **də**bā**rō* (> דְּבָרוֹ) "his word"
   - **ba**ra**katu* > **bə**rā**kā* (> בְּרָכָה) "blessing"
   - **bara**ka**tiyya* > **bara**ka**tī* > **bar**kā**tī* (> בִּרְכָתִי) "my blessing"
   - ****ša**mara* > ****ša**mar* > ****šā**mar* (> שָׁמַר) "he guarded"
   - ****ša**marta* > ****šā**martā* (> שָׁמַ֫רְתָּ) "you guarded"
   - ****ša**marti* > ****šā**mart* (> שָׁמַרְתְּ)
   - ****ša**martu* > ****šā**martī* (> שָׁמַ֫רְתִּי)
   - ****ya**qūmu* > ****ya**qūm* > ****yā**qūm* (> יָקוּם) "he will arise"
   - ****ya**bīnu* > ****ya**bīn* > ****yā**bīn* (> יָבִין) "he will understand"
   - **la**qa**ḥanī* > **lə**qā**ḥanī* (> לְקָחַ֫נִי) "he took me"
   - **yiq**qa**ḥinī* > **yiq**qā**ḥēnī* (> יִקָּחֵ֫נִי) "he will take me."[40]

In contrast to */i/ and */a/, historical short */u/ usually reduced in open pretonic syllables:

   2.3. */u/ > */ə/ or ø
   - ****bu**kuru* > ****bə**kōr* (> בְּכֹר) "firstborn"
   - ****mu**tay* > ****mə**tē* (> מְתֵי) "men of"
   - **yaš**mu**rihu* > **yiš**mə**rēhū* (> יִשְׁמְרֵהוּ) "he will guard him"
   - ****šu**mur* > ****šə**mōr* (> שְׁמֹר) "guarding"

---

40. The above occur in open pretonic syllables. In closed pretonic syllables, the vowel must remain short (as is true for all closed, unaccented syllables), and the quality of the vowel is less likely to change (e.g., **šəmartɛm* [> שְׁמַרְתֶּם]).

- **šu**mu**rahu* > **šomrō* (> שָׁמְרוֹ) "his guarding."[41]

The primary exceptions to these tendencies occur where a short */i/ is preceded by a syllable that is closed or that contains a historical long vowel that does not reduce. In these cases, the /i/ reduces to *shewa* or elides:

- **šā**pi**ṭīma* > **šō**pi**ṭīm* > **šō**pə**ṭīm* (> שֹׁפְטִים) "judges"
- **wayyit**ti**nihū* > **wayyit**tə**nēhū* (> וַיִּתְּנֵ֫הוּ)
- **wayyubaq**qi**šihū* > **waybaqšēhū* (> וַיְבַקְשֵׁ֫הוּ) "he sought him."

In other cases, the reduction of the pretonic vowel seems to be the result of the shifting place of stress in the verb.[42] Note that the stem vowel in *qåṭal* and *yiqṭol* verb forms reduces or elides where the stem is followed by a single vowel morpheme (e.g., *-*ī*, *-*ā*, *-*ū*):

- **ša**ma**rat* > **šā**ma**rā* > **šā**mə**rā* (> שָׁמְרָה) "she guarded"
- **ša**ma**rū* > **šā**ma**rū* > **šā**mə**rū* (> שָׁמְרוּ) "they guarded"
- **tit**ti**nīna* > **tit**ti**nī* > **tit**tə**nī* (> תִּתְּנִי) "you will give"
- **yaš**mu**rūna* > **yiš**mu**rū* > **yiš**mə**rū* (> יִשְׁמְרוּ) "they will guard"
- **yiš**la**ḥūna* > **yiš**la**ḥū* > **yiš**lə**ḥū* (> יִשְׁלְחוּ) "they will send"
- **yubaq**qi**šūna* > **yəbaq**qi**šū* > **yəbaqšū* (> יְבַקְשׁוּ) "they will seek."

Also, the same unexpected reduction is found with the noun + second-person masculine singular suffix:

- **daba**ra**ka* > **dəbā**ra**kā* > **dəbā**rə**kā* (> דְּבָרְךָ) "your word."

---

41. In general, this seems to reflect the tendency for any two historical high vowels (that is, /i/ and /u/) that appear in sequence to dissimilate, such that the first is no longer a high vowel (see W. Randall Garr, "Pretonic Vowels in Hebrew," *VT* 37 [1987]: 143, 150).

42. See §5, "Lengthening of Pretonic */i/ and */a/ Vowels and the Place of Stress," below. Another general exception to the rule that pretonic /u/ reduces to *shewa* is where the short */u/ vowel has been reanalyzed as a historical long vowel (e.g., **ga**du**līma* > **ga**dō**līm* > **gə**dō**līm* [> גְּדוֹלִים] "great").

3. In open syllables that are both nontonic and nonpretonic, the historical short vowels reduce to *shewa* or elide entirely:

- *****ġi****nabīma* > *****ʿă****nābīm* (> עֲנָבִים) "grapes"
- ****da****barīma* > ****də****bārīm* (> דְּבָרִים) "words"
- ****bara****katiyya* > ****bara****katī* > ****bar****kātī* > (> בִּרְכָתִי) "my blessing"[43]
- ****la****qaḥanī* > ****lə****qāḥanī* (> לְקָחַנִי) "he took me"
- ****bu****qarīma* > ****bə****qārīm* (> בְּקָרִים) "mornings"
- ****yu****baqqišūna* > ****yu****baqqišū* > ****yə****baqšū* (> יְבַקְשׁוּ) "they will seek."[44]

When exactly each of these developments took place is hard to know, but they are all reflected in one way or another in the Secunda. It is possible that vowels lengthened and/or lowered in the First Temple era, though this is hard to demonstrate given the nature of the evidence.[45] The lengthening of */i/ and */a/ in pretonic syllables must have taken place at the latest by circa 250 BCE, since the LXX of Genesis attests long vowels in its transcriptions of names: **qidar* > **qēdār* > Κηδαρ "Kedar" (cf. קֵדָר; note also עֵשָׂו and Ησαυ "Esau").[46] The reduction of pretonic */u/ is presupposed

43. In cases where two nontonic/nonpretonic open syllables both contain a short vowel, as in ****bara****katiyya*, the second of the two short vowels elides entirely and the first often shifts to /i/ in THT and in the Babylonian Hebrew (pronunciation) tradition (BHT).

44. In closed unaccented syllables, however, the vowel must be short and is relatively stable, as explained above.

45. As a comparison, note that in the first part of the first millennium BCE Phoenician (with which Hebrew shares many traits) experienced a shift from */a/ to /ō/ (or /o/) in accented open syllables (found mostly in nouns, but not in verbs [except the 3ms suffix-conjugation form]), as evidenced, e.g., in the name "Ahirom" in cuneiform script *ḫi-ru-um-ma* (from Tiglath-Pileser III's *Annals* 27, l. 2) and the corresponding name in Greek ειρωμος (from Josephus, *C. Ap.* 1:105). If Phoenician experienced such a shift in nouns (but not verbs) in the era 1000–500 BCE, then it is conceivable that Hebrew did too, though we assume a raising of /a/ to /o/ for Phoenician and a lowering of /i/ to /e/ and /u/ to /o/ for Hebrew. For the connection of the Hebrew and Phoenician evidence, see Garr, *Dialect Geography*, 34, who characterizes the similarity in terms of lengthening; for the examples, see Stanislav Segert, *A Grammar of Phoenician and Punic* (Munich: Beck, 1976), 74 and Jo Ann Hackett, "Phoenician," *CEWAL*, 371, who notes the Phoenician vowel as short /o/.

46. Blau, *Phonology and Morphology*, 124. Blau (128) suggests this emerged in the Second Temple era as a means of distinguishing Hebrew from Aramaic (where pretonic vowels in open syllables reduce); for more description, see ibid., 123–32.

in some words in the Secunda (e.g., **zukur* > ζχορ "remember!" Ps 89:48 [cf. זְכָר־]).[47] The reduction of short vowels in open nontonic/nonpretonic syllables to *shewa* is usually thought to have taken place sometime in the second half of the first millennium BCE.[48] The lack of clear evidence for vowel reduction in the first half of the first millennium BCE supports this.[49] The mixed evidence from the DSS, the Secunda, and Jerome suggests perhaps that short vowels were gradually lost over the course of the Second Temple era.

There are numerous further exceptions to the tendencies described above. But, the basic outline of these shifts and the most common exceptions should be carefully studied. Knowing something of this history helps one inflect words and predict what a given form should look like. Because the manner in which we pronounce the vowels does not precisely mirror the pronunciation of the Masoretes, there is often ambiguity in the minds of students over the exact articulation of a word's sounds and thus over the spelling of the word with Tiberian vowels. For example, if a student remembers that the *qal* third-person masculine plural *yiqṭol* of שׁמר is phonetically *yish-me-ˈroo* it can be difficult to remember whether the middle vowel should be written יִשְׁמֶרוּ* or יִשְׁמְרוּ.[50] Similarly with noun forms such as *de-va-ˈreem* and *de-va-ˈro*, it can be hard for a student to predict whether the first vowel should be written with a *shewa* or *segol* and whether the second vowel should be *patakh* (דְּבַרִים* or דֶּבַרִים* and דְּבַרוֹ* or דֶּבַרוֹ*) or *qamets* (דְּבָרִים or דֶּבָרִים* and דְּבָרוֹ or דֶּבָרוֹ*).

But the above rules and tendencies can help a student reproduce the proper vocalization and form of words. For *yish-me-ˈroo*, the vowel of "*-me-*" must be */ə/ since it is in an open pretonic syllable, where we expect a *shewa* and where we do not find (barring some exceptions) /ɛ/. The word *de-va-ˈreem* must reflect **də-bā-rīm* > דְּבָרִים and *de-va-ˈro* must reflect **də-bā-rō* > דְּבָרוֹ. That is, the "*de-*" must reflect a *shewa* since it is an open nontonic/nonpretonic syllable, where one finds only *shewa* and long vowels. The vowel of "*-va-*" must be */ā/ (> /å/) since it is in an open pretonic syllable, where we do not find */a/ and where we expect */ā/ (>

47. Brønno, *Studien*, 46.

48. See Sandra L. Gogel, *A Grammar of Epigraphic Hebrew*, RBS 23 (Atlanta: Scholars Press, 1998), 33; cf. T. Muraoka, *A Grammar of Qumran Aramaic*, ANESSupp 38 (Leuven: Peeters, 2011), 31–33.

49. See §6 below, "Vowel Reduction."

50. The mark ˈ precedes the accented syllable.

/å/). The following paragraphs will detail further the phonological developments outlined above.

3.4. Lengthening and Lowering of Vowels in Tonic Syllables

With respect to historical */i/ and */u/ vowels in tonic syllables, it seems that these short vowels sometimes lowered in their articulation but did not lengthen (i.e., */i/ > */e/, */i/ > /ɛ/, and */u/ > */o/).[51] As implied by the Secunda, this phenomenon appears primarily in nouns where the short vowel is followed in its historical form by two word-final consonants, that is, in geminate nouns:

- **libbu* > ****lebb*** > λεβ (cf. לֵב) "heart" Ps 32:11
- *ʿ***uzzu*** > *ʿ***ozz*** > οζ (cf. עֹז) "strength" Ps 30:8
- **maginnu* > **mag**enn*** > μαγεν (cf. מָגֵן) "shield" Ps 18:31
- **maʿ***uzzu*** > **maʿ***ozz*** > μαοζ (cf. מָעוֹז) "stronghold" Ps 31:3

and in segolate nouns:

- *****sitru*** > *****setr*** > σεθρ (cf. סֵ֫תֶר) "secret" Ps 32:7
- *****bukru*** > *****bokr*** > βοκρ (cf. בֹּ֫קֶר) "morning" Ps 46:6.[52]

In addition, the Septuagint evidences similar nouns with *epsilon*: νεδερ [cf. נֵ֫דֶר] "jar" (1 Sam 1:24) and εμακ [cf. הָעֵ֫מֶק] "Emak" or "valley" (Josh 13:19).[53] Contrast the realization of */i/ as /ē/ in words without geminated historical consonants in the Secunda:

- *ʾ***ilu*** > *ʾ***ēl*** > ηλ (cf. אֵל) "God of" Ps 29:3
- **ma**hiratu* > **mə**hērā* > μηηρα (cf. מְהֵרָה) "in haste" Ps 31:3
- *****nikaru* > *****nēkār* > νηχαρ (cf. נֵכָר) "foreigner" Ps 18:46.[54]

51. See the summary of correspondences between the vowels of the Secunda and those of THT in Brønno, *Studien*, 453–54.

52. Examples are drawn from Brønno, *Studien*, 25 (note also ιεθεν), 120, 122, 144, 149, 175, 177.

53. See Khan, "*Ṣere*," 140.

54. The construct state of the noun does not seem to be a relevant factor; note the absolute form with the same vowel: αηλ vs. הָאֵל "the God" Ps 18:31. The examples are again from Brønno, *Studien*, 59, 110, 155, 161. Short */u/ does not typically occur

The lowering of historical short vowels without lengthening also occurs regularly in finite verbal forms in context:

- **yittinu* > **yit**ten*** > ιεθθεν (cf. יִתֵּן) "he will give" Ps 18:33
- **yudab**bi**ru* > **yədab**ber*** > ιδαββερ (cf. יְדַבֵּר) "he will speak" Ps 49:4
- *ʾ***ir**du**pu*** > *ʾ***er**dop*** > ερδοφ (cf. אֶרְדּוֹף) "I will pursue" Ps 18:38.[55]

Participles and infinitives (being verbal adjectives and nouns) attest the vowels associated with nongeminate nouns and adjectives (i.e., *ēta* = /ē/ and *ōmega* = /ō/):

- *ʿ***ā**zi**ru*** > *ʿ***ō**zēr*** > ωζηρ (cf. עֹזֵר) "one helping" Ps 30:11
- **(wa)mušal**li**mu* > **(ū)məšal**lēm*** > ουσαλημ (cf. וּמְשַׁלֵּם) "and one preserving" Ps 31:24
- **(li)mu**ṣu**ʾi* > **(li)m**ṣō*** > λαμσω (cf. לִמְצֹא) "to find" Ps 36:3.[56]

In addition, finite verbal forms with pronominal object suffixes, attest lowering and lengthening in the tonic syllable:

- *ʾ*imḫuṣ**i**hum* > ʾ*emḫō**ṣēm*** > ʾ*emḥō**ṣēm*** > εμωσημ (cf. אֶמְחָצֵם) "I struck them" (Ps 18:39).[57]

Although it might not appear obvious at first, the distribution of vowels in THT seems to confirm an earlier distinction wherein finite verbal forms

---

as /ō/ in similar environments since it tends to reduce or elide (e.g., **bukur* > βχωρ [cf. בְּכוֹר] "firstborn" Ps 89:28 [Brønno, *Studien*, 161]). Note also the lengthening and lowering implied in the LXX: *νωκηδ* for נֹקֵד "sheep-raiser" in 2 Kgs 3:4.

55. Examples are drawn from Brønno, *Studien*, 25 (note also ιεθεν), 32, 71. Pausal forms show some variation, but frequently attest *ēta* and *ōmega* (see Khan, "*Ṣere*," 137–38). Note, e.g., pausal **yuḥallilūna* > **yəḥallēlū* > ιαλληλου (cf. יְחַלֵּלוּ) "they will profane" Ps 89:32 (see Brønno, *Studien*, 71). In the MT, one finds a similar discrepancy between forms that seem to be linked with a following word or phrase and exhibit /ɛ/ (e.g., דִּבֶּר "he spoke" passim; יְדַבֶּר־בִּי "he will speak to me" Hab 2:1; הִוָּלֶד לוֹ "being born to him" Gen 21:5) and corresponding forms with /e/ where there sometimes is and sometimes is not a prosodic link with what follows.

56. Brønno, *Studien*, 56, 59, 84.

57. Brønno, *Studien*, 32. The theme vowel in the Secunda form agrees with that of the Aramaic cognate, *mḥq*, as attested, e.g., in Jewish Palestinian Aramaic and Jewish Babylonian Aramaic (see *DJPA* and *DJBA*).

had short vowels in their stem and nonfinite forms had long vowels. Note, for example, the distinction between the finite *niphal* form נֶאֱמַן "he is faithful" and the participial form נֶאֱמָן "one who is faithful." The finite form implies a pre-Masoretic short */a/ and the participle a long */ā/. This implies an analogous distinction between finite forms and nonfinite forms, even in other conjugations (e.g., יִתֵּן < **yitten* "he will give" vs. נֹתֵן < **nōtēn* "one giving"; and אֶרְדּוֹף < *ʾ*erdop* "I will pursue" vs. רְדֹף < **rədōp* "pursuing"). Furthermore, although we might at first assume that finite forms like יִתֵּן and אֶרְדּוֹף evidence both lowering and lengthening of the historical */i/ and */u/ vowels, where the stem vowel is /a/ in analogous *yiqṭol* forms, the vowel that appears in THT is not *qamets*, but *patakh*: יִשְׁלַח "he will send." This implies that the *tsere* in יִתֵּן and the *holem* in אֶרְדּוֹף reflect an earlier short /e/ and /o/, respectively.[58]

Finally, a small group of words evidences the further lowering of */i/ to /ɛ/, especially where the historical */i/ is followed by two consonants in a row. In particular, this relates to some **qitl* nouns, feminine singular participles, and *qal* infinitives construct from I-*vav*/*yod* roots (and I-*nun* roots): **qirbu* > **qɛrb* (= קֶ֫רֶב) "midst" and **yāṯibtu* > **yōšibt* > *yōšɛbt* (> יוֹשֶׁבֶת) "one dwelling"; **ṯibtu* > **šibt* > **šɛbt* (> שֶׁבֶת) "dwelling."[59] In pause,

58. There is also some limited orthographic evidence that the historical /i/ vowel in finite forms was realized in a manner different from how it was realized in nonfinite forms. For example, *piel* finite forms of III-*khet* roots have a *patakh* in context (e.g., יְשַׁלַּח "he will send away" Exod 3:20), reflecting an earlier short vowel, but have a *tsere* in pause (יְשַׁלֵּחַ Isa 45:13), where we would expect an earlier long vowel. On the other hand, the same vowel in the participle and infinitives is often written both in context and in pause with a *tsere*, implying an earlier long vowel. Note especially the contextual forms: מְשַׁלֵּחַ "one sending away" (Exod 8:17); inf. cstr.: זַבֵּחַ "making sacrifices" (1 Kgs 12:32); inf. abs.: שַׁלֵּחַ "sending away" (1 Kgs 11:22). The exception here is the infinitive construct of שלח which has a *patakh* (perhaps to distinguish it from the infinitive absolute [?]). But, the other seven contextual forms of the *piel* inf. const. of III-*khet* roots have *tsere*. If the finite and nonfinite verbal forms had the same vowel length in the earlier Second Temple era, then we would expect a common realization of the last stem vowel in all the forms.

59. Although it is difficult to explain all the exceptions and although there are probably multiple causes, one explanation for this vowel in **qitl* nouns involves the quality of the second root consonant. If the second root consonant of a monosyllabic word is relatively sonorous (i.e., /l/, /m/, /n/, /r/), then the historical */i/ became /ɛ/ (e.g., **qirbu* > **qɛrb* [> קֶ֫רֶב]). See Thomas O. Lambdin, "Philippi's Law Reconsidered," in *Biblical Studies Presented to Samuel Iwry*, ed. Ann Kort and Samuel Morschauser (Winona Lake, IN: Eisenbrauns, 1985), 139–40. Other nouns, like נֶ֫דֶר "vow" (a byform

such vowels are represented with a *qamets* in THT (e.g., יוֹשָׁבֶת "one dwelling" Josh 2:15 and שָׁבֶת "to dwell" Isa 40:22).[60] There is no clear evidence of the shift */i/ to /ɛ/ in such forms in the Secunda.[61]

A similar shift of historical */i/ to */ɛ/ and then to THT /a/ may be reflected in other types of nouns and especially in verbs like the *piel qåṭal*: **dabbirta* > **dibbɛrtā* (> *dibbartå* = דִּבַּרְתָּ) "you spoke" (see §8 below, "'Phillipi's Law' and Similar Changes").

The pronominal affixes for verbs תֶּם- and תֶּן- and for nouns כֶם- and כֶן-, marking the second-person masculine and feminine plural, reflect a similar lowering from */i/ to /ɛ/, though the context of this shift is different from that of the above words (i.e., it does not appear in a syllable followed by two consonants).

The relevance of the above comparisons with the Secunda, of course, presumes some correspondence between the Hebrew implied by this transcription and that which led to THT. It is also conceivable that these traditions reflect entirely independent vocalic developments. For the present work, however, I assume some connection between the Hebrew of the Secunda and the tradition that led to THT. I primarily indicate the historical */i/ and */u/ vowels in geminate and segolate nouns as */e/ and */o/ respectively (i.e., without lengthening). Because we focus on the contextual forms of words from the late Second Temple era, I indicate the historical */i/ and */u/ vowels in the stem of finite verbal forms in the same manner (i.e., as */e/ and */o/).

3.5. Lengthening of Pretonic */i/ and */a/ and the Place of Stress

Historical short vowels in open pretonic syllables often lengthened in BH. It is especially the case that */a/ lengthened to */ā/ (before shifting to /å/ in THT). The historical */i/ vowel somewhat less frequently lengthened (and

---

of נֵ֫דֶר), formed on analogy to words like קֶ֫רֶב. In still other cases, a given word might have had byforms from earliest times (e.g., **dark* vs. **dirk* > דֶּ֫רֶךְ "path" [see Huehnergard, "Biblical Hebrew Nominal Patterns," 39]).

60. In some cases, **qitl* segolates reveal a *qamets* in pause in the first syllable, as with סָ֫תֶר "hiding place" vs. סֵ֫תֶר in context.

61. Note some of the limited evidence from the Secunda that seems to suggest the realization of an /a/ vowel: *νεεμαναθ* (cf. נֶאֱמֶ֫נֶת) "something trustworthy/enduring" Ps 89:19; σαθιβηηκι (cf. שְׂאֵתִי בְחֵיקִי) "my carrying in my breast" Ps 89:51; βρεδεθι (cf. בְּרִדְתִּי) "in my descent" Ps 30:10 (for the examples, see Brønno, *Studien*, 56, 107).

lowered) to */ē/, while */u/ often did not lengthen, but instead reduced to *shewa* (see §6, "Vowel Reduction"). These tendencies have been remarked on above.

In the inflection of the *qåṭal* verb, most forms exhibit the pretonic lengthening of the first */a/ vowel: **šamar* > **šāmar* (> שָׁמַר). Where this historical /a/ vowel is in the propretonic syllable, it reduces to *shewa*: **šamartumu* > **šəmartɛm* (> שְׁמַרְתֶּם). However, in the third-person feminine singular and third-person common plural, it appears that the pretonic /a/ vowel is reduced to *shewa* and the propretonic */a/ is lengthened: **šāmarā* > **šāmərā* (> שָׁמְרָה) and **šāmarū* > **šāmərū* (> שָׁמְרוּ). These inconsistencies are likely due to the shifting place of the stress in the history of Hebrew verbs.[62] When pretonic vowel lengthening was taking place, there was a full vowel in the second syllable and this penultimate syllable was accented, resulting in the pretonic lengthening of the first stem vowel (**šamarat* > **šāˈmarā* and **šamarū* > **šāˈmarū*). The penultimate accent is reflected in the pausal forms of these words (e.g., שָׁמָ֫רוּ Num 9:23). Only later (presumably close to the end of the Second Temple era) did the accent then shift to the last syllable, resulting in the reduction of the second */a/ vowel (**šāməˈrā* [> שָׁמְרָה], and **šāməˈrū* [> שָׁמְרוּ]).[63] In the Secunda, the transcription consistently reflects the reduction of these short vowels to zero (e.g., ασσα [cf. עָשְׁשָׁה] "becomes dark" Ps 31:10 and ταμνου [cf. טָמְנוּ] "they hid" Ps 31:5).[64] Although the orthography of the

62. Geoffrey Khan, "Pretonic Lengthening: Biblical Hebrew," *EHLL* 3:226.

63. Blau (*Phonology and Morphology*, 128) argues that what began as **ša-ˈmarat* shifted to **ša-ˈma-rā* (due to loss of *taw*) and then to **šā-ˈma-rā* (due to pretonic lengthening in Second Temple times) and then to **šā-mə-ˈrā* (with the shift of accent to the final syllable sometime later, when pretonic vowels no longer were lengthened but reduced, as in Aramaic). See his long description of stress and syllable structure in ibid., 123–29; and the description of the sequence of these changes at pp. 144–48. Alternatively, one may explain these forms by suggesting that the accent on third-person forms was initially on the first syllable; the long vowel of the first syllable (which is assumed from the THT *qamets*) is due to tonic lengthening/lowering (see Bergsträsser, *Hebriäsche Grammatik*, 116–18). One can imagine the development: *ˈ*ša-marat* > *ˈ*šā-ma-rā* (due to loss of *taw* and tonic lengthening/lowering) > *ˈ*šā-mə-rā* (due to vowel reduction of nontonic/nonpretonic vowels) > **šā-mə-ˈrā* (shift in stress, akin to the shift in stress presumed for *wəqåṭal* forms that show no vowel reduction, like וְשָׁמַרְתָּ֫ "and observe" Deut 6:3).

64. See Brønno, *Studien*, 19 and 22. Exceptions are only found in II-guttural roots where the MT contains a *khatef* vowel: ρααθα [cf. רָאֲתָה] "she saw" Ps 35:21; μααδου

DSS does not usually allow one to discern the theme vowel of *qåṭal* forms, the vowel is rarely indicated with a *mater*, implying its preservation and a penultimate accent for the verb (e.g., יכולו *yākōlū* [cf. יָכְלוּ] "they did [not] prevail" 11Q5 [11QPs[a]] at Ps 129:2).[65]

It seems likely that other verbal forms were similarly accented on their penultimate syllable and only subsequently did the theme vowel reduce when accent shifted from the penultimate to the final (i.e., ultimate) syllable:

- **yašmurūna* > **yišmurū* > **yišmərū* (> יִשְׁמְרוּ) "they will guard"
- **yišlaḥūna* > **yišlaḥū* > **yišləḥū* (> יִשְׁלְחוּ) "they will send"
- **tittinīna* > **tittinī* > **tittənī* (> תִּתְּנִי) "you will give"
- **yubaqqišūna* > **yubaqqišū* > **yəbaqšū* (> יְבַקְשׁוּ) "they will seek."[66]

The penultimate stress of such forms is implied in the pausal forms in THT (e.g., יִשְׁמֹ֫רוּ Ezek 44:24 and יְבַקֵּ֫שׁוּ Jer 4:30). In addition, the preservation of the theme vowel (and by association penultimate stress) is not infrequently reflected in the DSS (e.g., ישמורו [cf. יִשְׁמְרוּ] "they will guard" 11Q5 [11QPs[a]] at Ps 105:45) and in the Secunda (e.g., ιεφφολου [cf. יִפְּלוּ] "they will fall" Ps 18:39; ιουχαλευ [cf. to יָכְלוּ] "they are able" Ps 18:39).[67] However, the final stem vowel is not always reflected in the orthography of the DSS (ישמרו [cf. שָׁמְרוּ] "they will guard" 4Q70 [4QJer[a]] at Jer 8:7) or in the Secunda (e.g., **wəyiḫparū* > ουιεφρου [cf. וְיַחְפְּרוּ] "they will be ashamed" Ps 35:26).[68] As with the reduction (or nonreduction) of short

---

[cf. מָעֲדוּ] "they did not slip" Ps 18:37; ουνααθα [cf. וְנִחֲתָה] "it brings down" Ps 18:35 (ibid., 19, 22, 64).

65. See also the plene writing of the *qåṭal* of the same verb in a fragmentary context in 4Q385 6a II + 6c, 9 and 4Q401 14 II, 4.

66. Some of these forms, of course, may also be interpreted as reflecting the reduction of pretonic */i/ where the propretonic vowel cannot reduce (as in שֹׁפְטִים "judges") as well as reflecting the tendency for pretonic /u/ to reduce. Nevertheless, since the historical */a/ vowel also reduces in this same position (e.g., יִשְׁלְחוּ "they will send"), it seems more likely that the reduction of the pretonic theme vowel is due to the movement of stress/accent from the penultimate to the ultimate (i.e., last) syllable.

67. See Brønno, *Studien*, 35. Note also **yirʿašū* > ιερασου (cf. יִרְעֲשׁוּ) "they will shake" Ps 46:4.

68. See Brønno, *Studien*, 35 and Yuditsky, "Hebrew in Greek and Latin Transcriptions," 2:67. Presumably the elision of the vowel has led to the emergence of an epenthetic vowel before the second root consonant in other forms: e.g., *(*wa*)*yiśmaḫūna* >

vowels (discussed in the following subsection), in the Hebrew of the Second Temple era, there seems to have been some variation in where such verbal forms were accented.

In the inflection of nouns, one also finds incongruity in the singular noun with second-person masculine singular suffix. In all the other forms of the noun (both masc. and fem.) that bear a nonheavy pronominal suffix, the pretonic vowel is lengthened and the propretonic is reduced according to the tendencies outlined above: **dabarik* > **dəbārēk* (> דְּבָרֵךְ) "your word." The pausal form of the singular noun with second-person masculine singular suffix also exhibits the expected correspondences between syllables and vowels (i.e., **dabaraka* > **dəbārakā* > *dbå'rɛkå* = דְּבָרֶ֫ךָ "your word"). In the contextual form, however, the propretonic vowel seems to have been lengthened and the pretonic reduced to *shewa*: **dəbārə'kā* (> דְּבָרְךָ) "your word" and **ʿăṣātə'kā* (> עֲצָתְךָ) "your counsel." This also can be explained as due to the shifting place of stress within the word. The stress must have been over the penultimate syllable when pretonic vowels were lengthening and then the stress shifted and the suffix altered its form, such that what was once a penultimate short /a/ reduced to *shewa*:

- **dabaraka* > **dəbā'rakā* > **dəbārə'kā* (> דְּבָרְךָ)
- **ʿiṭataka* > **ʿăṣā'takā* > **ʿăṣātə'kā* (> עֲצָתְךָ).[69]

3.6. Vowel Reduction

Usually, vowel reduction is learned as a phenomenon affecting *qamets* and *tsere* vowels in the transformation of singular nouns into plurals (or from absolute forms into construct forms or forms with suffixes), as if a *qamets* of an absolute noun reduced to *shewa* in the plural (or construct or with suffixes). But, this is not how vowel reduction is described from a historical perspective. Vowel reduction affected pronunciation of Hebrew vowels long before */ā/ shifted to /å/ (*qamets*). In this context, it is not correct to say that the *qamets* reduces; instead, the vowel that reduces is the histori-

---

*(*wə*)*yisməḫū* [> *(*wə*)*yismḫū*] > *(*wə*)*yisimḥū* > ιεσεμου and ουειεσαμου "(and) they will rejoice" (Ps 35:24, 27 [cf. וְיִשְׂמְחוּ]).

69. It is interesting to note that the Secunda reflects an /a/ vowel before the suffixed *kaph* and usually no /a/ vowel after the *kaph*. This is reminiscent of the Aramaic 2ms pronominal suffix. For more on this, see ch. 4 §5, "Peculiarities of Some Possessive Suffixes."

cal short vowel that in other positions would eventually lengthen and then become *qamets*. For example, the singular form of "word" developed from a form with two short vowels in its stem, **dabaru*, into one with two long vowels, **dābār*, before becoming *dåbår* = דָּבָר. The plural developed from a similar base: **dabarīma*, though in this form the first /a/ vowel did not lengthen into /ā/, but it instead reduced to *shewa*, resulting eventually in the form **dəbārīm* and then *dbårim* = דְּבָרִים.

Moreover, when we speak of vowel reduction, we speak of one of two phenomena. The full, short vowel may reduce to a *shewa* (that is, a muttered vowel). Or, the full short vowel reduces to nothing; that is, the full vowel elides.

In general, */i/, */a/, and */u/ became muttered vowels (i.e., *shewa*) or elided entirely in open syllables that were both nontonic and nonpretonic. A historical */i/ reduced to *shewa* or elided in an open pretonic syllable when the vowel in the preceding syllable could not reduce (either because it was historically long or because it was in a closed syllable; e.g., **šāpiṭīma* > **šōpiṭīm* > **šōpəṭīm* [> שֹׁפְטִים] "judges"; **mazbiḥāt* > **mizbəḥōt* [> מִזְבְּחוֹת] "altar").[70] In addition, the */u/ vowel often reduced to *shewa* in open pretonic syllables (e.g., **bukur* > **bəkōr* [> בְּכֹר] "firstborn" and **yašmurihū* > **yišmərēhū* [> יִשְׁמְרֵהוּ] "they will guard him").

It might be pointed out here that where */u/ reduces, it is often (though not always) followed by another high vowel, an /i/- or /u/-class vowel. It seems that often there was a tendency to dissimilate two high vowels in a row, that is, to make two high vowels dissimilar to each other. For example, in cases where we presume the sequence of historical vowels **u-u*, we often find instead **ə-ō* (e.g., שְׁמֹר "guarding") or **i-ō*, where the first vowel cannot reduce (e.g., גִּבּוֹר "warrior").[71]

---

70. Note also *ʿ*awwirīm* > *ʿ*iwrīm* (> עִוְרִים) "blind"; and **passiḥīm* > **pisḥīm* (> פִּסְחִים) "limping"; and the *piel* inf. const. plus suffix, as in **dabbiraha* > **dabbərāh* (> דַּבְּרָהּ) "her speaking." The loss of gemination in some forms of the plural is described below in §15, "Loss of Gemination and *Shewa*."

71. See ch. 4 §11, "Nouns with Three Root Consonants, One of Which Is Geminated" and Garr, "Pretonic Vowels in Hebrew," 143, 150. Several idiosyncracies and apparent anomalies should be mentioned. The *niphal* masc. pl. ptc. of מצא does not attest pretonic lengthening in most of its occurrences: הַנִּמְצְאִים "those found" (vs. once as הַנִּמְצָאִים in Ezra 8:25, in pause). Garr (ibid., 153) notes that the participle with unexpected reduction of the pretonic vowel always precedes some phrase (like a prepositional phrase) to which it is closely associated. He also cites the cases of נִבְּאִים "those prophesying."

Where short */a/ or */i/ vowels occurred in two open syllables side-by-side, both syllables being nontonic and nonpretonic, then the second short vowel elided:

- **malakaykum* > **malakēkim* > **malkēkɛm* (> מַלְכֵיכֶם) "your kings" (Jer 44:21)
- **šibaṭaykum* > **šibaṭēkim* > **šibṭēkɛm* (> שִׁבְטֵיכֶם) "your tribes" (passim).

In the cases where */a/ was the vowel that remained, it often shifted to /i/ in THT (see the following subsection for more on this):

- **dabaray* > **dabrē* (> דִּבְרֵי) "words of" (passim)
- **barakat* > **barkat* (> בִּרְכַּת) "blessing of" (passim).

Finally, there are also the cases where what seems to be the pretonic vowel reduces where we do not expect such reduction: **šāmarū* > **šāmərū* (> שָׁמְרוּ) "they guarded"; **yišlaḥū* > **yišləḥū* (> יִשְׁלְחוּ) "they will send"; and **dəbāˈrakā* > **dəbārəˈkā* (> דְּבָרְךָ). As explained in the preceding section, these likely reflect the changing place of stress (near the close of the Second Temple era).

As stated above (in §3, "Development of Individual Vowels"), there is no clear evidence for vowel reduction in the First Temple era.[72] Furthermore, we should admit that short vowels in open, nontonic and nonpretonic syllables may have initially reduced to a muttered vowel and then, at a later time, been entirely lost.[73] Also, some variation in pronunciation (between a short vowel, a muttered vowel, and no vowel) seems implied by a variation of spelling in the DSS, in the Secunda, and in the MT itself.[74] The presence

---

72. Cuneiform inscriptions from the First Temple era are difficult to interpret (see Alan Millard, "Transcriptions into Cuneiform," *EHLL* 3:838–47). Still Michael D. Coogan (*West Semitic Personal Names in the Murašû Documents*, HSM 7 [Missoula, MT: Scholars Press, 1976], 107) concludes that the Akkadian Murašû documents do not reveal any evidence for vowel reduction. See also Gianto, "Archaic Biblical Hebrew," 1:22.

73. Aramaic may have lost short vowels gradually over the same span of time; see Stephen A. Kaufman, "On Vowel Reduction in Aramaic," *JAOS* 104 (1984): 87–95.

74. Notice, as a comparison, that contemporary English words can be pronounced with similar variation, as with "family," which the *OED* transcribes (for the USA pronunciation): [fæm(ə)li], presuming a pronunciation with an elided vowel (*fam-ly*) or a

of a short vowel in certain places presumes it was accented (e.g., **yišlaḥū* and **yišmurū* [> יִשְׁמְרוּ] "they will guard"); in this way, the variation in spelling also reflects a variation in the place of accent (see §5, "Lengthening of Pretonic */i/ and */a/ Vowels and the Place of Stress," above).

In the DSS, where we suppose the sequence full vowel + *aleph* + /ō/ (or /ū/) (e.g., מאור *māʾōr* "light"), the *aleph* is almost never lost.[75] But in cases where the *aleph* is preceded by what we would expect to be a reduced short vowel + *aleph* + /ō/ (or /ū/), the *aleph* (and preceding *shewa*) are occasionally elided (e.g., ונצה *ūnāṣā* "and contempt" [4Q175 25] for ונאצה* **ūnəʾāṣā*; and רויה *rūyā* "what was seen" [11Q19 LXVI, 9] for ראויה* **rəʾūyā*).[76] This implies that all historical short vowels in open propretonic syllables likely reduced, even where the *aleph* is preserved.

Whether short vowels in such syllables sometimes reduced to a muttered vowel or uniformly elided is another question. I assume that the vowels usually became muttered vowels and only in certain cases elided. This is based on the tendency toward unconventional (i.e., non-Masoretic) phonetic spelling in the DSS on the one hand, and the consistent (though not universal) preservation of *aleph* before historical short vowels in propretonic syllables on the other. Examples of misspellings such as רויה are

---

muttered vowel (*fa-mə-ly*), though it also can be articulated with a full vowel (*fa-mi-ly*) when pronounced slowly and emphatically.

75. See Reymond, *Qumran Hebrew*, 137–38.

76. In the second example, the vowel reduction and subsequent elision of the muttered vowel + *aleph* reflect the word's inflection. The cases where one finds the elision of the historical short vowel as well as the *aleph* are relatively uncommon (e.g., רובן *rūbēn* "Reuben" in 4Q221 4, 9 vs. THT רְאוּבֵן). One exception is שרית *šērīt* "remainder" (vs. THT שְׁאֵרִית), which occurs in about ten of its forty occurrences without *aleph* (e.g., 1QS V, 13). Conceivably, the latter word (and others phonetically similar to it: שאר "flesh" and באר "well") had lost the *aleph* in the vernacular already by the time of the scrolls (cf. שֵׁרִית "remainder" in 1 Chr 12:39; משרו *miššērō* "from his flesh" 4Q386 1 II, 4; שיר *šēr* "flesh of" 4Q477 2 II, 8; בירות *bērōt* "wells" 11Q20 XII, 25). A similar loss of a muttered vowel + *aleph* in THT is רָאשִׁים "heads" for an expected רְאָשִׁים*; in the DSS, however, there is only one case of the plural absolute spelled without *aleph* (4Q171 1 + 3–4 III, 5). (The *aleph* is elided elsewhere only in the const. pl., e.g., רשי "heads of" 4Q328 1, 1.) See Reymond, *Qumran Hebrew*, 79; Blau, *Phonology and Morphology*, 55; Blau, *On Pseudo-Corrections*, 28–29. Other examples may reflect other phenomena: תקרוא *tiqqārū* "you will be called" (1QIsa[a] at Isa 61:6) for the pausal form in MT תִּקָּרֵאוּ may reflect confusion of III-*vav*/*yod* and III-*aleph* roots, a phenomenon among the DSS especially prominent in 1QIsa[a] (see Reymond, *Qumran Hebrew*, 189–90).

uncommon. Much more common is to find the *aleph* preserved, as in the plural form מאורות (= *mə*ʾ*ōrōt*) "lights."[77]

On the other hand, among the DSS, spellings of *yiqṭol* forms with object suffixes (e.g., **yišmorkā* > יִשְׁמָרְךָ "he will guard you") sometimes imply the presence of the historical stem vowel and sometimes imply its elision. Where a *mater vav* appears after the second root consonant, we assume the preservation of the historical vowel as in THT (e.g., ישמורכה = *yišmorkā* or *yišmōrekā* "he will guard you" 1QS II, 3). In other cases, however, a *mater vav* appears after the first root consonant and we assume the elision of the historical vowel and the secondary emergence of an epenthetic vowel (e.g., ישומרכה = *yəšomrəkā* or *yəšomrekā* "he will guard you" 11Q5 [11QPs^a] at Ps 121:7 for MT יִשְׁמָרְךָ).[78]

Contradictory evidence is also found in the Secunda. The regular elision of short vowels is implied in many spellings (e.g., ταμνου [cf. טָמְנוּ] "they hid" Ps 31:5; ασσωμριμ [cf. הַשֹּׁמְרִים] "those who guard/give attention to" Ps 31:7; βνη [cf. בְּנֵי] "sons of" Ps 29:1; οιβαυ [cf. אוֹיְבָיו] "his enemies" Ps 89:43).[79] Nevertheless, in a substantial number of cases, where we would expect to find an elided vowel we find a full vowel (e.g., ιεφφολου [cf. יִפְּלוּ] "they will fall" Ps 18:39; βανη [cf. בְּנֵי] "sons of" Ps 18:46).[80] Among these, at least some *epsilon* and *iōta* vowels may mark a muttered vowel, as in:

- οϊεβαϊ (cf. אוֹיְבַי) "my enemies" (Ps 18:38)
- σεμω (cf. שְׁמוֹ) "his name" (Ps 29:2)
- γεδουδ (cf. גְּדוּד) "troop" (Ps 18:30)
- λεβουσι (cf. לְבוּשִׁי) "my clothing" (Ps 35:13)
- χισους (cf. כְּסוּס) "like a horse" (Ps 32:9).[81]

---

77. Reymond, *Qumran Hebrew*, 51–56, 77–87. Neither for מאורות nor for many other similar words do we see frequent unconventional spellings (i.e., **mōrōt* > מואראות* or > מורות*), which we might otherwise expect based on the unconventional spellings of other words (see the preceding footnote).

78. See ibid., 209–21 for a review of the evidence and possible explanations.

79. Yuditsky, "Transcription into Greek and Latin Script," 3:807. Yuditsky (808) writes that "Short vowel elision is quite common in the Hexapla." See also Khan, "Shewa," 3:551.

80. According to Brønno (*Studien*, 322–41), in 184 out of 270 examples vocal *shewa* in the MT corresponds with the absence of a vowel in the Secunda. See also Alexey Yuditsky, "Reduced Vowels in the Transcriptions from Hebrew in the Hexapla" (Hebrew), *Leshonenu* 67 (2005): 121–41.

81. See Khan, "Shewa," 3:550–51. Khan (550) writes: "Both [*epsilon* and *iōta*] seem

Even the MT provides contradicting evidence. Where we usually find an elided vowel (e.g., שִׂמְחֵי "those rejoicing of [mind]" Isa 24:7) we sometimes find a full vowel (e.g., שְׂמֵחֵי "those rejoicing at [my calamity]" Ps 35:26). Alternatively, where we expect an elided vowel (e.g., קִלְלַת [< *qalalatu] "curse of [God" Deut 21:23) sometimes we find a muttered vowel (e.g., קִֽלֲלַת "curse of [Jotham]" Judg 9:57).[82]

Strangely, one of the latest pieces of evidence, the transcriptions and descriptions from Jerome, give no consistent evidence for muttered vowels or elided vowels.[83] In the version of Biblical Hebrew reflected in Jerome's transcriptions, short vowels are generally retained. This, at the least, would seem to reflect the fact that the reduction of vowels did not follow a clean, linear path from full vowel to zero. The variation in the place of stress and in vowel reduction may reflect not only different dialects or pronunciation traditions, but also different registers spoken by single individuals.

3.7. "Attenuation" and Similar Changes

A relatively common shift in vowel quality is that of */a/ to /i/ (in what is sometimes referred to as "attenuation").[84] Most often this takes place where historical */a/ is followed by two consonants in a row. The shift */a/ to */i/ occurred in the first syllable of *qåṭal piel* verbs and *qåṭal hiphil* verbs, as well as in some nouns:

---

to reflect a realization close to that of the Palestinian and Sephardic *shewa*"; he suggests that the *alpha* that marks a historical /a/ vowel where THT has a *shewa* may be an archaism. Brønno (*Studien*, 327) notes various other factors, including the absence of a vowel in the Secunda, even where we really need one in order to pronounce the form, implying that not all vowels were transcribed. On the other hand, Yuditsky believes that "short vowels have either preserved their original quality or been elided" ("Transcription into Greek and Latin Script," 3:807); cf. Yuditsky, "Reduced Vowels," 121–41, where he offers more thorough explanations for his thesis.

82. Furthermore, note the presence of a muttered vowel (derived from an earlier short vowel) in other traditions of Biblical Hebrew, like that presumed for (Proto-) Samaritan: **mal'ak* > **måla'ak* > **måla'ak* > מלאך [*må'lå'k*] "angel" (cf. THT מַלְאָךְ). See Florentin, "Samaritan Tradition," 1:123.

83. Yuditsky, "Transcription into Greek and Latin Script," 3:807; Khan, "Shewa," 3:551; Harviainen, "Transcription into Latin Script," 3:823.

84. Aaron Koller ("Attenuation," *EHLL* 1:231–32) notes that this is not a true "law" since there are too many exceptions, but rather "the results of disparate processes."

- ****dab**bira* > ****dib**ber* (> דִּבֵּר in pause) "he spoke"
- ****haš**lika* > ****hiš**līk* (> הִשְׁלִיךְ) "he threw"
- **ʿ**aw**wiru* > **ʿ**iw**wēr* (> עִוֵּר) "blind."

Since this shift is attested widely in different traditions, it is assumed to be a relatively early phenomenon.[85] In all the cases above where an initial */a/ shifted to /i/, the second syllable of the word contained an etymological */i/ vowel. This shift may be due to the initial */a/ assimilating in pronunciation to the following */i/. In addition, perhaps this development was encouraged by the fact that it helped to disambiguate otherwise similar forms in the *piel* and *hiphil*, like the infinitive construct (and in the case of the *piel*, the ms impv. and inf. abs.).

Another early shift of */a/ to /i/ occurs in the prefix of *qal* short-*yiqṭol*, *wayyiqṭol*, and *yiqṭol* forms. The early PNWS forms **yiqtal*, **yaqtul*, and **yaqtil* are characterized by vowels that are distinct between the prefix and stem.[86] At some point early in the history of Hebrew or of its ancestor, the vowel of the prefix in **yaqtul* and **yaqtil* forms shifted to /i/: **yiqtul* and **yiqtil*, perhaps on analogy to **yiqtal*.[87] Weak roots still sometimes evidence this /a/ vowel, as with **yaqum* > **yāqom* > יָקֹם "let him arise" and **yaqūmu* > **yāqūm* > יָקוּם "he will arise."[88]

Sometimes similar developments of */a/ > /i/ are associated primarily with THT, and appear to have occurred relatively late in time, emerging perhaps in the mid-first millennium CE. For example, the shift of */a/ > /i/ in the prefix component to *mem*-preformative nouns (e.g., ****mad**baru* > ****mad**bār* > ***mid**bår* [= מִדְבָּר] "desert") seems at least superficially simi-

---

85. The same shift in vowel (/a/ > /i/) is found in the same contexts (*piel*, *hiphil* verbs, etc.) in other pronunciation traditions (e.g., Babylonian and Palestinian), as well as in the Secunda, where it is represented by *epsilon*; note the *piel* ελλελθ [cf. חִלַּלְתָּ] "you profaned" (Ps 89:40); the *hiphil*: εσθερθα [cf. הִסְתַּרְתָּ] "you hid" (Ps 30:8) (the examples are from Yuditsky, "Hebrew and Greek in Latin Transcriptions," 1:111). It is even implied in the orthography of the DSS (e.g., היראתי "I showed" in 4Q158 4, 6, if this is not a case of metathesis for הראיתי*). See Reymond, *Qumran Hebrew*, 39–40.

86. This is the Barth-Ginsberg Law; see Rebecca Hasselbach, "Barth-Ginsberg Law," *EHLL* 1:258–59.

87. See also, e.g., Blau, *Phonology and Morphology*, 221. The identical shift happened in *wayyiqṭol* and *yiqṭol* forms.

88. Note also I-guttural roots like עשׂה that attest /a/ in the prefix: יַעַשׂ "let him do."

lar to the shift */a/ to */i/ in the prefix of *qal* short-*yiqṭol*, *wayyiqṭol*, and *yiqṭol* forms just described. However, it shows a quite different distribution among the different traditions. The shift */a/ > /i/ in the initial syllable of *mem*-preformative nouns appears to be primarily a feature of THT.[89] In earlier varieties of Hebrew and in pronunciation traditions contemporaneous with THT (like BHT), the /a/ vowel in these words was preserved (e.g., **malḥamatu* > **malḥāmā* > **milḥåmå* [= מִלְחָמָה] vs. μαλαμα "war" in Secunda at Ps 18:35).[90] This historical */a/ vowel is still reflected in THT, however, in a variety of *mem*-preformative nouns like מַמְלָכָה "kingdom" and מָקוֹם "place."

Another rather late development is the shift of */a/ to /i/ in cases where the original */a/ was followed in the next syllable by an */a/ that elides (e.g., **dabaray* > **dabrē* [> *dibre* = דִּבְרֵי] "words of" passim; **barakat* > **barkat* [> *birkat* = בִּרְכַּת] "blessing of").[91] The evidence is limited from the Secunda, but may reflect the preservation of /a/ in this context (i.e., δαβρη "words of" Ps 35:20; cf. דִּבְרֵי).[92]

Similarly, the shift of */a/ to /ɛ/ (as in **malku* > **malk* > *mɛlk* [= מֶ֫לֶךְ] "king") is peculiar to THT.[93] In BHT and the Secunda, the vowel of these segolate nouns is usually /a/ (e.g., **gabr* > γαβρ corresponding to גֶּ֫בֶר "man"

89. See, e.g., McCarter, "Hebrew," 329. He refers to the phenomenon as "*qatqat* → *qitqat* dissimilation."

90. Brønno, *Studien*, 173. Note also *madbår* in the Samaritan Tradition (SP Exod 14:11; cf. THT מִדְבָּר); *madbår* in the Old Babylonian Tradition (Deut 9:28; cf. THT מִדְבָּר). For the examples, see Florentin, "Samaritan Tradition," 2:73; Heijmans, "Babylonian Tradition," *HBH* 2:91.

91. The reason words like **malkēkɛm* (> מַלְכֵיכֶם) "your kings" preserve the /a/ vowel is due presumably to the influence of forms like מַלְכִּי "my king."

92. See Brønno, *Studien*, 151. The feminine attests *epsilon*: βσεδκαθαχ corresponding to בְּצִדְקָתְךָ "in your righteousness" (Ps 31:2; ibid.), though this is likely a reflex of the preceding sibilant (see Yuditsky, "Transcription into Greek and Latin," 3:810) or (perhaps) the nonsonorous second root consonant (Huehnergard, "Biblical Hebrew Nominal Patterns," 39).

93. See Huehnergard, "Biblical Hebrew Nominal Patterns," 38–39; Lambdin, "Philippi's Law Reconsidered," 135–45. One assumes the same development for the second syllable of the byform of feminine *mem*-preformative nouns (used often as the construct form): **mamlaktu* > **mamlɛkt* (> מַמְלֶ֫כֶת) "dominion of." By contrast, Joüon (§ 29e) suggests the development of the /ɛ/ of the stem in מֶ֫לֶךְ is due to assimilation to the epenthetic vowel: **malku* > **malɛk* > **mɛlɛk*. See also W. Randall Garr, "The *Seghol* and Segholation in Hebrew," *JNES* 48 (1989): 109–16.

Ps 89:49).[94] A similar shift of */a/ to THT /ɛ/ is implied in a wide variety of other places. Note too the same shift in *hiphil* short-*yiqṭol* and *wayyiqṭol* forms from III-*vav*/*yod* roots: **tarb* > *tɛrb* = תֶּ֫רֶב "may you multiply" (Ps 71:21) [*hiphil* רבה] and **wayyarb* > *wayyɛrb* = וַיֶּ֫רֶב "he multiplied" (2 Sam 18:8) [*hiphil* רבה]. A related phonetic shift may also be reflected in energic verb forms: **yašmuranhū* > **yišmərannū* > *yišmrɛnnu* = יִשְׁמְרֶ֫נּוּ "he will guard him" (Exod 21:29).[95]

The shift of a historical */a/ to /ɛ/ in THT also occurs in some cases where we presume a historical doubling of a guttural (*aleph*, *he*, *khet*, *ayin*) followed by THT /å/. Since it is difficult to determine the presence of this shift in the Hebrew before the time of the Masoretes, it is unclear if this phenomenon was present in earlier varieties of Hebrew. Most commonly, this dissimilation is found in two environments: in the definite article before words that begin with a guttural (*he*, *khet*, *ayin*) + /å/, and with medial-guttural words of the **qattal*(*at*) base.[96] The most commonly occurring words associated with this phenomenon are (**hahharrīma* >) הֶהָרִים "the mountains" and (**haʿʿarrīma* >) הֶעָרִים "the cities." Note, also, other words like הֶהָמוֹן "the tumult," הֶהָרוּס "the (altar) that had been destroyed," הֶחָג "the festival," הֶחָצֵר "the court," הֶעָנָן "the cloud," הֶעָרֵל "the uncircumcised." Where the *he* or the *ayin* begins a tonic syllable, however, this shift does not take place (e.g., **hahharru* > **hāhār* [> הָהָר]; **haʿʿammu* > **hāʿām* [> הָעָם]). Nouns of the **qattal*(*at*) base exhibit simi-

94. Brønno, *Studien*, 173. Note also *napaš* (in the Old Babylonian Tradition at Deut 10:22 corresponding to נֶ֫פֶשׁ), as presented in Heijmans, "Babylonian Tradition," 2:92. It is also conceivable that in **qatl* nouns that have a relatively nonsonorous second root consonant (i.e., not /l/, /n/, /m/, /r/), the historical */a/ vowel shifted to */i/ in forms with suffix, as with **ṣadqī* > **ṣidqī* (> צִדְקִי) "my righteousness" vs. the expected development in the absolute, **ṣadq* > **ṣedq* (> צֶ֫דֶק) (see Huehnergard, "Biblical Hebrew Nominal Patterns," 39). On the other hand, in the Secunda, the tendency is for sibilants to shift historical */a/-class vowels to /ɛ/, as in εσδ corresponding to חֶ֫סֶד (< **ḥasd*) "piety" (Ps 32:10) and in σεδκι corresponding to צִדְקִי "my righteousness" (Ps 35:27) (see Yuditsky, "Transcription into Greek and Latin," 3:810).

95. The evidence from the Secunda is slender but seems to presuppose a shift from */a/ to /ɛ/ in energic forms: αωδεννου corresponding to אֲהוֹדֶ֫נּוּ "I will praise you" (Ps 28:7); note also αιωδεχχα, which corresponds to הֲיוֹדְךָ "will he praise you" (Ps 30:10), though the transliteration seems to presuppose an energic form, *הֲיוֹדֶ֫ךָּ (see Brønno, *Studien*, 195–97).

96. Given the environments in which it occurs, it seems to have been a shift that affected words relatively late (at least after the lengthening of vowels in the tonic and pretonic syllables). See Steven Fassberg, "Dissimilation," *EHLL* 1:766–67.

lar transformations: *kaḥḥāš (> כַּחַשׁ) "lying," *bahhālā (> בֶּהָלָה) "horror," *lahhābā (> לֶהָבָה) "flame." Among nouns with suffixes, note the relatively frequent (*ʾaḫḫayhu >) *ʾaḥḥāw (> אֶחָיו) "his brothers."

In still other cases, it is hard to know the reason for the vowel shift. Note, for example, the shift presumed in the vowel between the stem and suffix in pausal forms, like *dabaraka > *dəbārakā (> dbårɛkå = דְּבָרֶךָ) "your word" (Gen 30:34).[97] Unlike the examples discussed above, in this case the historical */a/ is not followed by two consonants.

3.8. "Philippi's Law" and Similar Changes

In many other cases, historical short */i/ became /a/ (in essence, the reverse of attenuation). It will be obvious to students, at the intermediate level, that often the presence of a guttural or *resh* will affect the vowel that precedes or follows it. Often, */i/ shifts to /a/ (e.g., *diʿtu > daʿt [= דַּעַת] "knowledge" and *pāriḫtu > *pōraḫt [> פֹּרַחַת] "one sprouting"). Presumably this tendency for the gutturals to attract the /a/ vowel is a relatively early phenomenon.[98]

A relatively late shift consists of the historical short */i/ becoming /a/ in construct forms and in the stem of some verbal forms. As indicated above (in §4, "Lengthening and Lowering of Vowels in Tonic Syllables"), it is assumed that */i/ initially became */ɛ/ in these forms before then becoming /a/.

---

97. Cf. the contextual form דְּבָרְךָ (in 1 Sam 9:10). In the Secunda, one finds that the 2ms suffix on singular nouns in pause is usually marked with -*αχ*, as in *αμμαχ* corresponding to עַמֶּךָ "your people" (Ps 28:9); but it appears once as -*αχα*, in *ιεσαχα* corresponding to יִשְׁעֶךָ "your salvation" (Ps 18:36) (see Brønno, *Studien*, 288); -*αχ* is also the most common form of the suffix on contextual nouns (ibid., 341). Similarly, on plural nouns both pausal and contextual, the 2ms suffix is usually marked with -*αχ*, as in *φαναχ* corresponding to פָּנֶיךָ "your face" (Ps 30:8) (ibid., 199). By contrast, most cases of the 2ms suffixes on *yiqṭol* verbs, whether in pause or context, are -*εχ*, as in *ωδεχ* corresponding to אוֹדְךָ "I will praise you" (Ps 35:18) but also pausal אוֹדֶךָּ (Ps 30:13) (ibid., 195).

98. At the least, the /a/ vowel occurred near gutturals in the late Second Temple era, as suggested by various transcriptions, including from the Secunda. Note the theme vowel in *θεβαρ* corresponding to תִּבְעַר "it will burn" Ps 89:47 and the epenthetic vowel represented by *ουβααρ* corresponding to וָבַעַר "and idiot" Ps 49:11 (Brønno, *Studien*, 28, 139). In other cases, sometimes */i/ lowered to /ɛ/ (e.g., חֶלְקָם "their portion" Gen 14:24).

- *za**qi**nu- > *za**qin**- > *za**qɛn**- (> **zqan**- = זְקַן־) "elder of"
- *za**qin**ta > *zā**qɛn**tā (> zå**qan**tå = זָקַ֫נְתָּ) "you are old"
- *yā**lid**taha > *yō**lɛd**taha (> yo**lad**tåh = יֹלַ֫דְתָּהּ) "one who bore her"
- *dab**bir**ta > *dib**bɛr**tā (> dib**bar**tå = דִּבַּ֫רְתָּ) "you spoke"
- *hag**gid**ta > *hig**gɛd**tā (> hig**gad**tå = הִגַּ֫דְתָּ) "you told"
- *ti**lik**na > *tē**lɛk**nā (> te**lak**nå = תֵּלַ֫כְנָה) "they will go."[99]

This shift is often described as a development of */i/ > /a/ in stressed syllables and is labeled "Philippi's Law."[100] Notice in relation to the forms above that the historical */i/ is, in each case, followed by two consonants in the interior of a word (assuming that the construct form זְקַן־ would be pronounced with a following word).[101] The phenomenon, it should be noted, admits of many exceptions (e.g., *likna > *leknā [> לֵ֫כְנָה] "go!" and *libbu > *leb [> לֵב] "heart"). Although the shift */i/ > /a/ used to be considered an extremely early phenomenon, it is now usually thought to be relatively late (at least where it occurs in the above listed forms), appearing in different distributions in different reading traditions, but not in the Secunda.[102] In the Secunda, the historical */i/ is usually realized as *epsilon*, which likely

99. See Lambdin, "Philippi's Law Reconsidered," 142. The shift in words such as זָקֵן may be due to analogy with nouns of the **qatal* base (See Huehnergard, "Biblical Hebrew Nominal Patterns," 43 n. 41, who cites Thomas O. Lambdin pers. comm.). Also, *ʾab**bi**da > *ʾib**bid** > *ʾib**bɛd** (> אִבַּד) "he destroyed" (in context), due to dominance of /a/ in stative and passive verbs (?); see Joüon § 52c.

100. See John Huehnergard, "Philippi's Law," *EHLL* 3:70–71 and Steven E. Fassberg, "Two Biblical Hebrew Sound Laws in Light of Modern Spoken Semitic" in *Nicht nur mit Engelszungen: Beiträge zur semitischen Dialektologie, Festschrift für Werner Arnold zum 60. Geburtstag*, ed., Renaud Kuty, Ulrich Seeger, and Shabo Talay (Wiesbaden: Harrassowitz, 2013), 97–99. The mnemonic "Philippi-Philappi" is sometimes used to remember the rule. Note still other isolated examples like **bint* > **bitt* (> בַּת) "daughter"; **pitt* (> פַּת) "piece" vs. פִּתִּים "pieces."

101. The shift of */i/ to /ɛ/ in contextual forms but to /å/ in pausal forms is also found in fs ptcs. and in inf. const. of the I-*vav*/*yod* and I-*nun* roots. See above §4, "Lengthening and Lowering of Vowels in Tonic Syllables."

102. Lambdin, "Philippi's Law Reconsidered," 143. Khan ("*Ṣere*," 139–40) suggests that the Secunda is an outlier and that other traditions (like that presumed for the LXX) evidence this shift to /a/ earlier than the Secunda. Blau (*Phonology and Morphology*, 134) views it as occurring after pausal lengthening had ceased to operate. The orthography of the DSS only makes explicit an /i/ vowel in these forms, though these forms can perhaps be attributed to Aramaic influence: והוליכתי "I will lead" (1QIsa[a] at Isa 42:16) vs. וְהוֹלַכְתִּי.

reflects a Hebrew /i/, /e/, or /ɛ/.[103] Note the *piel* ελλελθ (cf. חִלַּ֫לְתָּ) "you profaned" (Ps 89:40); the *hiphil*: εσθερθα (cf. הִסְתַּ֫רְתָּ) "you hid" (Ps 30:8).[104]

3.9. Canaanite Shift and Historical */ā/

The term "Canaanite shift" refers to the shift of */ā/ to */ō/.[105] This shift is attested in the indigenous language used by some Canaanite correspondents in the Amarna letters, letters written on behalf of various city rulers (like the ruler of Jerusalem) to the Egyptian pharaoh Akhnaten (ca. 1350s–1330s BCE). The letters are written in Sumero-Akkadian cuneiform in the Akkadian language (an East Semitic language, where the historical /ā/ was preserved). Nevertheless, sometimes the scribes would include words from their own Northwest Semitic dialect, where */ā/ had shifted to /ō/. Thus, in the cuneiform Akkadian script, *a-nu-ki* is written for what was presumably pronounced as *ʾanōki* "I," a pronoun that derives from an earlier form **ʾanāku*.[106] Similarly, *a-bu-ti-nu* was pronounced something like *ʾabōtinu* "our fathers" (from an earlier **ʾabātinu*) and *sú-ki-ni* like *sōkini* "steward" (from an earlier **sākinu*).[107] Eventually, this vowel would be represented with *holem* by the Masoretes: אֲבֹתֵ֫ינוּ ,אָנֹכִי, and סֹכֵן.

---

103. Writing in relation to verb forms such as יִתֵּן, Khan ("*Ṣere*," 139) notes that, although Tiberian *patakh* sometimes corresponds to *epsilon* in the Secunda, this is never the case with verbal forms like יִתֵּן; he writes: "Since *alpha* is never used in the final syllable of the verbal forms in question, it is likely that the *epsilon* here was intended to represented [sic] a closer vowel." In the case of verbal forms like those above, the Secunda represents the last stem vowel with *epsilon* in all but one case (out of twelve examples): μαγαρθα (cf. מִגַּ֫רְתָּה) "you threw" Ps 89:45, which form seems like a *qal* (see Brønno, *Studien*, 64–68, 88). Not counted are the two *hithpael* forms (ibid., 107), which attest /a/-vowels perhaps reflecting the tendency for /a/-class vowels in this conjugation.

104. Cf. the *hiphil* 3ms: εριμ "he thundered," Ps 29:3, corresponding to הִרְעִים. For the examples, see Yuditsky, "Hebrew and Greek in Latin Transcriptions," 1:111.

105. Blau (*Phonology and Morphology*, 48) argues that this only took place in accented syllables. However, Fassberg ("Two Biblical Hebrew Sound Laws," 95–97) has recently argued that it is more likely that all */ā/ vowels shifted to */ō/.

106. Sumero-Akkadian cuneiform has no independent symbols to mark the /o/ vowel and so scribes used the symbols for /u/.

107. For more examples, see Sivan, *Grammatical Analysis*, 29–34. Serpent incantations from the Pyramid Texts may suggest that the Canaanite Shift took place by at least the third millennium BCE (see Richard C. Steiner, *Early Northwest Semitic Serpent Spells in the Pyramid Texts*, HSS 61 [Winona Lake, IN: Eisenbrauns, 2011], 46).

Most commonly, the */ō/ (< */ā/) appears in the first syllable of the *qal* active participle: **šāmiru* > **šōmēr* (> שֹׁמֵר), and in the ending of feminine plural nouns/adjectives: **barakātu* > **bərākōt* (> בְּרָכוֹת). Note also the base **qatāl*, on which are formed nouns like **lāšōn* (> לָשׁוֹן) "tongue" and *ʾ*ādōn* (> אָדוֹן) "lord," as well as the *qal* infinitive absolute (e.g., **šāmōr* [> שָׁמוֹר]).[108] As with other vowels that derive from historical long vowels, the */ā/ that became */ō/ never reduced to *shewa* or further altered in quality in BH (e.g., יֹדְעֵי "knowers of" Isa 51:7). This is in contrast to the short /u/ that sometimes was realized as /o/, as in **ḥuqqu* > **ḥoqq* > **ḥoq* (> חֹק) "statute" but that remains /u/ in other forms such as the plural, **ḥuqqīma* > **ḥuqqīm* (> חֻקִּים).[109] Recognizing the most common bases and forms that include the */ō/ (< */ā/) vowel can help in the comprehension and reproduction of verbal and nominal forms.

It should be noted that in some exceptional words and forms a PS */ā/ is not realized as */ō/, but seems to remain */ā/ and in THT is realized as /å/ (i.e., *qamets*). In these cases, the reason may be influence from Aramaic or an Aramaic-like dialect. In ancient Aramaic, historical */ā/ remained */ā/. Influence from Aramaic gradually became stronger and stronger over the course of the first millennium BCE. All the same, some words probably migrated from Aramaic (or another similar dialect) in earlier periods.

Note the following examples, where the */ā/ derives from a historical long */ā/:

- **yiqāru* > **yəqār* (> יְקָר) "honor"
- **kitābu* > **kətāb* (> כְּתָב) "book"
- **maṣādu* > **məṣād* (> מְצָד) "mountain refuge"
- **sVpāru* > **səpār* (> סְפָר) "calculation"
- **qarābu* > **qərāb* (> קְרָב) "war."[110]

In these cases, the Aramaic influence is seen not only in the retention of */ā/, but also in the pretonic reduction of the historical short vowels */i/ and */a/. Such reduction is characteristic of Aramaic but uncharacteristic

---

108. Other bases like **qattāl* are less common.

109. In the construct form with the *maqqef*, the short */u/ lowered further in quality to /å/ in THT, as reflected in חָק־; with suffixes the vowel sometimes appears as a short */u/: **ḥuqqī* (> חֻקִּי). Similarly with the word "all": **kol* (> כֹּל) and **kullō* (כֻּלּוֹ).

110. See Stadel, "Aramaic Influence on Biblical Hebrew," 1:162–65; and Hornkohl, *Ancient Hebrew Periodization*, 152–58.

of Hebrew, where pretonic */i/ and */a/ usually lengthen to */ē/ and */ā/ (as described above). Other examples of */ā/ possibly derived from Aramaic influence include those Hebrew words exhibiting Aramaic infinitival patterns, like those of the D-stem infinitive **qattālā* and the H-stem infinitive **haqtālā*:

- **bahhālā* (> בֶּהָלָה) "horror"
- **baqqārā* (> בַּקָּרָה*) "care"
- **baqqāšā* (> בַּקָּשָׁה*) "request"
- **nahhāmā* (> נֶחָמָה*) "comfort"
- **hakkārā* (> הַכָּרָה*) "recognition"
- **hănāḥā* (> הֲנָחָה) "resting"
- **hănāpā* (> הֲנָפָה) "waving"
- **haṣṣālā* (> הַצָּלָה) "deliverance."[111]

In all these cases, the */ā/ does not reduce in construct or in other positions with suffix:

- **kətāb* (> כְּתָב־) "writing of [the law]" (Esth 4:8)
- **baqqārat* (> בַּקָּרַת) "care of [the shepherd]" (Ezek 34:12)
- **baqqāšātēk* (> בַּקָּשָׁתֵךְ) "your request" (Esth 5:6).[112]

In addition, II-*vav*/*yod* roots also attest what at first glance appears to be a historical */ā/ which developed due to various triphthong contractions:

- **ġawabu* > **ġāb* > *ʿ*āb* (> עָב) "cloud"
- **rawamatu* > **rāmā* (> רָמָה) "high place"
- **qawamu* > **qām* (> קָם) "one who arises"
- **ṯawabu* > **šāb* (> שָׁב) "one who returns."[113]

111. Stadel, "Aramaic Influence on Biblical Hebrew," 1:162–65. Huehnergard ("Biblical Hebrew Nominal Patterns," 51) suggests these might derive instead from **qattalat*, based on Akkadian evidence.

112. Stadel, "Aramaic Influence on Biblical Hebrew," 1:162–65.

113. For the adjective רָמָה, see Fox, *Semitic Noun Patterns*, 162; for the participles, see ibid. Another example may be the plural of עִיר "city," *ʿ*ayarīm* > *ʿ*ārīm* > עָרִים (cf. עֲיָרִים "cities" in Judg 10:4), but note that Huehnergard and others have suggested an alternative explanation of suppletion, from another root, ערר (see Huehnergard, "Biblical Hebrew Nominal Patterns," 32 n. 22 with literature).

As in the cases of the apparent Aramaisms above, in these Hebrew words the */ā/ does not reduce:

- *ʿābē (> עָבֵי) "clouds of [the heaven]" (Ps 18:12)
- *rāmātēk (> רָמָתֵךְ) "your high place" (Ezek 16:31)
- *qāmēhɛm (> קָמֵיהֶם) "those rising against them" (Exod 32:25)
- *šābē (> שָׁבֵי) "those returning from [transgression]" (Isa 59:20).[114]

This */ā/ is analogous to the */ē/ that appears in words like *mēt (> מֵת) "dead one" (*mētē [> מֵתֵי] "dead ones of").[115] Huehnergard and others categorize these words as from the Proto-Hebrew base *qal and *qil respectively.[116] All things being equal, the */ā/ resulting from contractions should have become /ō/ in Hebrew through the Canaanite Shift, suggesting a sequence of changes like the following: *qawama > *qāma > *qama (time of Canaanite Shift) > *qām > קָם.[117]

In only very rare cases does a historical short */a/ not reduce in an open syllable. The most notable example is found in the *niphal yiqṭol* and related forms, like the imperative: *hiššamirū > *hiššāmərū (> הִשָּׁמְרוּ) "be attentive!" (Exod 19:12).

3.10. Loss of Final Short Vowels

Most words in the precursor to Hebrew in the second millennium BCE would have ended with a short vowel. Singular nouns and adjectives would have ended in case vowels consisting of a single short vowel (e.g., *malku "king" in the nominative case vs. *malka "king" in the accusative case).[118] Verbs, too, often ended in short vowels, as with the *yiqṭol* form *yašmuru

---

114. Note also the potential parallel *ʿārē (> עָרֵי) "cities of [the Levites]" Lev 25:32 (see the preceding footnote).

115. See Huehnergard, "Biblical Hebrew Nominal Patterns," 29 and his article "Features of Central Semitic," 176–78.

116. See Huehnergard, "Features of Central Semitic," 176–78; Huehnergard, "Biblical Hebrew Nominal Patterns," 29.

117. Further inconsistencies are found in other traditions; in Samaritan Hebrew, e.g., the PNWS */ā/ does not shift to /ō/ in various words where the shift does happen in THT: [ånåki] (cf. אָנֹכִי) "I"; [lå] (cf. לֹא) "no" (see Florentin, "Samaritan Tradition," 1:124).

118. See ch. 4 §4, "Inflection of Basic Masculine and Feminine Nouns," for an elaboration of the case system.

"he will guard" (vs. short-*yiqṭol* **yašmur*). At some point near the beginning of the first millennium, these short vowels were lost from the ends of words. This contributed to a number of further changes that are documented below, including the obsolescence of the case system (**malk* could function as a nominative or accusative), and the general loss of distinction between the regular *yiqṭol* and the short-*yiqṭol*.

3.11. Feminine Singular *-*at* > *-*ā*

In the second millennium BCE, the feminine morpheme on singular nouns was often -*at*. Thus, a typical word like "queen" **malkā* (> מַלְכָּה) would have had the form **malkat* followed by a case vowel (e.g., **malkatu*). By the first millennium BCE, case vowels were lost and the feminine morpheme *-*at* had shifted to *-*a* and later *-*ā*. In essence, the *taw* was lost and the preceding vowel was preserved as short and later lengthened.[119] Cognizance of this earlier form for feminine singular nouns is helpful since it explains the form of feminine nouns in construct and with suffixes. It is helpful to remember that words with endings are often closer to their historical, etymological forms.[120] Thus, one finds the construct form *malkat* (= מַלְכַּת) "queen of" and we would expect to find, based on analogous nouns with suffixes, **malkātō* (> מַלְכָּתוֹ*) "his queen" and **malkātakā* > **malkātəkā* (> מַלְכָּתְךָ*) "your queen."[121]

3.12. Triphthongs and Diphthongs

At a relatively early date, by at least the beginning of the first millennium BCE, certain sequences of vowels and semivowels (i.e., /w/ and /y/) had contracted.[122] We have just described the early resolution of triphthongs in II-*vav*/*yod* roots that are eventually realized in BH as */ā/ and then /å/.

---

119. See Geoffrey Khan, "Compensatory Lengthening," *EHLL* 1:501.

120. Words in construct are similar to words bearing suffixes since the construct word is essentially attached to the following word. The linking of words means that the second (nonconstruct) word essentially functions like a suffix to the first word.

121. Cf. אַהֲבָתוֹ "his love" and אַהֲבָתְךָ "your love."

122. The two sounds /w/ and /y/ are called semivowels because they share qualities of both vowels and consonants. Note the examples of resolved diphthongs and triphthongs assembled by Sivan, *Grammatical Analysis and Glossary*, 12–19 (from the second millennium BCE) and Millard, "Transcriptions into Cuneiform," 3:838–47 (from the first millennium BCE).

In general, triphthongs that ended with */a/ became */ā/ and then /å/ in THT; triphthongs that ended with a short */i/ or */u/ developed into */ɛ̄/, which then became /ɛ/ by the time of the Secunda. In the latter case, the exact sequence of changes is hard to trace.[123]

- **banaya* > **banā* > **bānā* (> בָּנָה) "he built" (passim)
- **yabniyu* > **yibnɛ̄* > *yibnɛ* (= יִבְנֶה) "he will build"
- **yagluwu* > **yagluyu* > **yiglɛ̄* > *yiglɛ* (= יִגְלֶה) "he will reveal"
- **maʿśayu* > **maʿsɛ̄* > *maʿsɛ* (= מַעֲשֶׂה) "deed."

Where a triphthong ended in a long vowel, that long vowel eclipsed the preceding vowel and semivowel and the long vowel is all that remains:

- **yagluwūna* > **yagluyūna* > **yigluyū* > **yiglū* (> יִגְלוּ) "they will reveal"
- **qašiyīma* > **qāšīm* (> קָשִׁים) "hard"
- **qašiyātu* > **qašiyōt* > **qāšōt* (> קָשׁוֹת) "hard."

For nouns, one assumes a contraction with a case vowel (e.g., see **maʿśayu* above).[124] That the contraction of triphthongs involved case vowels implies the early date of these contractions since the case vowels (and all final short vowels) dropped off words relatively early in the history of Hebrew (by around the first millennium BCE).[125]

---

123. The contraction of triphthongs should result in a long vowel (e.g., /ɛ̄/). This seems to be evidenced in cuneiform transcriptions of Hebrew names (from ca. 800s–600s BCE), as with *mi-na-si-i*, *me-na-se-e*, *me-na-si-i'*, *mi-in-se-e*, *mu-na-se-e*, and *me-na-se-e* (for מְנַשֶּׁה "Manasseh"), where the sequence of consonant-vowel + vowel signs implies a long, final vowel (see Millard, "Transcriptions into Cuneiform," 3:840–41). This is also suggested by the transcription of III-*vav*/*yod* words in the LXX with final *ēta* (representing /ɛ̄/); see Khan, "*Ṣere*," 136–37. Were these resolved triphthongs always pronounced /ɛ̄/? In any case, the Secunda represented the vowel in question with *epsilon* (e.g., *μασε* [cf. מַחֲסֶה] "refuge" Ps 46:2).

124. On case vowels, see below in chapter 4 §4, "Inflection of Basic Masculine and Feminine Nouns." See, e.g., Blau, *Phonology and Morphology*, 98.

125. Although some words, such as חַי "alive," צַו "command!" (the apocopated form of the *piel* imperative), and קַו "line," might seem at first to be exceptions, these actually attested geminated *vavs*/*yods* (e.g., **ḥayyu*) at the time when the language had case vowels. The gemination of the consonant preserved the historical vowels (see Blau, *Phonology and Morphology*, 99–100).

Diphthong contraction (i.e., */ay/ > */ē/ and */aw/ > */ō/) is seen in THT in the inflection of short words such as יַ֫יִן "wine," בַּ֫יִת "house," זַ֫יִת "olive," מָ֫וֶת "death," and also in verbs:

- ******yaynu* > ****yayn*** > **yēn* (> יֵין) "wine of"
- ****baytiyya*** > ****baytī*** > **bētī* (> בֵּיתִי) "my house"
- ****mawtu*** > ****mawt*** > ****mōt*** (> מוֹת) "death of"
- ****hawšiʿa*** > ****hōšīʿ*** (> הוֹשִׁיעַ) "he delivered" [*hiphil* ישׁע]
- ****hayṭiba*** > ****hēṭīb*** (> הֵיטִיב) "he treated well" [*hiphil* יטב].

One frequently sees contraction of diphthongs in the plural noun plus pronominal suffix (e.g., **dabar**ay**kumu* > **dabrēkεm* [> דִּבְרֵיכֶם] "your words"). Only exceptionally does the /ay/ diphthong appear to have contracted to short /e/: **dabar**ay**ka* > ****dəbārekā*** (> דְּבָרֶ֫יךָ) "your words" and **dabar**ay**ha* > **dəbārehā* (> דְּבָרֶ֫יהָ) "her words."[126]

For the southern version of Classical Hebrew of the first part of the first millennium BCE the diphthongs /ay/ and /aw/ would have been preserved, presumably even when unaccented. This is suggested by the spelling of certain words in texts dating to the 700s–580s BCE. For example, in Hebrew letters from Arad (ca. 600 BCE) and Lachish (586 BCE), the word "wine" is spelled with a medial *yod*, *yyn*, both in the absolute state and in the construct state, implying the preservation of a diphthong: **yayn*.[127] Since *matres* are not predictably found within words in inscriptions to indicate /ē/ at this time, it is easier to argue that the second *yod* of *yyn* is a true consonant, not a *mater* for a resolved diphthong.[128] The THT version of the word in the absolute, יַ֫יִן, is essentially the same, with an epenthetic vowel, /i/, inserted between the final two consonants (though in construct the diphthong resolves, as noted above). In addition, Neo-Assyrian cuneiform transcriptions sometimes reveal the presence of diphthongs, as in the

126. Is it perhaps a case of dissimilation (i.e., **dabarayaha* > **dabarāhā* > *dbårεhå* [= דְּבָרֶ֫הָ]), akin to the dissimilation in הֶהָרִים (see §7 above, "'Attenuation' and Similar Changes")?

127. On the dates, see Shmuel Aḥituv, *Echoes from the Past: Hebrew and Cognate Inscriptions from the Biblical Period*, trans. Anson Rainey, Carta Handbook (Jerusalem: Carta, 2008), 59, 92. The word *yyn* is found in Lachish letter 25 and Arad 1, 2, 3, 4, 8, 10, 11. See also F. W. Dobbs-Allsopp et al., eds., *Hebrew Inscriptions: Texts from the Biblical Period of the Monarchy with Concordance* (New Haven: Yale University Press, 2005).

128. For the evidence, see Gogel, *Grammar of Epigraphic Hebrew*, 66–67.

transliteration of "Hosea" (THT הוֹשֵׁעַ) *a-ú-se-ʾ* (reflecting something like **hawšeʿ*).[129] In later times (probably by the middle of the first millennium BCE), these diphthongs were preserved only in stressed position. Thus, "wine" was **yayn* in the absolute, but **yēn* in construct or with pronominal suffixes.

In the north, however, it seems that these diphthongs had contracted early on, even in the accented syllable of the absolute noun. The same word "wine" is found in inscriptions from the north (in Samaria), dating approximately to 780–740 BCE; in these texts the diphthong did resolve as implied by the spelling with just one *yod*: *yn* (**yēn*) "wine."[130] A reduction of diphthongs is also found in dialects and languages of NWS even further north, as in Phoenician and Ugaritic. This small disparity between the northern and southern dialects of Hebrew is not preserved in the MT, but it is useful to know that within the time that the biblical texts were being written distinct dialects coexisted. Moreover, the resolution of accented diphthongs appears to have survived into Samaritan Hebrew, where, for example, "water" appears as [mem] (cf. THT מַ֫יִם).[131]

129. See Millard, "Transcriptions into Cuneiform," 3:840. Note that the same name is also spelled without a diphthong as *ú-se-ʾ*. In addition, the name of a Samarian, אֲחִיָּהוּ, is spelled *aḫi-i-ú*, presuming a pronunciation something like *ʾaḫḫiyyō*, where the *he* of the earlier *-yahū* has elided and the resulting diphthong has resolved (see ibid., 3:841).

130. On the date, see Aḥituv, *Echoes from the Past*, 259; and Dobbs-Allsopp et al., *Hebrew Inscriptions*, 423. The word *yn* is found in Samaria Ostraca 5, 12, 13, 14, 53, 54. See Garr, *Dialect Geography*, 38–39. Na'ama Pat-El ("Israelian Hebrew: A Re-Evaluation," *VT* 67 (2017: 227–63) emphasizes that there is counterevidence for this dialectal trait (i.e., the preservation of the diphthong /ay/ seems to be evidenced in the orthography of *byt* "house of" in two inscriptions from the north [from Beth Shean, Bshn 1:2, and Tell Qasil, Qas 2:1]; and the apparent resolution of the diphthong in the orthography of *qṣ* (< **qyṣ*) "summer" in a southern text [Gezer Calendar, Gez 7]). As Pat-El herself observes, however, the spellings with the diphthong in the north (with *byt*) are part of names and thus "less convincing" (ibid., 244 n. 49). See Garr (*Dialect Geography*, 38–39) for possible explanations of *byt* and for another anomaly from the south. Despite the inconsistencies with other words, the spelling of the word "wine" appears to reflect this distinction between the north and south regularly.

131. See Florentin, "Samaritan Tradition," 1:123. Note, too, that *ay > *ī in certain environments; see Richard C. Steiner, "On the Monophthongization of *ay to ī in Phoenician and Northern Hebrew and the Preservation of Arachaic / Dialectal Forms in the Masoretic Vocalization," *Orientalia* 76 (2007): 73–83.

3.13. Compensatory Lengthening

Compensatory lengthening refers to the lengthening (and sometimes lowering) of a vowel due to the loss of a following consonant. This is found not only in later varieties of Hebrew, but is already presupposed in the Canaanite pronunciation reflected in certain spellings of words in the Amarna correspondence, mentioned above (ca. 1350–1330 BCE). For example, the word "head," based on comparative evidence, would have been **raʾšu* in an early stage of the language. The word is found spelled with the first-person common plural pronominal suffix in the Amarna letters: *ru-šu-nu* "our head," reflecting the pronunciation *rōšu* for the word without suffix.[132] This presumes the development of **raʾšu* > **rāšu* (compensatory lengthening) > **rōš* (Canaanite shift) (> רֹאשׁ).[133]

Compensatory lengthening continued to operate in specific environments at specific times. Generally, compensatory lengthening is associated with guttural consonants (as well as *resh*), where these consonants should be pronounced at the end of a syllable. Compensatory lengthening was especially common before geminated gutturals, where the first of the two gutturals was lost and the preceding vowel lengthened. In essence, the difficulty of extending the articulation of a guttural consonant after a short vowel led to the shortening of the consonant and the lengthening of the vowel. Stated in another way, the loss of one component of a word (a consonant) led to its replacement with another component (the length of the vowel) such that the word retained its basic syllable structure and rhythm. Blau suggests that this took place in the syllable that bore the stress.[134]

The phenomenon seems, at first blush, to appear only randomly in the language and this can cause confusion for the student. Why, one may ask, does compensatory lengthening appear in (**birrika* >) **bērek* (> בֵּרֵךְ) "he blessed" and (**yubarriku* >) **yəbārek* (> יְבָרֵךְ) "he will bless" but not in (**biʿʿira* >) **biʿʿer* (> בִּעֵר) "he kindled" and (**yubaʿʿiru* >) **yəbaʿʿer* (> יְבַעֵר) "he will kindle"? Or, why does the etymological short */i/ of the *niphal yiqṭol* prefix become lengthened, as reflected in (**yiḥḥašibu* >)

132. See Sivan, *Grammatical Analysis*, 29–30. The final /u/ vowel is the nominative case vowel.

133. A similar development pertains to the word *ṣú-ú-nu*, pronounced *ṣōnu* "small herd animal" and eventually written צֹאן. See also Fox, *Semitic Noun Patterns*, 78. See more on this word in ch. 4 §18, "Segolate Nouns."

134. Blau, *Phonology and Morphology*, 87.

*yēḥāšeb (> יֵחָשֵׁב) "it will be considered," but the same vowel remain short in the *piel qåṭal* (*šaḥḥita >) *šiḥḥet (> שִׁחֵת) "he destroyed"?[135]

At least some of these inconsistencies can be explained by noting the place of articulation of the three short vowels and by postulating a specific sequence of developments related to the pronunciation of gutturals (+ *resh*). The short */i/, being a front vowel, is furthest in its place of articulation from the gutturals. It lengthens/lowers least often. On the other hand, short */u/, being a back vowel, is closest in its place of articulation to the gutturals; it lengthens/lowers most often. As for the gutturals themselves, they seem to have ceased gemination at different times.

At the earliest stages, the *aleph* and *resh* ceased being geminated (and, in the case of *aleph*, ceased being pronounced within a word in certain environments [e.g., **raʾšu*]) and this led to compensatory lengthening before *aleph* and *resh*.[136] As a consequence, compensatory lengthening is most common before these letters, resulting in the development of long-vowel versions of each of the short vowels:

- */i/ > */ē/ as in (**birrika* >) **bērek* (> בֵּרֵךְ) "he blessed";
- */a/ > */ā/ as in (**yubarriku* >) **yəbārek* (> יְבָרֵךְ) "he will bless";
- */u/ > */ō/ as in (**yuburraku* >) **yəbōrak* (> יְבֹרַךְ) "he will be blessed."[137]

At a later time, *ayin* ceased being pronounced as a geminated consonant.[138] Due to the relative lateness of this cessation and/or due to the inherent qualities of this consonant, compensatory lengthening appears only sporadically with *ayin* and only in association with certain vowels. The vowel */i/ often did not develop into */ē/ (e.g., the initial vowel in **biʿʿira* > **biʿʿer* [> *biʿer* = בִּעֵר] "he kindled"). Short */a/ only sometimes developed into */ā/, as evidenced by contrasting the *piel yiqṭol* form **yubaʿʿiru* > **yəbaʿʿer* (> **ybaʿer* = יְבַעֵר) "he will kindle" with the *piel* infinitive construct (= inf.

135. For more examples, see Sperber, *Historical Grammar*, 434.

136. On compensatory lengthening and its development, see Blau (*Phonology and Morphology*, 83) and Khan ("Compensatory Lengthening," 1:501).

137. Similarly with *aleph*, note **bēʾer* (> בֵּאֵר) "he explained"; **bāʾer* (> בָּאֵר) "explain!" Still, there are cases where compensatory lengthening did not take place: **baʾʾer* (> בַּאֵר) "clearly." Often the *piel* of נאץ "to spurn" does not evidence compensatory lengthening.

138. I assume that this is after /ʿ/ and /ġ/ had merged.

abs.) of the same verb **ba*ʿʿ*ira* > **bāʿēr* (> בָּעֵר) "to kindle."[139] However, one regularly finds compensatory lengthening of historical */a/ before *ayin* in the definite article (e.g., **haʿʿīru* > **hāʿīr* [> הָעִיר] "the city" and **haʿʿabdu* > **hāʿabd* [> הָעֶבֶד] "the servant"). In contrast to /i/ and /a/, the vowel */u/ regularly develops into */ō/, as with pausal (**mubuʿʿirtu* >) **məbōʿārt* (> מְבֹעָרֶת) "was kindled."

At the same time or a little later, *he* ceased being geminated. Neither */i/ nor */a/ regularly lengthen before this guttural (e.g., [**mihhara* >] **mihhar* [> **mihar* = מִהַר] "he hastened"; [**muʾahhibu* >] **məʾahhēb* [> **mʾaheb* = מְאַהֵב*] "lover"; [**hahhōliku* >] **hahhōlēk* [> **haholek* = הַהֹלֵךְ] "the one going").[140] Only short */u/ regularly lengthens to */ō/, as with (**mubuhhalīma* >) **məbōhālīm* (> מְבֹהָלִים) "making haste."

Finally, *khet* ceased being geminated.[141] Compensatory lengthening is relatively rare with this consonant (**yaḥḥilnū* > **yiḥḥalnū* [> *yiḥalnu* = יִחַלְנוּ] "we hoped"; *ʾ*uyaḥḥilu* > *ʾ*ăyaḥḥel* [>ʾ*yaḥel* = אֲיַחֵל] "I will hope" and **haḥḥušku* > **haḥḥošk* [> *haḥošk* = הַחֹשֶׁךְ] "the dark"; pausal **nuḥḥāmā* [> *nuḥåmå* = נֻחָמָה] "was not comforted"). This reflects the fact that it ceased gemination only at a very late date.[142] The label "virtual doubling" is used to describe the apparent gemination of *ayin*, *he* and *khet* in some of the above THT forms, where compensatory lengthening is not in evidence. Although it is "virtual" for THT, and thus the letters are not marked with a *daghesh* by the medieval scribes, the gutturals *ayin*, *he*, and *khet* were likely really geminated in the last centuries of the first millennium BCE, and *khet* likely into the Common Era.

Nevertheless, a consistent place where one does see compensatory lengthening, even with *ayin* (perhaps also /ġ/), *he*, and *khet*, is with pre-

---

139. Not all verbs with middle *ayin* attest this clear distinction in the paradigm between finite and infinitive forms. The point is that sometimes you find compensatory lengthening, though usually you do not. Note, e.g., that the verb תעב "to abhor" occurs in the *piel* twelve times in *yiqṭol*, participial, and infinitival forms and attests compensatory lengthening of */a/ to */ā/ only four times (once in a ptc., once in a *yiqṭol* form, and twice in a *wayyiqṭol* form); it does not attest the lowering/lengthening of */i/ to */ē/ in the three attested *qåṭal* forms.

140. The singular absolute form of the second to last word is based on the numerous attestations of the plural with suffix, e.g., מְאַהֲבַי.

141. I assume that this is after /ḥ/ and /ḫ/ had merged.

142. Note that the Secunda may reflect the gemination of *khet* by way of lack of compensatory lengthening in σεωθι corresponding to שַׁחוֹתִי "I bowed down" (Ps 35:14) (see Yuditsky, "Transcription into Greek and Latin," 3:806).

fixes containing the sequence *-in-*, either those associated with the *niphal yiqṭol* or the *min* preposition. Thus, one sees the historical */i/ vowel of the *niphal yiqṭol* prefix regularly realized as *tsere* (implying an earlier */ē/) in verbs beginning with not only *aleph* and *resh*, but also with *ayin*, *he*, and *khet*:

- **yēʾākel* (> יֵאָכֵל) "it will be eaten"
- **tērāʾɛ* (> תֵּרָאֶה) "it will appear"
- **yēʿāsɛ* (> יֵעָשֶׂה) "it will be done"
- **yēhāpek* (> יֵהָפֵךְ) "it will be turned"
- **yēḥāšeb* (> יֵחָשֵׁב) "it will be considered."[143]

Note also the relatively consistent presence of */ē/ with the *min* preposition:

- **mēʾīš* (> מֵאִישׁ) "from a man"
- **mērāḥōq* (> מֵרָחֹק) "from a distance"
- **mēġarb* (> מֵעֶ֫רֶב) "from evening"
- **mēhayyōm* (> מֵהַיּוֹם) "from the day"
- **mēḥālāb* (> מֵחָלָב) "than milk."[144]

Note the set of geminate nouns/pronouns that begin with *he* and exhibit compensatory lengthening in the singular with the definite article:

- (**harru*/**hahharru*) > **har*/**hāhār* (> הָהָר/הַר) "(the) mountain"
- (**himm*/**hahhimm*) > **hēm*/**hāhēm* (> הָהֵם/הֵם) "they"
- (**himma*/**hahhimma*) > **hēmā*/**hāhēmmā* (> הָהֵ֫מָּה/הֵ֫מָּה) "they"
- (**hinna*/**hahhinna*) > **hēnā*/**hāhēnnā* (> הָהֵ֫נָּה/הֵ֫נָּה) "they."[145]

All the examples above derive from environments where the guttural (or *resh*) was initially doubled. Compensatory lengthening also took place where the guttural came at the end of an accented syllable, but where it was not doubled. For example, in the verbal form **maṣaʾta* > **maṣāta* > **māṣātā* (> מָצָאתָ) "you found," the second syllable experiences com-

---

143. Curiously, this does not occur with the *qåṭal* of נחם, which appears as נִחַם (< **niḥḥam* < **ninḥam*) "he was comforted."

144. Note, however, the consistent presence of *hireq* in מִחוּץ "from the outside."

145. Similarly, note the independent pronoun "they" with definite article הָהֵם, but cf. הַהִיא, הַהוּא (Joüon, § 35d).

pensatory lengthening when the *aleph* dropped from pronunciation. It is retained in writing presumably because it is retained in pronunciation in other parts of the paradigm, like **maṣa'ū* > **māṣa'ū* > **māṣə'ū* (> מָצְאוּ) "they found."

Vowels lengthened to compensate for the absence of a geminated guttural (or *resh*) do not reduce, even in a propretonic syllable. This helps explain the difference between such forms as **pārātō* (> פָּרָתוֹ) "his cow" (Job 21:10) and **šənātō* (> שְׁנָתוֹ) "his year" (Num 6:12). If one just knew the singular absolute form of both nouns (**pārā* [> פָּרָה] and **šānā* [> שָׁנָה]), one might believe that they derive from the same base and that they should inflect in a similar manner. However, **pārā* (> פָּרָה) is really a geminate noun (from an earlier **parratu*) while **šānā* (> שָׁנָה) is not (it is from an earlier **šanatu*). A vowel compensatorily lengthened at the end of a word will even be retained in construct: (**mawṣa'* >) **mōṣā ham-mayim* (> מוֹצָא הַמַּיִם) "the spring of water" (2 Kgs 2:21); and (**kussi'* >) **kissē bēt yisrā'ēl* (> כִּסֵּא בֵית־יִשְׂרָאֵל) "the throne of the house of Israel" (Jer 33:17).[146]

Given the precedent of **ra'šu* > **rāšu* > **rōš* (> רֹאשׁ) "head" where the lengthened */ā/ shifts to */ō/ as part of the Canaanite Shift, one may also wonder: Why did the forms **maṣāta* and **mōṣā* not shift to **māṣōtā* and **mōṣō* through the Canaanite Shift? One explanation is that the syllable *-ṣa'*(-) was not accented and so did not experience compensatory lengthening when the Canaanite Shift was taking place. Only at a later time did the accent move to the syllable *-ṣa'-* and result in the shift to *-ṣā-*. Notice also that the initial syllable in the word **ma'kalu* > **ma'kāl* (> מַאֲכָל) "food" does not experience compensatory lengthening at all. Again, presumably this reflects the fact that the initial syllable was never accented.

In the Secunda, vowels are compensatorily lengthened in the manner reflected in THT.[147] In the DSS, the frequency of spelling mistakes involving gutturals parallels the frequency with which gutturals ceased being geminated. That is, words with *aleph* and *resh* are relatively often misspelled (often where the relevant letter is left out); words with *ayin* are misspelled slightly less often; and words with a *khet* are only very rarely misspelled.[148]

---

146. In contrast to, e.g., מוֹשַׁב בְּנֵי יִשְׂרָאֵל "the dwelling of the children of Israel (Exod 12:40); עִקֶּשׁ־לֵב "crooked of mind" (Prov 17:20).

147. Khan, "Compensatory Lengthening," 1:502–503.

148. Reymond, *Qumran Hebrew*, 71–114.

3.14. Epenthesis

At a relatively late date (in the last centuries of the first millennium BCE into the first centuries CE), vowels were sometimes added between consonants at the end of words to help break up clusters of consonants.[149] In most cases no vowel had previously existed where the epenthetic vowel appeared. The end result in the following forms is usually a sequence of two short vowels in the MT only the first of which was present in earlier varieties of Hebrew: (1) singular segolate nouns (e.g. מֶ֫לֶךְ "king" and בַּ֫עַל "master"); (2) *qal* infinitives construct from I-*vav*/*yod* and I-*nun* roots (e.g., שֶׁ֫בֶת "dwelling"); (3) feminine singular participles (e.g., נֹפֶ֫לֶת "one falling" and בֹּ֫רַחַת "one fleeing"); and (4) the short-*yiqṭol* form of III-*vav*/*yod* roots (e.g., יִ֫בֶן "let him build").

Another example of epenthesis is the furtive *patakh* that appears between a high or midvowel (/i/, /e/, /o/, /u/) and a following guttural (e.g., כֹּחַ "strength"). Epenthetic vowels also sometimes occur after gutturals in some verbs (e.g., the /ă/ of יַעֲמֹד "he will stand" and the second /a/ of יַעַמְדוּ "they will stand"). Even the vocal *shewa* functions as an epenthetic consonant, as in the case of יִשְׁמְרוּ "they will guard," where the *shewa* breaks up the cluster of *mem* followed by *resh*. In none of these cases, however, did the Masoretes consider the epenthetic vowel as constituting its own syllable.[150]

In separate traditions, the epenthetic vowel comes before the cluster of consonants, not between them, as reflected, for example, in the Secunda (e.g., *[*wə*]*yisimḥū* > ιεσεμου and ουειεσαμου "(and) they will rejoice" Ps 35:24, 27; cf. [וְיִשְׂמְחוּ]) and in BHT (e.g., *tiqirbu* "you will approach" Lev 18:6).[151] Even the name of Jeremiah in the LXX reflects this tendency: ιερεμιας < **yirimyāhū* (cf. יִרְמְיָהוּ where the second *shewa* constitutes the epenthetic vowel).[152]

149. See Geoffrey Khan, "Epenthesis: Biblical Hebrew," *EHLL* 1:831–33. Epenthetic vowels are attested in some LXX transliterations (e.g., γομορ corresponding to עֹמֶר "omer measure" [Exod 16:16]) as well as in some DSS forms (e.g., פועול "work of" 1QIsa[a] at Isa 59:6, corresponding to פֹּעַל) but not in most forms in Origen (e.g., γαβρ corresponding to גֶּבֶר). See, e.g., Kutscher, *Isaiah Scroll*, 502; Qimron, *Hebrew of the Dead Sea Scrolls*, 37; Reymond, *Qumran Hebrew*, 181–88; John Huehnergard, "Segholates: Pre-modern Hebrew," *EHLL* 3:520–22.

150. Geoffrey Khan, "Shewa," 3:544; Khan, "Syllable Structure," 3:666

151. Heijmans, "Babylonian Tradition," 1:142.

152. See Khan, "Epenthesis," 1:832.

3.15. Loss of Gemination and *Shewa*

When certain geminated consonants follow a *shewa*, the gemination may be optionally lost together with the *shewa*, at least in THT. For example, **min + ləmaʿlā* > **milləmaʿlā* > **milmaʿlā* > מִלְמַעְלָה "from above" versus **milləmaṭṭā* > מִלְמַטָּה "from below"; **ʿiwwēr* > עִוֵּר "blind" but **ʿiwrīm* > עִוְרִים.[153] The phenomenon is associated with several colloquial phrases, created ostensibly for mnemonic purposes, including "Skin 'em alive" and "Skin 'em Levi." Although these may help one remember that the set of consonants that may lose gemination in this way includes sibilants ("s"), liquids ("l," "m" and "n"), as well as *vav* ("v"), one might be forgiven for believing that *kaph* ("k") and *bet* ("v") are also included in this set of consonants. They are not. A more useful mnemonic makes explicit the consonants that are part of this set.[154]

3.16. *Qamets* in the Tiberian Hebrew Tradition and Earlier Vowels

The articulation of *qamets* in THT, as indicated above, was /å/ (= IPA [ɔ]). This vowel developed from two different historical vowels. The PS/PNWS short /a/ shifted to a long /ā/ at some point in the first millennium BCE. Its further transformation into /å/ took place sometime in the first millennium CE. Simultaneously, PS/PNWS short /u/ shifted first to /o/ in certain environments and then shifted further to /å/, making it identical in its articulation to the etymological */a/. Since the Tiberian Masoretes heard only one sound, they represented these two historical vowels with one symbol, the *qamets*. If we followed the Tiberian tradition more closely in our classroom pronunciation, we would not distinguish between *qamets gadol* (/a/) and *qamets qaton* or *qamets khatuf* (/o/). As mentioned earlier, our classroom pronunciation is influenced by modern Israeli Hebrew, which is, in turn, influenced by Sephardic tradition, which preserved the distinction between /a/ and /o/.

153. Cited in Joüon, §18m. Note the similar loss of gemination and elision of the vowel "e" in the two alternative pronunciations of the participial form of English "listen": *lis-sen-ing* vs. *lis-ning*.

154. I use the phrase "Shy queens swim alone," which, although not based in a colorful biblical act of mutilation, does include all the relevant letters (except *tsade*): *shin*, *yod*, *qoph*, *nun*, *samek*/*sin*, *vav*, *mem*, *lamed*.

That the two vowels (*/ā/ [< */a/] and */o/ [< */u/]), which would eventually be represented by *qamets* in the Tiberian tradition, were still distinguished in the first millennium BCE is reflected in, among other places, the orthography of the Dead Sea Scrolls. Note, for example, that nouns that are spelled with an initial *qamets* in THT but which we pronounce with an initial /o/ are spelled with a *vav mater* in the Scrolls. Consider the instances in the Temple Scroll (11Q19), where we find, for example, אוכלה "food" in LIX, 7 (cf. אָכְלָה in THT); חורבה "ruin" in LIX, 4 (cf. חָרְבָּה in THT). By contrast, the verbs that are spelled with an initial *qamets* but which we pronounce as /a/ are spelled universally without a *vav mater*. In the same scroll (11Q19), we find, for example, אסרה "she binds" in LIII, 16 and passim (cf. אָסְרָה in THT); געלה "it loathes" in LIX, 9 (cf. גָּעֲלָה in THT).

3.17. Pausal Forms

As mentioned in the preface, pausal forms usually occur at the end of a verse (marked with the *silluq* symbol, ˌ), in the middle of the verse (marked by the *atnach* symbol, ‸), and sometimes at the quarter point and three-quarter point of the verse (marked by the *zaqef* symbol, ˸). Often pausal forms are accented on the penultimate syllable. If the word in pause is inflected in a way that would typically result in reduction of the historical short vowel in the penultimate syllable, the vowel is preserved and was (earlier) long: יִשְׁבֹּתוּ "it will not stop" (Gen 8:22); יֵצֵאוּ "they will go forth" (Gen 17:6); תִּסְחָרוּ "you will trade" (Gen 42:34); דְּבָרֶךָ "your word" (Gen 30:34); שְׁלָחוּ "send!" (2 Kgs 2:17; cf. contextual שִׁלְחוּ). Also, in pause a short /a/ vowel that is accented will lengthen to */ā/ as reflected in תִּסְחָרוּ as well as in אָכָלְתּ "you eat" (Gen 3:11); אֲבֹתָי "my fathers" (Gen 49:29); and דְּבָרָיִךְ "your words" (1 Kgs 1:14). That such lengthening is not just a phenomenon connected with the Tiberian tradition but has roots in earlier stages of Hebrew is hard to determine but seems implied by the spellings in the Secunda (e.g., *ιεσμωρου* [יִשְׁמֹרוּ], and *ιαλληλου* [יְהַלֵּלוּ] [Ps 89:32]).[155] Pausal forms of **qaṭl* segolates sometimes exhibit the original vowel, lengthened: נָפֶשׁ "soul" (Job 3:20).[156] Conventionally it is believed

155. Khan ("*Ṣere*," 142) writes that "Pausal lengthening of the stressed vowel took place sometime before the general lengthening of stressed vowels."

156. This commonly occurs with other nouns, but curiously, this does not happen with others like מֶלֶךְ "king," which exhibit both *segols* in pause. Steven Fassberg ("Why Doesn't *Melex* Appear as *Ma:lex* in Pause in Tiberian Hebrew?" [Hebrew], *Lešonenu*

that the pausal forms represent a slightly more archaic version of words. This is true especially as regards vowel reduction in verbs and the place of stress. That is, the pausal forms reflect the preservation of penultimate vowels in verbs and penultimate word stress, both of which would have been part of an earlier stage of Hebrew. However, as the above examples demonstrate, pause does not result in the retention of short vowels in propretonic syllables, nor in the preservation of vowels that are reduced already in the absolute form (e.g., וּגְבוּל "and border" Josh 15:47). Furthermore, it is not always the case that the penultimate vowel that is lengthened in pause reflects the quality of the etymological vowel. Contrast **ʾākilatu* > אוֹכֵלָה "one eating" (Isa 30:30), above the *atnach* and **ʾākiltu* > אֹכָ֫לֶת (Isa 30:27), above the *silluq*.[157]

3.18. Chapter Summary

Historical Details

1. The vowels of the Tiberian system are not exactly the ones we typically use in class. Nor do the vowels of the Tiberian system (or the ones we use in class) mirror exactly the vocalic system of earlier phases of Hebrew.
2. Historical long vowels remained long in Biblical Hebrew (*/ō/ [< PNWS */ā/], */ī/, */ū/).
3. Historical short vowels */a/, */i/, and */u/ lengthened and/or lowered in tonic syllables in most nouns and some verbs: **daba**ru*** > **dā**bār*** (> דָּבָר) "word" and **baraka**tiyya*** > **bar**kātī*** (> **bir**kātī***) > בִּרְכָתִי) "my blessing"; **ka**bida*** > **kā**bed*** (> כָּבֵד) "it is heavy" (*qal* 3ms *qåṭal*/ms adj.) and **yak**tubu*** > **yik**tob*** (> יִכְתֹּב) "he will write." (Note the exceptions: in many verb forms, historical /a/ remained /a/, e.g., **ka**taba*** > **kā**tab*** [> כָּתַב] "he wrote," **yik**bad*** [> יִכְבַּד] "it will be heavy").

64 [2002]: 207–19) has proposed that this is in order to avoid a pronunciation of the word that would make it too close to the word "Moloch."

157. Notice also that although the verbs in pause often seem to reflect a more archaic morphology (שִׂמֳּ֫חָהוּ "it gladdened him" Jer 20:15 instead of ו-), such archaic features may in fact be secondary, as is suggested in places where a *nun* does not assimilate (e.g., תִּנְצְּ֫רֵנִי "you guard me" Ps 140:2). For more on pause, see the article (with references) by Steven E. Fassberg, "Pausal Forms," *EHLL* 3:54–55.

4. Historical short */a/ and */i/ lengthened to */ā/ and */ē/ respectively in pretonic open syllables: *___da___baru* > *___dā___bār* (> דָּבָר) "word," *_da**ba**rīma_ > *_də**bā**rīm_ (> דְּבָרִים) "words," *_ka**bi**dīma_ > *_kə**bē**dīm_ (> כְּבֵדִים) "heavy"; *___ka___taba* > *___kā___tab* (> כָּתַב) "he wrote" and *___ya___qūmu* > *___yā___qūm* (> יָקוּם) "he will arise."
5. Historical short vowels reduced to _shewa_ or elided in open syllables that were both nontonic and nonpretonic: *___da___barīma* > *___də___bārīm* (> דְּבָרִים) "words" and *___bara___katiyya* > *___bar___kātī* (> ___bir___kåti = בִּרְכָתִי) "my blessing."
6. Compensatory lengthening occured most regularly with _aleph_ and _resh_ and then, in order of decreasing frequency, with _ayin_, _he_, and _khet_. If a vowel was compensatorily lengthened, it did not reduce in an open propretonic syllable.
7. A very hypothetical sequence of some of the phenomena discussed above is presented here:

Canaanite Shift	ca. 1500 BCE
Triphthong contraction	ca. 1500 BCE
Loss of final short vowels	ca. 1000 BCE
Feminine *_-at_ > *_-a_ > *_-ā_	ca. 1000–500 BCE
Tonic lengthening/lowering	ca. 800–300 BCE
Merger of /ś/ and /s/	ca. 600–400 BCE
Pretonic lengthening/lowering	ca. 500–300 BCE
Spirantization	ca. 500 BCE–200 CE
Vowel reduction	ca. 400 BCE–400 CE
Compensatory lengthening of geminated gutturals	ca. 300 BCE–100 CE
Epenthesis	ca. 300 BCE–200 CE
Merger of /ġ/ and /ʿ/	ca. 200 BCE–1 BCE
Merger of /ḫ/ and /ḥ/	ca. 100 BCE–200 CE.

Learning Tips

1. Memorize the basic rules for syllables and vowels for Biblical Hebrew, especially the fact that:
   1.1. a nontonic open syllable can have only a _shewa_ (*_lamm**ə**lākīm_ [> לַמְּלָכִים] "for the kings") or a long vowel (*_lammə**lā**kīm_ [> לַמְּלָכִים])
   1.2. a nontonic closed syllable can have only a short vowel (*_**lam**məlākīm_ [> לַמְּלָכִים])

1.3. often, a tonic syllable will have a long vowel (reflected in THT by *qamets, tsere, hireq, holem, shureq*) (**lammәlā**kīm*** [> לַמְּלָכִים])
1.4. often, a pretonic open syllable will contain */ā/ or */ē/ (THT *qamets* or *tsere*) (**lammә**lā**kīm* [> לַמְּלָכִים]).

2. Remember that when a word bears a pronominal suffix or morpheme at its end, it typically will exhibit a form closer to its older, historical form. This is mentioned in relation to the shift from */-at/ of feminine singular nouns to */-ā/, where the earlier ending emerges in the construct and with suffixes (e.g., מַלְכָּתָהּ* "her queen" [< **malkatah*]), but this also occurs with geminate nouns (e.g., חֻקִּים "statutes" [< **ḥuqqīma*]) and with singular segolate nouns with suffixes (e.g., מַלְכִּי "my king" [< **malkiyya*]), as detailed in the next chapter.
3. Learn the basic rudiments of the PS/PNWS vowel system: three long vowels (*/ī/, */ā/, */ū/) and three short vowels (*/i/, */a/, */u/).
4. Learn to recognize the origin of most Tiberian vowels:
   4.1. *hireq* (with *yod*) usually derives from */ī/ while *hireq* (without *yod*) derives from */i/
   4.2. *tsere* derives from */i/ (or the contraction of */ay/)
   4.3. *segol* derives from */i/ (or from */a/ in segolate nouns like מֶ֫לֶךְ)
   4.4. *patakh* and *qamets* derive from */a/ (unless the *qamets* occurs in a closed, unaccented syllable, in which case it derives from */u/, as in חָכְמָה "wisdom")
   4.5. *shureq* derives usually from */ū/
   4.6. *qibbuts* usually derives from */u/ and somewhat less often from */ū/
   4.7. a muttered vowel (*shewa*) may derive from any short vowel in a historical open syllable.
5. Mnemonic Aids
   5.1. "Shy queens swim alone"—the consonants (+ *tsade*) that optionally lose their *daghesh* when followed by a *shewa*.
   5.2. הֶהָרִים exhibits the shift of historical */a/ to /ɛ/.

4
Morphology of Ancient Hebrew: The Noun

4.1. Morphology of the Hebrew Noun

In Biblical Hebrew, the morphology of the noun overlaps with the morphology of adjectives, with that of some adverbs, as well as with that of *qal* participles and infinitives. Here and in the charts that follow in chapter 6, these categories of words will be treated together. Moreover, the following pages categorize these words according to which abstract pattern they belong (i.e., **qal*, **qil*, **qul*, etc.), patterns that reflect their etymological bases. The abstract patterns, however, are not necessarily identical to their earliest forms. This pertains especially to II-*vav*/*yod* roots. For example, the *qal* participle of II-*vav*/*yod* roots is categorized under **qal* (e.g., **qam*) not **qatal* (**qawam*) or **qāl* (**qām*).[1] At the same time, the abstract patterns represent a form of the words long before the vowel reduction and lengthening associated with BH (e.g., דָּבָר is categorized as a **qatal* noun, not **qāṭāl* or *qåṭål*).[2]

It should be admitted at the beginning that attributing a given noun to a particular base is difficult because the different traditions of Hebrew often do not reveal consistency. What appears to be of the **qatl* base in THT (e.g., גֶּפֶן "vine") appears to be of the **qutl* base in the DSS (גופן in 1QIsa^a at Isa 34:4).[3] In truth, even the Hebrew Bible reveals different bases

1. This follows the method of Huehnergard, "Biblical Hebrew Nominal Patterns," 29–30. If the vowel was long in the immediate ancestor to BH, it would have presumably become /ō/ through the Canaanite Shift. Still, such forms would have contained a long vowel in an earlier version of Northwest Semitic (see ibid., 29 n. 7).

2. As noted in the preface, the paradigmatic root is **qtl* (and not **qṭl*), since the form with *tav* is likely the earliest form of this root (reflected in, e.g., Akkadian, Arabic, and Ethiopic).

3. See Reymond, *Qumran Hebrew*, 171–74.

for what seems to be the same word: חֶ֫סֶר "lack" (*qatl or *qitl) versus חֹ֫סֶר "lack" (*qutl).[4] When comparative evidence from other languages is considered, categorization becomes even more complex. In what follows, I make an educated guess about the base of the words informed especially by Hebrew evidence. It seems possible that at least for some words there were byforms from earliest times (e.g., דֶּ֫רֶךְ "way" < **dark* and/or < **dirk*).[5]

Although learning the base of words along with their meaning and inflection seems like an added burden for the student, these base patterns are rather limited in number and offer at least two advantages to the intermediate student. First, learning the basic outline of the system will allow the student to more easily remember vocabulary. For example, learning that short words ending in *tav*, like דַּ֫עַת, are often from I-*vav*/*yod* roots helps to recall that this word is from ידע and means "knowledge." Second, nouns of a common base pattern inflect in the same way; thus, learning that the segolate nouns (those of the **qatl*, **qitl*, and **qutl* bases) exhibit the sequence of vowels **ə-ā* in the absolute plural allows one to predict the correct plural form for a diverse set of nouns including חֳלִי "sickness," מֶ֫לֶךְ "king," בֹּ֫קֶר "morning" as well as feminine nouns like מַלְכָּה "queen," דִּמְעָה "tears," and חָרְבָּה "waste." All the same, it should be recognized that it is likely impossible to remember all the details laid out in the following pages.

4.2. Case and Number in Second-Millennium Northwest Semitic

In addition to those phonological developments mentioned in the preceding chapter, morphological developments mark a distinction between second-millennium BCE Canaanite languages and first-millennium BCE Hebrew. First, the earlier languages or dialects would have had three numbers: singular, dual, and plural. Although Hebrew preserves some examples of the dual (e.g., יָדַ֫יִם "two hands" vs. יָדוֹת "[multiple] hands"), this would have presumably been a more productive category in the second millennium BCE and would have also been reflected in verbal morphology, through which it would have been possible to communicate not only the ideas "s/he wrote" and "they wrote," but also "two (people) wrote."

In addition, the earlier second-millennium NWS languages had a case system. This system allowed speakers to distinguish three basic functions

4. See the list of similar forms in Sperber, *Historical Grammar*, 30–31. Similarly, the MT evidences many words that differ essentially only in their gender (ibid., 22–30).

5. Huehnergard, "Biblical Hebrew Nominal Patterns," 39.

of nouns in a sentence. Nouns that functioned as the grammatical subject of a verb were marked as distinct from nouns that functioned as the grammatical object of the verb and these were both distinct from nouns that were the last in a construct chain or that came after prepositions.[6] In outline, the case system for this version of proto-Hebrew would be similar to the case system known from Ugaritic.[7] The grammatical subject of a sentence is said to be in the nominative case, the grammatical object in the accusative case; the word after a construct form or after a preposition is in the genitive case. With respect to Ugaritic, on masculine singular absolute nouns, final short *-u* marked the nominative, *-i* marked the genitive, and *-a* the accusative (e.g., **malku*, **malki*, **malka* "king"); on masculine dual absolute nouns final *-āmi* marked the nominative and *-ēmi* (from < **-aymi*) marked the genitive and accusative (**malkāmi*, **malkēmi* [< **malkaymi*] "two kings").[8] Feminine nouns in the singular and dual absolute had endings analogous to those of the masculine singular and dual absolute, though the feminine nouns incorporated the feminine morpheme *-at* or *-t*. As for the plurals, on masculine plural absolute nouns *-ūma* marked the nominative and *-īma* marked the genitive/accusative (**malakūma*, **malakīma* "kings"); on feminine plural absolute nouns *-ātu* marked the nominative and *-āti* the genitive/accusative.[9] The case vowels also appeared on nouns in the construct state. For the singular noun, they were the same as the absolute form; for the dual and the masculine plural,

6. In the sentence, וַיַּךְ אֶת־הַפְּלִשְׁתִּי אֶל־מִצְחוֹ "he (i.e., David) struck the Philistine (i.e., Goliath) on his forehead" (1 Sam 17:49), the grammatical subject is "he (i.e., David)"; the grammatical object is "the Philistine (i.e., Goliath)"; the word "his forehead" follows the preposition "on."

7. The vowels of Ugaritic are known not only from Sumero-Akkadian cuneiform transliterations of Ugaritic words, but also the Ugaritic cuneiform script that marks the vowel following any *aleph* consonant; i.e., in Ugaritic cuneiform there is one symbol for *aleph* followed by /a/, another symbol for *aleph* followed by /i/, and a third symbol for *aleph* followed by /u/. For examples of ancient word lists from Ugarit written in Sumero-Akkadian cuneiform, where individual words are listed in different columns according to language (like a primitive dictionary), see John Huehnergard, *Ugaritic Vocabulary in Syllabic Transcription*, 2nd ed., HSS 32 (Winona Lake, IN: Eisenbrauns, 2008).

8. The endings on the dual are also attested, respectively, as *-āma* and *-ēma* (see ibid., 298–99, 402). I have based this paradigm on that of Pierre Bordreuil and Dennis Pardee, *A Manual of Ugaritic*, LSAWS 3 (Winona Lake, IN: Eisenbrauns, 2009), 32.

9. Alternatively, there was just one vowel within the stem of such plural nouns: **malkūma*, **malkīma* (see Bordreuil and Pardee, *Manual of Ugaritic*, 34).

the construct forms lost the final *-mi* or *-ma*: dual *-ā* (nom.), *-ē* (< **-ay*) (gen./acc.) and masculine plural *-ū* (nom.), *-ī* (gen./acc.).[10] It is likely that in the southern dialect of NWS spoken near the end of the second millennium BCE, the diphthongs were still preserved, unlike in Ugaritic. Thus, the dual genitive/accusative ending on a masculine dual noun would have been *-aymī* in the absolute and *-ay* in the construct.

Presuming a stem **dabar*, one may postulate the following hypothetical paradigm for the absolute and construct forms, based on the Ugaritic paradigm for nouns. The **ā* reflects the PS/PNWS vowel, before the Canaanite Shift.

		Masculine absolute		
	singular		dual	plural
nom.	**dabaru*	nom.	**dabarāmi*	**dabarūma*
gen.	**dabari*	gen./acc.	**dabaraymi*	**dabarīma*
acc.	**dabara*			
		Feminine absolute		
	singular		dual	plural
nom.	**dabaratu*	nom.	**dabaratāmi*	**dabarātu*
gen.	**dabarati*	gen./acc.	**dabarataymi*	**dabarāti*
acc.	**dabarata*			
		Masculine construct		
	singular		dual	plural
nom.	**dabaru*	nom.	**dabarā*	**dabarū*
gen.	**dabari*	gen./acc.	**dabaray*	**dabarī*
acc.	**dabara*			
		Feminine construct		
	singular		dual	plural
nom.	**dabaratu*	nom.	**dabaratā*	**dabarātu*
gen.	**dabarati*	gen./acc.	**dabaratay*	**dabarāti*
acc.	**dabarata*			

10. See ibid.

In essence, the inflected forms of the noun were composed of the stem (**dabar*) followed by the appropriate suffixal morpheme.

At some point close to the end of the second millennium BCE, the final short vowels on nouns and verbs ceased being pronounced. As described above in chapter 3, this meant that there was no longer a distinction in the singular noun between the different cases. This, in turn, led to the obsolescence of the entire case system (even though it would have been possible to continue distinguishing certain forms in the dual and plural, e.g., where the form ended with a long vowel). In short, speakers used fewer forms to communicate. Instead of having two forms to express the masculine plural absolute, speakers used just one. They ended up using the form that had previously marked the genitive/accusative case (i.e., **dabarīm* [< **dabarīma*]). Similarly, instead of four forms to express the masculine dual and plural construct, speakers used just one. Again, they ended up using the form that had marked the genitive/accusative case, specifically the form that once marked exclusively the dual (i.e., **dabaray*).

The new forms and their relationship to the preceding paradigm can be more easily grasped from looking at the following chart that duplicates the earlier paradigm, though in the following the obsolete aspects of the paradigm have been crossed out. Forms that are identical to other forms are put in parentheses after their first appearance.

		Masculine absolute		
	singular		dual	plural
~~nom.~~	*dabar~~u~~	~~nom.~~	*~~dabarāmi~~	*~~dabarūma~~
~~gen.~~	(*dabar~~i~~)	~~gen.~~/~~acc.~~	*dabaraym~~i~~	*dabarīm~~a~~
~~acc.~~	(*dabar~~a~~)			

		Feminine absolute		
	singular		dual	plural
~~nom.~~	*dabarat~~u~~	~~nom.~~	*~~dabaratāmi~~	*dabarāt~~u~~
~~gen.~~	(*dabarat~~i~~)	~~gen.~~/~~acc.~~	*~~dabarataymi~~	(*dabarāt~~i~~)
~~acc.~~	(*dabarat~~a~~)			

		Masculine construct		
	singular		dual	plural
~~nom.~~	*dabar~~u~~	~~nom.~~	*~~dabarā~~	*~~dabarū~~

~~gen~~.	(**dabar~~i~~*)	~~gen~~./~~acc~~.	**dabaray*	*~~*dabarī*~~
~~acc~~.	(**dabar~~a~~*)			

		Feminine construct		
	singular		dual	plural
~~nom~~.	**dabarat~~u~~*	~~nom~~.	*~~*dabaratā*~~	**dabarāt~~u~~*
~~gen~~.	(**dabarat~~i~~*)	~~gen~~./~~acc~~.	*~~*dabaratay*~~	(**dabarāt~~i~~*)
~~acc~~.	(**dabarat~~a~~*)			

The absolute form of masculine plural nouns in the genitive/accusative case developed into the absolute form of masculine plural Hebrew nouns: **dabarīma* > **dabarīm* > **dəbārīm* > דְּבָרִים "words." In a similar way, the genitive/accusative ending for dual nouns in construct (*-*ay*) became the standard ending for masculine plural nouns in construct in Hebrew as well as for masculine plural nouns with pronominal suffixes. That is, what would have been **dabaray* "two words of" (in the gen./acc. case) became the basis of the plural construct: **dabaray* "(multiple) words of," which through the process of diphthong contraction and vowel reduction would have subsequently become **dabrē* and then in THT (as well as BHT) דִּבְרֵי. This same form was used also for the plural form with pronominal suffixes: **dabarayya* "my two words" (in the gen./acc. case) became **dabaray* and then **dəbāray* "my (multiple) words," before finally becoming דְּבָרַי.[11] Due to the ubiquity of this *yod* in the masculine noun, even feminine plural nouns bear the same *yod*, though this has no precedent in the earlier morphology of NWS: **barakātaka* > בִּרְכוֹתֶיךָ "your blessings."

As illustrated below, the singular noun with pronominal suffixes also seems to retain some vestige of the older morphology. The initial vowels of the pronominal suffixes likely derive from the earlier case vowels on the singular noun. Thus, the vowel of the genitive case seems to have led to the initial /ē/ of the first-person common plural suffix: **dabar* + *i* + *nū* > **dabarinū* > **dəbārēnū* (> דְּבָרֵנוּ) "our word."

This historical explanation also helps make sense of the form of dual nouns in later Hebrew. The Biblical Hebrew absolute form (יָדַיִם "two hands") derives from the genitive/accusative form of the absolute (i.e., **yadaym* vs. the abs. dual nom. **yadāmi*). The BH construct form (יְדֵי "two hands of") derives from the construct form of the genitive/accusative case

11. See Blau, *Phonology and Morphology*, 170.

(i.e., **yaday* vs. the const. dual nom. **yadayā*); the dual with suffix derives from the same historical form (**yadayya* > יָדַי "my two hands").[12] In Biblical Hebrew, the dual construct and the dual with pronominal suffix look like the corresponding masculine plural forms, such that sometimes they are confused. For example, יְדֵיהֶם will sometimes be translated by students as if it meant "their (multiple) hands" and not more specifically "their two hands." (The pl. would be יְדוֹתָם "their [multiple] hands"). The fact that the dual + suffix looks like the plural + suffix in BH is no coincidence; the masculine plural endings in BH derive from the earlier (second millennium BCE) dual endings.[13]

The transformation of the feminine forms is less confusing than that of the masculine. First, note that in the above charts, the vowel in the feminine plural morpheme is */ā/; by the time of Hebrew in the first millennium BCE (and likely much earlier), that vowel had shifted to */ō/ through the Canaanite Shift. Thus, the plural absolute and construct forms would both be **dabarōt* (not **dabarāt*). Other than this, however, the feminine nouns are easy to understand. In essence, with the loss of case vowels, the singular forms (both absolute and construct) sounded the same; similarly, all the feminine plural forms sounded the same.

Although the exact realization of these words might have been different in the early first millennium BCE, it is pedagogically useful to imagine them in this hypothetical way since it helps make sense of their later forms, especially in light of the phonological shifts described earlier. Each of these basic entities (i.e., sg. abs., sg. + pronominal suf., sg. const., pl. abs., etc.) experienced the phonological shifts described in the preceding chapter. For example, **dabarīm* "words," **dabarēnū* "our words," and **dabarē* (const.) "words of" all experienced vowel reduction of */a/ and */i/ to *shewa* in open syllables that were nontonic and nonpretonic, as well as lengthening of */a/ and */i/ vowels in open pretonic syllables. Thus, **dabarīm* became **dəbarīm* (vowel reduction) and then *dəbārīm* (pretonic lengthening) (> דְּבָרִים).[14] Similarly, **dabarēnū* became **dəbarēnū* and then **dəbārēnū* (> דְּבָרֵ֫ינוּ), while the construct form **dabarē-* became **dabrē-*

12. These may be contrasted with the plural forms of the same word: abs. יָדוֹת "hands"; const. יְדוֹת; suf. יְדוֹתַי.

13. It goes without saying that the BH dual endings also derive from the earlier second millennium BCE dual endings.

14. These different shifts are imagined as occurring in this sequence simply for the sake of clarity.

(as reflected in δαβρη "words of" in the Secunda at Ps 35:20) which, in turn, became דִּבְרֵי (perhaps due to analogy with other nominal forms).

4.3. Noun Patterns

As explained above, nouns/adjectives in this study are categorized according to their etymological base patterns, since this helps elucidate certain underlying semantic and inflectional similarities and allows the student who has learned these patterns to more easily inflect the related words.[15] Hebrew nouns are categorized according to how many root consonants they attest and the number and nature of their vowels. (E.g., one category consists of nouns with two root consonants and a short vowel between them, another of nouns with two root consonants and a long vowel between them, yet another of nouns with three root consonants and a single short vowel between them, etc.) Each of these general categories is then broken down into subcategories, reflecting the etymological PNWS vowels, usually listed in the sequence according to the vowel: */a/, */i/, */u/ (e.g., **qal*, **qil*, **qul*; **qāl*, **qīl*, **qūl*; **qatal*, **qatil*, **qatul*; **qital*, **qutal*, **qutul*). With each of these smaller subcategories are associated feminine forms, that are derived from these bases through the suffixing of a *-t* or *-*at** morpheme (e.g., **qalt* and **qalat*, **qilt* and **qilat*, **qālat*, **qīlat*, **qūlat*; **qatalat*, **qatilt* and **qatilat*).

In most cases, each general category of noun exhibits a common inflection. For example, all segolate nouns/adjectives, that is, those of the base pattern **qatl* (e.g., מֶ֫לֶךְ "king"), **qitl* (סֵ֫פֶר "book"), **qutl* (בֹּ֫קֶר "morning"), exhibit the vowel sequence **ə-ā* (corresponding to the symbols *shewa-qamets* in THT) in the absolute plural. This also includes feminine forms and words from weak roots. Usually, where there is some distinction among the different subcategories of bases, it is the form with an */a/ vowel that exhibits idiosyncracies. Forms with an */i/ or */u/ vowel usually have similar inflections, reflecting the vowels' common place of articulation, with the tongue raised to the roof of the mouth.

In the charts in chapter 6, the various forms of nouns and adjectives (as well as *qal* verbal nouns and adjectives = infinitives and participles) are documented, beginning with the shortest (**qal*) and progressing to the

---

15. Another method is to list the nouns/adjectives according to their realization in BH.

more complex (e.g., **qātil*). The pages that follow in this chapter, however, follow a different sequence. First, I illustrate the inflection of three of the most common nominal base patterns in both their masculine (**qatal*, **qatil*, **qital*) and feminine forms (**qatalat*, **qatilat*). Next, I detail the inflection of bases with just two attested root consonants (**qal*, **qil*, **qul*, etc.), before addressing other base patterns with three root consonants (e.g., **qatul*, **qatāl* and **qutul*, **qitāl*, **qutāl*). In the next sections, I address nouns with preformative and afformative elements. Next, common features of weak roots are isolated. Then, I address two idiosyncratic noun classes: geminate nouns (e.g., **qall*) and segolate nouns (e.g., **qatl*).

4.4. Inflection of Basic Masculine and Feminine Nouns (Tables 6.15, 6.16, 6.17)

Here and in what follows, a basic masculine noun refers to a noun of a strong root with one of the base patterns **qatal*, **qatil*, or **qital*. Although classified as "nouns," note that many words of these bases are better construed as adjectives (e.g., חָזָק "strong"; חָכָם "wise"; כָּבֵד "heavy"; עָיֵף "weary"). In particular, the **qatil* base is associated with adjectives and the participle of stative verbs (e.g., כָּבֵד "one who is heavy"; זָקֵן "one who is old").

In most cases, the nouns of the **qatal*, **qatil*, or **qital* bases follow predictably the vowel shifts outlined in the previous chapter: loss of final short vowels, tonic-vowel lengthening/lowering, pretonic-vowel lengthening/lowering, vowel reduction in open syllables that are both nontonic and nonpretonic. As illustrated above, these vowel shifts affect both singular and plural forms, as well as nouns in construct and with suffixes. For construct forms (both sg. and pl.), nouns appear as though all their syllables are nontonic and nonpretonic. For singular nouns with suffixes, a vowel intercedes between the stem and the pronoun, likely deriving from the earlier genitive or accusative case vowel. For most plural nouns with pronominal suffixes, the genitive/accusative case ending of the masculine dual construct, **-ay-*, intercedes between the stem and pronoun. Note the following examples, which represent a simplified way of reconstructing the forms.

**dabaru* > **dābār* (> דָּבָר) "word"
**dabaru* > **dəbar* (> דְּבַר) "word of"
**dabar + i + ya* > **dabariy* > **dabarī* > **dəbārī* (> דְּבָרִי) "my word"

**dabar + a + ka > *dabaraka > *dəbārakā > *dəbārəkā* (> דְּבָרְךָ) "your word"[16]
**dabar + i + ki > *dabarik > *dəbārēk* (> דְּבָרֵךְ) "your word"
**dabar + a + hu > *dabarahu* (> **dabaraw*) > **dəbārō* (> דְּבָרוֹ) "his word"[17]
**dabar + a + ha > *dabarah > *dəbārāh* (> דְּבָרָהּ) "her word"
**dabar + i + nū > *dabarinū > *dəbārēnū* (> דְּבָרֵ֫נוּ) "our word"
**dabar + ? + kum > *dabarkim > *dəbarkɛm* (> דְּבַרְכֶם) "your word"[18]
**dabar + ? + kin > *dabarkin > *dəbarkɛn* (> דְּבַרְכֶן) "your word"
**dabar + a +* (*hu*)*m > *dabaram > *dəbārām* (> דְּבָרָם) "their word"
**dabar + a +* (*hi*)*n > *dabaran > *dəbārān* (> דְּבָרָן) "their word"

**dabarīma > *dəbārīm* (> דְּבָרִים) "words"
**dabaray > *dabrē* (> *dibre* = דִּבְרֵי) "words of"
**dabar + ay + ya > *dabaray > *dəbāray* (> דְּבָרַי) "my words"
**dabar + ay + ka > *dabarayka > *dəbārekā* (> דְּבָרֶ֫יךָ) "your words"[19]
**dabar + ay + ki > *dabarayk > *dəbārayk* (> דְּבָרַ֫יִךְ) "your words"
**dabar + ay + hu > *dabarawhu* (> **dabarawwu*) > **dabaraw > *dəbārāw* (> דְּבָרָיו) "his words"[20]
**dabar + ay + ha > *dabarayha > *dəbārehā* (> דְּבָרֶ֫יהָ) "her words"
**dabar + ay + nū > *dabaraynū > *dəbārēnū* (> דְּבָרֵ֫ינוּ) "our words"
**dabar + ay + kum > *dabaraykim > *dabrēkɛm* (> *dibrekɛm* = דִּבְרֵיכֶם) "your words"
**dabar + ay + kin > *dabaraykin > *dabrēkɛn* (> *dibrekɛn* = דִּבְרֵיכֶן) "your words"
**dabar + ay + hum > *dabarayhim > *dabrēhɛm* (> *dibrehɛm* = דִּבְרֵיהֶם) "their words"
**dabar + ay + hin > *dabarayhin > *dabrēhɛn* (> *dibrehɛn* = דִּבְרֵיהֶן) "their words"

---

16. See ch. 3 §5, "Lengthening of Pretonic */i/ and */a/ Vowels and the Place of Stress" and §5, "Peculiarities of Some Suffixes," below.

17. See Garr, *Dialect Geography*, 103 and note the alternative explanations listed in Jeremy Hutton, "Epigraphic Hebrew: Pre-Roman Period," *EHLL* 1:838.

18. The spirantized *kaph* of the pronoun would seem to imply a preceding vowel in this and the following form.

19. One would expect /ē/ to be the result of a contraction of /ay/, as in the 1cp pronominal suf. See ch. 3 §12, "Triphthongs and Diphthongs."

20. See Garr, *Dialect Geography*, 108.

**ṣadaqatu* > **ṣədāqā* (> צְדָקָה) "righteousness"
**ṣadaqatu* > **ṣadqat* (> *ṣidqat* = צִדְקַת) "righteousness of"

**ṣadaqat* + *i* + *ya* > **ṣadqatiy* > **ṣadqātī* (> *ṣidqåti* = צִדְקָתִי) "my righteousness"

**ṣadaqat* + *a* + *ka* > **ṣadqataka* > **ṣadqātakā* > **ṣadqātəkā* (> *ṣidqåtkå* = צִדְקָתְךָ) "your righteousness"

**ṣadaqat* + *i* + *ki* > **ṣadqatik* > **ṣadqātēk* (> *ṣidqåtek* = צִדְקָתֵךְ) "your righteousness"

**ṣadaqat* + *a* + *hu* > **ṣadqatahu* > **ṣadqātaw* > **ṣadqātō* (> *ṣidqåto* = צִדְקָתוֹ) "his righteousness"

**ṣadaqat* + *a* + *ha* > **ṣadqatah* > **ṣadqātāh* (> *ṣidqåtåh* = צִדְקָתָהּ) "her righteousness"

**ṣadaqat* + *i* + *nū* > **ṣadqatinū* > **ṣadqātēnū* (> *ṣidqåtenu* = צִדְקָתֵנוּ) "our righteousness"

**ṣadaqat* + ? + *kum* > **ṣadqatkim* > **ṣadqatkɛm* (> **ṣidqatkɛm* = צִדְקַתְכֶם) "your righteousness"

**ṣadaqat* + ? + *kin* > **ṣadqatkin* > **ṣadqatkɛn* (> *ṣidqatkɛn* = צִדְקַתְכֶן) "your righteousness"

**ṣadaqat* + *a* + (*hu*)*m* > **ṣadqatam* > **ṣadqātām* (> *ṣidqåtåm* = צִדְקָתָם) "their righteousness"

**ṣadaqat* + *a* + (*hi*)*n* > **ṣadqatan* > **ṣadqātān* (> *ṣidqåtån* = צִדְקָתָן) "their righteousness"

**ṣadaqātu* > **ṣədāqōt* (> צְדָקוֹת) "righteousnesses"
**ṣadaqātu* > **ṣadqōt* (> *ṣidqot* = צִדְקוֹת) "righteousnesses of"

**ṣadaqāt* + *ay* + *ya* > **ṣadqōtay* (> *ṣidqotay* = צִדְקוֹתַי) "my righteousnesses"

**ṣadaqāt* + *ay* + *ka* > **ṣadqōtayka* > **ṣadqōtekā* (> *ṣidqotɛkå* = צִדְקוֹתֶיךָ) "your righteousnesses"

**ṣadaqāt* + *ay* + *ki* > **ṣadqōtayk* (> *ṣidqotayk* = צִדְקוֹתַיִךְ) "your righteousnesses"

**ṣadaqāt* + *ay* + *hu* > **ṣadqōtawhu* (> **ṣadqōtawwu*) > **ṣadqōtaw* > **ṣadqōtāw* (> *ṣidqotåw* = צִדְקוֹתָיו) "his righteousness"

**ṣadaqāt* + *ay* + *ha* > **ṣadqōtayaha* > **ṣadqōtehā* (> *ṣidqotɛhå* = צִדְקוֹתֶיהָ) "her righteousnesses"

**ṣadaqāt* + *ay* + *nū* > **ṣadqōtaynū* > **ṣadqōtēnū* (> *ṣidqotenu* = צִדְקוֹתֵינוּ) "our righteousnesses"

**ṣadaqāt* + *ay* + *kum* > **ṣadqōtaykim* > **ṣadqōtēkɛm* (> *ṣidqotekɛm* = צִדְקוֹתֵיכֶם) "your righteousnesses" *ṣadaqāt + ay + kin > *ṣadqōtaykin > *ṣadqōtēkɛn (> ṣidqotekɛn = צִדְקוֹתֵיכֶן) "your righteousnesses"

*ṣadaqāt + a + (hu)m > *ṣadqōtām (> ṣidqotåm = צִדְקוֹתָם) "their righteousnesses"

*ṣadaqāt + a + (hi)n > *ṣadqōtān (> ṣidqotån = צִדְקוֹתָן) "their righteousnesses"

In almost all the singular forms above, the tonic syllable has a long vowel and the pretonic syllable is open and also has a long vowel. Excluding the forms plus second-person masculine singular suffix, the exceptions occur with heavy suffixes that consist of the sequence consonant + vowel + consonant (e.g., כֶם-). In these cases, the tonic syllable has a short vowel and the preceding syllable is closed with a short vowel. The stem of the noun with a heavy suffix often matches the stem of the construct form. In most plural nouns with suffix, the pretonic syllable is also open and has a long vowel. The exceptions again occur where the suffix is heavy.

The above discussion has focused on nouns with two */a/ vowels in their stem (i.e., of the pattern *qatal), but the same developments and inflections also pertain to words with the patterns *qatil and *qital. In the case of nouns of the *qatil base, the singular construct form usually is (somewhat unexpectedly) like that of nouns of the *qatal base. Thus, the singular construct form of זָקֵן is זְקַן "elder of." The other forms of *qatil base nouns, however, do not exhibit the shift of /a/ to /i/ (e.g., זְקֵנִים and the forms with suffix: זְקֵנִי*, זְקֵנֵךְ*, זְקֵנוֹ*, זְקֵנָהּ*, זְקֵנֵ֫נוּ*, זְקֵנָם*, זְקֵנָן*, etc.).[21]

Feminine singular nouns in the construct and with suffixes generally are either marked with final *-t* or final **-at*. The absolute form is the only form to end with **-ā* (> *-å*). Although it is not expected from its etymology, the feminine plural noun often incorporates the dual component **-ay-* before suffixes. We do not expect such a component since this is peculiar to masculine (dual) nouns (in the gen./acc. case), not the feminine. In fact, the third-person masculine plural and feminine plural suffixes often are not preceded by this syllable.

The feminine nouns (and adjs./stative ptcs.) of the *qatilat base are unusual in that they often do not exhibit vowel reduction of the histori-

21. Singular nouns of the *qatil* base with suffixes are especially uncommon; nevertheless, note, e.g., יְרֵכִי "my thigh"; יְרֵכֵךְ "your thigh"; יְרֵכוֹ "his thigh"; יְרֵכָהּ "her thigh"; כְּתֵפָם "their shoulder." The plural forms are more common: זְקֵנָיו, זְקֵנֶ֫יהָ, זְקֵנֵ֫ינוּ, זְקֵנַי, זְקֵנֶ֫יךָ.

cal */i/ vowel. Thus, the noun בְּרֵכָה "pool" (pl. abs. בְּרֵכוֹת) exhibits no reduction in the singular construct form בְּרֵכַת or in the plural construct form בְּרֵכוֹת. Similarly, with suffixes, the */ē/ (corresponding to the symbol *tsere* in THT) appears in the propretonic open syllable: גְּנֵבָתוֹ "his theft," מְלֵאָתְךָ "your full harvest." Note also with adjectives טְמֵאַת "unclean of" (abs. טְמֵאָה) and מְלֵאַת "full of" (abs. מְלֵאָה). There are exceptions to this, including the word נְבֵלָה "carcass," which usually appears with the expected vowel elision and shift of initial */a/ to /i/ (e.g., const. נִבְלַת, נִבְלָתוֹ).[22] Note, however, the form נְבֵלָתִי at Isa 26:19.

4.5. Peculiarities of Some Possessive Suffixes

Note that although most suffixes that occur on the single consonantal prepositions (i.e., בְּ "in, with" and לְ "to") are analogous to those suffixes that occur on singular nouns, there are four slight distinctions between the two paradigms. In each case, the suffix on the preposition takes an */ā/ connecting vowel and the suffix on the noun takes */ē/ or no vowel:

- לָךְ "to you (fs)" versus דָּמֵךְ "your (fs) blood"
- לָ֫נוּ "to us" versus יָדֵ֫נוּ "our hand"
- לָכֶם "to you (mp)" versus דִּמְכֶם (= *dimkɛm*) "your (mp) blood"
- לָהֶם "to them (mp)" versus יָדָם "their hand."[23]

The third masculine singular suffix occasionally appears with a *he mater*, instead of a *vav mater* (e.g., כֻּלֹּה "all of it" 2 Sam 2:9). This seems to be an inheritance from an earlier orthography, reflected in First Temple era ostraca and inscriptions, where the third-person masculine singular pronominal suffix was uniformly written with a *he mater*. The earlier form of the suffix, *-*ahu* (which became *-*ō* [perhaps due to elision of the *he* and contraction of the two vowels]), helps explain the use of *he* as a *mater* for this pronominal suffix. All the same, note that word final *-*ō* was also marked with *he* in the infinitive absolute of III-*vav*/*yod* verbs (e.g., רָאֹה "seeing"), as well as in words like פַּרְעֹה "Pharaoh."[24]

22. Nouns of the **qitalat* base are rare.

23. In addition, the 2fp and 3fp suffixes show a similar distribution between preposition and noun.

24. See Eric D. Reymond, "The 3ms Suffix on Nouns Written with *Heh* Mater," in *"Like ʾIlu Are You Wise": Studies in Northwest Semitic Languages and Literatures in*

The second-person masculine singular suffix on prepositions and nouns exhibits different vowels depending on whether it appears in context or pause. Most students learn the contextual form as part of the paradigm: לְךָ "to you (ms)" and יָדְךָ "your (ms) blood." In pause, the preposition plus second-person masculine singular suffix is identical to the second-person feminine singular suffix (in pause or context): לָךְ "to you (ms in pause or fs in pause or context)." In pause, the singular noun plus second-person masculine singular suffix attests an /ɛ/ (instead of *shewa*) after the last consonant of the word's stem: דָּמֶ֫ךָ "your (m.s.) blood"; דְּבָרֶ֫ךָ "your word"; עֲצָתֶ֫ךָ* "your counsel."

According to the rules of vowel reduction outlined above, the contextual form of the noun plus suffix is a bit difficult to account for; that is, יָדְךָ < **yādəˈkā* seems to evidence vowel reduction in the pretonic syllable and vowel lengthening in the propretonic syllable. This likely reflects an earlier form with a full short vowel in the penultimate syllable, which was accented (**yadaka* > **yāˈdakā*); the accent subsequently shifted to the final syllable and the formerly accented /a/ vowel reduced (**yādəˈkā*).[25] That the historical form of the suffix contained a preceding full vowel, not *shewa* (e.g., **-aka*) is suggested by the Secunda, where we find ιεσαχα (cf. יִשְׁעֶךָ [analogous to a pausal form, though in the MT it should be a contextual form]) "your salvation" (Ps 18:36) and elsewhere a shorter form, σεδκαχ (cf. צִדְקֶ֫ךָ, in pause) "your righteousness" (Ps 35:28).[26] It seems possible that a form like דְּבָרְךָ would have been articulated as something like *dəbārak* (with ultimate accent) in the era from 200 BCE to 100 CE (especially since this seems to reflect RH). However, the presence of a long vowel after the *kaph* in this same time period (i.e., */ā/, like that implied by the THT *qamets*) is presupposed by the many spellings of the suffix in the DSS with a final *he mater*: דברכה "your word" (e.g., 1QHᵃ XII, 36), implying perhaps the articulation **dəbārakā*.

When feminine plural nouns attest a third-person masculine/feminine plural suffix, sometimes the heavy suffix characteristic of the masculine plural nouns is used (i.e., ־הֶם- and ־הֶן-), though in a majority of cases (especially in earlier texts) the simple nonheavy suffix typical of singular

Honor of Dennis G. Pardee, ed. H. Hardy, Joseph Lam, and Eric D. Reymond (Chicago: Oriental Institute of the University of Chicago, forthcoming).

25. See the explanation above in ch. 3 §5, "Lengthening of Pretonic */i/ and */a/ Vowels and the Place of Stress."

26. Brønno, *Studien*, 144–45.

nouns appears (i.e., ָם- and ָן-). Some nouns attest both types of suffix: בְּנוֹתֵיהֶם "their daughters" (Judg 3:6) and בְּנֹתָם (Gen 34:21). Although it is hard to predict which suffix will appear on which noun, the longer, heavy suffix tends to occur in later texts.[27] For example, the plural of "father" appears with the heavy suffix (אֲבוֹתֵיהֶם) primarily in Ezra, Nehemiah, and Chronicles and with the shorter suffix (אֲבוֹתָם) throughout the MT.[28] On the other hand, certain words occur with primarily one suffix or the other: מִשְׁפָּחָה "clan" occurs with the short suffix over eighty times (מִשְׁפְּחוֹתָם) and with the longer heavy suffix only three times (מִשְׁפְּחוֹתֵיהֶם); contrast this with the distribution of "daughters": בְּנֹתָם occurs just once, but בְּנוֹתֵיהֶם occurs (with and without the *vav mater*) over twenty times.

In some cases the third-person masculine plural suffix appears with a following */ō/ vowel. This expanded form of the pronominal suffix appears on prepositions (e.g., לָמוֹ "to them" Deut 32:35), particles (אֵינֵמוֹ "they are not" Ps 73:5), nouns (e.g., פִּרְיָמוֹ "their fruit" Ps 21:11), and verbs (e.g., שִׁיתֵמוֹ "set them!" Ps 83:14).

4.6. Biconsonantal Bases (Tables 6.1, 6.2, 6.3, 6.4, 6.5, 6.6)

Words with just two obvious root consonants are relatively common in BH. The easiest to inflect are those with historical long vowels in their middle: **qāl*, **qīl*, **qūl*. These words often have a *mater* to mark the long vowel, which never alters or reduces: טוֹב (< **ṭāb*), טוֹבָה, טוֹבִים, טוֹבוֹת "good"; דִּין, דִּינִי "(my) judgment"; רוּחַ, רוּחוֹת "breath." These are classified here as from II-*vav*/*yod* roots, though the *vav* or *yod* is only rarely present as a consonant. *Qal* infinitives construct from II-*yod* and II-*vav* roots have the bases **qīl* and **qūl* (respectively); some of these are listed in dictionaries as nouns (e.g., גִּיל "rejoicing" from גיל and בּוּז "contempt" from בוז). Feminine versions of these bases are easy to identify (e.g., קוֹמָה "height" and קוֹמָתָהּ "her height"; בִּינָה "understanding" and בִּינָתִי "my understanding"; בּוֹשָׁה "shame").

Words from analogous bases with historical short vowels (**qal*, **qil*, **qul*) offer more variations, though they are comparatively fewer in number and follow the tendencies for vowels already outlined in chapter 3. However, note that the */a/ vowel developed in different ways in closed

27. For the appearance of the different suffixes in earlier versus later BH, see most recently Hornkohl, *Ancient Hebrew Periodization*, 135–39.

28. Ibid., 137.

unaccented syllables; it remained */a/ in construct forms (i.e., דַּם "blood of," יַד "hand of"), but seems to have been /i/ or /ɛ/ with suffixes (דִּמְכֶם, יֶדְכֶם).

Feminine nouns of this base, like אָמָה "maid servant," שָׂפָה "lip," and שָׁנָה "year," are inflected normally in the singular (אֲמָתָהּ "her handmaid"; שְׂפָתָם "their lip"; שְׁנָתוֹ "his year"). However, in the plural each of these nouns shows some irregularity. The word "maid servant" exhibits a *he* as a true consonant, אֲמָהוֹת, while "lip" attests a final *tav* as a root consonant, שִׂפְתוֹתָיו "his lips," and "year" has a masculine plural form, שָׁנִים, in addition to a regular feminine plural form, שָׁנוֹת.

Most **qil* nouns attest predictable patterns (e.g., **ʿiṣu* > **ʿiṣ* > **ʿēṣ* > עֵץ). In the cases of בֵּן and שֵׁם, however, the */i/ reduces even in an open pretonic syllable: בְּנִי "my son" and שְׁמִי "my name."[29] In general, the rarity of these types of nouns means that if one encounters an unknown masculine noun with two recognizable root consonants and an */ē/ vowel, most commonly this will be derived from a geminate root, **qill* (on which see below).

Feminine nouns of this base are often derived from I-*vav/yod* and I-*nun* roots. Specifically, nouns of the **qilat* base are often from I-*vav/yod* roots:

- דֵּעָה (from ידע) "knowledge"
- חֵמָה (from יחם) "rage"
- לֵדָה(from ילד) "birthing"
- עֵדָה (from יעד) "assembly"
- עֵצָה(from יעץ) "advice"
- שֵׁנָה (from ישן) "sleep"[30]

Most nouns from the **qilt* base, on the other hand, are *qal* infinitives construct from either I-*vav/yod* or I-*nun* roots:

- גַּ֫עַת (*qal* inf. const. נגע) "touching"[31]

---

29. These words have been described as possibly consisting not of a consonant + vowel + consonant sequence (i.e., **bin*, **šim*), but rather as a vowel-less consonant cluster **bn-* and **šm-*. See Testen, "Significance of Aramaic r < *n," 143–46; Fox, *Semitic Noun Patterns*, 73 n. 13.

30. Though contrast עֵדָה "witness" from עוד.

31. The /a/ vowels are a reflex of the guttural.

- גֶּ֫שֶׁת (*qal* inf. const. נגשׁ) "approaching"
- דַּ֫עַת (*qal* inf. const. ידע) "knowing"
- טַ֫עַת (*qal* inf. const. נטע) "planting"
- לֶ֫כֶת (*qal* inf. const. הלך) "going"
- עֵת (*ʿ*idt* from יעד or *ʿ*int* from ענה) "time"
- צֵאת (*qal* inf. const. יצא) "going out"
- רֶ֫דֶת (*qal* inf. const. ירד) "going down"
- רֶ֫שֶׁת (*qal* inf. const. ירשׁ) "inheriting"
- שֶׁ֫בֶת (*qal* inf. const. ישׁב) "dwelling"
- תֵּת (< **tint*; *qal* inf. const. נתן) "giving"

Note that many of these exhibit a vowel pattern like that of segolate nouns. This extends to forms with suffixes, where the etymological vowel is usually clear (e.g., שִׁבְתִּי "my dwelling" Ps 27:4). There is a general tendency for *qal* infinitives construct to attest segolate or segolate-like vowel patterns.[32]

There are very few words from the **qul* base. One is found in the plural noun מְתִים (< **mutīm*) "men," where the short */u/ vowel has reduced in an open pretonic syllable, as expected.

A subset of words from II-*vav*/*yod* roots exhibit an */ā/ or */ē/ (corresponding to the symbols *qamets* or *tsere* in THT) throughout their inflection; that is, there is no reduction of the vowel between the two root consonants.[33] Many of these words are attested as *qal* active participles of II-*vav*/*yod* roots. For example, the common root קום "to stand" attests a participle קָם, the underlying vowel of which does not reduce though it appears in an open, nontonic/nonpretonic syllable, as in קָמֵיהֶם. In a similar way, the participle of מות "to die," attests a participle, מֵת, whose vowel does not reduce, even in the plural construct מֵתֵי. Nouns that seem to reflect a similar development include the plural of "city" עָרִים (e.g., עָרֵי "cities of") and the nouns עָב "cloud" (עָבֵי) as well as עֵד "witness" (עֵדַי), and נֵר "lamp" (נֵרֹתֶ֫הָ).[34]

Students should remember that words exhibiting the vowel pattern **ē-ā* (corresponding to the symbols *tsere-qamets^he^* in THT), like דֵּעָה, are often from I-*vav*/*yod* roots, while words with the pattern *a-a* or *ε-ε* (in

32. See below on nouns of the **qutul* base and on segolate nouns.

33. See the comments in ch. 3 §9, "Canaanite Shift and Historical */ā/."

34. On the plural of "city," see Huehnergard, "Biblical Hebrew Nominal Patterns," 32 n. 22 with literature.

THT) that end in a *tav* (e.g., דַּ֫עַת) are often *qal* infinitives construct from I-*vav*/*yod* or I-*nun* roots. Also, words (including participles) from II-*vav*/*yod* roots will usually exhibit an */ā/ or */ē/ (corresponding to the symbols *qamets* or *tsere* in THT) that does not alter or reduce in the word's inflection.

4.7. Nouns of the **Qatul* and **Qatāl* Bases (Tables 6.15, 6.16, 6.17, 6.19)

Nouns of these bases exhibit the same forms, such that it is hard to know at first blush to which base a word belongs. In general, words of the **qatul* (fem. **qatulat*) base are adjectives (e.g., גָּבֹהַּ/גְּבֹהָה "high," גָּדוֹל/גְּדוֹלָה "great," טָהוֹר/טְהוֹרָה "clean," קָדוֹשׁ "holy," רָחוֹק/רְחוֹקָה "far," קָרוֹב "near"), while words of the **qatāl* base (excluding words with an Aramaic or Aramaic-like form [on which see below]) are usually *qal* infinitives absolute (e.g., שָׁמוֹר "guard," בָּנוֹה "build").[35] In other cases what appears to be a word from the **qatul* base appears in the plural with a doubled third root consonant and the /u/ vowel preserved: עָמֹק/עֲמֻקִּים "deep." These words are categorized here as from a similar base: **qatull* (see §11 below, "Nouns with Three Root Consonants, One of Which Is Geminated"). That words from the **qatul* base never exhibit vowel reduction of the historical short */u/ vowel is unexpected based on the relatively regular reduction of pretonic short */u/ in other bases. Still, note the lowering of */u/ to */o/ implied in construct forms like גְּדָל־ "great of (loving-kindness)" Ps 145:8; and the *ketiv* of טְהָור־ "pure of (heart)" Prov 22:11.

4.8. Nouns of the **Qutul*, **Qitāl*, and **Qutāl* Bases (Tables 6.17, 6.21)

Nouns of these bases are inflected in an identical manner such that we may discuss them together. In order to determine the base of a given word, one must rely on comparative information or consult a dictionary. As examples, note the following: בְּכוֹר "firstborn" and חֲלוֹם "dream" are of the **qutul* base, as are most *qal* infinitives construct from strong roots (e.g., שְׁמֹר "guarding" and שְׁלֹחַ "sending"). The nouns זְרוֹעַ "arm" and אֱלוֹהַּ "god" are of the **qitāl* base and אֱנוֹשׁ "people" and רְחוֹב "plaza"

35. The word גָּבֹהַּ is not written with a *vav mater*, while the other words commonly are. All the same, the other words are also sometimes written defectively (without the *vav mater*). Such disparity does not reflect distinct etymological bases.

are of the **qutāl* base.[36] Although identifying the precise historical base of words like these is difficult for the novice, inflecting these nouns is easy given the consistent vowel sequence **ə-ō* (corresponding to the symbols *shewa-holem* in THT). This sequence of vowels is found throughout the inflection of nonverbal nouns: the absolute (e.g., בְּכוֹר), construct singular (e.g., בְּכוֹר), construct plural (בְּכוֹרֵי/בְּכֹרוֹת), and suffixed forms (sg. בְּכֹרְךָ/בְּכוֹרִי; pl. בְּכוֹרֵיהֶם). The major exception is provided by the *qal* infinitives construct with suffixes, which usually exhibit the vowels one associates with **qutl* segolate nouns. Note, for example, **šomrō* > שָׁמְרוֹ "his guarding" (1 Sam 19:11) and **šolḥī* > שָׁלְחִי "my sending" (Num 32:8) and compare these to the **qutl* noun + suffix **qodšī* > קָדְשִׁי "my sanctuary" (Lev 20:3).

Nevertheless, the *qal* infinitive construct with suffix reflects the **qutul* base in other ways. First, note that in forms like שָׁמְרוֹ "his guarding," the historical first */u/ vowel is preserved, but the second is not. This may reflect the tendency for pretonic */u/ to dissimilate and reduce (i.e., **šumurahu* > **šumrō* > **šomrō* [> שָׁמְרוֹ]). In addition, with the second-person masculine singular and plural suffix, **qutul* base infinitives in context sometimes (especially after the *lamed* preposition but also without a preposition) attest a /u/-class vowel after the second root consonant (e.g., **lašumuraka* > **lišmorkā* > לִשְׁמָרְךָ "to guard you" Prov 6:24), while **qutl* base nouns in context do not (e.g., **qudšaka* > **qodšakā* > **qodšəkā* > קָדְשְׁךָ "your holy place" Isa 63:15). Furthermore, with other suffixes, **qutul* base infinitives that have a *begadkepat* letter as a third root consonant regularly attest the spirantized allophone, implying the presence of a vowel after the second root consonant in an earlier form of the word (e.g., **puqudiyya* > **poqdī* > פָּקְדִי "my visiting" Jer 27:22; **nuqubahu* > **noqbō* > נָקְבוֹ "his blaspheming" Lev 24:16), while **qutl* base nouns do not (e.g., **ḥuškiyya* > **ḥoškī* > חָשְׁכִּי "my darkness" 2 Sam 22:29; **ruḥbahu* > *roḥbō* > רָחְבּוֹ "its breadth" Exod 25:23).

As for feminine nouns of these bases, it is again difficult to determine their original base. Those of the **qutult* base (some of which might actually be of the **qutālt* base) include כְּתֹנֶת "tunic," נְחֹשֶׁת "copper," קְטֹרֶת "smoke."[37] The ending of these nouns resembles a **qutl* noun. Note, in particular, the presence of an epenthetic vowel (i.e., *segol* in THT) between

36. Huehnergard, "Biblical Hebrew Nominal Patterns," 45, 48–49.
37. Ibid., 45.

the last two consonants. The construct form is the same as the absolute (e.g., קְטֹ֫רֶת can mean "smoke" or "smoke of"). The form with suffixes attests a *qamets* (or *qibbuts*) in place of the *holem* (e.g., **nəḥošti* > נְחָשְׁתִּי, קְטָרְתִּי, נְחֻשְׁתִּי). Feminine nouns of the **qitālat* base, on the other hand, are inflected in a regular manner (e.g., עֲבוֹדָה "labor").[38]

In this group of bases (**qutul*, **qitāl*, and **qutāl*) the initial vowel is short and the second is long, either from its origin (*/ā/ > */ō/) or through later developments (*/u/ > */ō/). The pretonic /u/ vowel reduces, as expected. As noted above, there is a tendency for two high vowels in a word's stem to dissimilate, that is, to change such that the first high vowel becomes dissimilar to the second, in this case becoming *shewa*.[39] This tendency is present after the Canaanite shift has turned */ā/ to */ō/, since /ā/ is not a high vowel and, thus, would not trigger such dissimilation.

Students should remember that the vowel underlying the *holem* in the second syllable of most of these nouns (e.g., גָּדוֹל, חֲלֹם, זְרוֹעַ, אֱנוֹשׁ) does not shift or reduce in the inflection (the primary exception being in the *qal* inf. const.).

4.9. Nouns of the **Qātil* Base (Table 6.18)

Nouns of this base are primarily associated with *qal* active participles (e.g., כֹּתֵב "one who writes"; שֹׁמֵר "one who guards"). Nevertheless, in some cases, the nouns of this base are listed as individual words in dictionaries (e.g., אֹיֵב "enemy"; כֹּהֵן "priest"; שֹׁפֵט "judge"); still, they inflect just like participles.

Often the feminine singular form of the participle derives from the base **qātilt*, which results in an ending that exhibits a vowel pattern like that of a segolate noun: **yālidt* > **yōlidt* > **yōlɛdt* > יֹלֶ֫דֶת "one who bears." In rare cases, the feminine singular participle exhibits a form derived from **qātilat* (e.g., בֹּעֲרָה "one burning" Isa 30:33).

Usually, the */i/ of the stem (**qātil*) reduces to *shewa* when it is in the pretonic syllable because the initial vowel cannot reduce: **hālikīma* > **hōlikīm* > **hōləkīm* (> הֹלְכִים) "those going"; **hālikāt* > **hōlikōt* > **hōləkōt* (> הֹלְכוֹת). One irregularity, however, appears in the contextual form of the masculine singular **qātil* noun with second-person masculine singu-

38. Ibid., 48.

39. See ch. 3 §5, "Lengthening of Pretonic */i/ and */a/ Vowels and the Place of Stress." See also Garr, "Pretonic Vowels in Hebrew," 143, 150.

lar suffix. The vowel after the second root consonant is either an /i/, /ɛ/, or /a/ in THT: אֹיִבְךָ "your enemy" (Exod 23:4); יֹצֶרְךָ "one forming you" (Isa 43:1); בֹּרַאֲךָ "one creating you" (Isa 43:1).[40] This reflects the elision of a vowel between the stem and the suffix (i.e., *ʾōyibakā > *ʾōyibkā > אֹיִבְךָ). The pausal form, on the other hand, does reflect a vowel between the stem and base (i.e., *ʾōyibakā > ʾōyəbakā > ʾoybɛkå = אֹיְבֶךָ). In addition, when feminine plural participles are used as substantives, the historical */i/ sometimes does not reduce, helping to distinguish the substantival nature of the word (e.g., הוֹלֵלוֹת "madness"; עוֹלֵלוֹת "gleanings").[41]

In the feminine singular form with suffix, the short */i/ shifts to */ɛ/ then /a/ in THT: *yālidtaha > *yōlɛdtaha (> *yoladtåh = יֹלַדְתָּהּ) "one who bore her"; *yālidtVkum > *yōlɛdtVkem > *yōladtəkem (> יֹלַדְתְּכֶם) "one who bore you." Nevertheless, the *qātilat form of the feminine singular participle often expresses the historical */i/ vowel clearly: יוֹלֵדָה.

4.10. Other Nouns with Long Vowels (without Gemination) (Tables 6.20, 6.21)

Many nouns with three root consonants derive from a base that includes a long vowel. Since historical long vowels never reduce, the inflection of these nouns requires little comment. Note, for example, the regular absolute forms of the *qal* passive participle which derive from the *qatūl(at) base: כָּתוּב, כְּתוּבָה, כְּתוּבִים, כְּתוּבוֹת "that which is written." In the case of III-*vav*/*yod* roots, the *yod* appears as a third root consonant and the vowel sequence is preserved (e.g., בָּנוּי, בְּנוּיָה, בְּנוּיִם, "that which is built").[42] In addition, there are many nouns of this pattern: בְּתוּלָה "maiden," זָכוּר "remembrance," יְשׁוּעָה "salvation," שָׁבוּעַ "week," שְׁבוּעָה "oath."

Words of the *qatīl(at) base are often classified as adjectives: חָסִיד "pious"; יָמִין "south, right"; כָּלִיל "complete"; נָעִים "pleasant"; צָעִיר "little." However, a fair number are also commonly used as substantives to describe a type of person: אָסִיר "prisoner"; בָּחִיר "chosen one"; מָשִׁיחַ "anointed one"; נָבִיא "prophet"; נָגִיד "leader"; נָזִיר "Nazirite"; נָשִׂיא "prince"; סָרִיס "high official, eunuch"; פָּלִיט "survivor"; שָׂרִיד "survivor." Other words from this base are associated with agriculture: אָסִיף "harvest"; בָּצִיר "vintage"; זָמִיר

40. Note also שֹׁלֵחֲךָ "one sending you" (1 Sam 21:3).

41. See Garr, "Pretonic Vowels in Hebrew," 145.

42. In relation to בְּנוּיִם, it was scribal convention not to include a *vav* or *yod mater* when such a *mater* would have come directly after a true *vav* or *yod* consonant.

"trimming of vines"; חָרִישׁ "ploughing"; קָצִיר "harvest."[43] Roots whose third root consonant is *vav/yod* attest the same vowel sequence, though without a final root consonant: נָקִי "innocent"; עָנִי "poor." The underlying historical vowel sequence (**a-ī*) is also reflected in the feminine singular, the masculine and feminine plural, and with pronominal suffixes, in each case where the historical III-*yod* is preserved through gemination: עֲנִיָּה, עֲנִיִּים, עֲנִיָּו, and so on.

Nouns of the **qutūl* base often exhibit the reduction of the first */u/, as expected for a pretonic /u/ in an open syllable: גְּבוּל "territory"; גְּדוּד "band"; זְבוּב "flies"; יְבוּל "produce." Note the plural nouns that indicate a period in a person's life: בְּחוּרוֹת "youth (i.e., time of being young)"; בְּתוּלִים "virginity"; זְקוּנִים "old age"; נְעוּרִים "youth (i.e., time of being young)"; עֲלוּמִים "youth (i.e., time of being young)."

Nouns that look to be of the **qātal* base may ultimately derive from other roots (e.g., כּוֹכָב "star" from **kwb*; עוֹלָם "eternity" perhaps from **ʿwl*; עוֹלָל "child" from **ʿwl*) or from other languages (e.g., חוֹתָם "seal" is Egyptian in origin).[44]

Nouns of the **qatāl* base often refer to occupations and may be connected to, in some remote way, a similar nominal form in Aramaic. Note, for example, אָמוֹן "craftsman"; בָּגוֹדָה "traitor"; עָשׁוֹק "oppressor"; צָרוֹף "metalsmith."[45]

4.11. Nouns with Three Root Consonants, One of Which Is Geminated (Table 6.22)

Nouns from strong roots sometimes attest gemination of the second or third consonant. As for those that exhibit gemination of the second root consonant, their inflection is generally easy to predict since the gemination preserves the short vowel of the first syllable throughout the inflection. The vowel of the second syllable is lengthened or reduced, depending on the normal rules for vowel lengthening/reduction outlined above.

Of these words, nouns of the **qattal*, **qattil*, and **qattīl* bases are perhaps the most common. Words of the **qattal* base often indicate a

---

43. See *HGhS*, 471pα–rα. Still other words do not fit into any of these categories: הֲלִיכָה "going"; פְּתִיל "thread"; שָׂעִיר "billy-goat."

44. See Huehnergard, "Biblical Hebrew Nominal Patterns," 49–50; also, Fox, *Semitic Noun Patterns*, 289–90.

45. On words from this base, see Hornkohl, *Ancient Hebrew Periodization*, 148–52.

person who does the activity associated with the root (e.g., גַּנָּב "thief"; דַּיָּן "judge"; חַטָּא "sinner"; טַבָּח "cook"; עַוָּל "criminal"). Two frequent nouns of this base have a medial *resh* that results in compensatory lengthening of the initial */a/: חָרָשׁ "craftsperson" and פָּרָשׁ "horse rider."[46] Feminine nouns of the **qattalt* and **qattalat* base often have negative connotations: בַּלָּהָה "terror"; בַּצָּרָה "drought"; חַטָּאָה/חַטָּאת (< **ḫaṭṭaʾat*/**ḫaṭṭaʾt*) "sin"; יַבֶּלֶת "wart"; יַלֶּפֶת "scabs"; צָרַעַת "leprosy."[47] Note also the medial guttural nouns בֶּהָלָה "horror," לֶהָבָה "flame," which exhibit the shift of */a/ to /ɛ/ in THT as in the word הֶהָרִים (see above).

The relatively common noun שַׁבָּת "sabbath" seems to be a masculine noun from this base; however, the final feminine /t/ morpheme has dropped off in the absolute (**šabbattu* > **šabbāt*). With suffixes it is preserved: שַׁבַּתּוֹ "his sabbath." The word חַטָּאת "sin" exhibits compensatory lengthening in most singular forms (e.g., חַטָּאתָם "their sin"), except in the construct and in related forms (e.g., חַטַּאת "sin of" and חַטַּאתְכֶם "your sin"). In the plural, there is no compensatory lengthening because a vowel follows the *aleph*: **ḫaṭṭaʾātu* > **ḫaṭṭaʾōt* > **ḫaṭṭāʾōt* (> חַטָּאוֹת). But, another phonetic transformation is evidenced in the construct plural and in forms with suffixes: what should be a vocal *shewa* (derived from a historical short */a/ vowel) is elided, reflecting (all things being equal) the development: **ḫaṭṭaʾātu* > **ḫaṭṭaʾōt* > **ḫaṭṭəʾōt* > *ḫaṭṭōt* (> חַטֹּאות). Note the peculiar spelling. Although both the plural absolute and plural construct are spelled in THT with a *vav mater*, the *holem* appears after the *tet* in the plural construct.

In some words, the historical */a/ presupposed by the THT *qamets* does not reduce, as in בַּקָּרַת "care of" (Ezek 34:12); בַּקָּשָׁתִי "my request" (Esth 5:7 and elsewhere); בַּקָּשָׁתוֹ "his request" (Ezra 7:6); חָרָשֵׁי "engravers of" (2 Sam 5:11 and elsewhere); מַלָּחֵיהֶם "their sailors" (Ezek 27:9); נֶחָמָתִי "my comfort" (Ps 119:50; Job 6:10). These nouns, thus, look like Aramaic words, which attest a long vowel /ā/ that derives from PS (e.g., Aramaic

46. Although the word מַלָּח "sailor" is often construed as a member of this base, derived from the Hebrew word for salt (מֶלַח) like English "saltee" from "salt," it is rather a loanword, from Aramaic *mallāḥ* (or *mallāḫ*), which language also attests a verb *mlḥ*/*mlḫ* "to steer, guide." (The Aramaic word derives from Akkadian *malāḫu* which is in turn derived from Sumerian). See, e.g., Aaron D. Rubin, "Sumerian Loanwords," *EHLL* 3:665–66.

47. There are exceptions, of course, like חָרָבָה "dry ground," טַבַּעַת "seal ring," יַבָּשָׁה/יַבֶּשֶׁת "dry land."

דַּיָּנִין "judges" Ezra 7:25 and קַטָּלָה [the D-stem infinitive] "to execute" Dan 2:14).[48]

Nonverbal words of the *qattil base have undergone a shift such that the initial */a/ has shifted to */i/: ʿawwir > ʿiwwēr > עִוֵּר "blind." As in this example, many words of this base describe aspects of a person's physique: אִלֵּם "dumb"; גִּבֵּחַ "bald"; גִּבֵּן "hunch-backed"; חֵרֵשׁ "deaf"; כֵּהֶה "dim"; פִּסֵּחַ "lame"; פִּקֵּחַ "able to see"; קֵרֵחַ "bald." In other cases, the word is a simple adjective: גֵּאֶה "arrogant" and עִקֵּשׁ "twisted."[49] Often these words seem to have negative connotations. The same base supplies the forms of the *piel qåṭal*, דִּבֵּר "he spoke" (pausal), and infinitive construct, דַּבֵּר "speak." Due to an affinity between the infinitive construct and the *yiqṭol* (e.g., יְדַבֵּר), the *piel* infinitive construct has maintained the original first stem vowel.[50]

Words of the *qattīl base are often adjectives with positive connotations: אַבִּיר "strong"; אַדִּיר "mighty"; אַמִּיץ "strong"; כַּבִּיר "great"; צַדִּיק "righteous." As with *qatīl base words, some of these are used as substantives referring to persons: אַסִּיר "prisoner," שַׁלִּיט "ruler."

Among the other bases with geminated middle consonants, mention should be made of the *quttul base, which shifted to *qittul and then to *qittōl, as in גִּבּוֹר "warrior," צִפּוֹר "bird," and שִׁכּוֹר "drunk."[51] Feminine nouns include שִׁבֹּלֶת "ear of grain."[52] A similar shift took place with *quttūl nouns, which most commonly occur in the masculine plural: בִּכּוּרִים "first fruits"; גִּדּוּפִים "defamation"; כִּפֻּרִים "atonement"; מִלּוּאִים "consecration."

Bases of nouns whose third consonant geminates are often associated with other, previously described bases. In part, this is due to the regular loss of gemination at the end of a singular absolute word. Thus, *qatall nouns became *qatal in this environment and then went through the same transformations that led from *dabar to דָּבָר. Subsequently, these two cat-

---

48. Stadel, "Aramaic Influences on Biblical Hebrew," 1:162–65. As noted above (ch. 3 §9, "Canaanite Shift and Historical */ā/"), Huehnergard ("Biblical Hebrew Nominal Patterns," 51) suggests, based on Akkadian evidence, that such Hebrew words may ultimately derive from *qattal and *qattalat.

49. As with feminine plural words of the *qātil base, where the pretonic */i/ lowers and lengthens in substantives and does not reduce, so also with some masc. pl. words of the *qattil base that function as substantives. Thus, one finds שִׁלֵּשִׁים "third generations" and רִבֵּעִים "fourth generations" (see Garr, "Pretonic Vowels in Hebrew," 145).

50. See Huehnergard, "Biblical Hebrew Nominal Patterns," 52.

51. See ibid., 53–54.

52. See ibid., 54.

egories of nouns (i.e., **qatal* and **qatall*) became indistinguishable in the absolute. Words that exhibit the **qatall* base in their paradigm include: קָטָן "small" (קְטַנָּה, קְטַנֵּי, קְטַנִּם, etc.); גָּמָל "camel" (גְּמַלָּיו, גְּמַלִּים).[53]

Similar mergers and confusion pertain to **qatull*, which became **qatul* and then **qātōl*, making the absolute singular of such words look identical to historical **qatul* nouns. Here evidence from other Semitic languages suggests that many color terms are etymologically **qatull* (e.g., אָדֹם "red" [אֲדֻמִּים, אֲדֻמָּה]; and עָקֹד "striped" [עֲקֻדִּים]; as well as שָׁחֹר "black" [שְׁחֹרָה, שְׁחֹרִים]).[54]

As for other bases, the base **qutull* exhibits the same dissimilation of high vowels found in other nouns discussed above. Thus, the initial */u/ vowel is reduced to *shewa*: לְאֹם "people" (pl. לְאֻמִּים). As for the feminine base, **qutullat* is "found almost exclusively as an abstract action noun" (e.g., גְּאֻלָּה "redemption"; חֲנֻכָּה "dedication").[55]

4.12. *Aleph-*, *Yod-*, *Mem-*, and *Tav*-Preformative Nouns

Biblical Hebrew attests numerous words formed, in part, by the supplementation of a consonant to the beginning of the root. One of the rarest of these prefixal consonants is the *aleph*: אַכְזָב "deceitful," אַלְמָנָה "widow," אֶשְׁכֹּל "grape bunch." In some cases, *aleph*-preformative words are byforms of words that begin with a consonant + *shewa* אֶזְרוֹעַ/זְרוֹעַ "arm," צְעָדָה "anklet"/ אֶצְעָדָה "bracelet." Also rare are those nouns with a preformative *yod*: יִצְהָר "oil," יָרִיב "adversary," and יְקוּם "existence."

Mem-preformative nouns are the most frequent of this set and most fall into one of four categories, based on their historical vowels: **maqtal*, **maqtil*, **maqtul*, and **maqtāl*. For most strong roots, the historical short */a/ following the preformative *mem* has shifted to /i/ or /ɛ/ at a relatively late date (in the Common Era). Where the first root consonant is a guttural, however, the */a/ has often been preserved (מַעֲשֶׂה "deed"); the same sometimes happens when the first root consonant is a *lamed*, *mem*, or *nun* (e.g., מַמְלָכָה "kingdom," מַתָּן "gift"). In addition, nouns of II-*vav*/*yod* roots preserve the initial /a/ vowel (e.g., מָקוֹם "place"). There is also some incon-

53. See ibid., 56.
54. Fox, *Semitic Noun Patterns*, 285.
55. Ibid.

sistency evidenced in the MT itself (e.g., מִכְמֹ֫רֶת "net" Isa 19:8 and מַכְמֹרָיו "his nets" Ps 141:10).[56]

Words of the **maqtal* base are the most frequent. With the strong roots or with gutturals, it is often clear what the relevant root consonants are and there is rarely confusion about whether or not the initial *mem* might be a root consonant. Note, for example, מַאֲכָל "food," מִבְחָר "choice element," מִבְצָר "fortified city," מִבְטָח "trust," מִגְדָּל "tower," מִדְבָּר "desert," מַהֲלָךְ "passage," מַלְאָךְ "messenger," מִסְפָּר "number," מִשְׁמָר "guard," מִשְׁפָּט "judgment." In all these cases, the inflection of the nouns is entirely predictable. The vowel of the initial syllable is in a closed syllable and so it never alters or changes from the lexical (or dictionary) form. The historical */a/ in the second syllable is entirely like the second short */a/ vowel in **dabar*. Note, for example, מִשְׁפָּטִים and מִשְׁפָּטוֹ, מִשְׁפָּטָיו, as well as מִשְׁפְּטֵיכֶם.

Feminine nouns of this base (i.e., **maqtalt*, **maqtalat*) are also easily recognizable with strong roots or roots with gutturals. Note that **maqtalt* nouns (e.g., מַאֲכֶלֶת "food," מִשְׁמֶ֫רֶת "guard, obligation") seem to be fewer than **maqtalat* nouns (מַחֲשָׁבָה "thought," מִלְחָמָה "war," מַמְלָכָה "kingdom," מֶמְשָׁלָה "dominion"). Nevertheless, the two forms of feminine nouns are closely associated with each other since nouns of the **maqtalat* base appear to be of the **maqtalt* base in the construct and with suffixes (e.g., מַחֲשֶׁבֶת [const.] / מַחֲשַׁבְתּוֹ [+ 3ms]; מִלְחֶמֶת [const.] / מִלְחַמְתָּהּ [+ 3fs]; מַמְלֶכֶת [const.] / מַמְלַכְתּוֹ [+ 3ms]; מֶמְשֶׁלֶת [const.] / מֶמְשַׁלְתּוֹ [+ 3ms]). There is just one absolute plural form for these types of feminine noun: מִלְחָמוֹת, מַאֲכָלוֹת.

Words from I-*nun* roots are slightly more difficult to recognize as *mem*-preformative nouns since the same sequence of vowels may also reflect a **qattal* base. All the same, *mem*-preformative nouns from I-*nun* roots are comparatively common (e.g., מַכָּה "wound" from נכה *hiphil* "to strike"; מַשָּׂא "burden" from נשׂא "to lift"; מַתָּן "gift" from נתן "to give.").

Words from I-*vav*/*yod* roots exhibit a *vav* or *yod mater* after the *mem* prefix, reflecting the contraction of a diphthong. Thus, what was **mawṯabu* "dwelling place" has shifted to **mōšab*, then **mōšāb* and finally מוֹשָׁב. Similarly, **mayšarīma* "uprightness" shifted to **mēšarīm* before then becoming **mēšārīm* and then מֵישָׁרִים.

56. See Sperber, *Historical Grammar*, 451.

Words from II-*vav/yod* roots have shifted to **maqāl* and then **māqōl*. For example, note מָבוֹא "entrance," מָקוֹם "place," מָקוֹר "source," מָרוֹם "height." The historical */ā/ that shifted to */ō/ does not reduce or shift in the inflection of these nouns.

III-*vav/yod* nouns from the **maqtal/*maqtal(a)t* base offer little confusion in their absolute singular forms: מִבְנֶה "building," מַעֲלֶה "ascent," מַעֲלָה "stairs," מַעֲנֶה "answer," מַעֲשֶׂה "deed," מַרְאֶה "appearance, seeing." As explained above, the word-final vowel is the result of a triphthong contraction. Similar contractions have resulted in the loss of the final vowel of the original stem in the plural (and with suffixes) such that these nouns usually exhibit no trace of the third root consonant (e.g., מַעֲשֶׂהוּ, מַעֲשִׂים, מַעֲשָׂיו; מַעֲלֹתָו, מַעֲלוֹת).

Words from other *mem*-preformative bases attest similar patterns to those outlined above for **maqtal*. Note **maqtil* and **maqtil(a)t* (מַגֵּפָה [from נגף] "plague," מוֹעֵד [from יעד] "designated time," מִזְבֵּחַ "altar," מַצֵּבָה and מַצֶּבֶת [from נצב] "standing stone," מַרְפֵּא "healing," מַשְׂאֵת [from נשׂא] "elevation, tribute"). The short */i/ vowel reduces to *shewa* in the plural of **maqtil* nouns (מִזְבְּחוֹת/מִזְבֵּחַ "altar"), though sometimes the */i/ does not reduce (e.g., מַגֵּפֹתַי "my plagues" Exod 9:14). In some cases, the root is geminate. In these cases, the vowel sequence is distinct from those above, but the identification of the root and its inflection offer no problems (the initial two syllables are always the same): מְגִלָּה and construct מְגִלַּת (from גלל) "scroll (of)," מְזִמָּה and pl. abs./const. מְזִמּוֹת (from זמם) "plot(s [of])"; מְסִלָּה and מְסִלּוֹתָם (from סלל) "(their) highway(s)."

Words associated with the **maqtul* base are relatively rare. It is noteworthy, however that several feminine nouns of this base (which derive from II-*vav/yod* roots) are byforms of **maqtal/*maqāl* nouns: מְנוּחָה versus מָנוֹחַ "resting place"; מְנוּסָה versus מָנוֹס "flight"; מְצוּדָה versus מָצוֹד "mountain stronghold"; מְצוּקָה versus מָצוֹק "distress"; מְצוּרָה versus מָצוֹר "distress." Words of the **maqtāl* base, on the other hand, are sometimes byforms of strong root **maqtal* nouns: מִבְחוֹר versus מִבְחָר "choice thing"; מִשְׁקוֹל versus מִשְׁקָל "weight." In other cases, no byform exists: מִזְמוֹר "song," מִכְשׁוֹל "stumbling."

Tav-preformative nouns are less frequent than the *mem*-preformatives. They also attest words from I-*vav* (תּוֹרָה "law") and I-*yod* (תֵּימָן "south") roots. The same types of bases found with *mem*-preformatives are also found for *tav*-preformatives (e.g., **taqtalat* תִּפְאָרָה "glory"; **taqtilat* תּוֹכֵחָה "rebuke" [also **taqtilt* תּוֹכַחַת "rebuke"]; **taqtulat* from II-*vav/yod* roots תְּשׁוּבָה "return"). Note also the nouns from geminate roots: תְּהִלָּה

"beginning," תְּפִלָּה "prayer." Moreover, the *taqtūl* base (e.g., תַּעֲנוּג "pleasure," תַּחֲנוּנִים "pleading," תַּנְחוּמִים "comforts") seems more common than the analogous *maqtūl* base (e.g., מַלְבּוּשׁ "robe"). As can be seen from this brief list, these *tav*-preformative words are often feminine in gender and often express an act or abstraction. Like some *mem*-preformative words (מַצֵּבָה and מַצֶּבֶת "standing stone"), some *tav*-preformative nouns exhibit byforms; note especially תִּפְאָרָה and תִּפְאֶרֶת "beauty." Inflection of these nouns is entirely predictable.

Students should remember especially that feminine *mem*-preformative nouns of the **maqtalat* pattern will often exhibit a **maqtalt* pattern in the construct and before suffixes (מַחְשָׁבָה vs. מַחֲשֶׁבֶת [const.] and מַחֲשַׁבְתּוֹ). In addition, notice that a *mater vav* or *yod* after a word-initial *mem* or *tav* often signals a I-*vav*/*yod* root (e.g., תּוֹרָה/מוֹשָׁב; and תֵּימָן/מֵישָׁרִים).

4.13. Nouns with Afformatives

Hebrew nouns attest a wide variety of afformative elements that attach to the stem of a noun. The most common is *-*ōn* (< *-*ān*), appearing as part of the base **qatalān*, **qattalān* and as part of a variety of other bases. The nouns from the **qattalān* base almost always appear only in the absolute singular; the other forms of the noun are based on **qatalān* (e.g., זִכָּרוֹן "remembrance" vs. זִכְרוֹן [const.] and זִכְרוֹנֵךְ as well as זִכְרֹנוֹת [abs. pl.] and זִכְרֹנֵיכֶם). In this and most other words of this base, the initial historical */a/ has shifted to /i/ (חִזָּיוֹן "vision," נִקָּיוֹן "innocence," עִוָּרוֹן "blindness," שִׁבָּרוֹן "destruction"), though there are exceptions (שַׁבָּתוֹן "rest"). Words from II-*vav*/*yod* roots include שָׂשׂוֹן "joy" and זָדוֹן "arrogance." In the inflection of these words, the historical */a/ of the first syllable reduces to *shewa* (e.g., שְׂשׂוֹן [const.] and זְדוֹנְךָ). In some cases listed above, the III-*yod* is preserved (e.g., חִזָּיוֹן); in other cases, the III-*yod* has elided entirely and the second root consonant does not geminate (e.g., גָּאוֹן [from גאה] "pride"; הָמוֹן [from המה] "turmoil, noise, crowd"; חָזוֹן [from חזה] "vision"; רָצוֹן [from רצה] "favor"). The inflection of these III-*vav*/*yod* words is otherwise entirely regular. As can be seen from this list, most of these words are abstractions or intangible items.

Many adjectives are formed with the afformative *-*ōn* (<*-*ān*). These include אֶבְיוֹן "poor," אַחֲרוֹן "last," חִיצוֹן "outside," עֶלְיוֹן "most high," *קַדְמוֹן "eastern," רִאשׁוֹן "first," תִּיכוֹן "middle." A variety of nouns also bear this suffix, including אִישׁוֹן "pupil of eye (lit., little person)," יִתְרוֹן "profit." The inflection of these nouns is entirely regular. The vowel of the initial closed syllable remains stable in BH (e.g., אַחֲרֹנָה and אַחֲרֹנִים "last"). A small minority of words contain an *-*ān* ending (> THT -*ån*) in the suffix instead of *-*ōn*, as though the word derives from Aramaic: בִּנְיָן "building"; קִנְיָן "property"; קָרְבָּן "offering"; שֻׁלְחָן "table." However, in contrast to other forms associated with Aramaic, these nouns exhibit shortening of the vowel of the afformative in the construct and with heavy suffixes (e.g., קִנְיַן [const.], קָרְבַּנְכֶם).

Other frequently encountered afformatives include the *-*iyy* > *-*ī* gentilic ending (e.g., אֲרַמִּי "Aramaean," כְּנַעֲנִי "Canaanite," עִבְרִי "Hebrew"). The ending is also a part of various other adjectives (e.g., אַכְזָרִי "cruel," חָפְשִׁי "free," נָכְרִי "foreign," שְׁלִישִׁי "third"), some of which are used as substantives (e.g., רַגְלִי "foot soldier"). The inflection of these kinds of words usually results in the doubling of the *yod*: עִבְרִיָּה, עִבְרִיִּים, and עִבְרִיּוֹת.[57] Often in the masculine plural, the *-*iyyī*- sequence of vowels and *yod* contracted to simply *-*ī*-, as in עִבְרִים. Sometimes the feminine form of such a noun ends with *-*īt*: מוֹאָבִית "Moabite" (vs. מוֹאֲבִיָּה). In some cases, the *-*ī* afformative was attached to the *-*ōn* afformative, like קַדְמוֹנִי "eastern," אַדְמוֹנִי "red."

Two endings are associated with abstract nouns, *-*īt* (e.g., אַחֲרִית "end," חִתִּית "terror," רֵאשִׁית "beginning," שְׁאֵרִית "remnant") and *-*ūt* (e.g., דְּמוּת "likeness," זְנוּת "unfaithfulness," יַלְדוּת "childhood, youth," כְּסוּת "covering," מַלְכוּת "kingship"). These words are regular in their inflection; usually the initial closed syllable means that there is little change in the stem with a suffix (e.g., אַחֲרִיתָהּ "its end"). In some cases, an */ā/ (> THT /å/) appears in the initial syllable and is present throughout the inflection (e.g., גָּלוּת "exile," גָּלוּתֵנוּ "our exile"; חָזוּת "vision," חָזוּתְכֶם "your vision").

The last afformative element we address marks adverbs and seems to be derived from the old accusative ending */a/ followed by a word final *mem*.[58] This developed into Hebrew *-*ām* (> -*åm*) and is found on words like אָמְנָם/אֻמְנָם "truly," חִנָּם "undeservedly," יוֹמָם "daily," פִּתְאֹם "suddenly," רֵיקָם "in vain."

---

57. The gemination of *yod* is also found in *qatīl* base nouns/adjectives from III-*vav*/*yod* roots: עֲנִיָּה. In these cases, the gemination helps preserve the preceding /i/ vowel. See Bergsträsser, *Hebräische Grammatik*, 1:102.

58. See *IBHS*, 93 n. 29. This *mem* is often called enclitic. It has no discernible semantic value in other languages, like Ugaritic.

4.14. I-*Aleph*, I-*Nun*, and I-*Vav*/*Yod* Nouns

Nouns from I-*aleph* roots sometimes exhibit full vowels where we would otherwise expect a *shewa* or *khatef* vowel. For example, as explained above, the initial */i/ of the *qitāl base usually is realized in BH as a *shewa* (e.g., זְרוֹעַ "arm"). In the case of אֵזוֹר "loincloth," however, the */i/ has become */ē/. Similarly, the short */u/ shifts to a reduced vowel in most *qutūl nouns (e.g., גְּבוּל "territory"), but with a I-*aleph*, the */u/ shifts to */i/ and then to */ē/ (e.g., אֵסוּר "bonds").[59]

Nouns from roots with a *nun* or *vav*/*yod* as initial root consonant exhibit peculiar forms, which can sometimes make identifying their root difficult. This, in turn, creates difficulty in making an educated guess about the meaning of an unfamiliar word. In many instances, words from I-*nun* roots have lost the initial root consonant, such that they look like they are not from a I-*nun* root. This is sometimes the case with words of the *qilt base (גֶּשֶׁת "approaching" *qal* inf. const. נגשׁ), discussed above. Where the base has a preformative *mem*, the *nun* will often assimilate: מַכָּה "wound" from נכה *hiphil* "to strike" and מַתָּן "gift" from נתן "to give."[60]

Words from I-*vav*/*yod* roots appear from the *qilat (עֵדָה "assembly") and *qilt bases (רֶ֫דֶת "going down" *qal* inf. const. ירד), as discussed above, where the first root consonant has totally disappeared. Where a preformative *mem* or *tav* attaches to the beginning of such a root, one can recognize the historical root consonant. A I-*vav* root will often attest an */ō/ vowel with *vav mater* (e.g., מוֹשָׁב "dwelling place" from ישׁב "to dwell"; תּוֹדָה "thanksgiving" from ידה *hiphil* "to give thanks") and a I-*yod* root will attest */ē/ with a *yod mater* (מֵישָׁרִים "integrity" from ישׁר "to be straight"; תֵּימָן "south" from ימן *hiphil* "to go to the right").

4.15. II-*Vav*/*Yod* Nouns

Nouns of II-*vav*/*yod* roots often appear with a historical long vowel between their first and last consonants, as discussed above (e.g., טוֹב "good" from טוב and בִּינָה "understanding" from בין), though there are rare exceptions (e.g., עָוֶל "iniquity"). Words from *qal and *qil bases attest */ā/ and */ē/ vowels throughout their inflection (e.g., the participles קָם and מֵת as well

59. See Huehnergard, "Biblical Hebrew Nominal Patterns," 49.

60. On nouns with preformative elements, see above.

as the nouns עָב "cloud" and נֵר "lamp"). Note, for example, the construct form of the feminine singular participle of זוב in the famous expression אֶ֫רֶץ זָבַת חָלָב וּדְבָשׁ "a land flowing with milk and honey."

4.16. III-*Vav*/*Yod* Nouns

With few exceptions, nouns from III-*vav*/*yod* roots are inflected in a similar way, regardless of base. Generally, masculine formed nouns will end with an /ɛ/, which is marked by a *he mater*. Thus, **qatal* nouns have the vowel sequence **ā-ɛ* (in THT *å-ɛ*), as in חָזֶה "(animal) breast"; קָנֶה "reed(s), stem(s)."[61] Words of other bases often have a similar ending: **qatil* (קָשֶׁה "hard, stiff"), **qital* (מֵעֶה* "innards" [cf. מֵעָיו]), **qātil* (בֹּנֶה "one who builds," עֹשֶׂה "one who does"), **qattil* (גֵּאֶה "arrogant").[62]

The inflection of these more regular III-*vav*/*yod* words that end in /ɛ/ is very easy to learn. In essence, the final triphthong resolves such that only the vowel of the final morpheme remains (e.g., **qašiyīm* > **qāšīm* > קָשִׁים). Note the feminine singular forms קָשָׁה "hard, stiff" עֹשָׂה "one who does"; the plural forms קָשׁוֹת/קָשִׁים and עֹשׂת/עֹשִׂים; the suffixed forms קָנָהּ "its stem(s)," עֹשָׂהּ "who made it."[63] This inflection reflects presumably the regular contractions of earlier triphthongs, as described above. One nuance in relation to the noun + possessive suffixes is the fuller form of the third-person masculine singular suffix, as seen on the word for "pasture": נָוֵ֫הוּ "his pasture" (abs. נָוֶה). Sometimes the third-person feminine singular has a similarly extended form: מַרְאֶ֫הָ "its appearance" (Lev 13:20).

The construct singular is usually distinguished from the absolute by the distinction of */ē/ instead of /ɛ/, which in Tiberian Hebrew is realized as the difference between *tsere* and *segol*. In some words that contain an etymological short vowel in an open pretonic syllable (e.g., **qašiyu* > קָשֶׁה "hard, stiff"), the construct form will also be marked by the reduction of the initial vowel, as in the adjective קָשֶׁה in the expression עַם־קְשֵׁה־עֹ֫רֶף "a people, stiff of neck" (Exod 32:9). In other cases, however, the initial syllable will not contain a vowel that reduces and the only signal that the word is in construct is the */ē/ in place of /ɛ/: עֹשֵׂה הַשָּׁמַ֫יִם "the maker of the heavens" (Ps 136:5).

---

61. Huehnergard, "Biblical Hebrew Nominal Patterns," 44.

62. Ibid., 44–53.

63. Note too the plural forms with suffix: עֹשָׂיו and קְנוֹתָם.

The words and bases whose last stem vowel is long exhibit different endings. In each, the vowel sequence found in nouns of the strong root is also found in the III-*vav/yod* roots, making the identification of the word usually very easy: **qatūl* (בָּנוּי "that which is built" *qal* passive ptc.); **qatīl* (עָנִי "poor"); **qātōl* (בָּנֹה "building" *qal* inf. abs.). The inflection of these nouns is often similar to the inflection of the same bases with strong roots: בְּנוּיָה ,בְּנוּיִם and עֲנִיָּה ,עֲנִיִּים ,עֲנִיָּו.[64]

4.17. Geminate Nouns with One Vowel in the Stem (Tables 6.7, 6.8)

Some geminate nouns attest a vowel between the second and third root consonants (e.g., לֵבָב "heart"). Such nouns are entirely predictable in their inflection. Another group of geminate nouns has only a single vowel in their stem. These exhibit certain characteristics that make learning them together useful. Nouns of these bases have either a historical short */a/, */i/, or */u/: **qall*, **qill*, **qull*; **qallat*, **qillat*, **qullat*. We first consider the masculine forms and then the feminine.

The above masculine singular bases (**qall*, **qill*, **qull*) develop in slightly different ways in BH, depending on the vowel. First, note that the historical gemination at the end of the word is lost in the masculine absolute noun. This is due to the relative difficulty of pronouncing geminated consonants without a following vowel. During the second millennium BCE, when there was a case system, it would still be easy to articulate the gemination (e.g., *ʿammu* "people"). With the loss of the case system, the final consonant and vowel were eventually both lost.[65]

The vowels shift in different ways. The vowel */a/ usually remains stable, while */i/ and */u/ are lowered in quality. Thus, **ṭappu* "children" and **kappu* "palm" became, respectively, **ṭapp* > **ṭap* (> טַף) and **kapp* >

64. The gemination of *yod* in עֲנִיָּה, etc. helps preserve the preceding /i/ vowel. See §13, "Nouns with Afformatives," above. In rare cases, a final III-*vav/yod* is preserved in other bases: **qatal* (עָנָו "humble"); **qātilat* (עֹטְיָה "one who wraps," הוֹמִיָּה "one who moans/is tumultuous"); **qattal* (דַּוָּי "weak").

65. A similar thing seems to happen in English too. In contemporary English, the noun "bed" derives from an Old English word that exhibited gemination of the "d": *bedd*. See, e.g., Rob Getz and Stephen Pelle, *The Dictionary of Old English* (Toronto: University of Toronto), s.v. bedd; http://tinyurl.com/SBL0395a. In Old English, the final gemination was preserved due to a case system consisting of final vowels/consonants (e.g., *beddes*). The gemination is lost entirely in contemporary English except in forms of the word where there is a following syllable; contrast "beds" with "bedding."

**kap* (> כַּף). But, **qinnu* "nest" and **libbu* "heart" became, respectively, **qenn* > **qen* (> קֵן) and **lebb* > **leb* (> לֵב); similarly, **kullu* "all" and **ḥuqqu* "statute" became **koll* > **kol* (> כֹּל) and **ḥoqq* > **ḥoq* (> חֹק).

The construct form of the singular **qall* nouns **ṭap*/**kap* is identical to the absolute form in almost all circumstances (e.g., כַּף "palm of"). But, the construct forms of the other two bases show some alternation. Usually, the construct form of the **qill* base is the same as the absolute (e.g., לֵב "heart of"). Occasionally, with *maqqeph* the THT spelling with *segol* presumes a shift from */i/ to /ɛ/ (e.g., לֶב־ "heart of"); in other cases the historical */i/ shifted to /a/, at least in THT (e.g., קַן־ "nest of"). The construct form of **qull* nouns may also be identical to the absolute (e.g., כֹּל "all of" and חֹק "statute of"), but often with *maqqeph*, the */u/ is realized in THT as /å/ (e.g., כָּל־ and חָק־).

Vowel lengthening affects the geminate **qall* base, at least in THT, though this is primarily restricted to where the second/third root consonant is a *mem*. Although עַם is found regularly where it is followed by an attributive adjective or relative clause, the form *ʿåm* (= עָם) is found (even in context) where it is followed by prepositional phrases and conjunctions. In addition, *ʿåm* always occurs when accompanied by the definite article.[66] The /å/ is even more regular in other geminate **qall* nouns that end with a *mem*: יָם "sea" (< **yammu*) and תָּם "complete" (< **tammu*).[67]

In contrast to the singular, the plural forms of the masculine geminate nouns are very straight forward. With the suffixed morpheme **-īma*, the original vowel and gemination were retained so that the historical form and the realization in BH are very close: **ʿammīma* > **ʿammīm* > עַמִּים; **qinnīma* > **qinnīm* > קִנִּים and **ḥuqqīma* > **ḥuqqīm* > חֻקִּים. In the construct plural, the historical vowel and gemination are also preserved, as they are in the noun with suffixes. For example, note: עַמֵּי "peoples of," עַמּוֹ and עַמָּיו "his people(s)"; לִבּוֹת "hearts of," לִבָּם and לִבּוֹתָם "their heart(s); חֻקִּי and חֻקַּי "my statute(s). Even for the heavy suffixes, the historical form is often retained: כֻּלְּכֶם "all of you." Occasionally, the historical */u/ will appear as /å/ in THT (e.g., חָקְךָ and חָקְכֶם "your statute").

---

66. In this way, it is like a set of nouns that attest a *qamets* after the first root consonant in the singular only when accompanied by the definite article. Especially noteworthy are the geminate nouns הַגָּן/גַּן "(the) garden" (< **gann*); הָהָר/הַר "(the) mountain" (< **harr*); הֶחָג/חַג "(the) festival" (< **ḥagg*); הַפָּר/פַּר "(the) bull" (< **parr*). Note too הָאָרוֹן/אֲרוֹן "(the) ark" and the ubiquitous הָאָרֶץ/אֶרֶץ "(the) land."

67. See Huehnergard, "Biblical Hebrew Nominal Patterns," 36.

Variations from these basic patterns mostly involve roots with a geminated guttural root consonant, which causes compensatory lengthening. In particular, note the words **parru* > **par* > פַּר "bovine" and the plural **parrīma* > **parrīm* > **pārīm* > פָּרִים; and the word **śarru* > **śar* > **sar* > שַׂר "prince" and the plural **śarrīma* > **śarrīm* > **śārīm* > **sārīm* > שָׂרִים. When vowels are lengthened to compensate for a missing consonant, they never reduce (e.g., שָׂרֵי "princes of").

Feminine marked geminate nouns are generally easy to identify. Due to the fact that their absolute form already contains the historical vowel and gemination, it is easy to predict their inflection. For example, note אַמָּה (const. אַמַּת) "cubit" and אַמּוֹת (const. אַמּוֹת) "cubits"; פִּנָּה (const. פִּנַּת, suff. פִּנָּתָהּ) "corner" and פִּנּוֹת (const. פִּנּוֹת, suffix פִּנּוֹתָיו) "corners"; חֻקָּה (const. חֻקַּת) "statute" and חֻקּוֹת* (const. חֻקּוֹת, suffix חֻקּוֹתַי) "statutes." Again, the only forms difficult to identify are those with guttural consonants, as with the masculine geminates discussed above. Note, in particular פָּרָה "cow" and שָׂרָה "princess." The */ā/ (> THT /å/) that is the result of compensatory lengthening does not reduce (e.g., שָׂרוֹתֶיהָ "her princesses").

Students should remember that the inflected forms of these words usually always reflect their base (**qall*, **qill*, **qull*), with preservation of the historical short vowel and gemination of the second root consonant. This makes identification and production of these words relatively easy. Identifying the masculine absolute singular as from a geminate root, however, is more tricky. Still, (excepting the extremely frequent בֵּן "son" and שֵׁם "name"), nouns with two apparent root consonants and a *tsere* or *holem* are more often than not from a geminate root.

4.18. Segolate Nouns (Tables 6.9, 6.10, 6.11, 6.12, 6.13, 6.14)

Segolate nouns are like geminate nouns in that they derive from bases with short vowels and two consecutive consonants at their end, though in the case of segolates these final, consecutive consonants are not identical: **qatl*, **qitl*, **qutl*. As with geminates, the segolates exhibit greater development in their absolute and construct forms than in their suffixed forms, which generally are quite similar to their historical bases. In particular, the **qatl* base seems to have gone through several stages of development, which (according to one model) involved a shift from **malku* to **malk* to *mɛlk* (= מֶלֶךְ) "king." In THT, a vowel appears between the two final consonants, though this is an epenthetic vowel that does not constitute its own syllable, analogous in this way to the furtive patakh.[68] Where the second root consonant is a guttural, the */a/ vowel is often still attested, as with *baʿl (> בַּ֫עַל) "lord." More predictably, *qitl and *qutl nouns seem to have developed along lines similar to geminate nouns: *sipru > sepr = סֵ֫פֶר "book" and *buqru > boqr = בֹּ֫קֶר "morning."[69] Nevertheless, it should be emphasized again that in different dialects and different eras a given segolate noun might have been articulated with different vowels. That is, what was a *qatl noun in one era might have been a *qutl noun in another (cf. גֶּ֫פֶן "vine" in the MT with גופן in 1QIsa[a] at Isa 34:4). As mentioned above, even the MT evidences different stem vowels for what appear to be the same word (e.g., חֶ֫סֶר "lack" and חֹ֫סֶר "lack"). Furthermore, notice that there are often discrepancies between pausal and suffixed forms of the same word; for example, נֶ֫גַע "plague" appears with a *qamets* in pause (e.g., הַנָּ֫גַע Lev 13:50, implying a *qatl base), but appears with a *hiriq* with suffixes (נִגְעִי Ps 38:12, implying a *qitl base).[70] Note similarly, פֶּ֫שַׁע "crime," פֶּ֫תַח "opening," קֶ֫דֶם "in front."[71]

Similar to geminates, the construct forms of singular segolate nouns are identical in almost every case to the absolute forms (מֶ֫לֶךְ "king" and "king of"). Also, with suffixes the segolates, like the geminates, reveal a form closer to or identical with their historical base. Thus, "my king" began as *malkiyya* and developed to *malkī* (> מַלְכִּי); "my book" began as *sipriyya* and developed to *siprī* (> סִפְרִי). *Qutl* segolates offer a slight variation: "my morning" began as *buqriyya* and developed to *buqrī* then to *boqrī* (> בָּקְרִי*).[72] Even heavy suffixes are attached to this historical base (e.g., מַלְכְּכֶם "your king").

The plural forms of the segolates are easy to predict as well. Unlike other nouns whose plural form is based on the stem of the singular, most segolate nouns have separate bases for their plural forms. Thus, although the singular of "king" would have been *malku*, the plural seems to have

---

68. See the discussion in chapter 3 §3, "Developments of Individual Vowels."

69. Note the exceptions in THT where the historical */i/ became eventually /ɛ/ (e.g., *qirbu* > *qɛrb* [> קֶ֫רֶב]).

70. See ch. 3 §4, "Lengthening and Lowering of Vowels in Tonic Syllables." For consideration of comparative evidence, see Lambdin, "Philippi's Law Reconsidered," 135–45 and Huehnergard, "Biblical Hebrew Nominal Patterns," 38–39.

71. The last word appears with *tsere*, as קֵ֫דְמָה with the locative *he* (e.g., Num 34:3).

72. The word is used for consistency; cf. קָדְשִׁי "my sanctuary" (Lev 20:3).

been **malakīma*, with two short */a/ vowels in the stem. The result is that the base form develops just as דְּבָרִים develops: **malakīma* > **məlākīm* > מְלָכִים. The other segolate plural bases develop similarly:

- **siparīma* > **səpārīm* > סְפָרִים
- **buqarīma* > **bəqārīm* > בְּקָרִים

The forms with nonheavy suffixes are again similar in their development to the plural of דָּבָר with suffixes:

- **malakaynū* > **məlākēnū* > מְלָכֵ֫ינוּ
- **siparaynū* > **səpārēnū* > סְפָרֵ֫ינוּ*
- **buqaraynū* > **bəqārēnū* > בְּקָרֵ֫ינוּ*.[73]

With heavy suffixes and with the construct, by contrast, the historical vowel (or, in the case of **qutl* bases, the */o/ vowel) is retained:

- **malakay* > **malkē* > מַלְכֵי
- **malakaykum* > **malkēkεm* > מַלְכֵיכֶם
- **siparay* > **siprē* > סִפְרֵי*
- **siparaykum* > **siprēkεm* > סִפְרֵיכֶם*
- **buqaray* > **buqrē* > **boqrē* > בָּקְרֵי*
- **buqaraykum* > **buqrēkεm* > **boqrēkεm* > בָּקְרֵיכֶם*.

Feminine segolate nouns are identifiable in BH based on the following characteristics: the first syllable begins with a root consonant and is a closed syllable. Unlike masculine-formed segolates, the feminine-formed segolates are stressed on their second syllable. Since the initial syllable will always be closed and unaccented, it will always have a short vowel:

- **malkatu* > **malkā* > מַלְכָּה "queen"
- **dimʿatu* > **dimʿā* > דִּמְעָה "tears"
- **ḫurbatu* > **ḫorbā* > חָרְבָּה "waste."

73. These nouns are used for consistency and due to their lack of guttural consonants.

Like the masculine-based nouns, most feminine-based segolates attest the vowel sequence *ə-ā for the plural:

- **malakātu* > **məlākōt* > מְלָכוֹת
- **dimaʿātu* > **dəmāʿōt* > דְּמָעוֹת
- **ḫurabātu* > **ḫŏrābōt* > חֳרָבוֹת.

It so happens, perhaps for euphonic reasons, that most **qutl* and **qutlat* nouns have an initial guttural consonant, or they begin with *qoph* or *resh*. (The */u/, */o/ vowels and guttural consonants, as well as *qoph* and *resh*, are all pronounced in the back of the mouth). Due to this, where a **qutl* base would normally take a *shewa* after the initial root consonant, the reduced vowel is represented by a *khatef-qamets* in THT (e.g., חֳדָשִׁים "months"; הַקֳּדָשִׁים "the holy things"). Where the first root consonant is not a guttural, *qoph*, or *resh*, the initial vowel may be a *shewa*: בְּקָרִים (< **bəqārīm* < **buqarīma*) "mornings"; or it may have a *khatef-qamets* by analogy to the many other **qutl* nouns: גֳּרָנוֹת (< **gŏrānōt* < **guranātu*) "threshing floors."

Two nouns deserve separate mention for the irregular forms of their plural. These are קֹ֫דֶשׁ "holiness" and שֹׁ֫רֶשׁ "root." In each case, the stem of the plural form exhibits the sequence *å-å* (represented by *qamets-qamets*) in THT, which presumably reflects an earlier sequence **ŏ-ā*; it would seem, therefore, that what was a muttered vowel has lengthened into a full vowel in THT. The word "holiness" appears as קָדָשִׁים, and with suffixes קָדָשַׁי;[74] the word "root" appears in the plural only with suffixes שָׁרָשָׁיו. The word קֹ֫דֶשׁ also attests the more expected plural forms with the definite article and suffixes: הַקֳּדָשִׁים and קֳדָשָׁיו. Once in 2 Chr 5:7, the word even occurs with a *shewa* beneath the *qoph*: הַקְּדָשִׁים.[75]

In only very rare cases does a segolate noun attest a plural base that is analogous to the singular, that is, **qatlīm/*qatlōt*, **qitlīm/*qitlōt*, **qutlīm/*qutlōt*. It is this rarer plural pattern that is attested in THT in the

---

74. The plural form of קֹ֫דֶשׁ with suffix shows a full *qamets* in exilic (קָדָשַׁי Ezek 22:8, 26; 44:8, 13) and postexilic works (קָדָשָׁיו in 2 Chr 15:18), but the expected form with *khatef-qamets* appears in Genesis–2 Kings (e.g., קֳדָשָׁיו Num 5:10 and 2 Kgs 12:19). A *metheg* accompanies the form with full *qamets* in Deut 12:26, קָֽדָשֶׁ֫יךָ.

75. The forms with suffix and *khatef-qamets* are all preceded by some particle, while those with just *qamets* in the first syllable are not preceded by a particle. At the same time, this pattern does not hold for the plural forms of שֹׁ֫רֶשׁ with suffix, which always attest a *qamets* under the first consonant.

following words: רַחֲמִים (sg. רֶ֫חֶם and רַ֫חַם) "bowels"; שִׁקְמִים (sg. שִׁקְמָה*) "sycamores"; פִּשְׁתִּים (sg. פֵּ֫שֶׁת) "flax"; חָכְמוֹת (sg. חָכְמָה) "wisdom."[76] These nouns exhibit no medial */ā/ (> THT /å/) with suffixes (e.g., רַחֲמֶ֫יךָ and רַחֲמָיו).[77]

Weak root consonants (primarily *aleph*, *vav*, and *yod*) often result in masculine singular absolute forms that are unusual. In THT, they do not appear with one of the characteristic vowel sequences: *ε-ε*, *a-a*, *e-ε*, *e-a*, *o-ε*, *o-a* (מֶ֫לֶךְ, בַּ֫עַל, סֵ֫פֶר, קֶ֫רַח "ice," בֹּ֫קֶר "morning," and פֹּ֫עַל "deed"). Nevertheless, most nouns with weak consonants share the other characteristics of the segolate nouns: the absolute and construct forms are the same in the masculine singular; the plural (masculine and feminine) exhibits the vowel sequence *ə-ā*; the original short vowel is preserved in the first syllable of the singular with suffix.

When *aleph* is a first root consonant, the form of the segolate sometimes exhibits a full vowel where analogous forms have a *shewa* or *khatef* vowel. For example, note אֹהָלָיו (sg. abs. אֹ֫הֶל) "his tents"; אֹרְחֹתָיו (sg. abs. אֹ֫רַח) "his paths."

When an *aleph* is a second root consonant, the form of the word usually looks like a segolate noun from Aramaic, with the sequence *shewa-sere* for **qitl* bases (בְּאֵר "well," זְאֵב "wolf," כְּאֵב "pain," שְׁאֵר "flesh") or *shewa-holem* for **qutl* bases (בְּאֹשׁ "stench," מְאֹד "very," and מְלֹא "fullness"). Although it is conceivable that some of these words arrived in Hebrew as Aramaic loanwords, it also seems likely that many are the result of a more complicated process, where medial *aleph* was lost in pronunciation sometime in the first millennium BCE, but was retained in spelling with the result that the nouns appear in an Aramaic-like form in the MT.[78] Thus, what was earlier **muʾdu* "much" and **šiʾru* "flesh" (with nom. case vowels) became, respectively, **mōd* and **šēr*; the representation of the words presumed by THT, however,

76. See Joüon § 96Ab.

77. It seems that in other traditions of Hebrew, reflected in the transcriptions of Hebrew words in Greek in passages from the church fathers, this pattern for segolates was more common. Alexey Yuditsky ("On Origen's Transliterations as Preserved in the Works of the Church Fathers" [Hebrew], *Leshonenu* 69 [2007]: 306) cites as one example the transcription αρβωθ for what is חֳרָבוֹת "wastes" in the MT at Ps 9:7. For similar, but less clear examples in the Secunda, see ibid., 305 and Brønno, *Studien*, 136–38. This pattern is also the common realization of segolate plurals in Aramaic.

78. Cf. Blau, *Phonology and Morphology*, 55; Blau, *On Pseudo-Corrections*, 28–29.

presumes the articulation of the *aleph*: *m'od* = מְאֹד and *š'er* = שְׁאֵר.[79] That such elision of internal *aleph* took place at least during the first millennium BCE (if not earlier) is, in part, confirmed by spellings of these words among the DSS, where they are often written without the *aleph* (e.g., שר, שיר, מוד).[80] The plurals of the Aramaic-like segolates are rare (note especially זְאֵבִים and זְאֵבֵי). With suffixes, usually the word retains the vowel pattern of the absolute: כְּאֵבִי "my pain"; שְׁאֵרוֹ "his flesh"; שְׁאֵרָהּ "her flesh"; מְלֹאוֹ "its fullness," reflecting presumably the pronunciation of these words when the *aleph* was not normally articulated (i.e., שְׁאֵרוֹ < **šērō*; cf. ומשרו = *ūmiššērō* "and from his flesh" 4Q386 1 ii, 4). The word בְּאֹשׁ "stench" is one exception: בָּאְשׁוֹ "his stench" and בָּאְשָׁם "their stench."

A similar elision took place even earlier with **qatl* nouns that had a historical medial *aleph*: **raʾšu* "head" and **ṣaʾnu* "flock" must have experienced elision of *aleph* and compensatory lengthening of /a/ to /ā/ (**rāš*, **ṣān*) before the Canaanite shift, as suggested by the spelling of these words among the Amarna tablets where the pronunciation is assumed to have been *rōšu* and *ṣōnu*, respectively.[81] The spelling with *aleph* in alphabetic orthographies (e.g., ראש and צאן) was preserved presumably based on influence of its other forms, like the plural **raʾašīm*, which seems to have experienced the loss of internal *aleph* much later, after vowel reduction and vowel lengthening: **raʾašīm* > **rəʾāšīm* > **rāšīm* (> רָאשִׁים). The loss of an *aleph* when preceded by a reduced short vowel is attested in a variety of forms in LBH and among the DSS.[82]

If the middle root consonant is *vav*, the word appeared as all other segolates in pre-Masoretic Hebrew, with a short vowel followed by two different consonants (e.g., **mawt* "death"). In THT, of course, two vowels are represented graphically, the first of which is /å/ and the second of which

79. Nevertheless, the phonetic realization was [*šeʾeːr*] and [*moʾoːd*] (see Khan, "Tiberian Reading Tradition," 3:774). The preservation of the *aleph* was perhaps due to a more conservative pronunciation in a higher register of the language in the first millennium BCE and its continued articulation into the first millennium CE is perhaps encouraged by the secondary insertion of an epenthetic vowel after the first consonant (cf. Blau, *Phonology and Morphology*, 55).

80. Reymond, *Qumran Hebrew*, 185–86. Note the similar loss of *aleph* in words like שְׁאֵרִית "remainder" in late books of the Bible, as reflected in the spelling שֵׁרִית in 1 Chr 12:39.

81. See ch. 3 §9, "Canaanite Shift and Historical */ā/"; also, Sivan, *Grammatical Analysis and Vocabulary*, 71.

82. See n. 76 in ch. 3 §6, "Vowel Reduction." Reymond, *Qumran Hebrew*, 77–87.

is an epenthetic /ɛ/: **mawt* > מָ֫וֶת. If the middle root consonant is *yod*, the earlier form was as expected (e.g., **zayt* "olive"); in THT again two vowels are graphically present, *a-i*: **zayt* > זַ֫יִת. The plural of these nouns will often look like the uncommon plural form mentioned above (with a single vowel in the historical base of the stem): **mawtīma* > **mōtīm* > מוֹתִים and **zaytīma* > **zētīm* > זֵיתִים. In both cases, notice that the relevant diphthong (*/aw/ or */ay/) has contracted where it occurs in a syllable that does not bear the tone. Sometimes, II-*vav/yod* segolates will exhibit the more common vowel sequence **ə-ā* in the plural, in which the middle *vav/yod* is treated as a regular consonant: חֲיָלִים/חַ֫יִל "strength"; עֲיָנוֹת/עַ֫יִן "eye, spring"; עֲיָרִים/עַ֫יִר "young donkey"; תְּיָשִׁים/תַּ֫יִשׁ "he-goat."[83]

The construct forms of most of these nouns exhibit the same diphthong contractions seen in the absolute plural (**mawt* [const.] > **mōt* and **zayt* [const.] > **zēt*); here again, the original diphthong is not in a syllable that bears the tone. Occasional exceptions appear; for example, עָ֫וֶל "injustice" has the construct form עֲוֶל. This noun is also interesting in that its suffixed form does not exhibit diphthong contraction (i.e., עַוְלוֹ) and neither does its feminine cognate (i.e., עַוְלָה "injustice").[84] Compare this feminine noun with the feminine nouns from II-*yod* roots: צֵידָה "meat" and שֵׂיבָה "old age."[85]

When the third root consonant is a *vav* or *yod*, the segolate noun has yet another form. Excluding the familial terms אָב "father," אָח "brother," חָם "father-in-law," as well as a few other nouns that exhibit uncommon patterns, most III-*vav/yod* segolates appear as III-*yod* and had the vowel sequence **ə-i* in the absolute masculine singular (e.g., **qatl*/**qitl*: בְּכִי "weeping," גְּדִי "goat kid," לְחִי "jawbone," עֲדִי "ornament," צְבִי "beauty," שְׁבִי "captivity"; **qutl*: חֳלִי "sickness," עֳנִי "affliction," צֳרִי "balsam").[86] These segolates exhibit most other traits common to strong-root segolates: their absolute singular form is the same as their construct singular form; they exhibit their original vowel in the singular with suffixes (שִׁבְיָם "their captivity," חָלְיוֹ "his sickness," חֳלָיֵ֫נוּ "our sicknesses," עָנְיֵ֫נוּ "our affliction") and in the construct plural (צִבְאוֹת "beauty");[87] these same nouns exhibited the

83. See Huehnergard, "Biblical Hebrew Nominal Patterns," 34–35.

84. See ibid., 34 n. 26.

85. See ibid., 35.

86. The noun פֶּ֫תִי "simple" is also part of this group, but attests penultimate stress (as if in pause) in all its occurrences in the sg. abs. in the MT.

87. For the shift of *yod* to *aleph*, see ch. 2 §10, "Variation of Orthography and Pronunciation within Roots."

common vowel sequence *ə-ā in the absolute plural (פְּתָיִם, עֲדָיִים, גְּדָיִים, חֲלָיִם).[88] Notice that in both the suffixed and the plural absolute forms the final *yod* has become consonantal.

A minority of III-*yod* roots attest alternative forms. For example, the construct form of the plural would rarely retain the */ā/ (> THT /å/): גְּדָיֵי "kids of" and לְחָיֵי "jawbones of." The III-*aleph* noun חֵטְא "sin" follows the same pattern in the plural construct, חֲטָאֵי, and even with the second-person masculine plural suffix, חֲטָאֵיכֶם. Note also those words that seem formed on analogy to other III-*vav*/*yod* nouns with final -ɛ in THT: בֶּ֫כֶה "mourning," הֶ֫גֶה "moaning," קֵ֫צֶה "end."[89]

In the nouns אָב "father," אָח "brother," and חָם "husband's father-in-law" an */-ī/ vowel is implied after the second root consonant in the singular construct and forms with suffixes (e.g., אֲבִי "father of," אָבִיו "his father"; אֲחִי "brother of," אָבִיךָ "your brother"; חָמִ֫יהָ "her father-in-law"). The typical reflexes of historical */a/ help to distinguish the construct from the noun plus first-person common singular suffix: אֲבִי "father of" versus אָבִי "my father." The */-ī/ vowel is either the remnant of a genitive vowel and/or a reflection of its third root consonant (reflecting an early shift from III-*w* to III-*y*). Huehnergard reconstructs the development of the Hebrew word: **ʾabwum* > **ʾabūm* > **ʾabum* > **ʾab* > אָב.[90]

The absolute plural of אָב is feminine in appearance: אָבוֹת. The word אָח in the plural mostly appears derived from a root **ʾḫḫ*, as with the absolute אַחִים and with suffixes: אַחַי "my brothers"; אֶחָיו "his brothers" (with the shift of */a/ to /ɛ/ in THT, as with the definite article in הֶהָרִים "the mountains"). But, the construct plural appears to be from the root **ʾḫw* (אֲחֵי), as does the form of the plural with heavy suffixes (אֲחֵיכֶם).

Nouns that clearly reflect a derivation from III-*vav* roots are comparatively fewer. Those that seem obviously derived from III-*vav* roots attest in THT a full vowel in their initial syllable and a *shuruq* at their end: אָ֫חוּ "reeds, meadow"; שָׂ֫חוּ "swimming"; תֹּ֫הוּ "formlessness"; בֹּ֫הוּ "void."[91]

---

88. The forms פְּתָיִם and חֲלָיִם are defective, but reflect the common scribal practice of not writing two *vav*s or *yod*s when the first is consonantal and the second a *mater*. The words are also spelled plene: פְּתָיִים and חֲלָיִים.

89. See Huehnergard, "Biblical Hebrew Nominal Patterns," 37.

90. Ibid., 35. Bordreuil and Pardee (*Manual of Ugaritic*, 294) tentatively propose an etymology for the similar Ugaritic word: **ʾaḫawu* > **ʾaḫū*.

91. For this last pair, see Huehnergard, "Biblical Hebrew Nominal Patterns," 41.

Feminine-formed segolates from III-*yod* roots are relatively rare. Note, for example, שִׁבְיָה "captivity," and those with final *-*īt*, בְּכִית "mourning," בְּרִית "covenant," שְׁבִית "captivity," and final gemination, צְבִיָּה "gazelle," and אֳנִיָּה "ship."[92] Of III-*vav* roots, note the noun שַׁלְוָה "quiet," which exhibits a consonantal *vav*.[93] The feminine noun "sister" (אָחוֹת) also exhibits consonantal *yod* (from an earlier *vav*) in some of its plural forms with suffixes (e.g., אַחְיֹתָיו <*ʾ*aḫyōtāw*).[94]

Although most *qal* infinitives construct derive from the **qutul* base, a substantial number attest a segolate or segolate-like vowel pattern. First, recall that the *qal* infinitive construct with suffix appears to be of the **qutl* base, though it is really of the **qutul* base (e.g., לְשָׁמְרוֹ "to guard him" 1 Sam 19:11; cf. the **qutl* noun: לְקָדְשׁוֹ "for his holy place" Ps 114:2).[95] In addition, note the many cases of I-*vav*/*yod* and I-*nun* roots of the **qilt* base that bear the sequence of vowels one associates with segolates (e.g., גֶּשֶׁת *qal* inf. const. of נגשׁ "approaching" and גִּשְׁתּוֹ "his approaching"; שֶׁבֶת *qal* inf. const. of ישׁב "dwelling" and שִׁבְתּוֹ "his dwelling"). Also, several examples of infinitives construct appear to be from feminine segolate bases (e.g., **qatlat*: אַהֲבָה "loving"; **qitlat*: יִרְאָה "fearing"; **qutlat*: מָשְׁחָה "anointing").

Students should pay close attention to this important and somewhat complex base. The masculine absolute singular forms of these nouns can appear with a variety of different vowels, the second of which is usually an epenthetic vowel that is unaccented and does not mark an independent syllable: מֶ֫לֶךְ "king," בַּ֫עַל "lord," סֵ֫פֶר "book," קֶ֫רַח "ice," בֹּ֫קֶר "morning," פֹּ֫עַל "deed," בְּאֵר "well," בְּאֹשׁ "stench," מָ֫וֶת "death," זַ֫יִת "olive," עָ֫וֶל "injustice," שְׁבִי "captivity," חֳלִי "sickness," תֹּ֫הוּ "formlessness," בֹּ֫הוּ "void." Feminine segolate nouns are usually recognizable from the word-initial closed syllable (where the initial consonant is a root consonant): מַלְכָּה "queen," דִּמְעָה "tears," חָרְבָּה "waste," שִׁבְיָה "captivity," שַׁלְוָה "quiet."

Despite the apparent variety and discrepancies in the above singular forms, most of these nouns share the following characteristics:

---

92. See ibid., 37, 42.

93. Cf. the III-*yod* אַלְיָה "fat tail" (ibid., 35).

94. Note the forms without *yod* (e.g., אֲחוֹתַ֫יִךְ). Cf. ibid.

95. See the discussion of *qal* inf. const. in §8, "Nouns of the **qutul*, **qitāl*, and **qutāl* Bases," above. Note also that some *qal* inf. const. attest patterns similar to those of the **qitl* and **qatl* base (e.g., מִכְרָם "their selling" Neh 13:15; רַקְעֲךָ "your stamping" Ezek 25:6).

1. The absolute and construct forms are the same in the masculine singular and vary in the feminine singular only in their ending (*-*ā* in the absolute and -*at* in the construct).
2. The absolute plural (in both masculine and feminine nouns) exhibited the vowel sequence *ə-ā* in the stem.
3. In the singular noun with suffixes, the original short vowel is preserved in the first syllable.
4. In the construct plural the original short vowel is also preserved.

4.19. Suppletive Plurals and Construct Forms in Nouns

In Hebrew, unlike in some other Semitic languages (e.g., Arabic), the plural forms for most nouns are clearly derived from the singular forms (e.g., **dabar* + *īma* > **dabarīm* > דְּבָרִים). However, in some cases, one finds words where the singular form is from one base and the plural is from another. The only class of nouns where this happens regularly in Hebrew is the segolates (see above: **malk* vs. **malakīm*). Some rarer exceptions to this rule are listed here.

Some geminate nouns that have a single vowel in their stem in the singular attest two in the plural: צֵל "shade" in the singular but צְלָלִים in the plural. Sometimes even segolate nouns do not attest their expected base in the plural. Nouns of the **qiṭl* base sometimes have plurals of the **qaṭīl* base, as with פֶּסֶל and פְּסִילִים "idol(s)"; נְטִיעִים/נֶטַע (and נִטְעֵי) "plant(s)"; הֲרִיסֹתָיו/הֶרֶס "destruction(s)."[96]

In other cases, the construct form of a word seems to be derived from a base different from that of the absolute. This is regularly the case with *mem*-preformative feminine nouns, as remarked on above (מַחֲשָׁבָה, const. מַחֲשֶׁבֶת, with 3ms מַחֲשַׁבְתּוֹ "thought"). But, this also occurs with other words and bases. Note the following cases where the construct form appears to exhibit a segolate-base or a segolate-like word-final consonant cluster: אַיֶּלֶת "doe of," the construct form of אַיָּלָה "doe"; אֶרֶךְ "long of," the construct form of אָרֵךְ "long"; יֶרֶךְ "thigh of" and יָרֵךְ "thigh"; כֶּתֶף "thigh of" and כָּתֵף "thigh"; צֶלַע "rib of" and צֵלָע "rib."[97] Among segolates, note

---

96. See John Huehnergard, "*Qāṭîl* and *Qəṭîl* Nouns in Biblical Hebrew," in Maman, *Sha'arei Lashon*, *24 (with references). Perhaps also חֲרִיטִים/חֶרֶט "bag(s)" (?); צֵן* (< **ṣinn* as suggested by צִנִּים "hooks, barbs") /צְנִינִים "thorns." See ibid., *8.

97. See Fox, *Semitic Noun Patterns*, 109.

that many of the byforms that appear as construct forms are similar in pronunciation and vowel sequence to Aramaic segolates: גְּבַר "man of" (Ps 18:26) versus גֶּ֫בֶר "man"; הֲבֵל "vanity of" (Qoh 1:2; 12:8) versus הֶ֫בֶל "vanity"; חֲדַר "room of" versus חֶ֫דֶר "room (of)";[98] שְׁבַע "seven of" versus שֶׁ֫בַע "seven"; תְּשַׁע "nine of" versus תֵּ֫שַׁע "nine."[99]

4.20. Aramaic-Like Forms

A wide variety of nouns attest Aramaic-like forms, as observed in passing in the previous pages. These may be true loans from Aramaic (as with נְצִיב "pillar, overseer") or words formed on analogy to other words, as with אֱוִיל "fool," on analogy to כְּסִיל "stupid."[100] Note also these other Aramaic-influenced words: כְּתָב "writing," גָּלוּת "exile," and some other nouns like זְמָן "time."[101]

4.21. Chapter Summary

Historical Details

1. In some early ancestor of Hebrew, there were three different cases in the singular (nom. [marked by word final *-u*], gen. [*-i*], and acc. [*-a*]) and two cases in the dual (nom. [*-āmi*], gen./acc. [*-aymi*]) and plural (masc. nom. [*-ūma*], masc. gen./acc. [*-īma*]; fem. nom. [*-ātu*], fem. gen./acc. [*-āti*]).
2. These case endings eventually contribute to the various noun forms we are familiar with from THT; for example, the masculine plural morpheme *-īm* derives from the absolute masculine plural genitive/accusative ending *-īma*: **dabar + īma* > **dabarīma* > **dabarīm* > **dəbārīm* > דְּבָרִים.

98. Huehnergard, ("Biblical Hebrew Nominal Patterns," 36) lists this as a **qiṭl* noun, though it appears in most of its suffixed-occurrences (and in the const. pl.) with a *patakh* in the first syllable; only once does it have a *segol* (Joel 2:16).

99. In these types of words, the last letter is often a sonorous consonant (often /l/, /n/, or /r/). Note also חֲסַר "want of" const. (vs. חֶ֫סֶר abs.); שְׁגַר "offspring of" const. (vs. שֶׁ֫גֶר abs.). See Richard Steiner, "On the Origin of the *Ḥéðɛr ~ Ḥăðár* Alternation in Hebrew," *AfAsL* 3 (1976): 2; Fox, *Semitic Noun Patterns*, 137.

100. See Huehnergard, "*Qāṭîl* and *Qəṭîl* Nouns in Biblical Hebrew," *25.

101. See Fox, *Semitic Noun Patterns*, 284; Stadel, "Aramaic Influences on Biblical Hebrew," 1:162–65.

3. A word with any suffix or suffixal morpheme will usually reveal a form close to its etymological origin (e.g., the *tav* in אַהֲבָתִי [< *ʾahbātī < *ʾahbatiyya] "my love" and the vowel and gemination in עַמִּי [< *ʿammī < *ʿammiyya] "my people").

Learning Tips

1. For most masculine nouns (excluding segolates):
   1.1. The vowel sequence in the stem of the plural is the same vowel sequence one sees with nonheavy suffixes.
   1.2. The vowel sequence associated with the construct form is the same vowel sequence one sees with heavy suffixes.
2. Most feminine singular nouns that end with *-ā* (ָה-) in the absolute have *-āt-* (ָת-) before nonheavy suffixes and *-at-* (ַת-) before heavy suffixes (e.g., צִדְקַתְכֶם/צִדְקָתִי/צְדָקָה "righteousness"). Most feminine singular nouns that end with ֶת- in the absolute, have -ת- before all suffixes (יֹלַדְתְּכֶם/יֹלַדְתָּהּ/יֹלֶדֶת "one bearing").
3. For most feminine plural nouns, the vowel sequence in the stem of the construct plural is the same sequence found in the noun with suffixes (e.g., בִּרְכוֹת "blessings of" and בִּרְכוֹתַי "my blessings").
4. The historical */i/ vowel reduces to *shewa* in the pretonic syllable in the following bases: *qātil (שֹׁפְטִים/שֹׁפֵט "judge[s]"); *qattil (עִוְרִים/עִוֵּר "blind" and פִּסְחִים/פִּסֵּחַ "limping" as well as דַּבְּרָהּ/דַּבֵּר "her speaking" *piel* inf. cons.); *maqtil (מִזְבְּחוֹת/מִזְבֵּחַ "altar[s]").[102]
5. If a root seems to be missing one root consonant, consider the following clues:
   5.1. Words similar in form to עַם "people," קֵן "nest," חֹק "statute" are likely geminates; their etymology is usually clear in the plural and with suffixes (עַמִּים "peoples," עַמִּי "my people"; קִנִּים "nests," חִצִּי "my arrow"; חֻקִּים "statutes," חֻקִּי "my statute").
   5.2. The vowel sequence *ē-ā (corresponding to the symbols *tsere-qamets*^{he} in THT) in a word with two obvious root consonants (e.g., דֵּעָה) usually implies a I-*vav*/*yod* root, while *a-a* or *ɛ-ɛ* in THT with a final *tav* (e.g., דַּעַת) often imply a *qal* infinitive construct from a I-*vav*/*yod* root.

102. Though contrast מַגֵּפָה "plague."

5.3. A *vav* or *yod mater* in the middle of a word or even at its end will often indicate a *vav* or *yod* root consonant (e.g., מוֹשָׁב "dwelling place" from ישב and מֵישָׁרִים "integrity" from ישר; and טוֹב "good" from טוב; and שִׁיר "song" from שיר; and מָקוֹם "place" from קום; and מְרִיבָה "strife" from ריב; and עָנִי "poor" from ענה; and עֳנִי "misery" from ענה; and עֲדִי "ornament" from עדה).

5.4. Words that end in -ɛ are likely from III-*vav*/*yod* roots (e.g., עֹשֶׂה "one who does" *qal* active ptc. from עשה). But, this vowel appears only in the absolute singular; in the construct singular one finds *-ē (e.g., עֹשֵׂה "maker of"). There is no evidence of either -ɛ or *-ē with plural morphemes or pronominal suffixes. Instead, these endings seem to attach directly to the stem (e.g., עֹשָׂה "[she] makes," עֹשִׂים "[they] make," עֹשׂת "[they] make," עֹשָׂהּ "who made it").

5.5. A word that begins with a *mem* and is followed by a geminated consonant likely is a *mem*-preformative noun from a I-*nun* root (e.g., מַכָּה "wound" from נכה and מַתָּן "gift" from נתן).

6. Among segolates, the historical short vowel (or something close to it) is preserved in the singular with suffixes (מַלְכִּי "my king," סִפְרִי "my book," קָדְשִׁי "my holiness"); and in the plural construct (מַלְכֵי, סִפְרֵי, קָדְשֵׁי); as well as in most forms of the feminine (מַלְכָּה "queen," מַלְכָּתִי "my queen"; דִּמְעָה "tears," דִּמְעָתִי "my tears"; חָכְמָה "wisdom," חָכְמָתִי "my wisdom").

7. Segolate nouns come in a variety of forms.

7.1. Masculine nouns usually have two Tiberian vowels with the accent on the first:

7.1.1. **qatl*: מֶ֫לֶךְ "king"; בַּ֫עַל "master"; תָּ֫וֶךְ "midst," בַּ֫יִת "house"; עַ֫יִן "spring, eye"; שָׂ֫חוּ "swimming"; אָ֫חוּ "reeds"

7.1.2. **qitl*: סֵ֫פֶר "book"; שֵׁ֫מַע "news"; חֶ֫דֶר "room," זֶ֫בַח "sacrifice"; עֲדִי "ornament"; פֶּ֫תִי "simple"; cf. בְּאֵר "well"

7.1.3. **qutl*: קֹ֫דֶשׁ "holiness"; בֹּ֫קֶר "morning"; אֹ֫רַח "way"; חֳלִי "sickness"; בֹּ֫הוּ "emptiness"; cf. בְּאשׁ "stench"

7.2. Feminine nouns usually have a closed first syllable that begins with a root consonant:

7.2.1. **qatlat*: מַלְכָּה "queen"; אַהֲבָה "love, loving"

7.2.2. **qitlat*: דִּמְעָה "tear"; יִרְאָה "fear, fearing"

7.2.3. **qutlat*: חָכְמָה "wisdom"; טָהֳרָה "purity"; טֻמְאָה "impurity."

7.3. most absolute plural segolates exhibit the sequence of vowel symbols *shewa-qamets* in their stems: מְלָכִים, סְפָרִים, עֲדָיִים, דְּמָעוֹת, מְלָכוֹת, חֲלָיִים, בְּקָרִים.

8. Mnemonic Aids

8.1. **qatil* in construct: "I am heavy of mouth (כְּבַד־פֶּה [abs. כָּבֵד]) and heavy of tongue (כְּבַד לָשׁוֹן)" Exod 4:10

8.2. **qātil* with suffix: "his enemies (אֹיְבָיו [pl. abs. אֹיְבִים, sg. abs. אֹיֵב]) lick the dust" Ps 72:9

8.3. feminine noun with suffix:

8.3.1. "I await your salvation (יְשׁוּעָתְךָ [abs. יְשׁוּעָה])" Gen 49:18

8.3.2. "my hope is from him (מִמֶּנּוּ תִּקְוָתִי [abs. תִּקְוָה])" Ps 62:6

8.3.3. "in your goodness (טוֹבָתְךָ [abs. טוֹבָה]) you provide for the poor" Ps 68:11

8.3.4. "trust in the lord with all your heart and do not rely on your own understanding (בִּינָתְךָ [abs. בִּינָה])" Prov 3:5

8.4. III-*vav*/*yod* nouns

8.4.1. in construct: "a people, stiff of neck (קְשֵׁה־עֹרֶף [abs. קָשֶׁה])" Exod 32:9

8.4.2. with suffix: "the lord is my shepherd (רֹעִי [abs. רֹעֶה])" Ps 23:1

8.4.3. "you repay each person according to his work (כְּמַעֲשֵׂהוּ [abs. מַעֲשֶׂה])" Ps 62:13

8.5. Geminate nouns

8.5.1. **qall*

- plural: "the race does not go to the swift (קַלִּים [sg. קַל]) … but time and chance occur to all of them" Qoh 9:11
- dual/plural + suffix: "you will eat by the sweat of your brow (אַפֶּיךָ [lit., your two noses = your face; dual abs. אַפַּיִם; sg. abs. אַף; root is אנף])" Gen 3:19

8.5.2. **qill* + suffix: "I have escaped by the skin of my teeth (עוֹר שִׁנַּי* [abs. pl. שִׁנַּיִם, abs. sg. שֵׁן])" Job 19:20 (pause שִׁנָּי)

8.5.3. **qull* + suffix: "the lord is my strength (עֻזִּי) and my shield" Ps 28:7

8.6. Segolate nouns

8.6.1. **qatl*

- singular construct: "the land of the living (אֶ֫רֶץ הַחַיִּים)" Job 28:13
- plural construct: "ends of (the) earth (אַפְסֵי אֶ֫רֶץ*)" Deut 33:17 (pause אָ֫רֶץ)
- singular + suffix: "for his kindness is forever (כִּי עוֹלָם חַסְדּוֹ)" Ps 136
- singular + suffix: "let us make humans in our image (בְּצַלְמֵ֫נוּ [abs. צֶ֫לֶם])" Gen 1:26
- plural + suffix: "bone of my bones (עֶ֫צֶם מֵעֲצָמַי)" Gen 2:23

8.6.2. **qutl*

- singular construct: "pride (גֹּבַהּ רוּחַ lit. haughtiness of spirit) (goes) before a fall" Prov 16:18
- singular + suffix: "my holy mountain (הַר קָדְשִׁי) Isa 11:9
- **qutlat* singular + suffix: "at their wits' (חָכְמָתָם) end (lit., all their wisdom was engulfed [תִּתְבַּלָּע])" Ps 107:27

8.6.3. III-*vav/yod* plural + suffix: "Surely our sicknesses (חֳלָיֵ֫נוּ [abs. pl. חֳלָיִם or חֳלָיִים, abs. sg. חֳלִי]) he lifts and our pains, he carries them. We consider him stricken, struck by God, and afflicted." Isa 53:4

8.7. Irregular nouns

8.7.1. woman/wife (אִשָּׁה):

- construct: "wife of your bosom (אֵ֫שֶׁת חֵיקְךָ* [abs. אִשָּׁה])" Deut 13:7 [pause חֵיקֶ֫ךָ])
- + suffix: "a person abandons his father and mother and clings to his wife (אִשְׁתּוֹ [const. אֵ֫שֶׁת, abs. אִשָּׁה])

8.7.2. daughter (בַּת < **bint*): "as the mother, thus is her daughter (בִּתָּהּ)" Ezek 16:44

8.7.3. mouth (פֶּה):

- construct: "from the mouth of children (מִפִּי עֹלְלִים) you founded a bulwark" Ps 8:3
- + suffix: "Joab put the words into her mouth (בְּפִיהָ)" in 2 Sam 14:3
- + suffix: "let another praise you, not your mouth (פִּיךָ)" Prov 27:2

5
Morphology of Ancient Hebrew: Verbs

5.1. Terms for the Verb

The verb forms described below will be referred to in relation to the THT articulation in the *qal* third masculine singular of the Hebrew root *qṭl*. Thus, what is sometimes referred to as the suffix-conjugation or perfect verb form will be referred to here as *qåṭal*; the prefix-conjugation or imperfect will be referred to as *yiqṭol*, the *vav*-consecutive imperfect as *wayyiqṭol*, and the *vav*-consecutive perfect as *wəqåṭal*. The jussive/preterite verb form (on which see below) will be referred to as the short-*yiqṭol* since in weak verb classes (especially II-*vav*/*yod*, III-*vav*/*yod*) and in the *hiphil* conjugation it is phonetically and graphically shorter than the comparable *yiqṭol* form.[1]

This language attempts to avoid the confusion inherent in many other labels, which connect the verbal form with just one function (e.g., "perfect," as though the *qåṭal* form only represented perfect or perfective events). Since each form can express several different nuances, it makes sense to label each according to one generic phonetic contour.[2] Even here,

1. Compare the *qal* short-*yiqṭol* in its jussive function תָּשֶׁת "do [not] set" (Exod 23:1) with the *yiqṭol* תָּשִׁית "you will set" (Ps 21:4) (שׁית); compare also the *qal* short-*yiqṭol* in its preterite function יָשֶׁת "he set" (Ps 18:12) with the *yiqṭol* יָשִׁית "he will set" (Gen 46:4) (שׁית). Similarly, contrast יִבֶן "let him build" (Ezra 3:1) with יִבְנֶה "he will build" (2 Sam 7:13) (בנה) and the *hiphil*: תַּשְׁחֵת "may you [not] destroy" (Ps 57:1 and passim) with תַּשְׁחִית "you will [not] destroy" (Deut 20:19) (שׁחת).

2. As an example of a single form being able to express different nuances, consider *qåṭal*. Although the *qåṭal* form may express the perfective nuance, it may also be used "to express events that are remote" and in this sense "its function then approaches that of the preterite" (Jan Joosten, "Verbal System: Biblical Hebrew," *EHLL* 3:923). In addition, it can express certainty in the present tense when used in a performative expression (e.g., נָתַתִּי "I hereby give") (see ibid.). It can even be used to express epistemic

however, the terms are not perfectly clear: the short-*yiqṭol* will often be identical in form to the regular *yiqṭol* and it seems possible that at least some (if not most) speakers would not have recognized an independent short-*yiqṭol* form for most strong roots.[3] As for the labels of other verbal forms, there is less confusion as to the function and form of the imperative, cohortative, participle, and infinitives; thus, these labels are used.

The language employed to describe the functions of the various verbal forms should also be addressed, as should the correspondences between verbal functions and verbal forms. The terms perfective and imperfective refer to aspect, that is, how a speaker views a given event, either as complete or incomplete, respectively.[4] The perfective is typically communicated through the *qåṭal* and *wayyiqṭol*, the imperfective by *yiqṭol*, *wəqåṭal*, and the participle. The term preterite implies a verb that indicates past time reference, irrespective of its aspect (i.e., whether or not the event is viewed as complete).[5] It is typically communicated by the *qåṭal*, *wayyiqṭol*, and short-*yiqṭol*.[6] The term volitive refers to verbs that indicate

---

modality: "he might …" "he should …" "he could …" (see Jan Joosten, *The Verbal System of Biblical Hebrew: A New Synthesis Elaborated on the Basis of Classical Prose*, JBS 10 [Jerusalem: Simor, 2012], 208–12).

3. Nevertheless, a variety of factors (including the consistent appearance of paragogic-*nun* forms in nonvolitive contexts, e.g., לֹא תִלָּחֲמוּן "you will not fight" 1 Kgs 12:24 and לֹא מוֹת תְּמֻתוּן "you certainly will not die" Gen 3:4) imply that some sophisticated speakers/writers would have recognized the existence of such short-*yiqṭol* forms, even for strong roots (at least in their jussive function in the high literary register of the language). Note also the regular distinction in word order; the short-*yiqṭol* in its jussive function usually appears first in its clause, while the *yiqṭol* usually appears in noninitial position (see Joosten, *Verbal System*, 12).

4. More complex definitions and descriptions are available; see Joosten, *Verbal System*, 28–31.

5. See David Crystal, *A Dictionary of Linguistics and Phonetics*, 6th ed. (Oxford: Blackwell, 2008), https://doi.org/10.1002/9781444302776.

6. A more complex description of the various Hebrew forms and functions is found in Joosten, *Verbal System* and in John A. Cook, "The Hebrew Verb: A Grammaticalization Approach," *ZAH* 14 (2001): 117–43, and Cook, *Time and the Biblical Hebrew Verb*, LSAWS 7 (Winona Lake, IN: Eisenbrauns, 2010). For instance, Joosten writes that the *qåṭal* and *wayyiqṭol* express the same temporal and aspectual nuances, but *qåṭal* functions to indicate "anteriority with respect to the reference time" and *wayyiqṭol* indicates simply a past time (Joosten, *Verbal System*, 45); similarly, *qåṭal* can indicate (in dialogue) something that happened before the dialogue started, but *wayyiqṭol* is not used (independent of an initial *qåṭal*) for this (ibid., 48). A participle too can be used in the same context as a *qåṭal* form, though the participle implies that the action/event is

the volition of the speaker. In BH this function is expressed through the short-*yiqṭol*, *wəqåṭal*, the imperative, and the cohortative. The short-*yiqṭol* is sometimes called the jussive when it functions as a volitive; it occurs primarily in the third- and second-persons and thus can be translated by the English expressions "let it ...," "let her ...," "let him ...," "may you ..."[7] The imperative, on the other hand, occurs only in the second-person and the cohortative only in the first-person. Because English does not have a form that corresponds to the cohortative, it must be translated periphrastically (like the short-*yiqṭol* in its jussive function). The cohortative is often translated "let me ...," "let us ...," though it can also be translated by other phrases depending on the context.

Of all the forms and functions, the most uncommon is the short-*yiqṭol* where it functions as a preterite. Commonly recognized short-*yiqṭol* forms functioning as preterites from the Hebrew Bible include the following.

- יָ֫שֶׁת "he set" from שִׁית (Ps 18:12 vs. וַיָּ֫שֶׁת in 2 Sam 22:12)
- תֶּ֫שִׁי "you forgot" from שׁיה (Deut 32:18, parallel to וַתִּשְׁכַּח "you forgot")

For most strong verbs the short-*yiqṭol* merged entirely in its form with the regular *yiqṭol* and, as mentioned above, one cannot distinguish the two by the form alone; only context can guide one's translation and understanding in these instances. In most cases, where one finds the negative particle אַל followed by a verbal form, that verbal form should be identified as a short-*yiqṭol* (in its jussive function). Identifying the short-*yiqṭol* in its preterite function is more difficult. In Deut 32:10, one finds יִמְצָאֵהוּ in the context of God apportioning lots to the various nations; it is clear that it refers to an event from the past and should be construed as a short-*yiqṭol*.[8] Thus, we translate "he found him."[9]

---

contemporaneous with respect to the reference time and the *qåṭal* that it was anterior (ibid., 51). In archaic texts, *qåṭal* also indicates anteriority, but functions as a "present perfect" (ibid., 418); e.g., קִנְאוּנִי "they have made me jealous" (Deut 32:21).

7. Verb forms bearing the characteristics of the short-*yiqṭol* are also rarely found in the first-person (e.g., וְאַט "I bent" Hos 11:4 and נַשְׁאֵר "let us [not] leave" 1 Sam 14:36).

8. For the example, see Joosten, *Verbal System*, 74–75. The short-*yiqṭol* with preterite function is also thought to be attested after certain particles, like אָז and טֶ֫רֶם (see, e.g., Seow, *Grammar for Biblical Hebrew*, 225; see Joosten, *Verbal System*, 110 n. 81 for more references). Nevertheless, constructions with טרם are perhaps better explained as having a prospective function, expressing that something "had not yet happened

5.2. History of the Verbal Forms

This chapter treats the morphology of verbal forms, excluding for the most part those already treated in chapter 4 (i.e., *qal* infinitives and participles).[10] The verbal paradigms treated here can be broken down into two basic categories: (1) *qåṭal* forms and (2) all other forms (e.g., *yiqṭol*, imperative). In most cases, the transformations experienced by the verb in its inflections are fewer and less dramatic than those of the noun and adjective. Nevertheless, some knowledge of the history of the forms helps one produce and remember the verb in its various articulations.

The Hebrew *qåṭal* derives from adjectival forms, to which pronominal suffixes were attached.[11] This kind of construction is attested in Akkadian, where suffixes are applied to verbal adjectives and even nouns. For example, the Akkadian word for king is *šarrum*. To say "you (ms) are king" one adds the pronominal suffix *-āta* to the end of the stem: *šarrāta*. As with the nouns studied above, there were different basic vowel patterns that led to different verb forms in later West Semitic languages. In BH, there are basically two categories of *qåṭal* verbs, active (expressed by the pattern **a-a* > **ā-a* [> *å-a*, e.g., כָּתַב "he wrote"]) and stative (expressed by the vowel patterns **a-i* > **ā-e* [> *å-e*, e.g., זָקֵן "he is old"] and **a-u* > **ā-o* [> *å-o*, e.g., יָכֹל "he is able"]).

Cognizance of this history for Hebrew helps make sense of the forms of the Hebrew *qåṭal*, that is, as a combination of a nominal base plus a pronominal element: **katab* + *ta* = **katabta* > **kātabtā* > *kåtabtå* = כָּתַבְתָּ "you wrote." In addition, this background also helps explain the fact that many Hebrew adjectives and nouns have the same form in THT as the *qal* third masculine singular *qåṭal* of the same root (e.g., זָקֵן [< **zāqēn*] "elder" passim vs. זָקֵן [< **zāqen*] "he was old," 1 Sam 4:18 [cf. Prov 23:22 with זָקְנָה "she is old"]; טוֹב "good" passim vs. וְטוֹב "so that it will be good" Deut 5:33;

or that it would happen" (Joosten, *Verbal System*, 282). The constructions with אז are more difficult to explain; Joosten (*Verbal System*, 109–11) highlights the problems with previous explanations.

9. In LBH, the regular *yiqṭol* is sometimes used in this way: תַּסִּיעַ "you brought forth" (Ps 80:9); see Joosten, "Verbal System: Biblical Hebrew," 3:924. For more examples, see Sperber, *Historical Grammar*, 436.

10. See especially the discussion of nouns of the **qilt*, **qutul*, and **qātil* bases, as well as the discussion of infinitives that appears in ch. 4 §18, "Segolate Nouns."

11. Huehnergard, "Afro-Asiatic," 152.

רַע "evil" passim and וְרַע "it will be evil" Prov 24:18). That the *qåṭal* verb form developed from an adjectival/nominal form also helps make sense of certain tendencies, like the similarity between the noun + possessive suffix and *qåṭal* + object suffix. When an object suffix is attached to the third masculine singular *qåṭal* verb in Hebrew, the verb sometimes appears like a noun in its vowel pattern: חֲקָרָהּ "he explored it" (Job 28:27; cf. noun + suffix הֲדָרָהּ "her majesty" Isa 5:14); רָאָהּ "he saw it" (Job 28:27; cf. קָנָהּ "its stem" Exod 25:31). Similarly, with the *piel*: שִׁלְּחָהּ "he sent her away" (Deut 24:4).[12]

The other verbal forms all seem linked in some way. The *yiqṭol*, the short-*yiqṭol*, and the *wayyiqṭol* all derive ultimately from the PS form corresponding most closely to the short-*yiqṭol*. For this reason note the identical shape of the stem of the three forms in the strong root: יִשְׁמֹר, יִשְׁמֹר, וַיִּשְׁמֹר. The imperative (e.g., שְׁמֹר) is also tangentially linked to this form, as is the cohortative (e.g., אֶשְׁמְרָה). The infinitives and participle of the derived conjugations also share the vowel sequences of the short-*yiqṭol* (and *yiqṭol*) forms (as explained below).

In order to understand the history of BH verbal forms, it is necessary to take a step back and consider the verbal system of PS. In PS, as it is reconstructed, it is believed that there was one verbal form that expressed the durative sense and another that expressed the preterite (or perfective aspect). Both were characterized by prefixal morphemes. The durative sense was communicated through a form having the basic pattern like **yaqattal* "he kills" (cf. Akkadian *iparras* "he cuts off").[13] No morphological counterpart is found in West Semitic (= WS). If it had continued into WS, then the BH *qal* future/modal function may have been articulated as a form such as **yəqaṭṭal* > *יְקַטֵּל.

In PS, the preterite (or perfective) function was expressed by a verb form having the basic pattern **yaqtul* "he killed"; this same verb form also had a jussive function "let him kill."[14] This form became the BH short-

12. Though the nominal forms with this pattern (e.g., עִוֵּר "blind") do not typically take suffixes.

13. John Huehnergard and Christopher Woods, "Akkadian and Eblaite," *CEWAL*, 254; Joosten, *Verbal System*, 13.

14. In Akkadian, we find analogous verbal forms and functions. The preterite is expressed in forms like *iprus* "he cut off"; what is called the precative is analogous to the Hebrew jussive and has the same form as the preterite with an initial /l/: *liprus* "let him cut off." Joosten, *Verbal System*, 15. Joosten ("Verbal System," 3:921) refers to the

yiqṭol. Like its PS ancestor, the BH short-*yiqṭol* can function either as a preterite or as a jussive, but in BH the preterite function appears only rarely, and primarily in poetry.

In addition to the basic pattern **yaqtul*, the forms **yiqtal* and **yaqtil* also presumably occurred in PS and were present in PNWS. The three possible theme vowels of the stem are still reflected in BH in verb forms that derive from the short-*yiqṭol* (in the following cases with jussive function): תִּזְכֹּר "do (not) remember (iniquity)" (Isa 64:8); תִּשְׁלַח "do (not) set (a hand on the lad)" (Gen 22:12); יֵצֵא "may (no fugitive) go forth" (2 Kgs 9:15). Verbs that exhibit the **yaqtul* pattern often are active; verbs that exhibit the **yiqtal* pattern are often stative or contain a II- or III-guttural root consonant; verbs exhibiting the **yaqtil* pattern are usually I-*vav*/*yod* roots (plus הלך "to go" and נתן "to give"). As observed above, the prefix vowel shifted to */i/ in **yaqtul* and **yaqtil* forms at some point early in the history of the language, though the original */a/ is still reflected in some weak roots, as with the short-*yiqṭol* of קום: **yaqum* > **yāqom* > יָקֹם "let him arise."[15]

This PS **yaqtul* form also lies behind BH *wayyiqṭol*. The initial component of this form consists of the *vav* conjunction followed by the vowel /a/ and a following *-*n*- particle (or, conceivably another particle or even simply a doubling of the prefix of the verbal form in order to preserve the preceding /a/ vowel).[16] The *yiqṭol* component of the *wayyiqṭol* is from the PS jussive/preterite **yaqtul*. It is, of course, the preterite function that was retained in this BH verbal form. Thus, at least from a historical perspective, labels like "*vav*-conversive imperfect" and "converted imperfect" are really misnomers since they imply either a transformation in function (from imperfective to perfective/preterite) or a transformation in form (from a longer to a shorter verbal stem). But, there really was no conver-

"optative function of the preterite" and refers to the article by Amikam Gai, "The Connection between Past and Optative in the Classical Semitic Languages," *ZDMG* 150 (2000): 17–28; see esp. 20–23; see also Joosten, *Verbal System*, 211.

15. See ch. 3 §7, "'Attenuation' and Similar Changes."

16. David D. Testen (*Parallels in Semitic Linguistics: The Development of Arabic la- and Related Semitic Particles*, SSLL 26 [Leiden: Brill, 1998], 193–96) summarizes the different proposals, including *vav* + *ʾaz* ("then") and Testen's own suggestion *vav* + *al*. More recently, Kryzstoff Baranowski ("The Biblical Hebrew *wayyiqtol* and the Evidence of the Amarna Letters from Canaan," *JHS* 16 [2016]: 12–13, https://doi.org/10.5508/jhs.2015.v15.a12) suggests that the prefix of the verbal component is doubled in order to preserve the distinctive /a/ vowel following the conjunction.

sion in function or form. Instead, the PS jussive/preterite **yaqtul* simply continued to be used as a preterite in BH when preceded by the combination *wa* plus doubled verbal prefix.

In fact, in contrast to what one might expect, it is actually the *yiqṭol* that is the result of a conversion or transformation in function, not the *wayyiqṭol.* In PS, verbal forms in subordinate clauses were marked with a final /u/ vowel. Thus, the PS jussive/preterite in a subordinate clause would appear as **yaqtulu*, **yiqtalu*, or **yaqtilu* (depending on the root).[17] It was this form that was used to express the future or imperfective sense in WS and which became the BH *yiqṭol.* In relation to when such forms were used, notice that the earlier **yaqtul* and **yaqtulu* forms seem to be reflected in the Amarna letters (i.e., in the letters sent from the rulers of Levantine cities like Jerusalem, ca. 1350 BCE).[18]

This history helps explain why in cases of weak roots the short-*yiqṭol* and the *wayyiqṭol* have a similar (if not identical) form (e.g., יִ֫בֶן "let him build" and וַיִּ֫בֶן "he built") that differs from the *yiqṭol* (e.g., יִבְנֶה "he will build"). In weak roots, the difference in forms is the result of different phonetic developments, as explained above.[19] In general, the *yiqṭol* is longer than the short-*yiqṭol* in both its historical articulation and in its graphic representation. Compare the forms of II-*vav*/*yod* roots like קום: the *yiqṭol* typically has a *mater vav* (**yāqūmu* > יָקוּם), while the short-*yiqṭol* and *wayyiqṭol* do not (**yāqum* > יָקֹם* and **wayyāqum* > וַיָּקָם).[20]

17. Again, Akkadian offers an analogous morpheme, as with the subjunctive preterite *iprusu* "[who] cut off." (In Akkadian, the subjunctive verb forms are used in subordinate clauses.)

18. See Anson Rainey, *Canaanite in the Amarna Letters: A Linguistic Analysis of the Mixed Dialect Used by Scribes from Canaan*, 4 vols., HdO 1.25 (Leiden: Brill, 1996), 2:221 and passim; see also Baranowski, "Biblical Hebrew *wayyiqtol*"; and Hélène Dallaire, *Syntax of Volitives in Biblical Hebrew and Amarna Canaanite Prose*, LSAWS 9 (Winona Lake, IN: Eisenbrauns, 2014), 184–90, 216–17.

19. For example, in the case of the III-*vav*/*yod* verbs, the early triphthong sequence vowel-*yod*-vowel at the end of the *yiqṭol* form **yabniyu* contracted to a single final vowel on the *yiqṭol*: **yibnē* > *yibnɛ* = יִבְנֶה. By contrast, the shorter sequence vowel-*yod* at the end of the short-*yiqṭol* form **yabniy* eventually dropped off entirely: (**yabn* >) *yibn* = יִ֫בֶן. Phonetically, the latter form can be represented [jivɛn], though again the last vowel does not constitute a separate syllable. Stated another way, the *segol* in יִבְנֶה is the reflex of *-iyu* and constitutes the second syllable of the verb form, while the *segol* in יִ֫בֶן is an epenthetic vowel, which does not reflect a separate syllable in THT or in PS.

20. The primary exceptions to this general principle are the 1cs *wayyiqṭol* verbs. In III-*vav*/*yod* roots, first-person forms that are explicitly short-*yiqṭol* and that lack

This general tendency of the *yiqṭol* being acoustically and graphically longer than the short-*yiqṭol* and the *wayyiqṭol* is also found in the *hiphil*, where the *yiqṭol* often has a *mater* (e.g., **yašlīku* > **yašlīk* > יַשְׁלִיךְ "he will throw") and the short-*yiqṭol* and *wayyiqṭol* do not (e.g., **yašlik* > **yašlek* > יַשְׁלֵךְ "let him throw" and **wayyašlik* > **wayyašlek* > וַיַּשְׁלֵךְ "he threw"). This superficial rule also applies to the various *hiphil* forms of the II-*vav*/*yod* verbs (**yaqīmu* > **yāqīm* > יָקִים "he will raise" vs. **yaqim* > **yāqem* > יָקֵם "let him raise" and **wayyaqim* > **wayyāqɛm* > וַיָּ֫קֶם "he raised") and III-*vav*/*yod* verbs (**yabniyu* > *יַבְנֶה "he will cause to build" vs. **yabniy* > **yabn* > **yɛbn* = *יֶ֫בֶן "let him cause to build" and **wayyabniy* > **wayyabn* > **wayyɛbn* = *וַיֶּ֫בֶן "he caused to build").[21]

The distinctive brevity of the short-*yiqṭol* and *wayyiqṭol* is only found where there is no word-final vocalic morpheme or object suffix. The short-*yiqṭol* and *wayyiqṭol* are often identical to the *yiqṭol* where the short-*yiqṭol* or *wayyiqṭol* has a simple vocalic morpheme at its end, that is -*ī* (in the 2fs) or -*ū* (in the 3mp and 2mp), or where it bears an object suffix. Thus, יָ֫קוּמוּ, which bears the final-*ū* morpheme, may either be a short-*yiqṭol* or a regular *yiqṭol*; the same applies to תָּ֫קוּמִי, as well as יִבְנוּ and תִּבְנוּ, and also תְּשִׂימֵ֫נִי [*qal* שׂים] "you will set me" or "may you set me." In the *hiphil*, the same thing happens. Any short-*yiqṭol* with a suffixal component will appear as a regular *yiqṭol*. Contrast, for example, the clearly marked short-*yiqṭol* אַל תַּאֲמֵן "do not trust!" (Jer 12:6) with the ambiguous verbal form אַל תַּאֲמִינוּ "do not trust!" (Mic 7:5). Note also the distinct form of the *hiphil wayyiqṭol* וַיַּשְׁלֵךְ "he threw" (Exod 15:25) with the form וַיַּשְׁלִכֵם "he threw them" (Deut 29:27), which has the same stem vowels as the regular *yiqṭol* form.

In an earlier era, a final -*na* would have distinguished the regular *yiqṭol* of second feminine singular, third masculine plural, and second masculine plural (e.g., **takrutūna* "you will cut"). In fact, sometimes BH has pre-

---

the final syllable (e.g., וָאֲצַו "I commanded" Deut 3:18) occur with about as much frequency as forms that have a sequence of vowels like that of the regular *yiqṭol* (e.g., וָאֲצַוֶּה Deut 1:18). In II-*vav*/*yod* roots, the defective orthography in early books (e.g., וָאָקֻם "I arose" 1 Kgs 3:21) and plene orthography in later books (e.g., וָאָקוּם Neh 2:12) suggests that perhaps the distinction between *wayyiqṭol* and *yiqṭol* in the 1cs was lost in the Second Temple era.

21. The *hiphil* of בנה is used for the sake of comparison; note, e.g., the forms that do occur: יַרְבֶּה "he will multiply" (Hos 12:2); תֶּ֫רֶב "may you multiply" (Ps 71:21); וַיֶּ֫רֶב "he multiplied" (2 Sam 18:8).

served the *nun* of this ending: *takrutūna > *tikrutūn > tikrōtūn (> תִּכְרֹתוּן [in pause]) "you will cut" (Exod 34:13). The short-*yiqṭol* (and by extension *wayyiqṭol*) always lacked this *nun* (וַתִּכְרְתוּ "you cut" Jer 34:15). After this final *nun* was lost (from most 2fs, 3mp, 2mp *yiqṭol* forms), there was no longer a clear distinction between these short-*yiqṭol* and *yiqṭol* forms. Where the *nun* is preserved in the MT, it is called a paragogic *nun* (on which, see below).

As for the imperative, the basic PS form was akin to that of the short-*yiqṭol* (minus the prefix), which, for our purposes we can represent through the examples: **šmur*, **škab*, **tin* (for the equivalent of the *qal* conjugation); alternatively the forms might have been realized as **šumur*, **šakab*, **nitin*.[22] In either case, an initial muttered vowel is implied in the Hebrew masculine singular (e.g., שְׁמֹר and שְׁכַב; but cf. תֵּן) and in the far less common feminine plural (שְׁמֹרְנָה* and שְׁכַבְנָה*). The feminine singular (שִׁמְרִי* and שִׁכְבִי as well as תְּנִי) and the masculine plural forms (e.g., שִׁמְרוּ and שִׁכְבוּ* as well as תְּנוּ) exhibit the reduction of the stem's historical short vowel (as in the corresponding forms of the short-*yiqṭol* and *yiqṭol*); those imperatives with three root consonants attest an /i/ vowel in the first syllable.[23]

The cohortative likely derives from a form like PS **yaqtul* followed by a final *-*a* or *-*ā*.[24] In an earlier era, this was part of a complete verbal paradigm (with third- and second-person forms), each form of which ended in a similar way. In the MT, third-person forms are only very rarely found (e.g., יָחִישָׁה "let him hasten" Isa 5:19 and תָּבוֹאָה "let it come" Isa 5:19).[25] As with the other vocalic morphemes at the end of the *yiqṭol* form, this suffixed /a/-class vowel resulted in the reduction of the verb's theme vowel (e.g., אֵלְכָה "let me go" Gen 24:56 and נִכְרְתָה "let us cut" Gen 26:28).

Several more details of *yiqṭol* morphology can be explained easily by reference to the history of the language. As mentioned above, one not infrequently finds second feminine singular, third masculine plural, and second masculine plural *yiqṭol* verb forms containing a final *nun* (i.e., a *nun* following the -*ī* or -*ū* morpheme).

---

22. Huehnergard ("Afro-Asiatic," 152) posits for PS an epenthetic vowel (e.g., **kutub*) or prothetic glottal stop (*ʾ*uktub*) to resolve the consonant cluster.

23.Note the evidence of the Secunda: σιμου "hear" (cf. שִׁמְעוּ); see Brønno, *Studien*, 52.

24. Alternatively, it is related to the energic forms. See Steven E. Fassberg, "Cohortative," *EHLL* 1:476–77.

25. Ibid. See also Job 11:17.

- תִּדְבָּקִין "you will cling" (Ruth 2:21)
- יִשְׁמְעוּן "they will hear" (Deut 2:25)
- יֶהֱמָיוּן "they roar" (Isa 17:12)
- תִּכְרֹתוּן "you will cut" (Exod 34:13)
- תֶּאֱהָבוּן "you will love" (Ps 4:3)[26]

The *nun* in these cases is referred to as a paragogic *nun* and occurs exclusively on such forms (i.e., 2fs, 3mp, 2mp *yiqṭol* verbs).[27] There are many such examples.[28] How these function in BH and what significance they have for the verbal system are unclear and debated.[29]

As explained above, this *nun* is actually part of the older paradigm of the *yiqṭol*. In an older stage of the language, the second feminine singular and third and second masculine plural *yiqṭol* forms would have regularly ended with this *nun* (i.e., *-īna*, *-ūna*, *-ūna*). By contrast, the second feminine singular and third and second masculine plural forms in the short-*yiqṭol* (and *wayyiqṭol*) lacked this final *nun*.

---

26. Among BH verb forms, it is only the 3fp and 2fp that typically end in a *nun* (e.g., תִּקְטֹלְנָה), which may reflect either the short-*yiqṭol* or regular *yiqṭol*. The 3fp and 2fp *yiqṭol* and related forms are used for both indicative and jussive functions (e.g., אַל־תִּשְׁלַחְנָה "do not send" Obad 13).

27. The term "paragogic" often refers to "a letter or syllable added to a word" (*OED*). Technically, this is an inaccurate description of the *nun* in question since verb forms with this *nun* are closer to the earlier base forms of the nonvolitive *yiqṭols*; however, it should be recognized that some scribes/speakers could have added such a *nun* to the *yiqṭols* for phonological reasons or due to a perceived sense that these forms were more sophisticated or "correct."

28. See *IBHS*, 514–17. Tamar Zewi (*A Syntactical Study of Verbal Forms Affixed by -n(n) Endings in Classical Arabic, Biblical Hebrew, El-Amarna Akkadian and Ugaritic*, AOAT 260 [Münster: Ugarit-Verlag, 1999], 114–39 and passim) lists and discusses each example.

29. In addition to Zewi, *Syntactical Study*, see Stephen A. Kaufman, "Paragogic *Nun* in Biblical Hebrew: Hypercorrection as a Clue to a Lost Scribal Practice," in *Solving Riddles, Untying Knots: Biblical, Epigraphic, and Semitic Studies in Honor of Jonas C. Greenfield*, ed. Ziony Zevit, Seymour Gitin, and Michael Sokoloff (Winona Lake, IN: Eisenbrauns, 1995), 95–99; W. Randall Garr, "The Paragogic *nun* in Rhetorical Perspective," in *Biblical Hebrew in Its Northwest Semitic Setting: Typological and Historical Perspectives*, ed. Steven E. Fassberg and Avi Hurvitz (Winona Lake, IN: Eisenbrauns, 2006), 65–74; V. De Caen, "Moveable *Nun* and Intrusive *Nun*: The Nature and Distribution of Verbal Nunation in Joel and Job," *JNSL* 29 (2003): 121–32.

Proof that the origin of the *nun* is in a distinction between *yiqṭol* and short-*yiqṭol* paradigms comes from comparative evidence and inner-Hebrew evidence. In other languages like Aramaic and Arabic, a final *nun* on second feminine singular and third and second masculine plural verb forms marks the verb as nonvolitive (or as indicative). By contrast, the jussive or volitive forms lack the *nun* (and are, therefore, shorter than the nonvolitive forms). That the Hebrew forms with the so-called paragogic *nun* go back to such earlier (nonvolitive) *yiqṭol* forms is supported by the fact that verbs with the paragogic *nun* are almost universally negated with לֹא in the MT, not with אַל (which is associated especially with the short-*yiqṭol* in its jussive function). In addition, paragogic-*nun* forms are only very rarely found as *wayyiqṭol* forms.[30]

Another feature of BH that is related to verbal endings and with which the paragogic *nun* is sometimes confused is the energic *nun*. In BH, the energic *nun* appears almost exclusively with *yiqṭol* forms that take an object suffix.[31] With the first- and second-person object suffixes, the energic *nun* usually assimilates into the following consonant of the pronominal suffix (e.g., **ʾăbārikan + kā* > **ʾăbārikakkā* [> אֲבָרְכֶךָּ] "I will bless you" Gen 26:3).[32] With third-person suffixes, assimilation usually happens in the opposite direction: the first consonant of the suffix assimilates backward into the *nun* (e.g., **təbārikan + hū* > ** təbārikannū* > תְּבָרְכֶנּוּ "you will bless him" 2 Kgs 4:29). This assimilation is possible because no vowel ever followed the energic *nun*.[33]

Like the paragogic *nun*, the energic *nun* occurs almost exclusively on the *yiqṭol* (i.e., not on the short-*yiqṭol* or *wayyiqṭol*).[34] It is distinct from

30. There are only nine examples in the MT (see Joüon §44e). Note, too, that many verb forms from III-*vav/yod* roots that attest a paragogic *nun*, also preserve a third *yod* root consonant (e.g., יֶחֱזָיוּן "they will [not] see" Isa 26:11). Also at Deut 8:13; Isa 17:12; 21:12; 31:3; 33:7; 40:18; 41:5; Pss 36:8, 9; 39:7; 78:44; 83:3; Job 19:2; 31:38. See also Zewi, *Syntactical Study*, 73.

31. Note, however, some have proposed that certain forms that look like 3fp forms are actually energic forms without suffix, like תִּשְׁלַחְנָה "she sent" (Judg 5:26). See Joüon §61f. For all the examples of the energic *nun*, see Zewi, *Syntactical Study*, 75–114, 141–52.

32. Contrast this with the nonenergic form: אֲבָרֶכְךָ "I will bless you" Gen 22:17.

33. In pause the *nun* sometimes does not appear to assimilate, though this is extremely rare (e.g., יַעַבְרֶנְהוּ "it will [not] pass" Jer 5:22; note also in Exod 15:2, Deut 32:10, and Ps 72:15; Zewi, *Syntactical Study*, 75 n. 57).

34. The energic *nun* occurs only three times on a verb form preceded by the nega-

the paragogic *nun* in several ways. First, whereas the paragogic *nun* occurs only on forms with a final vowel morpheme (i.e., final /ī/ or /ū/), the energic *nun* occurs only on forms without a final vowel morpheme, including third and second masculine singular, third feminine singular, and first common singular and plural forms. Second, the energic *nun* occurs only between the stem and object suffix. It does not occur on verbal forms without an object suffix.[35] The energic *nun* is really part of an earlier and separate verbal paradigm, each verb form of which ended in *-*an* or *-*n* (e.g., **yišmuran* "he will guard"). Again, it is other Semitic languages that suggest this origin. In Arabic, for example, the energic forms constitute two entire verbal paradigms, one a long form (ending –*anna*) and the other a short form (ending –*an*). Similar forms appear in Ugaritic with suffixes. In the end, BH only seems to reflect the short form. These energic endings in BH have no easily discernible semantic significance for the verbs to which they are attached.[36] One may note, however, that given the *nun*'s distribution, it can often be assumed that a verbal form with an energic ending is a regular *yiqṭol* form.[37]

The energic endings are usually easy to identify since they are often analogous to the forms of suffixes attached to the preposition *min*.

- מִמֶּ֫נִּי "from me" and יוֹעִדֶ֫נִּי "he will summon me" (Jer 50:44) [*hiphil* יעד][38]

---

tive particle אַל (all three occurrences appear in Job); the energic *nun* appears only nine times on a *wayyiqṭol* form (seven out of the nine times in poetry). In a further sixteen cases (almost all in poetry), close proximity with volitive forms suggests that the verbal form with energic nun and suffix is really a short-*yiqṭol* (e.g., Job 12:8). Contrast these figures with the 533 occurrences of the energic *nun* with the regular *yiqṭol*. Cf. the *wayyiqṭol* + suffix, וַיִּשְׁלָחֵ֫הוּ "so, he sent him" (Gen 37:14), with the regular *yiqṭol* + energic *nun* + suffix: יִשְׁלָחֶ֫נּוּ "he would send him" (1 Sam 18:5). See Blau, *Phonology and Morphology*, 172.

35. See n. 31 above for possible exceptions.

36. See Zewi (*Syntactical Study*, 75–114, 141–52) for a thorough review of where and how these forms are used.

37. This does not mean, however, that every form without an energic *nun* is a short-*yiqṭol*; the regular *yiqṭol* can also occur without an energic *nun*. But, note this significant tendency: in prose texts, the 3ms object suf. on a regular *yiqṭol* will almost always have an energic *nun* before it (See Blau, *Phonology and Morphology*, 172).

38. Often, however, the suffix has a *patakh*, as in תְּבָרְכַ֫נִי "you will bless me" (Gen 27:31).

- מִמֶּךָּ "from you" (pausal) and אֲצַוֶּךָּ "I will command you" (Exod 7:2) [*piel* צוה]
- מִמֶּנָּה "from her" and יַקְטִירֶנָּה "he will offer it" (Exod 30:7) [*hiph*il קטר]
- מִמֶּנּוּ "from him" and תְבָרֲכֶנּוּ "you will [not] bless him" (2 Kgs 4:29) [*piel* ברך][39]

Where one finds a *nun* between a third masculine plural or second masculine plural verbal stem and a suffix, it is usually identified as a paragogic *nun*, not an energic *nun* (e.g., יְשַׁחֲרֻנְנִי "they will seek me" Prov 1:28; וּתְדַכְּאוּנַנִי "and you will crush me" Job 19:2).[40] In cases like יְשַׁחֲרֻנְנִי one assumes an earlier form with a historical short vowel after the *nun* (one assumes /a/ of the paragogic *nun*-ending, **yušaḥḥirūnanī*). The energic *nun* was not followed by a short vowel and, thus, would have resulted in assimilation.[41] Despite the different origins, likely by the mid-first millennium BCE, the verbs with energic *nun* + suffix and those with paragogic *nun* + suffix were conceived of as part of a single paradigm. Note, for instance, that in Jer 5:22 a pausal verb with paragogic *nun* + suffix, יַעַבְרֻנְהוּ "they will [not] pass it," is immediately preceded by (and is poetically parallel to) a pausal verb with energic *nun* + suffix, יַעַבְרֶנְהוּ "it will [not] pass it."

39. Energic *nun* does not appear with most plural suffixes; there is only one example of the 1cp suffix (Hab 3:16), and none of the 2mp, 2fp, 3mp, 3fp.

40. Note also יְשָׁרְתוּנֶךָ (pause) "they will serve you" Isa 60:7; יִמְצָאֻנְנִי (pause) "they will find me" Prov 8:17. The energic *nun* is never followed by a vowel. Zewi (*Syntactic Study*, 116–17) lists some of the examples (though others can be found: Hos 5:15; Ps 63:4; Prov 8:17).

41. Alternatively, examples like יַעַבְרֻנְהוּ are representative of a second energic paradigm, like that in Arabic, which ended in -(*a*)*nna* (i.e., **yaʿburunnahū* > **yaʿburunnəhū* > **yaʿbərunhū*). Or, the above pausal forms like יְשַׁחֲרֻנְנִי are due to a secondary archaizing formation of the energic paradigm.

In outline, then, the historical development of BH finite verbs can be presented in the following manner:

Time period	*qåṭal*	short-*yiqṭol*	*yiqṭol*	imperative	energic[42]
			third masculine singular		
PNWS	**šamara*	**yašmur*	**yašmuru*		**yašmuran*
BH 100 BCE	**šāmar*	**yišmor*	**yišmor*		**yišmərɛn(+nū)*
THT	*šåmar*	*yišmor*	*yišmor*		*yišmrɛn(+nu)*
			third feminine singular		
PNWS	**šamarat*	**tašmur*	**tašmuru*		**tašmuran*
BH 100 BCE	**šāmərā*[43]	**tišmor*	**tišmor*		**tišmərɛn(+nū)*
THT	*šåmrå*	*tišmor*	*tišmor*		*tišmrɛn(+nu)*
			second masculine singular		
PNWS	**šamarta*	**tašmur*	**tašmuru*	**š(u)mur*	**tašmuran*
BH 100 BCE	**šāmartā*	**tišmor*	**tišmor*	**šəmor*	**tišmərɛn(+nū)*
THT	*šåmartå*	*tišmor*	*tišmor*	*šmor*	*tišmrɛn(+nu)*
			second feminine singular		
PNWS	**šamarti*	**tašmurī*	**tašmurīna*	**š(u)murī*	**tašmurin*
BH 100 BCE	**šāmart*	**tišmərī*	**tišmərī*	**šimrī*	-
THT	*šåmart*	*tišmrī*	*tišmrī*	*šimrī*	-
			first common singular		
PNWS	**šamartu*	*ʾ*ašmur*	*ʾ*ašmuru*		*ʾ*ašmuran*
BH 100 BCE	**šāmartī*	*ʾ*ešmor*	*ʾ*ešmor*		-
THT	*šåmarti*	ʾ*ešmor*	ʾ*ešmor*		-
			third masculine plural		
PNWS	**šamarū*	**yašmurū*	**yašmurūna*		**yašmurun*
BH 100 BCE	**šāmərū*	**yišmərū*	**yišmərū*		-
THT	*šåmru*	*yišmru*	*yišmru*		-

42. One could also include a separate column for the earlier paradigm from which the cohortative derived: **yašmura*, etc.

43. During this time period, this and similar forms were presumably also sometimes pronounced with a full vowel in the penultimate syllable, as reflected in some forms of the Secunda. The same applies to the 3cp *qåṭal* and the 2fs, 3mp, and 2mp short-*yiqṭol*, *yiqṭol*, etc.

		third feminine plural			
PNWS	**šamarā*	**yašmurna*	**yašmurna*		-
BH 100 BCE	-	**tišmornā*	**tišmornā*[44]		-
THT	-	*tišmornå*	*tišmornå*		-
		second masculine plural			
PNWS	**šamartumu*	**tašmurū*	**tašmurūna*	**š(u)murū*	**tašmurun*
BH 100 BCE	**šəmartɛm*	**tišmərū*	**tišmərū*	**šimrū*	-
THT	**šmartɛm*	*tišmru*	*tišmru*	*šimru*	-
		second feminine plural			
PNWS	**šamartinna*	**tašmurna*	**tašmurna*	**š(u)murna*	-
BH 100 BCE	**šəmartɛn*	**tišmornā*[45]	**tišmornā*	**šəmornā*	-
THT	**šmartɛn*	*tišmornå*	*tišmornå*	*šmornå*	-
		first common plural			
PNWS	**šamarnū*	**našmur*	**našmuru*		**našmuran*
BH 100 BCE	**šāmarnū*	**nišmor*	**nišmor*		**nišmərɛn(+nū)*
THT	*šåmarnu*	*nišmor*	*nišmor*		*nišmrɛn(+nu)*

Although the above verbal forms are based on the strong root for the basic stem (BH *qal*), the other conjugations (*piel*, *hiphil*, etc.) would have attested similar features and paradigms. That is, the third masculine singular *hiphil qåṭal* would have ended in an /a/ vowel, **hašmira*, just as the above third masculine singular form does. Similarly, the energic would also have occurred in the *hiphil*, **yašmiran*.

The most essential thing for students to remember from this history is the underlying correspondences between the short-*yiqṭol*, *wayyiqṭol*, *yiqṭol*, imperative, and cohortative forms. Usually, these forms contain the same stem vowel(s) and inflect in a similar manner. From a pragmatic perspective, due to these correspondences, one can often predict the various forms of the verb based on a knowledge of just the third masculine singular and third masculine plural *yiqṭol*. In addition, it is important to remember

44. The 3fp *yiqṭol* begins with *tav*, due presumably to an association of this letter with feminine marked verbs. The earlier form with prefix *yod* is reflected in only three forms in the MT (e.g., וַיִּשַּׁרְנָה "they went straight" 1 Sam 6:12; see Joüon §44d).

45. The 2fp short-*yiqṭol* and regular *yiqṭol* are the same. Note, e.g., אַל־תִּשְׁלַחְנָה "do not send" Obad 13 vs. לֹא תֶחֱזֶינָה "you will not see" Ezek 13:33.

the even closer connection between the short-*yiqṭol* and *wayyiqṭol*. In general (and as the label implies), the short-*yiqṭol* and *wayyiqṭol* are shorter than the regular *yiqṭol*. In both strong and weak roots, the short-*yiqṭol* and *wayyiqṭol* do not typically attest the paragogic *nun* or the energic *nun*. Graphically, the theme vowel of short-*yiqṭol* and *wayyiqṭol* weak verbs is often not marked with a *mater*, though such marking is regular in the *yiqṭol* (e.g., יָקֹם "let him arise" and וַיָּ֫קָם "he arose" vs. יָקוּם "he will arise"). With III-*vav*/*yod* roots, the short-*yiqṭol* and *wayyiqṭol* lack all trace of the third root consonant (e.g., יִ֫גֶל "he reveals" Job 36:15 and וַיִּ֫גֶל "he reveals" Job 36:10 vs. יִגְלֶה "he will [not] reveal" 1 Sam 20:2).

5.3. Verb with Object Suffixes

Object suffixes on the *qåṭal* are for the most part the same as those on the noun. The primary exceptions include the following: the first common singular suffix has a *nun* (e.g., שְׁלָחַ֫נִי "he sent me" Num 16:28) and the third masculine singular suffix sometimes has a *he* (e.g., הֲרָגָ֫תְהוּ "she killed him" Judg 9:54; and עֲבָד֫וּהוּ "they did [not] serve him" Judg 10:6).[46] In other cases, the third masculine singular *qåṭal* has a simple vowel, like the suffix on the noun (e.g., הֲרָגוֹ "he killed him" Gen 4:25).[47] Sometimes, the vowel suffix is due to assimilation of *he* (i.e., **gamalat + hū* > **gəmālattū* > גְּמָלַ֫תּוּ "she weaned him" 1 Sam 1:24).

Often, if there is a full vowel between the *qåṭal* verbal form and suffix, it matches the vowel of the earlier PNWS form. For the third masculine singular and second masculine singular *qåṭal*, the vowel is an /a/-class vowel (cf. **šamara* and **šamarta*).

- עָשָׂ֫הוּ "he made it" (Ps 95:5)
- שְׁלָחַ֫נִי "he sent me" (Gen 45:5)
- שְׁלַחְתָּ֫נִי "you sent me" (Exod 5:22)

This is important to remember because it can sometimes help disambiguate otherwise similar forms. For example, עֲנִיתָם (the 2ms of ענה +

46. The 3ms suffix on nouns also exhibits a *he* if the noun to which it is attached is from an etymological III-*vav*/*yod* root, e.g., שָׂדֵ֫הוּ "his field."

47. This is perhaps derived from a form with an /a/ linking vowel (i.e., **haragahū* [> **haragau*] > **haragaw* > **hărāgō* > [הֲרָגוֹ]); see Garr, *Dialect Geography*, 103 and note the alternative explanations listed in Hutton, "Epigraphic Hebrew," 1:838.

the 3mp object suf.) "you answered them" (Ps 99:8) has a *qamets* and is thus distinct from the second masculine plural *qåṭal* (without object suf.) עֲנִיתֶם "you did (not) answer" (Isa 65:12). Similarly, the /a/-class linking vowel of the *qåṭal* + object suffix is distinct from the /i/-class linking vowel of the imperative + object suffix. Compare, for example, the *qåṭal* form שְׁלָחַנִי "he sent me" (Gen 45:5) with the imperatival form שְׁלָחֵנִי "send me!" (Isa 6:8); also with weak roots: עָנָנִי "he answered me" (1 Kgs 2:30) versus עֲנֵנִי "answer me!" (1 Kgs 18:26). Because the third masculine singular /ō/ suffix (e.g., הֲרָגוֹ < **haragahu* "he killed him") is likely derived from a form with an /a/ linking vowel, one does not find it on forms ending in a historical /i/ or /u/ (e.g., וַאֲכָלֻהוּ "they will eat it" Lev 24:9). Imperatives and non-*qåṭal* forms also do not attest the third masculine singular /ō/ suffix since they usually attest an /i/ linking vowel (e.g., עָבְדֵהוּ "serve him!" 1 Chr 28:9).

The second feminine singular *qåṭal* also seems to reflect its earlier vowel: יְלִדְתִּנִי "you bore me" (Jer 15:10). The second masculine plural is the same: הֶעֱלִיתֻנוּ "you brought us up" (Num 20:5). Of course, the final /ū/-vowel of the third common plural is preserved before suffixes (e.g., וַאֲכָלֻהוּ "they will eat it"; וְשָׁבוּם "they will capture them" in 1 Kgs 8:46 [שׁבה]). The primary exception to this general principle is the first common singular, which shows the vowel of its later articulation (*/ī/ not */u/): צִוִּיתִיךָ "I commanded you" (Gen 3:11).

With these object suffixes, the *qåṭal* often reveals a vowel pattern within its stem similar to that of nouns + suffix. This is due to the common development of both categories of words. Thus, the addition of a suffix to the third masculine singular verb results in the initial sequence of vowels **ə-ā*. Note, for example, **haragahu* > **haragō* > **hărāgō* > הֲרָגוֹ "he killed him" (Gen 4:25). Note similarly the form חֲקָרָהּ "he explored it" (Job 28:27). The vowel patterns of these verbal forms are analogous to those of דְּבָרוֹ "his word" דְּבָרָהּ and "her word." The initial sequence **ə-ā* is also found in most other *qal* third-person verbal forms with object suffixes (e.g., הֲרָגַתְהוּ "she killed him" and עֲבָדוּהוּ "they served him"). Unlike the third-person forms, the first- and second-person forms begin with the sequence **ə-a* (e.g., יְדַעְתּוֹ "you do [not] know him" Deut 22:2). Remembering these vowel sequences is especially helpful for distinguishing quickly a third feminine singular verb from a second masculine singular or first common singular verb. With the weak root, the vowel sequence also resembles that of a noun: רָאָהּ "he saw it" (Job 28:27; cf. קָנָהּ "its stem" Exod 25:31); עֲנִיתָם "you answered them" (Ps 99:8; cf. בְּרִיתוֹ "his covenant" Deut 4:13).

Usually the lexicon of BH is such that the *qåṭal* form with object suffix is not homophonous with a noun plus possessive suffix. For example, when a third-person masculine singular object suffix is added to the *yiqṭol* verb ידע, one gets the form יְדָעוֹ "he knew him" (Deut 34:10); no noun exists that would result in the form יְדָעוֹ. Instead, the same root attests nouns like דַּעַת "knowledge" and מַדָּע "knowledge."[48] Similarly, the verb דבר is articulated in the *piel* (e.g., דִּבֶּר "he spoke" and דִּבְּרוֹ "he [did] not speak it" Deut 18:22) or as the *qal* in the participle (e.g., דֹּבֵר "one speaking"). This means that there is never confusion with דְּבָרוֹ "his word."

Object suffixes on *yiqṭol* verb forms are easily recognizable and are the same as those for the *qåṭal*. If there is a full vowel linking the verbal form with the suffix, it is usually an /i/-class vowel, represented in THT by either *segol* or *tsere* (e.g., יִשְׁפְּטֵנִי "he will judge me" 1 Sam 24:16; תִּשְׁלָחֵנוּ "you will send us" Josh 1:16), in contrast to the /a/-class vowel commonly found between a suffix and a third masculine singular or second masculine singular *qåṭal* form.[49]

For those prefix verbal forms that have an /o/ theme vowel, the underlying /u/ vowel generally reduced before suffixes (e.g., יִשְׁפְּטֵנִי). This is consistent with the pattern we observed above, where a historical short */u/ will often reduce in the pretonic position.[50] In those cases, where the theme vowel of the *yiqṭol* is /a/ (e.g., יִשְׁלַח "he will send" and יִשְׁמַע "he will hear"), the form with suffix will reflect */ā/; note, for example, תִּשְׁלָחֵנוּ "you will send us" (Josh 1:16) and יִשְׁמָעֵנִי "he will hear me" (Exod 6:12). This also follows the vowel pattern, noted above, where a pretonic historical */a/ in an open syllable is usually lengthened to */ā/.

With suffixal morphemes and pronominal object suffixes, the short-*yiqṭol* and *wayyiqṭol* have forms identical to those of the *yiqṭol*. As mentioned above, however, in prose the regular *yiqṭol* plus third masculine

---

48. In a similar way, the *yiqṭol* verb ילד with 2ms object suffix is יְלָדְךָ "he engendered him" (Deut 32:18). The root ילד attests nouns that, with the application of the 2ms suffix, would not result in an analogous form (e.g., יֶלֶד with the 2ms would be *יַלְדְּךָ and in the plural יְלָדֶיךָ).

49. There are exceptions, of course: תִּדְבָּקַנִי "lest it cling to me" Gen 19:19; יִלְבָּשָׁם "he will wear them" Exod 29:30; אֲמִילַם "I will cut them off" Ps 118:10, 11, 12.

50. An /i/-class theme vowel will also reduce to shewa with object suffixes (e.g., יִתֵּן vs. יִתְּנֵנִי "he will set me" Jer 9:1), again reflecting the tendency for pretonic /i/ to reduce in open syllables where the vowel of the propretonic syllable cannot reduce (cf. **šāpiṭīma* > **šōpəṭīm* > שֹׁפְטִים "judges").

singular suffix usually exhibits an energic *nun*: *-*ɛnnū* (e.g. יִשְׁלָחֶנּוּ), while the short-*yiqṭol* and *wayyiqṭol* appear without it: *-*ēhū* (e.g., וַיִּשְׁלָחֵהוּ).[51]

The object suffixes attached to the imperative are again those associated with the other verb forms. Since the imperative is related to the *yiqṭol*, it also attests an /i/-class linking vowel between verb and suffix. This is useful in distinguishing the imperative from the *qåṭal*, as mentioned above (e.g., שְׁלָחַנִי "he sent me" vs. שְׁלָחֵנִי "send me!" and עָנָנִי "he answered me" vs. עֲנֵנִי "answer me!"). Notice, however, that the third feminine singular object suffix often exhibits an /a/-vowel (e.g., לָכְדָהּ "take it!" 2 Sam 12:28; לַמְּדָהּ "teach it!" Deut 31:19).

With suffixes, the stem of the *qal* imperative exhibits different forms, in each case associated with the theme vowel of the verb in the *yiqṭol*. The verbs with an /o/ theme vowel in the *yiqṭol* are characterized by an /o/ vowel in the first syllable of an imperative + suffix form (e.g., זָכְרֵנִי < **zokrēnī* < **zukrēnī* < **zukurini* "remember me" Judg 16:28). Verbs with an /a/ theme vowel in the *yiqṭol* are characterized by the same sequence of vowels as found in the *qåṭal* and suffix (e.g., שְׁמָעֵנִי < **šəmāʿēnī* < **šamaʿini* "hear me!"). This reflects the same tendencies for pretonic /u/ to reduce and for pretonic /a/ to lengthen (in open syllables) noted above.

Where the masculine singular imperative takes the long form with final */ā/, the verbs with an /o/ theme vowel in the *yiqṭol* attest the same pattern of vowel shift in their stem as with object suffixes: שָׁמְרָה "guard!" (Ps 25:20). But, verbs with an /a/ theme vowel show a different pattern. Usually, the imperative looks like a feminine **qåṭal* segolate (e.g., שִׁמְעָה "hear!" Ps 17:1).[52]

Students should remember that often the *qåṭal* + suffix contains an /a/-class vowel between the stem and suffix, but the *yiqṭol* and imperative contain an /i/-class vowel.

5.4. Verbs in the Non-*Qal* Conjugations (or Binyanim): General Comments

Certain consistencies between all strong and guttural roots in the different conjugations should be pointed out since this makes learning and predict-

51. See Blau, *Phonology and Morphology*, 172.

52. Sometimes, it reflects the same sequence of vowels as the *qåṭal* + suffix and imperative + suffix, that is, *ə-ā (e.g., רְפָאָה "heal!" Ps 41:5; שְׁמָעָה "hear!" and סְלָחָה "pardon!" Dan 9:19).

ing the various inflections comparatively easy. These consistencies, moreover, usually have historical explanations that have already been introduced elsewhere.

1. In all conjugations (except the *qal*), the vowels of the name of the conjugation indicate the sequence of vowels in the third masculine singular *qåṭal* (e.g., *niphal* implies **i-a* as in נִשְׁמַר).[53] In the *pual*, *hophal*, and *hithpael* the sequence of vowels in the name are present throughout the entire paradigm (i.e., in the *qåṭal*, [short-] *yiqṭol*, *wayyiqṭol*, impv., inf. constr., and ptc.).
2. With the exception of the *hiphil*, all conjugations (including most *qal* active roots) exhibit a *shewa* in the penultimate syllable of the third feminine singular and third common plural *yiqṭol* (e.g., *piel qåṭal*: דִּבְּרָה and דִּבְּרוּ).[54]
3. With the exception of the *hiphil*, all conjugations also exhibit a *shewa* in the penultimate syllable in the third feminine singular and third- and second-person masculine plural *yiqṭol* (and related forms) (e.g., *piel yiqṭol*: יְדַבְּרוּ).[55]
4. In all conjugations (including the *qal*), the last stem vowel of second- and first-person *qåṭal* forms is almost always /a/ (e.g., שָׁמַ֫רְתָּ [*qal*]; דִּבַּ֫רְתָּ [*piel*]; הִקְרַ֫בְתָּ [*hiphil*]; נִשְׁמַ֫רְתָּ [*niphal*]; שֻׁלַּ֫חְתִּי [*pual*]; הָכְלָ֫מְנוּ [*hophal*]; וְהִתְחַזַּקְתֶּם [*hithpael*]).[56]
5. If a conjugation attests an /a/-class vowel in the stem of the participle, it will always reflect */ā/ (e.g., נִלְחָם "one fighting" Exod 14:25). In the *niphal*, this can distinguish the masculine singular participle from the third masculine singular *qåṭal* (נִלְחָם vs. נִלְחַם

53. An /a/-vowel in the name presumes a short /a/.

54. These muttered vowels likely reflect secondary vowel reduction after the place of stress in verbs had shifted from the penultimate (e.g., **yiqṭol*) to the ultimate syllable (**yiqṭol*).

55. The reduction is, again, likely due to a shifting place of the stress. For infinitive and participial forms (e.g., *piel* inf. const.: דַּבְּרוֹ), this may reflect the tendency for historical */i/ to reduce in pretonic syllables where the vowel of the propretonic syllable cannot reduce.

56. In the case of the *qal* and conjugations associated with passivity, the /a/ vowel reflects the original vowel and was likely present in the Second Temple era and earlier. In the case of the non-*qal* conjugations associated with an active voice, the /a/ is a result of a shift (from an earlier */ɛ/ [< */i/]) and may be of a relatively late date. See ch. 3 §3, "Development of Individual Vowels."

"he fought" 2 Kgs 13:12). This reflects the consistent presence of */ā/ in the tonic syllable of nouns and adjectives, and contrasts with the short */a/ found in accented syllables in finite verbs.[57]

5.5. Verbs in the Non-*Qal* Conjugations: Passive *Qal*

In Hebrew, most stems associated with an active voice have a passive counterpart. That is, the *piel* has the *pual* and the *hiphil* has the *hophal*. It is often assumed that the *niphal* is the passive of the *qal*, but this is not exactly true. The *niphal* often indicates a passive voice, but it also indicates a middle voice (i.e., a reciprocal and/or reflexive sense) and presumably this was closer to its earliest meaning. The *qal*, in fact, once had a passive version of itself, the biblical examples of which were later reinterpreted as instances of the *niphal*, *pual*, or *hophal*.[58] This passive *qal* stem, it should be pointed out, is entirely distinct from the verbal adjective that is referred to as the "*qal* passive participle" (e.g., שָׁמוּר "one guarded").

The passive *qal* conjugation, as it can be perceived today, had a *qåṭal* form, a *yiqṭol* form, and a participial form. The basic vowel sequence in the stem of the passive *qal* was **u-a*. It was distinguished from the *pual* (which had the same vowel sequence in its stem) by the fact that the passive *qal* did not exhibit doubling of the middle root consonant (as happens in the *pual*). The participle would have had the vowel sequence **u-ā* without a prefixed *mem*, while the *yiqṭol* form would have had the form **yuqṭal*, which would have made it virtually identical to the *hophal yiqṭol*.[59]

---

57. Other more minor consistencies can also be found. In particular, verbs with an /a/ theme vowel in the *qal yiqṭol* sometimes occur in other conjugations with an /a/ vowel in the contextual *qåṭal* 3ms, where we might expect an /i/-class vowel. For example, אִבַּד "he destroyed" (note *qal* יֹאבַד "he will perish"); לִמַּד "he taught" (note *qal* יִלְמַד "he will learn"); קִדַּשׁ "he sanctified" (note *qal* יִקְדַּשׁ "he will be holy"); וְהֵצַר "he will cause distress" (note *qal* יֵצַר "he is pressed"); הֵקַל "he treated with contempt" (note וַתֵּקַל "she was slight"). See Joüon §§ 52c and 82d.

58. For a recent summary of the passive *qal* stem, see Eric D. Reymond, "The Passive *Qal* in the Hebrew of the Second Temple Period, Especially as Found in the Wisdom of Ben Sira," in *Sibyls, Scriptures, and Scrolls: John Collins at Seventy*, ed. Joel Baden, Hindy Najman, and Eibert Tigchelaar, JSJSup 175 (Leiden: Brill, 2016), 2:1110–27.

59. Though, the *hophal yiqṭol* would have been expressed with a *he* at some earlier point, i.e., **yuhuqṭal*. Cf. the *he* found in the *hiphil yiqṭol* of some forms: אֲהוֹדֶנּוּ "I will thank him" (Ps 28:7).

In any case, almost all the forms have been reanalyzed as true *niphal*, *pual*, or *hophal* forms in the Tiberian vocalization and thus, regardless of their etymology, their passive sense is usually clear.

Essentially, the passive *qal* is identified by looking for forms that appear to be *pual* or *hophal* but that are not attested in the respective active conjugations (i.e., *piel* or *hiphil*).

- לֻקַּח (< **luqaḥa*) "he was taken" (Gen 3:23)
- יֻקַּח (< **yuqqaḥu*) "it will be taken" (Gen 18:4)
- אֻכְּלוּ (< *ʾ*ukalū*) "they are consumed" (Nah 1:10)
- תְּאֻכְּלוּ (< **tuʾkalūna*) "you will be consumed" (Isa 1:20)

In addition, in their contexts, the meaning of the verbs corresponds to that of the *qal*, not to any of the senses typical of the *piel/pual* or *hiphil/hophal* (i.e., יֻקַּח = "it was taken," not "it was caused to be taken").

When the passive *qal* was lost from Hebrew is difficult to say, but at least it was lost by late Second Temple times. Its existence in the first half of the first millennium BCE is implied by various correspondences between 1–2 Samuel and 1–2 Chronicles. In the former, often one finds a passive *qal* form and in the latter a *niphal* (or something similar).

יֻלְּדוּ "they were born" (2 Sam 3:5)	versus	נוֹלַד (1 Chr 3:4)
יֻלַּד "he was born" (2 Sam 21:20)	versus	נוֹלַד (1 Chr 20:6)
יֻלְּדוּ "they were born" (2 Sam 21:22)	versus	נוּלְּדוּ (1 Chr 20:8)

5.6. Verbs in the Non-*Qal* Conjugations: *Piel*

The *piel* (like the *pual* as well as the *hithpael*) is morphologically distinct in containing a historical doubling of the middle root consonant. For this reason, the *piel* is sometimes referred to as the D-stem or "Double" stem. (The *pual* is referred to as the Dp-stem or "Double passive" stem, and the *hithpael* as the tD-stem.) Nevertheless, it is not uncommon for the doubling of the second root consonant not to be represented in the orthography and/or not articulated in the ancient pronunciation. This occurs with guttural roots (e.g., תְּכַחֲשׁוּן "you will renounce" Josh 24:27) and with III-*vav/yod* roots, where one commonly finds the elision of the final syllable (e.g., וַיְצַו "he commanded" Gen 2:16 [צוה]; and וַיְגַל "he revealed" Num 22:31 [גלה]). The loss of gemination also occurs in cases where the historical */i/ vowel of the second syllable has elided (e.g., **yubaqqišūna* > יְבַקְשׁוּ

"let them seek" 1 Sam 16:16).[60] For these reasons, it is better not to rely on the doubling of the middle root consonant to identify this conjugation. Far more consistent are the vowel sequences associated with the *piel*.

The vowel sequence reflected in the third masculine singular *piel qåṭal* is typically **i-e*; the short /i/ of the stem derives from /a/ (i.e., בִּקֵּשׁ < **biqqeš* < **baqqiša* "he sought"), making it analogous in its origin to nouns like עִוֵּר (< **ʿiwwēr* < **ʿawwiru*) "blind," described above.[61] The stem vowels of the *yiqṭol* and other forms (i.e., **a-e*) more clearly correspond to this earlier vowel sequence.

Although the third masculine singular *qåṭal* form is typically characterized as exhibiting the sequence of vowel symbols *hireq-tsere* in THT, the extremely frequent verbs דִּבֶּר "he spoke" and כִּפֶּר "he atoned for," are realized instead with the sequence *hireq-segol* (= *i-ɛ*). This seems to reflect the fact that the verbs were so familiar that they were produced with a rushed pronunciation such that the verb was articulated without a clear stressed syllable, as though it were in construct with the following word (e.g., דִּבֶּר־לָךְ Deut 29:12 "he spoke to you").[62] In other verbs, the pausal forms exhibit a *tsere* in THT, but a *patakh* in contextual forms, as with אִבֵּד (pause)/אִבַּד (context) "he destroyed" and בֵּרֵךְ (pause) /בֵּרַךְ (context) "he blessed."

A guttural as a third root consonant often results in the sequence *i-a* in context (e.g., פִּתַּח "he opened" Job 30:11), though in pause one finds the expected /i/-class vowel (i.e., פִּתֵּחַ "he opened" Job 12:18). With III-*aleph* roots, however, the vowel usually reflects */ē/, as in מִלֵּא "he filled" (Exod 35:35), in this case long due to compensatory lengthening (**malliʾa* > **milliʾ* > **millē*). In the verb בֵּרֵךְ (pause) /בֵּרַךְ (context) "he blessed," the *resh* cannot double and so the preceding */i/ lengthens and shifts to */ē/.[63]

The *piel yiqṭol* is characterized by the vowel sequence **ə-a-e* (e.g., יְדַבֵּר), as are the short-*yiqṭol* and *wayyiqṭol*. The vowels of the stem are

---

60. The loss of gemination occurs with the "Shy queens swim alone" consonants, as described in ch. 3 §15, "Loss of Gemination and *Shewa*."

61. The last vowel is represented by *epsilon* in the Secunda (e.g., ουκ.σσες [cf. וְקִצֵּץ] "and he will break" Ps 46:10) (see Brønno, *Studien*, 64). Alternatively, it is conceivable that the *piel qåṭal* originated as **qattala*, as in Arabic.

62. Such verb forms only rarely attest a *maqqef* and regularly bear cantillation marks. But, note that the pausal forms attests a *tsere*: דִּבֵּר. Note similar forms יְדַבֶּר־בִּי "he will speak to me" Hab 2:1; הִוָּלֶד לוֹ "was born to him" Gen 21:5).

63. Note the long vowel, e.g., in the Secunda's ηρφου vs. חֵרְפוּ "they reproach" Ps 89:52 (Brønno, *Studien*, 64).

also the same as those of the imperative (דַּבֵּר). Although the vowels of the infinitive construct (דַּבֵּר), infinitive absolute (דַּבֵּר), and participle (מְדַבֵּר) appear the same as those of the imperative in THT, the infinitives and participle presumably exhibited /ē/ as a final vowel, not /e/.[64]

For the *piel*, the vowel of any prefix element is always *shewa*. The word-initial vowel sequence *ə-a is quite consistent and typifies (and thus helps one to identify) the *yiqṭol* and *wayyiqṭol* since the second vowel of the stem (*/i/) will often be absent, as mentioned above (e.g., וַיְצַו "he commanded" passim [צוה]; and וַיְגַל "he uncovered" Isa 22:8 [גלה]).

Object suffixes on the *piel* usually do not dramatically affect the vowels of the stem, as in דִּבְּרוֹ "he spoke it" (Deut 18:22) and יְשַׁלְּחֵם "he will send them" (Exod 6:1).

5.7. Verbs in the Non-*Qal* Conjugations: *Hiphil*

The *hiphil* conjugation is formally unique among the other conjugations for several different reasons and, thus, sometimes it exhibits exceptions to some general principles. The *hiphil qåṭal* is characterized by the vowel sequence **i-ī* (e.g., הִשְׁמִיר).[65] In contrast to all the other conjugations, the theme vowel is long, not short. For this reason, in the third feminine singular and third common plural, there is no reduction of the vowel (הִשְׁמִ֫ירָה is 3fs; הִשְׁמִ֫ירוּ is 3cp). Furthermore, unlike in the other conjugations, the stress or tone remains over this second syllable. Nevertheless, in the other parts of the *hiphil qåṭal* paradigm, the historical */i/ vowel of the second syllable shifts to /a/ in THT (similar to the shift from historical */i/ to /a/ in the *piel* conjugation): for example, **higgidtā* > **higgɛdtā* > הִגַּ֫דְתָּ "you told." Application of object suffixes does not affect any of the vowels of the stem (e.g., הִשְׁמִידוֹ "he destroyed him" Deut 4:3; הִפְקַדְתּוֹ "you assigned him" 1 Sam 29:4).

Although the conjugation is easily recognizable in the *qåṭal* due to the initial *he*, this component of the conjugation is not normally present in the *yiqṭol* and related forms. There was once a *he* prefix in the *yiqṭol*, presumably, but this dropped off in most cases. It is only rarely attested in the MT (e.g., יְהוֹשִׁיעַ "he will deliver" 1 Sam 17:47, Ps 116:6).[66]

---

64. This is based on the tendencies observed above in ch. 3 for finite forms in the Secunda to exhibit /e/ and verbal adjectives and participles to exhibit /ē/.

65. In some cases in the *hiphil* the earlier */ī/ is not marked with a *mater yod*.

66. Note also יְהוֹדֶה Neh 11:17 and יְהֵילִילוּ Isa 52:5. See Joüon §54b.

The other forms of the *hiphil* all attest an /i/-class vowel (*/ī/, */e/, or */ē/) in the verbal stem, and /a/ in the prefix (e.g., יַשְׁמִיר* and וַיַּשְׁמֵר*), including the imperative, infinitive construct, infinitive absolute, and the participle. The short /a/ vowel of the prefix in the *hiphil yiqṭol* may be contrasted with the /i/ found in the prefix of the *qåṭal* form (**hišmīr* vs. **yašmīr*). It is likely that the original sequence of vowels in the *hiphil* was actually **a-i*, even in the *qåṭal* (cf. Aramaic *haphel*: הַנְפֵּק "he took out" Dan 5:2).[67]

As in the *hiphil qåṭal*, the *hiphil yiqṭol* paradigm attests no reduction where one sees it in other conjugations, that is, in forms with a final vowel (תַּשְׁמִירִי* in 2fs, יַשְׁמִירוּ* in 3mp, תַּשְׁמִירוּ* in 2mp). In these forms, the tone or stress remains on the penultimate syllable (like the *hiphil qåṭal* 3fs, 3cp). With object suffixes, again, there is no change in the stem vowels (e.g., יַעֲמִידֵנִי "he will make me stand" Ps 18:34).

The *hiphil* short-*yiqṭol* and *wayyiqṭol* forms are consistently distinct from the regular *yiqṭol* forms, even in the strong root. The short-*yiqṭol* and *wayyiqṭol* forms attest an */e/ where the regular *yiqṭol* has /ī/. In the *wayyiqṭol* we find וַיַּשְׁבֵּת "he put an end to" versus *yiqṭol* יַשְׁבִּית "he will put an end to."[68] This follows the pattern, as mentioned above, wherein the short-*yiqṭol* and *wayyiqṭol* forms are usually graphically shorter (if not also phonetically shorter) than regular *yiqṭol* forms. But, this */e/ (and, by extension, the shorter form) is evidenced only where the verb has no suffixed element (i.e., no suffixed morphological component or object suffix): תַּשְׁחֵת "do [not] destroy" (Deut 15:3); וַיַּבְדֵּל "he separated" (Gen 1:4). Where any type of suffix appears on the verb, the stem vowel of the verb is */ī/ (as in the regular *yiqṭol*): תַּשְׁחִיתֵהוּ "do [not] destroy him" (Isa 65:8); וַיַּבְדִּילוּ "they separated" (Neh 13:3).[69] In these cases, often the */ī/ will not be represented by a *yod mater* (e.g., וַיַּשְׁלִכוּ "they threw" Gen 37:24). In addition, note that the first common singular *wayyiqṭol* forms usually do not attest the */e/ theme vowel, but rather the */ī/ associated with the regular *yiqṭol*, sometimes without a *mater*: וָאַצִּיל "I rescued"

67. The shift from */a/ to /i/ is akin to the vowel shift found in the first syllable of the *piel* perfect and of most **qattil* nouns, as mentioned above.

68. The theme vowel would presumably be represented by *epsilon* in the Secunda (cf. the impv. form εεζεκ "take hold of" Ps 35:2, corresponding to הַחֲזֵק) (see Brønno, *Studien*, 100).

69. The respective verbal forms are still parsed or identified as short-*yiqṭol* and *wayyiqṭol*, despite their graphic similarity to the regular *yiqṭol*.

(1 Sam 10:18) and וָאַצִּל (Judg 6:9). If the third root consonant is a guttural, the theme vowel of the short-*yiqṭol* and *wayyiqṭol* is /a/ (e.g., וַיַּצְמַח "he made sprout" Gen 2:9), but the other forms are identical to the strong root.

Unlike in the other conjugations where the imperative and the infinitive construct are identical in graphic form (differing only in the length of the final stem vowel), in the *hiphil* the imperative and infinitive construct are actually distinct graphically and phonetically, at least when the imperative lacks a suffix or word-final morpheme. Both forms have an initial *he* followed by /a/; this /a/ is identical to the vowel found after the prefix in the *yiqṭol*. For the theme vowel, the imperative reflects an */e/ in its stem: הַרְכֵּב "mount!" (2 Kgs 13:16). The vowel sequence of the imperative, therefore, matches that of the short-*yiqṭol* and *wayyiqṭol* (e.g., וַיַּרְכֵּב "he made [him] mount" Gen 41:43); since the short-*yiqṭol* is like the imperative in indicating volition, it makes sense that the short-*yiqṭol* and the imperative have a similar articulation. When it takes any type of suffix or word-final morpheme, however, the imperative attests */ī/ in its stem (sometimes without *yod mater*: הַגִּדָה "tell!" [*hiphil* נגד + paragogic *he*] vs. הַגֵּד "tell!"). The infinitive construct, by contrast, always attests an */ī/: הַשְׁמִיד "to destroy" (2 Sam 14:16). The *hiphil* masculine singular imperative is, however, graphically identical to the infinitive absolute (again differing in pre-Masoretic Hebrew only in the length of the stem vowel). This formal similarity also overlaps with a semantic similarity since the infinitive absolute sometimes functions as an imperative.

The similarities between the different verbal forms of the *hiphil* can sometimes lead to confusion and students should notice the following distinctions. First, the key feature that helps to distinguish the *qåṭal* from the infinitives and imperative is the vowel that follows the initial *he*. Typically, if it is an /i/-class vowel, then the form is *qåṭal*, but if it is an /a/-class vowel, then the form is either an infinitive or imperative.

- הִשְׁמִיעֲךָ "he made you hear" (Deut 4:36) versus הַשְׁמִיעֻ֫נוּ "cause us to hear!" (Isa 41:22)
- הִשְׁמִידוֹ "he destroyed it" (Deut 4:3) vs. הַשְׁמִידוֹ "to destroy him" (Deut 9:20) (inf.)
- הֵשִׁיב "he brought back" (Gen 14:16) vs. הָשִׁיב "to bring back" (1 Kgs 12:21) (inf.)

- הֱשִׁיבוֹ "he brought him back" (1 Kgs 13:20) vs. הֲשִׁיבוֹ "to bring him back" (2 Sam 12:23) (inf.) and הֲשִׁיבֻ֫הוּ "bring him back!" (1 Kgs 22:26).[70]

Ambiguity is found primarily in I-*vav* roots, where the initial *he* is always followed by an */ō/ vowel (e.g., הוֹרִדֻ֫הוּ "they brought him down" Gen 39:1 vs. הוֹרִדֻ֫הוּ "bring him down!" Gen 44:21 and cf. הוֹרִדִי "my bringing down" Ezek 31:16).

Since the infinitive construct and imperative both share this initial *ha-* syllable, discriminating between them when they bear a suffix can sometimes be difficult. Usually, the type of suffix and especially the linking vowel between stem and suffix will reveal the correct identity of the form. If the vowel that links the verb to the suffix is an /i/-class vowel, then the form is likely an imperative. If the vowel is an /a/-class vowel, then the form is likely an infinitive construct. Compare הַקְרִיבֵ֫הוּ "offer it!" (Mal 1:8) with הַקְרִיבוֹ (< **haqribahu*) "his offering" (Lev 7:16). Nevertheless, note that the first-person suffixes on infinitives construct are sometimes identical to those of the *yiqṭol* and imperative, especially when the suffix on the infinitive marks the object of the verb (e.g., הַכְעִסֵנִי "to anger me" Jer 7:18; הַעֲבִרֵנוּ "to let us pass through" Deut 2:30). Similarly, there is also ambiguity with the third feminine singular suffix (e.g., הַשְׁחִיתָהּ "destroy it!" 2 Kgs 18:25; הַשְׁחִיתָהּ "to destroy it" Isa 36:10). In these cases, only context can guide interpretation. Remember that a verb form preceded by a preposition will be either a participle or an infinitive construct. Finite forms of the verb (*qåṭal*, *yiqṭol* and impv.) are never preceded by a preposition.[71]

70. Very rarely the scribes got confused. In Jer 52:3, one finds a form that must be an inf. cons., but which is pointed as though it were a *qåṭal* הִשְׁלִיכוֹ "his throwing"; cf. הַשְׁלִיכוּ "throw!" Gen 37:22.

71. Finite forms are preceded by conjunctions. In Hebrew, as in English, there is some overlap between prepositions and conjunctions (e.g., עַד "until" can function as either a preposition or conjunction, just like the English equivalent). But, the prepositions that attach directly to the following word, בְּ and כְּ and לְ, never function as conjunctions and never attach to finite verbal forms.

5.8. Verbs in the Non-*Qal* Conjugations: *Niphal*

The *niphal qåṭal* is characterized by the pattern *ni-a* (e.g., נִשְׁמַר), though the earlier form would have had /a/ in the prefix, as reflected in the historical form of I-*vav* roots, like **nawlada* > *nōlad* > נוֹלַד "he was born." The participle is like the *qåṭal* but exhibits a long vowel (e.g., נִשְׁמָר). The other forms, including the *yiqṭol*, short-*yiqṭol*, *wayyiqṭol*, and imperative are characterized by the following sequence of vowels in the prefix and stem: **i-ā-e*, as in תִּשָּׁמֵר "she will be careful" (Judg 13:13).[72] The infinitive construct is graphically the same in THT, differing only in pre-Masoretic Hebrew by the length of the final vowel: **i-ā-ē*. The sequence of three full vowels under three consecutive graphic consonants is rather uncommon in BH and may be remembered for this reason alone. Such a sequence is possible because the first vowel always appears in a closed syllable (due to the assimilation of the *nun* of the conjugation) and because the following */ā/ (< */a/) never reduces. What was **tinšamiru* shifted to **tiššāmer* and then to תִּשָּׁמֵר. The preservation of the */ā/ (< */a/) is unusual, but serves to distinguish the *niphal* from the *hithpael*, which shares almost the same sequence of vowels; compare **i-a-e*, as in יִתְהַלֵּךְ "he will go around" (Prov 23:31).[73]

In THT, the *niphal* masculine singular imperative and infinitive construct are identical in form. Again, the infinitive construct in pre-Masoretic Hebrew was distinguished by a final long vowel: **i-ā-ē*. In both the masculine singular imperative and infinitive construct, the first vowel of the sequence (/i/) is preserved through the addition of a word-initial *he*: הִשָּׁמֵר. The distinct morphological components of the prefix are the /i/ vowel followed by an assimilated *nun* (*-*in*-).

At least for THT, it is often the case that the accent moves forward in the *wayyiqṭol*, imperative, and infinitive construct such that the vowel reflected in the second syllable is often /ɛ/, not /e/.

---

72. The last vowel is represented by *epsilon* in the Secunda (e.g., θεσθερ [cf. תִּסָּתֵר] "you hide yourself" Ps 89:47) (see Brønno, *Studien*, 104–5; presumably a mistake for *θεσσαθερ).

73. Since the *tav* of the *hithpael* will rarely assimilate into the first root consonant (e.g., יִדַּכְּאוּ "they will be crushed" Job 5:4 [*hithpael* of דכא] and תִּכַּסֶּה "it will be covered" Prov 26:26 [*hithpael* of כסה]), the distinction in length between */ā/ and */a/ is important for distinguishing the two conjugations. The *tav* of the *hithpael* conjugation also assimilates with a following *ṭet* (יִטַּמָּא "he will [not] defile himself" Lev 21:1), and rarely *nun* (תִּנַּשֵּׂא "it will be exalted" Num 24:7). See Joüon §53e.

- וַיִּלָּחֶם "he fought" (Josh 10:38)
- הִלָּחֶם "fight!" (Judg 9:38)
- הִלָּחֶם "to fight" (Num 22:11).

The *niphal* infinitive absolute is attested in a variety of forms (e.g., הִמּוֹל "to circumcise oneself" Gen 17:13; נִכְסֹף "to long for" Gen 31:30; הִמָּצֵא "to be found" Exod 22:3) and is harder to predict for any given verb.

5.9. Verbs in the Non-*Qal* Conjugations: *Pual* and *Hophal*

These conjugations are the passive counterparts to the *piel* and *hiphil*, respectively. All verb forms (including the *qåṭal* and the participle) are characterized by the sequence of vowels found in their respective names. Thus, the *pual* is characterized by the vowel sequence *u-a*. Like the *piel*, the vowel of any prefix element is always *shewa* (e.g., יְשֻׁמַּר).

The *hophal* is characterized by the vowel sequence **o-a* (e.g., הָשְׁמַר). A /u/-class prefix vowel is found in all forms, including in the infinitive construct where a *he* precedes the vowel (meaning that it is formally identical to the 3ms *qåṭal*). Usually, the /u/-class vowel is realized as */o/, though in the case of I-*nun* roots the prefix vowel is /u/ (e.g., יֻקַּם "he will be avenged" Gen 4:24 [from נקם]) and in the case of I-*vav*/*yod*, II-*vav*/*yod*, and geminate roots it is */ū/ (e.g., הוּרַד "he was taken down" Gen 39:1 [ירד] and וַיּוּשַׁב "he was returned" Exod 10:8 [שׁוב]). This gives rise to a limited number of ambiguous forms, such as תּוּשָׁב "it (or, you) will be inhabited" from ישׁב (Isa 44:26), which might otherwise be interpreted as the *hophal* of שׁוב.[74]

5.10. Verbs in the Non-*Qal* Conjugations: *Hithpael* and *Hishtaphel*

The *hithpael* is also consistent across its different forms in its vowel sequence: **i-a-e* (or, **i-a-ē*).[75] In THT, the third masculine singular *qåṭal* is identical to the imperative and infinitive construct (i.e., וְהִתְהַלֵּךְ "he will walk around" Exod 21:19; הִתְהַלֵּךְ "walk around!" Gen 13:17; הִתְהַלֵּךְ "walking around" Zech 1:10), though in an earlier era the length of the

74. The *qamets* in this form is unusual.

75. As noted above in the discussion of the *niphal*, the */a/ in the stem is important in that it helps to distinguish the *hithpael* from the *niphal*, the latter which exhibits the sequence **i-ā-e*.

final vowel would have distinguished the infinitive construct from these other forms. The *yiqṭol* is characterized by its distinctive prefixes and suffixes, but the vowels of the stem are the same as those of the other finite verbal forms (e.g., יִתְהַלֵּךְ "he will go around" Prov 23:31).

Occasionally what is ordinarily */e/ appears as /a/ or /å/ in THT; usually, if this occurs, it can be attributed to pause (e.g., הִתְעַבָּר "he became enraged" Ps 78:62). In other cases, it seems that a particular root is expressed with /å/ (e.g., יִטַּמָּא "he will make himself unclean" Lev 21:4 [in context]).[76]

With roots that begin with a sibilant, the *tav* of the prefix and the initial sibilant switch places (i.e., metathesize).[77] This metathesis in BH sometimes creates forms whose roots are difficult to recognize (e.g., וָאֶשְׁתַּמֵּר "I kept myself" Ps 18:24 [שׁמר]). Nevertheless, the fact that there are more than three possible root consonants leads one to suspect that one of the letters is part of the verbal paradigm.

The *hithpael* is the remnant of a broader group of conjugations that were characterized by a prefixed *tav* and that were used to indicate middle and reflexive nuances. In an earlier stage of the language, there would have been prefix-*tav* conjugations corresponding to each major active conjugation (*qal*, *piel*, *hiphil*), as there are, for example, in Aramaic and Ugaritic.[78] The *hithpael* is the prefix-*tav* conjugation that corresponds to the *piel*; those that corresponded with the *qal* and *hiphil* have disappeared.[79] The link between the Hebrew *hithpael* and the *piel* is clear in several ways. First, note that the middle root consonant in the *hithpael* is doubled, if possible, and if not, the preceding /a/ is compensatorily lengthened to */ā/: הִתְבָּרֵךְ "he blessed himself" and יִתְבָּרֵךְ "he will bless himself." Second, the sequence of stem vowels throughout the *hithpael* is the same sequence

76. Joüon (§ 53b–c) notes that the /a/ vowel may be due to Babylonian influence, since in the Babylonian tradition of Biblical Hebrew the **a-a* vowel sequence is the normal one in this conjugation. This Babylonian Biblical Hebrew vowel pattern may, itself, be derived from Aramaic where the conjugation corresponding to the *hithpael* has predominantly an /a/ vowel, which is, in turn, derived probably through analogy to the theme vowel of Aramaic passive stems like the *pual* and *huphal*.

77. The same phenomenon is present in English with the switching of "s" and "k" in the common pronunciation of the word "asterisk" as if it were spelled *asteriks or *asterix.

78. Note, e.g., Syriac's *etqṭel*, *etqaṭṭal*, and *ettaqṭal* conjugations.

79. Note, however, that some have proposed that וַיִּתְפָּקֵד "it was enrolled" (Judg 21:9) and similar examples are the remnants of a *t*-prefix *qal* stem (see Joüon § 53g).

found in the stem of the *piel yiqṭol*, imperative, infinitives, and participle: **a-e* (or, **a-ē*).

Although the prefix-*tav* conjugations corresponding to the *qal* and *hiphil* are not attested in BH, there is one relic of a prefix-*tav* conjugation that corresponds to an earlier causative conjugation. This is the so-called *hishtaphel* conjugation attested primarily (if not exclusively) in the root חוה ("to bow down"), for example, וְהִשְׁתַּחֲוָה "and he will bow down" (Ezek 46:2) and הִשְׁתַּחֲווּ "they bowed down" (Jer 8:2). The equivalent to the *hiphil* conjugation was, in an earlier phase of Semitic, marked not by an initial *h*-, but by an initial *š*-.[80] In Akkadian and Ugaritic, this is the prefix component to the causative conjugation. The prefix-*tav* conjugation that corresponded to this initial *š*-conjugation is called the Št-conjugation. In Ugaritic, the same verb, *ḥwy* "to bow down," appears in this Št-conjugation (e.g., *tštḥwy* = *tištaḥwiyā* "[they] do homage"), with the same sense as found in BH.[81] It is due to this correspondence that scholars recognized that the root of this word in BH must be חוה (not שׁחה, as listed in BDB), and that consequently the *šin* of the word was part of the conjugation, not the root. Since BH otherwise universally attests the shift from an earlier *š*-initial causative conjugation to a *he*-initial causative conjugation (i.e., the *hiphil*), it seems likely that this word is borrowed from another language (similar to Ugaritic), rather than an inheritance from an earlier stage of Hebrew.

5.11. Verbs in the Non-*Qal* Conjugations: *Polel, Pilpel, Poel, Polal, Pilpal*, and *Poal*

The rarer conjugations, including the *polel*, *pilpel*, and *poel* are also associated with the *piel*. In general, these conjugations function as the *piel* for middle weak and geminate roots.

- עֹרֵר "he aroused" [עור] (in 2 Sam 23:18)
- יְכַלְכֵּל "he will provide" [כול] (Zech 11:16)
- עוֹנֵן "he did witchcraft" [ענן] (in 2 Kgs 21:6)

80. This shift is part of a broader shift of /š/ to /h/. Compare, e.g., the Akkadian 3ms independent pronoun *šu* with the cognate in BH: הוא. See Huehnergard, "Afro-Asiatic," 143.

81. See Bordreuil and Pardee, *Manual of Ugaritic*, 164, 166.

The *polel* and *poel* are identical superficially, though the *polel* (as its name implies) involves the reduplication of the last root consonant and the *poel* involves only a different sequence of vowels applied to three root consonants. Thus, the *polel* is the term used for middle-weak roots (since the last root consonant is reduplicated) and the *poel* for geminate roots (which have three root consonants). As in the *hithpael*, the third masculine singular form of the *qåṭal* (עֹרֵר "he aroused" 2 Sam 23:18), the infinitive (עֹרֵר "to arouse" Job 3:8), and the imperative (עֹרֵר* "arouse!" [cf. כּוֹנֵן "establish!" Job 8:8]) look identical, differing only in the underlying length of the final vowel (*/e/ vs. */ē/). In addition, these can all easily be mistaken for masculine singular *qal* participles. Of course, most other forms of the *qåṭal* will not be confused with participles (וְשׁוֹבַבְתִּיךָ "I will bring you back" [*polel wəqåṭal* of שׁוב] Ezek 38:4). Like the *piel*, these paradigms exhibit a *shewa* as the prefix vowel for the *yiqṭol* and participle, but no prefix at all for the imperative and infinitives.

The *pilpel* is used usually with II-*vav*/*yod* and geminate roots. As its name implies, it involves reduplication of the two primary consonants of a root. The sequence of vowels is again analogous to the *piel* (i.e., **i-a* appears in the second- and first-person forms of the *qåṭal*, as in וְכִלְכַּלְתִּי "I will provide" Gen 45:11, and **a-e* appears in the stem of the *yiqṭol*, as in יְכַלְכֵּל "it will survive" Prov 18:14).

The *polal*, *poal*, and *polpal* are the passive counterparts to these stems. Like other passive conjugations, these cojugations exhibit /a/ as a theme vowel (e.g., *polal*: כּוֹנָנוּ "they were ready" Ezek 28:13 [pausal] and *poal*: נוֹדַד "he flutters away" Nah 3:17). The *hithpolel* (e.g., מִתְעוֹרֵר "one who is excited" [עור] Isa 64:6) and *hithpalpel* (e.g., הִתְמַהְמְהוּ "they waited" [מהה] Judg 19:8) are the counterparts to the *hithpael*.[82]

5.12. Weak Roots: General Comments

Weak roots are characterized by vowel patterns that are distinct from those of the strong root. Generally, roots containing gutturals diverge least from the standard patterns. I-*nun* roots exhibit the assimilation of the *nun* in specific forms, but are otherwise similar to strong roots. The presence of a *vav* or *yod* as a historical root consonant, on the other hand, creates

82. Other conjugations also occur, but more rarely (see GKC §55).

significant variations from the basic verbal paradigm. One should keep the following three points in mind regarding these roots.

1. Originally the two letters (*vav/yod*) were distinguished in every position. However, at some point before the language was committed to writing, historical *vavs* shifted to *yods* in most words and forms. This happened especially in I-*vav/yod* roots and III-*vav/yod* roots. In II-*vav/yod* roots, on the other hand, medial *vav* or *yod* was generally lost through contractions and/or assimilation.
2. The idiosyncratic features of these roots usually derive from the contraction of diphthongs or triphthongs at the beginning, in the middle, or at the end of the root.
   - **hawṯibani* > **hōšībanī* > הוֹשִׁיבַנִי "he caused me to dwell" (Ps 143:3)
   - **yaqwumu* > **yaqūmu* > **yāqūm* > יָקוּם "he will arise" (passim)
   - **banaya* > **banā* > **bānā* > בָּנָה "he built" (passim)

   Vowels that are the result of contractions at the beginning or in the middle of a root are rather stable throughout a given verb's inflection (e.g., the medial /ū/ is present throughout the *qal yiqṭol* in II-*vav* roots: יָקוּמוּ "they will arise" passim). On the other hand, at the end of the root, the triphthongs contracted in different ways, as explained above (see §3.12, "Triphthongs and Diphthongs").
   - **yagluwu* > **yagluyu* > **yiglē* > *yiglɛ* = יִגְלֶה "he will reveal"
   - **yagluwūna* > **yagluyūna* > **yagluyū* > **yiglū* > יִגְלוּ "they will reveal"
3. In all roots with a historical *vav* or *yod*, but especially in II- and III-*vav/yod* roots, the short-*yiqṭol* and *wayyiqṭol* forms are typically shorter than the regular *yiqṭol*.

5.13. Weak Roots: Gutturals and I-*Nun*

Guttural root letters will sometimes result in unexpected vowels in the stem and prefix of verbs. For example, a guttural as a first root consonant, will sometimes result in /a/ beneath the prefix of the *qal yiqṭol* and related forms, as with יַעֲמֹד "he will stand."[83] In the third masculine plural (and

83. In relation to I-*khet* verbs, the presence of a *khatef* vowel in THT is due to a

similar forms), two short vowels follow one another in THT (e.g., יַעַמְדוּ), the second of which is an epenthetic vowel (like the *khatef-patakh* in the form יַעֲמֹד). Although the *hiphil* paradigm also exhibits /a/ in the prefix element, the *hiphil* will never attest a *shewa* between the second and third root consonants; instead it will reflect either */e/ or */ī/ (e.g., יַעֲמֵד "let him cause to stand" [short-*yiqṭol*] and יַעֲמִיד "he will ..." [*yiqṭol*]).

In the *niphal yiqṭol*, all gutturals as well as *resh* will trigger compensatory lengthening in the prefix vowel (e.g., יֵרָאֶה "it will be seen" Exod 13:7).

In the *qal*, a guttural as a second or third root consonant will result in the *yiqṭol* and imperative (but not the inf. cons.) exhibiting an /a/ theme vowel: יִבְחַר "he will choose," בְּחַר "choose!," but the infinitive construct *בְּחֹר "choosing"; and יִשְׁלַח "he will send," שְׁלַח "send!," but the infinitive construct: שְׁלֹחַ "sending." In the *piel*, *pual*, and *hithpael*, a guttural (or *resh*) as a middle root consonant can result in compensatory lengthening (e.g., בֵּרֵךְ "he blessed"; יְבָרֵךְ "he will bless"; תְּבֹרַךְ "may she be blessed"). In these conjugations, a guttural as a second root consonant does not affect the vowel of the last stem syllable (e.g., שִׁחֵת "he acted corruptly"; contrast this with the *qal* where an /a/ vowel is always present, as in יִבְחַר "he will choose"). However, a guttural as a third root consonant will result (as in the *qal*) with a final /a/ vowel in contextual forms: שִׁלַּח "he sent away"; יְשַׁלַּח "he will send away"; הִתְגַּלַּע "quarreling" [inf. cons.]).[84]

An *aleph* as a root consonant is somewhat different from the other gutturals. In some *aleph*-initial roots the *qal yiqṭol* exhibits */ō/ after the initial consonant of the prefix. The phenomenon is quite commonly found in the expression וַיֹּאמֶר "he said." As in this example, the *aleph* has elided and receives no vowel. The verbs that often attest this */ō/ vowel are the following: אבד "to perish," אבה "to be willing," אחז "to seize," אכל "to eat," אמר "to say," אפה "to bake." The verbs can be remembered by any mnemonic that links the verbs in a single sentence.[85]

---

shift in sonority between the first two root consonants; generally, where the second consonant is more sonorous, the guttural receives a *khatef* vowel. See the short summary in Lutz Edzard, "Phonology, Optimality Theory: Biblical Hebrew," *EHLL* 3:134–38 and the fuller treatment in Silje Avestad and Lutz Edzard, *la-ḥšōḇ, but la-ḥăzōr? Sonority, Optimality, and the Hebrew* פ"ח *forms*, AKM 66 (Wiesbaden: Harrassowitz, 2009).

84. In pause, one finds a *tsere* in THT: אֲשַׁלֵּחַ "I will [not] send away" (Exod 5:2).

85. E.g., "Did you say you're not willing to eat what I bake? I will seize you, and you will perish."

As elsewhere, when the *aleph* should double, it also precipitates compensatory lengthening in the preceding vowel (e.g., יֵאָסְפוּ < **yēʾāsəpū* < **yiʾʾasipū* "they will be gathered" Gen 29:8 and יְמָאֲנוּ < **yəmāʾănū* < **yumaʾʾinū* "they will refuse" Jer 25:28).

Similarly, like the other gutturals, the *aleph* as a second consonant precipitates an /a/ theme vowel in the stem of the *yiqṭol* verb (e.g., יִשְׁאַל "he will request" Exod 22:13). When an *aleph* is a third root consonant, this /a/ vowel lengthens to */ā/ (e.g., יִמְצָא). This compensatory lengthening is due to the *aleph*'s quiescence at the end of a syllable (i.e., יִמְצָא < **yimṣā* < **yimṣaʾ* < **yimṣaʾu*). When the *aleph* initiates a syllable, we do not see (typically) such compensation (e.g., יִמְצְאוּ < **yimṣəʾū* < **yimṣaʾū* "they will find" Judg 5:30).

Occasionally III-*aleph* roots appear to be vocalized on analogy to III-*vav*/*yod* roots (e.g., חֹטְאִים "who are sinning" 1 Sam 14:33; מְלֹאת "to be fulfilled" Num 6:13). This is found with particular frequency in the *niphal*, where one finds נִמְצֵאתִי "I was found" (Isa 65:1) instead of נִמְצָאתִי* as one might have expected (cf. the III-*vav*/*yod* root: נִגְלֵיתִי "I revealed myself" 1 Sam 2:27). The *niphal* masculine plural participle consistently appears with a *shewa* where we would expect a *qamets*: הַנִּמְצְאִים "those found" (2 Kgs 25:19), instead of הַנִּמְצָאִים (which occurs just once at Ezra 8:25, in pause).[86] In other cases, as mentioned above, byforms exist in the lexicon between III-*aleph* and III-*vav*/*yod* roots, as with קרא "to encounter, meet" and קרה "to encounter, meet."

A *nun* that abuts another, following consonant will often assimilate into that following consonant. This occurs frequently with verbs, as in the *qal yiqṭol* form of נתן, for example יִתֵּן < **yinten*, or the *hiphil qåṭal* or *yiqṭol* forms of נצל, for example הִצִּיל < **hinṣīl* "he delivered" and יַצִּיל < **yanṣīl* "he will deliver." However, where a vowel comes immediately after such a *nun*, there is no assimilation, as in the *qal qåṭal* נָתַן "he gave" and the *piel yiqṭol* form of נצל, for example יְנַצְּלוּ < **yənaṣṣəlū* "they will save." The assimilation or preservation of a first *nun* is rather regular and predictable within these parameters. One must note, however, that in cases where the

---

86. Does the form הַנִּמְצְאִים reflect a pronunciation like that of III-*vav*/*yod* participles (i.e., **hannimṣim*; cf. נִרְפִּים "who are lazy" Exod 5:8) that was secondarily altered to **hannimṣəʾim*? See Blau, *Phonology and Morphology*, 88. As noted above, in ch. 3 §5, "Lengthening of Pretonic */i/ and */a/ Vowels and the Place of Stress," Garr notes that such participles always precede phrases to which they are closely linked (Garr, "Pretonic Vowels in Hebrew," 135).

verb contains a *nun* as a first root consonant and a guttural as a second root consonant, the *nun* does not assimilate. Thus, we find in the *qal* תְּנְאַץ "do [not] spurn" (Jer 14:21); יִנְהַג "he will lead" (Isa 20:4); נִנְחַל "we will [not] inherit" (Num 32:19); יִנְעָם "it will be pleasant" (Prov 2:10) (pausal). The same happens in the *hiphil*: יַנְחִיל "he will dispossess" (Deut 3:28).[87]

Since the form of an imperative is usually directly related to the short-*yiqṭol* (and/or the *yiqṭol*) form of the verb, it is not surprising that those verbs that see assimilation of the *nun* in the (short-)*yiqṭol* attest no *nun* in the imperative: יִתֵּן and תֵּן "give!"; also יַצֵּל and הַצֵּל "deliver!" Where the *nun* appears in the (short-)*yiqṭol*, then the *nun* appears in the imperative: נְהַג "lead" (2 Kgs 4:24).[88] The infinitives construct for the most common roots have a *segolate*-like (**qilt*) base in the *qal*.

- תֵּת < **tint* "to give" (+1cs תִּתִּי "my giving")
- שֵׂאת and שְׂאֵת < **śiʾt* "to lift" (+1cs שְׂאֵתִי)
- גֶּשֶׁת < **gišt* "to approach" (+ 3ms גִּשְׁתּוֹ)

Most other verbs usually attest the *nun* in the infinitive construct, even where the *nun* usually assimilates in the *yiqṭol* (e.g., יִפֹּל "he will fall" but נְפֹל "to fall").

5.14. Weak Roots: I-*Vav*/*Yod*

Roots that are originally I-*vav* are more numerous than original I-*yod* roots. The I-*vav* roots are characterized by several unexpected features in the *yiqṭol* and related forms. In the *qal*, the third masculine singular *yiqṭol* presumes the prefix-/stem-vowel sequence **ē-e* (e.g., יֵשֵׁב "he will dwell"), or, with final guttural, **ē-a* (e.g., יֵדַע "he will know"). Neither vowel sequence is shared by other *yiqṭol* forms. At least superficially, the initial **ē* vowel would seem to be due to the contraction of an earlier diphthong, **yayṯibu* > **yēšeb* (> יֵשֵׁב), which in turn implies the earlier transformation of the first *vav* to *yod* (**yawṯibu* > **yayṯibu*). However, we might have expected some memory of the first *vav* root consonant since we find evidence of this consonant throughout the non-*qal* conjugations that attest a prefix (through a *mater vav* or consonantal *vav*). Thus, in the *niphal* one

---

87. One exception to the rule is in the *niphal qåṭal* of נחם, where the *nun* root consonant does assimilate (e.g., נִחַם "he was consoled" 2 Sam 13:29).

88. There are several exceptions, e.g., נִפְלוּ "fall!"

finds in the *qåṭal* נוֹדַע < **nawdaʿa* "it is known" (Exod 2:14) and in the *yiqṭol* and related forms יִוָּדַע "it will be known" (Jer 28:9); הִוָּדְעִי "my being known" (Jer 31:19). In the *hiphil*, one finds הוֹדִיעַ < **hawdiʿa* "he made known" (Ps 98:2) and יוֹדִיעַ < **yawdiʿu* "he will make known" (Isa 38:19).[89] In the prefix to the *hophal*, one finds */ū/ instead of */ō/: הוּרַד < **huwrada* "he was brought down" (Gen 39:1).

The *qal* short-*yiqṭol* is often not distinguished from the regular *yiqṭol* in THT,[90] but the *wayyiqṭol* often has the accent on the prefix and a *segol* as a theme vowel (e.g., וַתֵּ֫רֶד "and she came down" Gen 24:18). The *qal* imperative exhibits the stem vowel of the *yiqṭol* (שֵׁב and שְׁבִי "dwell!"); the *qal* infinitive construct exhibits the **qilt* base, resulting in a form that looks like a segolate noun: שֶׁ֫בֶת "to dwell" (+1cs suf. שִׁבְתִּי).[91]

In the *qal*, a subclass of I-*vav*/*yod* roots experiences the assimilation of the *vav* as though it were a *nun*. In particular, this is common with roots whose second root consonant is *tsade*: אֶצֹּק "I will pour" (Isa 44:3) from יצק; also וַיִּ֫צֶר "he formed" (Gen 2:19) from יצר. Other roots often included in this same subclass include יצג *hiphil* "to set"; יצע *hiphil* "to make a bed"; יצת "to burn."[92] In addition, other roots whose second root consonant is a sibilant attest similar assimilation: וַיִּשַּׁ֫רְנָה "they went straight" (1 Sam 6:12) [*piel* of ישר]; and יְסִּרֵ֫נִי "he will instruct me" (Isa 8:11) [*piel* of יסר].[93]

Verbs in the *yiqṭol* with the prefix-/stem-vowel sequence **ē-e* and **ē-a* are originally I-*vav*. Original I-*yod* roots are comparatively rare. Joüon cites the following "primitive" I-*yod* roots: יבשׁ "to be dry"; ינק "to suck"; יטב "to be good"; יקץ "to wake up"; ילל *hiphil* "to wail"; ימן *hiphil* "to go to the right."[94] The prefix-/stem-vowel sequence in the *yiqṭol* of these roots is usually *ī-a*. Furthermore, the first etymological consonant usually appears graphically in the spelling of the *yiqṭol*, though it is best interpreted as a *mater* in these cases: יִיבַשׁ < **yībaš* < **yiybašu* "it will dry up" [*qal* יבשׁ];

---

89. That the original vowel of the prefix of the *hiphil qåṭal* was /a/ and not /i/ is reflected in some of the above forms which presuppose a contraction of an earlier diphthong (i.e., **aw* > **ō*): הוֹדִיעַ.

90. A rare example is תֵּ֫רֵד "may it come down" (2 Kgs 1:10).

91. This same base is used for the inf. cons. in some common I-*nun* roots like נתן.

92. Joüon (§77b) notes that יצג and יצת might be truly I-*nun* roots.

93. Ibid. §77a2. Note also מַסָּד "foundation" (1 Kgs 7:9).

94. Joüon §76d.

and הֵיטִיב < *hēṭīb < *hayṭiba "he treated well" [*hiphil* יטב].[95] In addition to these verbs, etymological I-*vav* roots that are stative appear as though they are I-*yod* in Hebrew, including יִירָא "he will fear"; יִיעַף "he will faint"; יִיקַר "he will be precious;" יִישַׁן "he will sleep." Other verbs that appear to be (at least morphologically) stative I-*vav* roots with this same vowel pattern are translated as active verbs in English: יִירַשׁ "he will inherit" and אִיעֲצָה "let me counsel" (Ps 32:8) [*qal* cohort. יעץ].

5.15. Weak Roots: II-*Vav*/*Yod*

II-*vav*/*yod* roots present some problems for the historical outline of Hebrew, since it seems at least possible that they ultimately derive not from a three-consonant root, but actually from a two-consonant root. In either case, a second root consonant is rarely in evidence. Instead there is almost always a full vowel (i.e., not a muttered vowel/*shewa*) that separates the first and last consonants.[96] For example, in the *qal qåṭal*, only the first and third root consonants are evidenced (e.g., קָם "he arose").

Throughout the different conjugations, the third-person forms of the *qåṭal* are regularly different from the second/first-person forms. In II-*vav*/*yod* roots in the *qal*, the third-person *qåṭal* forms reflect */ā/ between the two stable root consonants (i.e., קָם "he arose"; קָ֫מָה "she arose"; קָ֫מוּ "they arose"), while the other forms attest */a/ (e.g., קַ֫מְתָּ "you arose"). Notice that all these forms in the *qal* are accented on their first syllable (the exception being the 2mp/2fp forms, e.g., קַמְתֶּם). The *qal* participle is identical to the third-person masculine and feminine singular *qåṭal*, but the participle is accented on the last syllable (i.e., קָמָה vs. the 3fs *qåṭal* קָ֫מָה). Here again, the participle is articulated like most other adjectives and nouns, and the *qåṭal* diverges from this pattern.

In the non-*qal* conjugations (especially the *hiphil* and *niphal*), the *qåṭal* third-person forms are again distinct from the *qåṭal* second and first-person forms.[97] In these conjugations, the second- and first-person forms often attest an */ō/ (< */ā/) connecting vowel, between the stem and

95. The distinction between /ī/ and /iy/ would seem to be quite small (cf. Bergsträsser, *Hebräische Grammatik*, 1:102).

96. Note, however, the rare exceptions, like מות in the *hophal*: יוּמְתוּ "they will be put to death" (Lev 20:12).

97. When such verbs occur in the *piel*, the *vav*/*yod* is a regular root consonant (e.g., שִׁוַּ֫עְתִּי "I cried out" Jon 2:3).

the suffixed pronominal element of the verb, but the third-person forms do not.

In the *hiphil qåṭal*, the third-person forms follow the sequence **ē-ī*, as in הֵקִים "he raised" (Josh 5:7); הֵקִ֫ימוּ "they erected" (Isa 23:13). The initial **ē* in the third-person forms reflects the basic qualities of the first syllable; since the syllable in these forms is open and pretonic, we expect a long vowel, not *הִקִים. Compare the second- and first-person forms: וַהֲקֵמֹ֫תָ "you will erect" (Deut 27:2) and הֲקִמֹ֫תִי "I established" (Gen 9:17). Not only does an */ō/ vowel appear between the stem and suffixal morpheme, but the initial vowel is a muttered vowel, not **ē*. (Note also the alternation between */ī/ and */ē/ in the stem.)

For the *niphal qåṭal*, the third-person forms exhibit the sequence **ā-o*, without a connecting vowel (e.g., נָסוֹג "it turned back" Ps 44:19 and נָסֹ֫גוּ "they turned back" Isa 42:17), but the second- and first-person forms exhibit **ə-ū* followed by the connecting vowel */ō/ (e.g., נְסוּגֹ֫תִי "I did [not] turn back" Isa 50:5).[98] Again, the initial vowel of the prefix has reduced to *shewa* and an /ō/ follows the stem.

In the *hophal qåṭal* of II-*vav*/*yod* roots one finds the sequence **ū-a*: וְהוּכַן "it will be established" (Isa 16:5); יוּמַת "he will be put to death" (Judg 6:31, passim). The participle, since it follows the morphology of nouns and adjectives, contains an */ā/ in its stem: מוּכָן "one made ready" (Prov 21:31).

II-*vav*/*yod* roots are relatively easy to identify in their *yiqṭol* and related forms since they often have a full vowel with *mater* between the first and third root consonants.

qal

יָקוּם	"he will arise"
יָבִין	"he will understand"

niphal

יִכּוֹן	"he will be established" (Ps 102:29)
יִכֹּ֫נוּ	"they will be established" (Prov 4:26)
הִכּוֹן	"be ready!" (Amos 4:12).

98. The short /o/ is assumed based on the *niphal yiqṭol* of יִכּוֹן in the Secunda: ιεχχον (Ps 89:38) (see Brønno, *Studien*, 104).

hiphil

תָּקִים "you will erect" (Exod 40:2)
תָּקִ֫ימוּ "you will erect" (Lev 26:1)
הָקִים "the erecting of" (Num 9:15)

II-*vav* and II-*yod* roots can be distinguished from each other only in the *qal yiqṭol* and related forms (short-*yiqṭol*, and *wayyiqṭol*, as well as in the imperative and infinitives). In the *qal yiqṭol*, the II-*yod* roots will look identical to corresponding *hiphil* forms. Because בין occurs in both the *qal* and *hiphil* with the sense "to understand," it is difficult to be sure of the parsing of given forms (e.g., וַיָּ֫בֶן "he understood" 2 Sam 12:19 [*qal* or *hiphil*?]).

In the *qal*, the stative pattern is exhibited especially by בוש "to be ashamed." In this case, the *qåṭal* and *yiqṭol* both retain a long /ō/ vowel in the stem: בֹּשׁ "he was ashamed," בֹּ֫שׁוּ "they were ashamed," בֹּ֫שְׁתִּי "I was ashamed," and יֵבוֹשׁ "he will be ashamed," יֵבֹ֫שׁוּ "they will be ashamed." Notice that in the *yiqṭol*, the prefix reflects *ē. The other verbal forms of this root are predictable, each exhibiting the long /ō/ vowel, even the participle (בּוֹשְׁים "those ashamed" Ezek 32:30).

In the *qal*, the three forms *yiqṭol*, short-*yiqṭol*, and *wayyiqṭol* can be imagined in sequence progressing from longer to shorter forms: יָקוּם to יָקֹם to וַיָּ֫קָם and יָבִין to יָבֵן to וַיָּ֫בֶן. The short-*yiqṭol* and *wayyiqṭol* are distinguished from each other basically just by the place of the accent in THT. The historical form of both would have been the same: *yaqwum > *yaqum > *yāqom and *yabyin > *yabin > *yāben. In the *hiphil*, the three forms are similarly distributed and resemble *qal* II-*yod* roots: יָקִים versus יָקֵם versus וַיָּ֫קֶם. Although the imperative of the *qal* is related to that of the *yiqṭol* (i.e., קוּם → יָקוּם "rise"), in the *hiphil*, the vowels of the imperative (e.g., הָקֵם "erect!") match those of the short-*yiqṭol*.

As noted above in relation to the strong root in the *hiphil*, the form of the short-*yiqṭol* is identical to that of the regular *yiqṭol* in the second feminine singular, and third and second masculine plural, as well as when the short-*yiqṭol* occurs with object suffixes. Similarly, with the *wayyiqṭol* and the imperative. Thus, one finds the *wayyiqṭol* with a long middle vowel (sometimes written without a *mater*) in the third masculine plural *qal* וַיָּ֫קוּמוּ or וַיָּקֻ֫מוּ (instead of וַיָּ֫קְמוּ*) and in the *hiphil* וַיָּקִ֫ימוּ or וַיָּקִ֫מוּ (instead of וַיָּקֵ֫מוּ*). In the *hiphil* imperative, one finds הָקִ֫ימוּ (instead of הָקֵ֫מוּ*).

Although most *hiphil* participles typically exhibit the vowel sequence found in the *yiqṭol* (i.e., *a-ī, as in מַשְׁמִיעַ), with the II-*vav*/*yod* roots, the vowel sequence is that of the *qåṭal* (e.g., הֵבִין "he understood" and מֵבִין "one who understands"). As elsewhere, the vowel of the prefix is a *shewa* in the propretonic syllable: מְבִינִים "those who understand."

Another peculiarity of II-*vav*/*yod* roots, found in all the different conjugations, is the ending of many third- and second-person feminine plural *yiqṭol* (and *wayyiqṭol*) forms. Often, but not always, these forms will attest an ending that is more common with etymological III-*vav*/*yod* roots (*-ɛ̄nā > -ɛnå = ־ֶינָה). Thus, one finds in the same verse (e.g., Ezek 16:55) a form without this ending and a form with this ending: תָּשֹׁבְןָ "they will return" and תְּשׁוּבֶינָה "you will return." Similarly, note תָּבֹאנָה "they will come" (Isa 47:9) and תְּבֹאֶינָה "they will come" (Ps 45:16).

Although II-*vav*/*yod* roots sometimes appear in the *piel* (e.g., שִׁוַּעְתִּי "I cried out" Hab 1:2), more often these roots occur in the *polel* (in an active sense: וַתְּרוֹמֵם "you lifted up" Ps 107:25) and *polal* conjugations (in a passive sense: תְּרוֹמַמְנָה "they were exalted" Ps 75:11). Similarly, the *hithpolel* (in a reflexive sense: יִתְרוֹמֵם "he will exalt himself" Dan 11:36) occurs more commonly than the *hithpael*. These conjugations are extremely regular and the vowels often change very little in their inflection.

5.16. Weak Roots: III-*Vav*/*Yod*

Etymological III-*vav*/*yod* roots are regular at their beginning and exhibit all the characteristic prefix vowels of the various verb forms and conjugations associated with the strong root. It is primarily in relation to their endings that these roots look unusual. The endings are the result of contractions involving diphthongs and triphthongs. In general, there is consistency among the endings; each particular verbal form ends in the same way across all the different conjugations. For example, all third masculine singular *qåṭal* verbs end in the same way, even though they derive from slightly different triphthongs.

- *-aya > *-ā (e.g., *banaya > *banā > *bānā > בָּנָה "he built")
- *-iya > *-ā (e.g., *galliya > *gillā > גִּלָּה "he revealed")

The endings on third masculine singular *yiqṭol* forms are also consistent.

- *-iyu > -ɛ (e.g., *yabniyu > yibnɛ̄ > yibnɛ = יִבְנֶה "he built")
- *-ayu > -ɛ (e.g., *yuputtayu > *yuputtɛ̄ > *yəputtɛ > יְפֻתֶּה "he will be persuaded")

- **-uyu* > *-ɛ* (e.g., **yagluyu* > *yiglɛ̄* > *yiglɛ* = יִגְלֶה "he will reveal")

When a long vowel comes last in a triphthong, the long vowel is preserved and the preceding sounds are lost.

- **-ayū* > **-ū* (e.g., **banayū* > **bānū* > בָּנוּ "they built")
- **-iyū* > **-ū* (e.g., **yabniyūna* > **yabniyū* > **yibnū* > יִבְנוּ "they will build")
- **-iyī* > **-ī* (e.g., **tabniyīna* > **tabniyī* > **tibnī* > תִּבְנִי "you will build")

The consistency with which these contractions take place at the ends of words means that memorizing the endings in one conjugation (e.g., the *qal*) can help predict the endings in all the other conjugations.

This consistency is also reflected where contractions have taken place within a word or form. For example, second- and first-person *qåṭal* forms show the expected contractions of */iy/ to */ī/ and */ay/ to */ē/.

- **-iy* > **-ī* (e.g., **galliytu* > **gillītī* > גִּלִּ֫יתִי "I revealed")[99]
- **-ay* > **-ē* (e.g., **naglaytu* > **niglētī* > נִגְלֵ֫יתִי "I revealed myself")

Due perhaps to different bases or due to analogy, not infrequently there is some variation such that what should be */ī/ is instead */ē/ (e.g., גִּלֵּ֫יתִי) and vice versa, what should be */ē/ is instead */ī/ (וְנִגְלִ֫ינוּ and also **banaytu* > **banītī* > בָּנִ֫יתִי "I built").

Triphthongs also contract in a regular manner within verbs with object suffixes. In these cases, nothing remains of the third root consonant.

- **raʾayam* > **rāʾām* > רָאָם "he saw them" (Gen 32:3)
- **raʾayūka* > **rāʾūkā* > רָא֫וּךָ "they saw you" (Ps 77:17)
- **yaʿniyuka* > **yaʿnɛ̄ka* > **yaʿnɛka* > **yaʿnəka* > יַעַנְךָ "he will answer you" (1 Sam 20:10)[100]

In addition to reflecting various contractions, III-*vav*/*yod* roots also exhibit other peculiar characteristics. First, note that the final *yod* of the

99. If the *piel* base is, instead **qattal*, then the /ē/ would be expected and the /ī/ would not.

100. Note the pausal form יַרְבֶּ֫ךָּ "may he multiply you" Gen 28:3.

regular *yiqṭol* is preserved in rare cases (e.g., יִשְׁלָיוּ "they will be at ease" Job 12:6 [*qal* שלה]; and יֶאֱתָיוּ "they will come" Job 16:22 [*qal* אתה]). This also happens with the paragogic *nun* (e.g., יִבְכָּיוּן "they will weep" Isa 33:7 [*qal* בכה]; and תּוֹגְיוּן "you will torment" Job 19:2 [*hiphil* יגה]).

The third feminine singular *qåṭal* seems to have ended with a *tav* in the early part of the first millennium BCE (e.g., הית [= *hayāt* ? < **hayiyat*] "it was" Siloam Tunnel Inscription, l. 3). Such forms are occasionally found in the MT, too (e.g., וְעָשָׂת "and it will make" Lev 25:21; וְהָיָת [*ketiv*] "and it will be" 2 Kgs 9:37; וְהִרְצָת "it will enjoy" Lev 26:34).[101] But, by the latter part of the first millennium BCE, the third feminine singular contained two feminine morphemes: a *tav* and a final */ā/, גָּלְתָה "she revealed."

The third common plural *qal qåṭal* is exemplified by גָּלוּ "they revealed"; the only difference from the third common plural of a II-*vav*/*yod* root is the accent on the first syllable in the II-*vav*/*yod* form: קָ֫מוּ "they arose." In other conjugations the ending on III-*vav*/*yod* roots is the same, but there is less confusion with other forms: נִגְלוּ "they were revealed"; הִגְלוּ "they exiled."

As with II-*vav*/*yod* roots, there is a distinction between *yiqṭol* and short-*yiqṭol* (= *wayyiqṭol*) forms among III-*vav*/*yod* roots. The short-*yiqṭol*, as described above, began as the PS jussive/preterite and, in the singular, lacked a final vowel. In the case of III-*vav*/*yod* roots, this means that the preterite would have ended with a *vav* or *yod* (e.g., **yagluw* and **yabniy*). In these cases, the sequence of a vowel followed by word-final semivowel eventually was lost, leaving a single syllable consisting of the prefix followed by the first and second root consonants (**yagl* > **yigl* and **yabn* > **yibn*). In THT, such forms are often realized with a *hireq* in the prefix and an epenthetic vowel between first and second root consonants (e.g., a *segol*: יִ֫גֶל "let him reveal" and יִ֫בֶן "let him build"). The same form appears in the *wayyiqṭol* (וַיִּ֫גֶל "he revealed" and וַיִּ֫בֶן "he built").[102] These short-*yiqṭol* forms contrast with the longer regular *yiqṭol* יִגְלֶה "he will

101. Note also הֶלְאָת "it wearies" Ezek 24:12.

102. The cases where no epenthetic vowel is written in THT are also cases where the first root consonant is of a greater sonority than the second and pronouncing them without an epenthetic vowel is comparatively easy (e.g., וַיֵּ֫שְׁתְּ "he drank" Gen 9:21). See the short summary in Lutz Edzard, "Phonology, Optimality Theory: Biblical Hebrew," *EHLL* 3:134–38. In either case, these short-*yiqṭol* and *wayyiqṭol* forms of III-*vav*/*yod* roots are considered monosyllabic at the phonological level (see Khan, "Shewa," 3:544; Khan, "Syllable Structure," 3:666, 669).

reveal" and יִבְנֶה "he will build." As explained above, the short-*yiqṭol* and *wayyiqṭol* with a suffixal morpheme or pronoun appear the same as the *yiqṭol*. Thus, a form like יִגְלוּ can be, on formal grounds, either a *yiqṭol* or short-*yiqṭol*. Historically, they would have been distinguished through a (paragogic) *nun* at the end of the *yiqṭol* form.

Distinct short-*yiqṭol* and *wayyiqṭol* forms appear in all the conjugations. Since the endings are often lost, one must rely on the initial sequence of vowels to identify the conjugation.

qal

יִ֫רֶב	"let it be many" (Gen 1:22)
וַתֵּ֫רֶב	"it was numerous" (Gen 43:34)
יַ֫עַל	"let him go up" (Gen 44:33)
וַיַּ֫עַל	"he went up" (Gen 13:1)
יְהִי	"let it be" (Gen 1:3)
וַיְהִי	"it was" (passim)

piel

יְצַו	"may he command" (Deut 28:8)
וַיְצַו	"he commanded" (passim)

hiphil

תֶּ֫רֶב	"may you increase" (Ps 71:21)
וַיֶּ֫רֶב	"he increased" (2 Sam 18:8)
וַיַּ֫שְׁקְ	"he supplied drink" (Ps 78:15)
יַ֫עַל	"let him offer up" (2 Sam 24:22)
וַיַּ֫עַל	"he offered up" (Gen 8:20)
תֶּ֫רֶב	"may you increase" (Ps 71:21)
וַיֶּ֫רֶב	"he multiplied" (Lam 2:5)

hithpael

תִּתְחַר	"do [not] be angry" (Ps 37:7)
וַיִּתְכַּס	"he covered himself" (2 Kgs 19:1)

niphal

יֵרָא "let it appear" (Lev 9:6)
וַיֵּרָא "he appeared" (Gen 18:1)

Note, in particular, that the *qal* will usually reflect /i/ in the prefix (but also /e/, /a/, and */ə/), while the *hiphil* will usually reflect /a/ (rarely /ɛ/). In most of these cases the vowel sequence is similar to that of segolate nouns. The same even applies to the short-*yiqṭol* and *wayyiqṭol* of היה "to be" and חיה "to live" (compare יְהִי "let it be" Gen 1:3 with בְּכִי "weeping").

Some verbs are particularly difficult to recognize. The combination of a *nun* as first root consonant and *vav/yod* as third consonant result in short-*yiqṭol* and *wayyiqṭol* forms that attest just one root consonant. For example, the *qal* of נטה appears as תֵּט "do (not) stretch" (Prov 4:5) and וַיֵּט "he stretched" (Gen 12:8); the *hiphil* appears as תַּט "do (not) stretch" (Ps 141:4) and וַיֵּט "he stretched" (Ezra 9:9). The root נכה appears in the *hiphil*: יַךְ "it will strike" (Hos 14:6) and וַיַּךְ "it struck" (Exod 9:25). With suffixes, the *dagesh* is present, hinting at the missing *nun*: יַכֵּם "it will strike them" (Isa 49:10).

Those roots which are both I-*vav/yod* and III-*vav/yod* are also difficult to recognize in the short-*yiqṭol* and *wayyiqṭol* forms. In the *hiphil*, the initial */ō/ of the prefix is not always marked by a *mater* (e.g., וַיּוֹר "he shot" 2 Kgs 13:17; וַיֹּרֵם "he shot them" Ps 64:8; יֹרוּ "they were shooting" 2 Sam 11:20 [*hiphil* ירה]).

As with other verb types, the vowels of the *yiqṭol* stem usually allow one to predict the vowels of the imperative and infinitive construct. For III-*vav/yod* roots, the imperative masculine singular is distinct from the *yiqṭol* stem only in the length of the vowel. The *yiqṭol* reflects */e/ and the imperative */ē/: **tigle* > תִּגְלֶה versus **gəlē* > גְּלֵה "reveal!"[103] However, in many cases, the vowels of the imperative masculine singular match the vowels of the short-*yiqṭol* (and *wayyiqṭol*).[104] Note, for example, the shortened forms of the imperative.

---

103. The same distinction is also implied in the Secunda ιερε (יִרְאֶה Ps 49:10) vs. αιη (הֱיֵה Ps 30:11) (see Brønno, *Studien*, 25, 47). Note also in other conjugations: יְקַוֶּה "he will await" (Mal 5:6) vs. קַוֵּה "await" (Ps 27:14); תַּטֶּה "you will extend" (Prov 2:2) vs. הַטֵּה "extend" (Ps 33:3); יֵרָאֶה "it will be seen" (Gen 22:14) vs. הֵרָאֵה "be seen" 1 Kgs 18:1)

104. In the *hiphil* impv. masc. sing. one also sees this in the strong root: e.g., הַרְכֵּב "mount!" (2 Kgs 13:16) and וַיַּרְכֵּב "he made [him] mount" (Gen 41:43).

חַל "appease!" (1 Kgs 13:6 [*piel* חלה])
וַיְחַל "he entreated" (2 Kgs 13:4)

צַו "command!" (Lev 6:2 [*piel* צוה])
וַיְצַו "he commanded" (Gen 2:16)

הַ֫עַל "bring up!" (Exod 8:1 [*hiphil* עלה])
יַ֫עַל "let him bring up" (2 Sam 24:22)

הַךְ "strike!" (Exod 8:12 [*hiphil* נכה])
יַךְ "let him strike" (Hos 14:5)

הֶ֫רֶף "leave (us) alone!" (1 Sam 11:13 [*hiphil* רפה])
תֶּ֫רֶף "do [not] let go" (Josh 10:6).

The infinitive construct, however, shows a clear distinction from the *yiqṭol*. The *qal* infinitive construct of III-*vav*/*yod* roots reflects the sequence of vowels found with the strong root (e.g., **ə-ō*; cf. שְׁמֹר), though with an extra final /t/: גְּלוֹת "exiling," the result of which is that the infinitives construct look at first glance like feminine plural nouns.[105] The same ending also appears in all the derived conjugations (e.g., הַגְלוֹת "to exile"). The infinitive absolute often reflects the vowel sequence associated with the strong root. Thus, the *qal* reflects the sequence **ā-ō* (but with a *he mater*), גָּלֹה "reveal" (cf. שָׁמוֹר "guard"), but the *hiphil* the sequence **a-ē*, הַכֵּה "strike" and הַרְבֵּה "many" (cf. הַשְׁלֵךְ "throw"). The participles in all conjugations end like other etymological III-*vav*/*yod* nouns.

5.17. Weak Roots: Geminate

Verbs from geminate roots are the most complex of the root types. In part, this is due to the fact that they reflect different patterns of assimilation. As in the strong root, the geminates reflect two basic paradigms, associated with active and stative verbs. Verbs with an active sense often exhibit a *qal qåṭal* form that is analogous to the strong root in the third-person (e.g.,

105. Recall that *qal* inf. cons. from weak roots often bear a feminine morphological feature, usually a final *tav* (שֶׁבֶת "dwelling"), but also sometimes a final *-ā* (e.g., יִרְאָה "fearing").

סָבַב "he went around" and סָבְבוּ "they went around"), but a form closer to II-*vav*/*yod* roots in the second- and first-person forms (e.g., סַבּ֫וֹתִי "I went around"; cf. קַ֫מְתִּי "I arose" [*qal* קום] and הֲקִמֹ֫תִי "I established" [*hiphil* קום]).[106] Notice the */ō/ (< */ā/) linking vowel between stem and suffix.

The stative verbs in the *qal qåṭal* seem more consistent and most often do not exhibit forms based on the strong root. Instead, these verb forms look like adjectives from geminate roots (e.g., רַע "it [ms] is evil" vs. רַע "evil"; רָעָה "it [fs] is evil" vs. רָעָה "evil"; רַבָּה "it [fs] is many" vs. רַבָּה "many"). The form of the third common plural *qåṭal* exhibits the same /a/ vowel and gemination (e.g., רָעוּ [< **rāʿū* < **raʿʿū*] "they are evil" and רַבּוּ "they are many"). Second- and first-person forms are analogous to the active verbs, with gemination and the */ō/ (< */ā/) linking vowel (e.g., קַלּ֫וֹתִי "I am small").

The *qal yiqṭol* also exhibits separate patterns based on the active/stative dichotomy, with the /u/ theme vowel associated with active verbs and /a/ with stative verbs. In addition, the *yiqṭol* attests two alternative forms. (This means that there are essentially two patterns for the active *yiqṭol* and two for the stative.) Most often, the geminate consonants in the *yiqṭol* appear in Hebrew without a vowel separating them.

- **yasubbūna* > **yāsobbū* (> יָס֫בּוּ) "they will go around" (Job 16:13)
- **yiḥammūna* > **yēḥammū* (> יֵחַ֫מּוּ) "they will be hot" (Hos 7:7)[107]

In the singular, the doubling of the second and third root consonants is lost due to the lack of a final vowel (similar to how there is no gemination in singular nouns like עַם [< **ʿamm*] "people"): **yasubbu* > **yasobb* > **yāsob* (> יָסֹב) "he will go around" (1 Kgs 7:15) and **yiḥammu* > **yiḥamm* > **yēḥam* יֵחַם "he will be hot" (Deut 19:6).[108] This is often characterized as the "true" Hebrew manner of inflecting geminate roots.

Somewhat less frequently in these verbs, the theme vowel separates the two geminate consonants and the first of these (i.e., the second root consonant) assimilates backwards into the first root consonant. The vowel

106. There are numerous exceptions, where, e.g., the 3cp exhibits a geminated consonant: יַדּוּ "they threw" (Joel 4:3); שַׁחוּ "they bowed down" (Hab 3:6).

107. In pause, the stative pattern appears as יֵקַ֫לּוּ "they will be light" (1 Sam 2:30). Note also the form with suffixes: **yasubbanhū* > **yəsubbɛnnū* (> יְסֻבֶּ֫נּוּ) "it will go around it" (Jer 52:21).

108. Note also the form יֵרַע "he will do evil" (2 Sam 20:6).

of the prefix is expressed as /i/ in the closed, unaccented syllable. This is often referred to as an Aramaic-like inflection (since this is the characteristic inflection of geminate roots in Aramaic), but the resulting verbal forms appear in Hebrew like I-*nun* roots.

- **yas**b**u**bu* > **ya**ss**ub* > **yi**ss**ob* (> יִסֹּב) "he will go around" (2 Sam 14:24)
- **yiḥm**amu* > **yiḥḥ**am* (> יֵחַם) "it will be warm" (1 Kgs 1:1)[109]
- **yadm**umūna* > **yadd**umū* > **yidd**əmū* (> יִדְּמוּ) "they will be silent" (Ps 31:18)
- *(*way*)*yitmamū* > *(*way*)*yittamū* > *(*way*)*yittəmū* (> וַיִּתְּמוּ) "they were complete" (Deut 34:8)[110]

Notice that where a *dagesh* appears in these forms, it does not reflect the assimilation of a preceding *nun* but the backward assimilation of the second root consonant (identical to that of the last root consonant).

The student of Hebrew will perhaps not find it surprising that some forms in the MT evidence mixing of these two basic types, where one too many consonants has been doubled: תִּדֹּ֫מִּי "you will be silent" (Jer 48:2) and יִתַּ֫מּוּ "they will be complete" (Jer 44:12). In these cases, it seems possible that some confusion with the *niphal* paradigm has taken place (cf. יִסַּ֫בּוּ "they went around" Ezek 1:12 [*niph.* סבב]).

In THT, the *qal* short-*yiqṭol* and *wayyiqṭol* forms are sometimes accented on their prefix if the form lacks any suffixal morpheme or pronoun (e.g., וַיָּ֫סָב "he went around" Judg 11:18; וַיָּ֫מָד "he measured" Ezek 40:8; וַיֵּ֫צֶר "it was distressing" Gen 32:8; יֵ֫צֶר "it was distressing" Job 20:22; יַרְדְּ "he subdued" Isa 41:2). However, the short-*yiqṭol* and *wayyiqṭol* are often identical to the *yiqṭol*, especially with stative verbs (e.g., וַתֵּקַל "she

109. Note also **yadmumu* > **yaddum* > **yiddom* (> יִדֹּם) "he will be silent" (Amos 5:13) and **yimlalu* > **yimmal* (> יִמַּל) "it will wither" (Job 18:16).

110. Note also the *wayyiqṭol* form, וַיִּקְּדוּ "they bowed down" (Exod 4:31) and the pausal form: **yimlalū* > **yimmalū* (> יִמָּ֫לוּ) "they will wither" (Job 24:24). There are still other forms, more difficult to explain: תֵּזְלִי "you act gluttonously" (Jer 2:36) and תֵּצְרִי "you will be limited" (Isa 49:19); יֵרְעוּ "they will be evil" (Neh 2:3). Usually, the different manners of inflecting these roots do not imply different senses, though in סבב there does seem to be some consistency between form and meaning, with the Hebrew type of inflection being used in an active transitive sense and the Aramaic-like inflection being used in a reflexive sense (see Joüon §82h).

treated lightly" Gen 16:4) and those forms that have an Aramaic-like (or I-*nun*-like) form (e.g., וַיִּסֹּב "he turned away" Gen 42:24).

The imperative has the stem vowel of the *yiqṭol* form and usually exhibits a doubling of the second and third consonants like that of the "true" Hebrew pattern of the *yiqṭol* (e.g., סֹב and סֹבּוּ). The infinitive construct attests an */ō/ vowel (e.g., סֹב) even in stative verbs (e.g., תֹּם).

The non-*qal* conjugations exhibit different reflexes with respect to geminate roots. Geminate roots are entirely regular in the *piel* (e.g., חִלַּלְתִּי "I profaned" Isa 47:6). In the *hiphil qåṭal* third masculine singular, geminate roots exhibit no gemination (e.g., הֵחֵל "he began"), though gemination does reemerge in the third feminine singular and third common plural forms, where one finds penultimate stress (e.g., הֵחֵ֫לָּה "she began" and הֵחֵ֫לּוּ "they began"). In the second- and first-person forms, the linking vowel */ō/ (< */ā/) is also attested (e.g., הֲסִבֹּתָ "you turned around"), as with II-*vav*/*yod* roots (e.g., הֲקֵמֹ֫תִי "I established"). Here again, the vowel of the prefix reduces.

The *hiphil yiqṭol* again exhibits two basic patterns, one associated with Hebrew morphology, where the two geminate consonants are not separated and the other associated with Aramaic, where a vowel separates the two geminate consonants, the first one assimilating backward into the first root consonant.

- **yaḥillu* > **yaḥell* > **yāḥel* (> יָחֵל) "he will begin" (Judg 13:5) (*hiphil* חלל)
- **taḥillūna* > **taḥillū* > **tāḥellū* (> תָּחֵ֫לּוּ) "you will begin" (Ezek 9:6) (*hiphil* חלל)

versus

- **tatmimu* > **tattem* (> תַּתֵּם) "you will make blameless" (Job 22:3) (*hiphil* תמם)

The *wayyiqṭol* forms are sometimes accented on the prefix in THT (e.g., וַיָּ֫חֶל "he began" Gen 9:20), though this does not happen with forms that attest the gemination pattern typical of Aramaic (e.g., וַיַּסֵּב "he made go around" Josh 6:11). The imperative (ms) and infinitive construct are identical in THT (e.g., הָסֵב), differing in Second Temple times just in the vowel of the last syllable (/e/ for the imperative and /ē/ for the infinitive construct). The participle exhibits the vowels associated with the *qåṭal* (e.g., מֵסֵב "one making go around" Jer 21:4), in a manner similar to that of II-*vav/yod* roots in the *hiphil* (e.g., מֵבִין "one who understands" [*hiphil* בין]).[111]

The *niphal* of geminate roots shows diverse vowel patterns, in part influenced by the vowels of other verb forms. Most commonly, the *qåṭal* third-person form reflects the sequence of *ā-a, as in נָסַב "it changes direction" (Josh 16:6) and וְנָסַבּוּ "they will be turned over" (Jer 6:12).[112] However, note how the *niphal* of מסס only sometimes appears with the expected sequence of vowels (e.g., נָמָס "it melted" Exod 16:21 [in pause]); elsewhere, it also appears as though it were a *qal* stative verb from the root נמס, as with נָמֵס "it melts" (Ps 22:15). More dramatic (and confusing) are those cases where the geminate verb is inflected as though it were from another existing Hebrew root, as with וְנִחֲלוּ "they will be profaned" [חלל] (Ezek 7:24) vs. the *piel* נִחֲלוּ "they distributed" [נחל] (Josh 19:51).[113] In other cases, the *niphal* of geminate roots follows the vowel sequence of the II-*vav/yod* roots, as with נָזֹלּוּ "they shook" (Isa 64:3); נָבֹזּוּ "they will be ransacked" (Amos 3:11); נָגֹזּוּ "they will be cut off" (Nah 1:12); and וְנָרֹץ "it will be crushed" (Qoh 12:6).[114]

In the *niphal yiqṭol* and related forms, the vowels of the prefix and stem are typically *i-a (e.g., יִגַּל "let it roll" Amos 5:24; יִסַּבּוּ "they turn around" Ezek 1:9).[115] As is common with other roots, an initial guttural root consonant will trigger compensatory lengthening, such that the */i/ becomes */ē/, as with יֵחַת "he will be in awe" (Isa 30:31) and יֵחַתּוּ "they will be in awe" (1 Sam 2:10). Rarely, the vowel of the stem will be /o/, following the pattern of II-*vav/yod* roots (e.g., תִּבּוֹז "she will be plundered" Isa 24:3 [בזז]).

111. Again, we presume /e/ for the final syllable of the *qåṭal* and /ē/ for the participle.

112. Second- and first-person forms are much less frequent, but usually attest an */ō/ linking vowel, as in the other conjugations.

113. Both roots presumably reflect /ḥ/. Note also נִחַת "he was in awe of" (Mal 2:5) [*niphal* חתת] vs. נִחַת "he bent" (in 2 Sam 22:35) [*piel* of נחת].

114. Here, there is sometimes some similarity with other roots. Note, e.g., נָזְלוּ "they dripped" (Judg 5:5) [*qal* of נזל]; and גֹזִי "[you] cut me" (Ps 71:6) (*qal* ptc. גזה). Although בוז "to despise" does not occur in the *niphal*, as a *qåṭal* 3cp it would be *נָבֹזּוּ "they were despised"; similarly, רצה "to delight" occurs in the *niphal qåṭal* only in the 3ms, but the 3cp would be *נִרְצוּ.

115. In יִסַּבּוּ, the *dagesh* in the *samek* derives from the *nun* prefix of the *niphal* and the *dagesh* in the *bet* derives from the geminated consonants of the root. Contrast with the *qal* יִסֹּבּוּ, described above, where the *dagesh* in the *bet* is perhaps just due to confusion with the *niphal* paradigm.

Like II-*vav*/*yod* roots, geminate roots sometimes appear in the *polel* (מְקֹשֵׁשׁ "one gathering" Num 15:32) and *hithpolel* (in a reflexive sense: הִתְקוֹשְׁשׁוּ "gather yourself" Zeph 2:11). However, unlike the II-*vav*/*yod* roots, geminate roots frequently appear in the *piel* (especially with roots ending with *lamedh*, like הלל "to praise," חלל "to profane," and פלל "to pray") and the *hithpael* (וַיִּתְפַּלֵּל "he prayed" Num 21:7). These conjugations are extremely regular and the vowels often change little in the inflection.

5.18. Aramaic and Aramaic-Like Forms

As was the case for nouns, certain verbal forms seem to derive from Aramaic or, at the least, appear like corresponding Aramaic forms. We have just mentioned the cases of geminate verbs that seem to exhibit patterns more commonly found with Aramaic verbs. In addition, there are a limited number of *qåṭal* second feminine singular forms with final *yod* (e.g., the *ketiv* of וְיָרַדְתִּי "you will go down" Ruth 3:3). These match what we would expect in Aramaic. Furthermore, various historical features of BH are shared with Aramaic. For example, the rare third feminine singular *qåṭal* forms of III-*vav*/*yod* roots that end with final *tav* (e.g., וְעָשָׂת "and it will make" Lev 25:21) are presumably typical of First Temple era Hebrew, but are also typical of Aramaic. Note also that the paragogic *nun*, which appears on second feminine singular, and third and second masculine plural *yiqṭol* verbs in BH, is commonly found on nonjussive forms in Aramaic.

5.19. Chapter Summary

Historical Details

1. The *qåṭal* form of the verb derives from a verbal adjective to which suffixes were attached. This helps explain the similarity in form between stative *qåṭal* verbs, participles, and adjectives (e.g., זָקֵן "he is old" and "elder"; מֵת "he is dead" and "dead one").
2. The short-*yiqṭol* and *wayyiqṭol* derive from a preterite/jussive form (e.g., **yaqtul*). In weak roots, the stem of short-*yiqṭol* and *wayyiqṭol* verbs are often shorter (graphically and phonetically) than the regular *yiqṭol* (e.g., יַעַשׂ and וַיַּעַשׂ vs. יַעֲשֶׂה).
3. The regular *yiqṭol* is also derived from the preterite/jussive form **yaqtul* plus a final /u/ vowel (which marked the verb of a subordinate clause in PS): **yaqtulu*.

4. The initial vowel of the *hiphil qåṭal* likely originated as /a/, as did that of the *niphal*. This is based, in part, on the resolved diphthongs in I-*vav*/*yod* roots (הוֹשִׁיעַ [< *hawšiʿa]; הֵיטִיב [< *hayṭiba]; נוֹדַע [< *nawdaʿa]).

Learning Tips

1. The verb forms with object suffixes tend to reflect vowel tendencies typical of the noun and adjective. The *qal qåṭal* plus object suffix often exhibits the sequence of stem vowels *ə-ā (*shewa-qamets*) in the third-person and *ə-a (*shewa-patakh*) for second- and first-person forms.
2. The third masculine singular *qåṭal* plus object suffix uses an /a/-class linking vowel between the verbal stem and the suffix, while the imperative (like the *yiqṭol*) exhibits an /i/-class linking vowel.
3. In all conjugations with an /a/-class vowel in the stem (i.e., the *niphal*, *pual*, *hophal*), the participle exhibits */ā/ (*qamets*) but */a/ (*patakh*) in the *qåṭal*. This can be used to distinguish the *niphal qåṭal* from the *niphal* participle.
4. The *yiqṭol*, short-*yiqṭol*, *wayyiqṭol*, imperative, and infinitive construct (and sometimes inf. abs. and ptc.) usually share a similar if not identical vowel pattern, finite forms usually exhibiting a final short stem vowel and nonfinite forms a long vowel.
5. Vowel sequences are useful in distinguishing between different conjugations (more so than other features like the doubling of the middle consonant of the *piel* or the initial *he* of the *hiphil qåṭal*).
   5.1. The third-person *qåṭal* forms of both the *piel* and *hiphil* exhibit the sequence of two /i/-class vowels (*piel*: *i-e [> *hireq-tsere*]; *hiphil*: *i-ī [> *hireq-hireq*^{yod}]).
   5.2. Second- and first-person *qåṭal* forms (for strong roots) almost universally contain short /a/ as the last stem vowel.
   5.3. The vowel sequences characteristic of the *yiqṭol*, short-*yiqṭol*, *wayyiqṭol*, imperative, and infinitive construct in the derived conjugations are the following.
      5.3.1. *piel*: *a-e or *a-ē (> *patakh-tsere*)
      5.3.2. *hiphil*: *a-ī (> *patakh-hireq*^{yod}); the short-*yiqṭol*, *wayyiqṭol*, and imperative have instead *a-e (> *patakh-tsere*), without suffixed morpheme or pronoun.
      5.3.3. *niphal*: *i-ā-e or *i-ā-ē (> *hireq-qamets-tsere*)

6. The *pual* (*u-a), *hophal* (*o-a), *hithpael* (*i-a-e[/ē]), *polel* (*o-e[/ē]), *pilpel* (*i-e[/ē]), and related conjugations exhibit the vowel sequence implied in their names in every verbal form (*qåṭal*, *yiqṭol*, ptc., etc.), except where pretonic vowels reduce.
7. Weak roots containing a *vav/yod* usually exhibit in THT a form of the short-*yiqṭol* and *yiqṭol* that is accented on the prefix and that has a short vowel in the stem.
8. Mnemonic Aids
   8.1. *qal* I-*vav/yod*
      8.1.1. *yiqṭol*: "as one has come, so one will go (יֵלֵךְ [from הלך])" Qoh 5:15
      8.1.2. *yiqṭol*: "the meek will inherit (יִירְשׁוּ) the earth" Ps 37:11
      8.1.3. infinitive construct: "teach them to your children, speak them when you dwell (שִׁבְתְּךָ) in your house" Deut 6:7
   8.2. *qal* II-*vav/yod*
      8.2.1. *wəqåṭal*: "set (וְשַׂמְתֶּם) these, my words on your heart" Deut 11:18
      8.2.2. imperative (fs): "rise and shine (קוּמִי אוֹרִי)" Isa 60:1
      8.2.3. *wayyiqṭol*: "Joab put (וַיָּשֶׂם) the words into her mouth" 2 Sam 14:3
   8.3. III-*vav/yod*
      8.3.1. *qal wəqåṭal*: "the anger of the Lord will burn (וְחָרָה) against you" Deut 11:17
      8.3.2. *qal* short-*yiqṭol*: "let there be light (יְהִי אוֹר)" Gen 1:3
      8.3.3. *qal* cohortative: "let us make (נַעֲשֶׂה) humans in our image" Gen 1:26
      8.3.4. *qal yiqṭol*: "the race does not go to the swift … but time and chance occur (יִקְרֶה) to all of them" Qoh 9:11
      8.3.5. *piel qåṭal*: "I await (קִוִּיתִי) your salvation" Gen 49:18
      8.3.6. *piel* participle + suffix: "These words that I am commanding you (מְצַוְּךָ) today must be kept over your heart" Deut 6:6
      8.3.7. *hophal* and *pual* participles: "Surely our sicknesses he lifts and our pains, he carries them. We consider him stricken, struck (מֻכֵּה) by God, and afflicted (מְעֻנֶּה)" Isa 53:4.

6
Charts of Nouns and Verbs

It is sometimes difficult for a student to grasp the principles of the morphological system by being given just a few examples in the paragraphs of a grammar. The following charts, therefore, are provided in order for the student to see for him/herself the inflection of different common Biblical Hebrew nouns and verbs.[1] I spell and vocalize words as they occur in the MT, even if this means that a given form does not exactly match what we might expect. It will be immediately obvious that not all the forms are attested and those that are not are marked with an asterisk (*). The vocalization of these unattested forms is made possible first by analogy to other words from the same base with the same vowels and, if these are absent, by analogy to other words from the same base with different vowels. The words used to help pinpoint a particular vocalization are often, but not always, supplied in the footnotes. With certain suffixes I have neglected to offer reconstructions given the absence of adequate data. If a form is attested in its pausal form, I present it in its contextual form in the tables. In some cases, a word is chosen due to its convenience (e.g., because it has both a singular and plural form or because it is clearly related to another noun that is listed), even though it is not well attested with suffixes. The spelling is generally plene in the charts (except in the geminate verbs), though I do write forms defective if they are only attested in this way. The reconstructed historical forms of the nouns are not cited with the final short vowels marking case, but the reconstructed historical forms of verbs are cited with their final short vowels.

Because most elementary grammars include charts of the verbs according to their root type and conjugation, I have not included a com-

1. Much of the following is informed by Huehnergard, "Biblical Hebrew Nominal Patterns"; Fox, *Semitic Noun Patterns*; and *HGhS*.

prehensive set of similar charts here. Instead, many of the verbal charts below juxtapose paradigms of different verbs in order to highlight commonalities and distinctions between them. Due to the predictable nature of verbal inflection, verbal forms that are unattested can be reconstructed with some confidence based on the expectations of the paradigm. Where there are uncertainties, I have indicated specific parallels in the footnotes. Especially in the case of geminate verbs I have listed specific passages where the verb forms are found. In cases of inadequate data, I have not reconstructed anything.

I have listed forms of the short-*yiqṭol* and *wayyiqṭol* together, separate from the *yiqṭol*, if the the short-*yiqṭol* and *wayyiqṭol* have similar forms and are distinct from those of the regular *yiqṭol*. Since the short-*yiqṭol* and *wayyiqṭol* forms of the second-person feminine singular, third-person masculine/feminine plural, and second-person masculine/feminine plural are identical to the regular *yiqṭol*, they are never listed separately. If a given verb occurs in the short-*yiqṭol* in a form distinct from the *wayyiqṭol*, then the two forms are listed separately.

Table 6.1. Biconsonantal Bases with Short Vowel, Part 1[2]

	**qal* sg./pl. "blood" **dam/*damīm*		**qalat* sg./pl. "year" **šanat/*šanīm* and **šanāt*		**qalt* sg./du./pl. "door" **dalt/*dalataym/*dalatāt*[3]		
abs.	דָּם	דָּמִים	שָׁנָה	שָׁנִים	דֶּ֫לֶת	דְּלָתַ֫יִם	דְּלָתוֹת
const.	דַּם	דְּמֵי	שְׁנַת	שְׁנוֹת / שְׁנֵי	*דֶּ֫לֶת	דַּלְתֵי	דַּלְתוֹת
+1cs	דָּמִי	*דָּמַי	*שְׁנָתִי	שְׁנוֹתַי	*דַּלְתִּי	דְּלָתַי	דַּלְתוֹתַי
+2ms	דָּמְךָ	דָּמֶ֫יךָ	*שְׁנָתְךָ	שְׁנוֹתֶ֫יךָ	*דַּלְתְּךָ	דְּלָתֶ֫יךָ	*דַּלְתוֹתֶ֫יךָ
+2fs	דָּמֵךְ	דָּמַ֫יִךְ	*שְׁנָתֵךְ	שְׁנוֹתַ֫יִךְ	*דַּלְתֵּךְ	*דְּלָתַ֫יִךְ	*דַּלְתוֹתַ֫יִךְ

2. The chart is supplemented by the following forms: שָׁדַי "my breasts"; אֲמָתִי "my handmaiden"; אֲמָתְךָ "your handmaiden"; שְׂפָתָם "their tongue"; קֶ֫שֶׁת "bow of"; קַשְׁתִּי "my bow"; קַשְׁתְּךָ "your bow"; קַשְׁתּוֹ "his bow"; קַשְׁתָּם "their bow."

3. The word דֶּ֫לֶת is like other **qal* words ending in a feminine *tav* morpheme. That is, when these words are pluralized, the feminine *tav* morpheme is treated as though it were part of the root. Note, e.g., וּקְשָׁתוֹת (Isa 13:18, passim); קַשְּׁתֹתָיו (Isa 5:28, and other forms passim). See *HGhS*, 610t for other examples.

+3ms	דָּמוֹ	דָּמָיו	שְׁנָתוֹ	שְׁנוֹתָיו	*דַּלְתּוֹ	*דְּלָתָיו	דַּלְתוֹתָיו
+3fs	דָּמָהּ	דָּמֶ֫יהָ	שְׁנָתָהּ	*שְׁנוֹתֶ֫יהָ	*דַּלְתָּהּ	דְּלָתֶ֫יהָ	*דַּלְתוֹתֶ֫יהָ
+1cp	*דָּמֵ֫נוּ	*דָּמֵ֫ינוּ	*שְׁנָתֵ֫נוּ	שְׁנוֹתֵ֫ינוּ	*דַּלְתֵּ֫נוּ	*דְּלָתֵ֫ינוּ	*דַּלְתוֹתֵ֫ינוּ
+2mp	דִּמְכֶם	*דְּמֵיכֶם	*שְׁנַתְכֶם	*שְׁנוֹתֵיכֶם	*דַּלְתְּכֶם	*דַּלְתֵיכֶם	*דַּלְתוֹתֵיכֶם
+2fp	*דִּמְכֶן	*דְּמֵיכֶן	*שְׁנַתְכֶן	*שְׁנוֹתֵיכֶן	*דַּלְתְּכֶן	*דַּלְתֵיכֶן	*דַּלְתוֹתֵיכֶן
+3mp	דָּמָם	דְּמֵיהֶם	*שְׁנָתָם	שְׁנוֹתָם	*דַּלְתָּם	*דַּלְתֵיהֶם	דַּלְתוֹתֵיהֶם
+3fp	*דָּמָן	*דְּמֵיהֶן	*שְׁנָתָן	*שְׁנוֹתָן	*דַּלְתָּן	*דַּלְתֵיהֶן	*דַּלְתוֹתֵיהֶן

More Examples (see also table 6.2)

- **qal*: דָּג "fish"; יָד "hand" (see below); שֶׂה "sheep" (< **śay*);[4] *שַׁד "breast"
- **qalat*: אָמָה "handmaid" (pl. אֲמָהוֹת); and שָׂפָה "lip"
- **qalāt*: אָחוֹת "sister"; and חָמוֹת "husband's mother-in-law"[5]
- **qalt*: קֶ֫שֶׁת "bow"; נַ֫חַת "rest"; שַׁ֫חַת "pit"[6]

Table 6.2. Biconsonantal Bases with Short Vowel, Part 2[7]

	**qal* sg./pl. "one who arises" **qam/*qamīm*		**qalat* sg./pl. "one who arises" **qamat/*qamāt*		**qal* sg./du./pl. "hand" **yad /*yadaym/*yadāt*		
abs.	*קָם	קָמִים	קָמָה	*קָמוֹת	יָד	יָדַ֫יִם	יָדוֹת
const.	*קָם	*קָמֵי	*קָמַת	*קָמוֹת	יַד	יְדֵי	יְדוֹת
+1cs	—	קָמַי	*קָמָתִי	*קָמוֹתַי	יָדִי	יָדַי	*יְדוֹתַי
+2ms	—	קָמֶ֫יךָ	*קָמָתְךָ	*קָמוֹתֶ֫יךָ	יָדְךָ	יָדֶ֫יךָ	*יְדוֹתֶ֫יךָ

4. The forms of שֶׂה "sheep" are: const. sg. שֵׂה (Deut 14:4); + 3ms שֵׂיוֹ (Deut 22:1) and שְׂיֵהוּ (in 1 Sam 14:34).

5. The fem. familial terms: אָחוֹת "sister" and חָמוֹת "husband's mother-in-law" have an etymological *-āt* ending, which, in these cases, does not indicate plurality.

6. The last two examples derive from II-*vav*/*yod* roots; see Huehnergard, "Biblical Hebrew Nominal Patterns," 30.

7. The chart is supplemented by the following forms: עָב "cloud of" (const.); שָׁבֵי "those returning of"; זָבַת "flowing with"; רָמָתֵךְ "your height"; עָלוֹת "those suckling"; רָמוֹתַ֫יִךְ "your heights."

+2fs	—	*קָמַ֫יִךְ	*קָמָתֵךְ	*קָמוֹתַ֫יִךְ	יָדֵךְ	יָדַ֫יִךְ	*יְדוֹתַ֫יִךְ
+3ms	—	קָמָיו	*קָמָתוֹ	*קָמוֹתָיו	יָדוֹ	יָדָיו	יְדוֹתָיו
+3fs	—	*קָמֶ֫יהָ	*קָמָתָהּ	*קָמוֹתֶ֫יהָ	יָדָהּ	יָדֶ֫יהָ	יְדוֹתֶ֫יהָ
+1cp	—	קָמֵ֫ינוּ	*קָמָתֵ֫נוּ	*קָמוֹתֵ֫ינוּ	יָדֵ֫נוּ	יָדֵ֫ינוּ	*יְדוֹתֵ֫ינוּ
+2mp	—	*קָמֵיכֶם	*קָמַתְכֶם	*קָמוֹתֵיכֶם	יֶדְכֶם	יְדֵיכֶם	*יְדוֹתֵיכֶם
+2fp	—	*קָמֵיכֶן	*קָמַתְכֶן	*קָמוֹתֵיכֶן	יֶדְכֶן	*יְדֵיכֶן	*יְדוֹתֵיכֶן
+3mp	—	קָמֵיהֶם	*קָמָתָם	*קָמוֹתָם	יָדָם	יְדֵיהֶם	יְדוֹתָם
+3fp	—	*קָמֵיהֶן	*קָמָתָן	*קָמוֹתָן	*יָדָן	יְדֵיהֶן	*יְדוֹתָן

More Examples

- **qal*: עָב "cloud"; *qal* participles of II-*vav/yod* roots (like בוא "to enter"; גור "to sojourn"; זוב "to flow"; סור "to turn back"; עול "to nurse"; שׁוב "to return")
- **qalat*: רָמָה "height"

Table 6.3. Biconsonantal Bases with Short Vowel, Part 3[8]

	**qil* sg./pl. "tree" (עצה?) *ʿ*iṣ*/*ʿ*iṣīm*		**qilat* sg./pl. "counsel" (יעץ) *ʿ*iṯat*/*ʿ*iṯāt*		**qilt* sg. "dwelling" (ישׁב) **ṯibt*
abs.	עֵץ	עֵצִים	עֵצָה	עֵצוֹת	שֶׁ֫בֶת
const.	עֵץ	עֲצֵי	עֲצַת	—	שֶׁ֫בֶת
+1cs	*עֵצִי	*עֵצַי	עֲצָתִי	—	שִׁבְתִּי
+2ms	עֵצְךָ	עֵצֶ֫יךָ	עֲצָתְךָ	—	שִׁבְתְּךָ
+2fs	*עֵצֵךְ	עֵצַ֫יִךְ	*עֲצָתֵךְ	—	*שִׁבְתֵּךְ
+3ms	עֵצוֹ	עֵצָיו	עֲצָתוֹ	—	שִׁבְתּוֹ

8. The chart is supplemented by the following forms: אֵלִי "my God"; שִׁמְכֶם "your name" (see table 6.4). The form of certain words is ambiguous. Words like רֵעִי, רֵעֲךָ, (pausal רֵעֶ֫ךָ) may be from רֵעַ or רֵעֶה (from **riʿay*, i.e., the **qiṭal* base). Note the form רֵעֵיהֶם "their friends" (Jer 29:23; Ps 28:3).

+3fs	עֵצָהּ	עֵצֶ֫יהָ	*עֲצָתָהּ	—	שִׁבְתָּהּ
+1cp	*עֵצֵ֫נוּ	עֵצֵ֫ינוּ	*עֲצָתֵ֫נוּ	—	שִׁבְתֵּ֫נוּ
+2mp	*עֶצְכֶם	*עֲצֵיכֶם	*עֲצַתְכֶם	—	שִׁבְתְּכֶם
+2fp	*עֶצְכֶן	*עֲצֵיכֶן	*עֲצַתְכֶן	—	*שִׁבְתְּכֶן
+3mp	*עֵצָם	*עֲצֵיהֶם	עֲצָתָם	—	שִׁבְתָּם
+3fp	*עֵצָן	*עֲצֵיהֶן	*עֲצָתָן	—	*שִׁבְתָּן

More Examples (see also tables 6.4–6.5)

- **qil*: אֵל "god"; גֵּר "sojourner"; מֵת "dead one"; נֵר "lamp"
- **qilat*: חֵמָה (from יחם) "rage"; מֵאָה "one hundred"; עֵדָה (from יעד) "assembly"; עֵדָה (from עוד) "witness"; פֵּאָה "corner"
- **qilt*: גַּ֫עַת (*qal* inf. const. נגע) "touching"; גֶּ֫שֶׁת (*qal* inf. const. נגשׁ) "approaching"; דַּ֫עַת (*qal* inf. const. ידע) "knowing"; טַ֫עַת (*qal* inf. const. נטע) "planting"; צֵאת (*qal* inf. const. יצא) "going out"; לֶ֫כֶת (*qal* inf. const. הלך) "going"; עֵת (*ʿ*int* from ענה or *ʿ*idt* from יעד) "time"; רֶ֫דֶת (*qal* inf. const. ירד) "going down"; רֶ֫שֶׁת (*qal* inf. const. ירשׁ) "inheriting"; שֶׁ֫בֶת (*qal* inf. const. ישׁב) "dwelling"; תֵּת (< **tint*; *qal* inf. const. נתן) "giving"[9]

Table 6.4. Biconsonantal Bases with Short Vowel, Part 4

	**qil* sg./pl. "son" **bin/*banīm*		**qil* sg./pl. "name" **šim/*šimāt*		**qul* pl. "man" **mutīm*
abs.	בֵּן	בָּנִים	שֵׁם	שֵׁמוֹת	מְתִים
const.	בֵּן/בֶּן	בְּנֵי	שֵׁם/שֶׁם	שְׁמוֹת	מְתֵי
+1cs	בְּנִי	בָּנַי	שְׁמִי	*שְׁמוֹתַי	*מְתַי
+2ms	בִּנְךָ	בָּנֶ֫יךָ	שִׁמְךָ	*שְׁמוֹתֶ֫יךָ	*מְתֶ֫יךָ

9. The words עֵת "time" (< *ʿ*itt* < *ʿ*int* or *ʿ*idt*) and תֵּת "giving" (< **titt* < **tint*) exhibit forms akin to the geminate **qill* nouns due to the assimilation of their third root consonant into the feminine *tav* morpheme (e.g., עִתּוֹ, עִתָּם and תִּתּוֹ, תִּתָּם). For עֵת, the *tav* is taken as a root consonant in the plural forms (e.g., עִתִּים and עִתּוֹת), similar to the *tav* in *qalt* nouns like קֶ֫שֶׁת "bow."

+2fs	בְּנֵךְ	בָּנַ֫יִךְ	שְׁמֵךְ	*שְׁמוֹתַ֫יִךְ	מְתַ֫יִךְ
+3ms	בְּנוֹ	בָּנָיו	שְׁמוֹ	*שְׁמוֹתָיו	מְתָיו
+3fs	בְּנָהּ	בָּנֶ֫יהָ	שְׁמָהּ	*שְׁמוֹתֶ֫יהָ	*מְתֶ֫יהָ
+1cp	בְּנֵ֫נוּ	בָּנֵ֫ינוּ	שְׁמֵ֫נוּ	*שְׁמוֹתֵ֫ינוּ	*מְתֵ֫ינוּ
+2mp	*בִּנְכֶם	בְּנֵיכֶם	שִׁמְכֶם	*שְׁמוֹתֵיכֶם	*מְתֵיכֶם
+2fp	*בִּנְכֶן	*בְּנֵיכֶן	*שִׁמְכֶן	*שְׁמוֹתֵיכֶן	*מְתֵיכֶן
+3mp	*בְּנָם	בְּנֵיהֶם	שְׁמָם	שְׁמוֹתָם	*מְתֵיהֶם
+3fp	*בְּנָן	בְּנֵיהֶן	*שְׁמָן	*שְׁמוֹתָן	*מְתֵיהֶן

More Examples

- *qul*: תֹּר/תּוֹר "dove"

Table 6.5. Biconsonantal Bases with Short Vowel, Part 5[10]

	qil sg./pl. "mouth" *piy/*piyāt*		*qil* sg./pl. "one dead" *mit/*mitīm*		*qil* sg./pl. "witness" *ʿid/*ʿidīm*	
abs.	פֶּה	פֵּיוֹת/פִּיּוֹת	מֵת	מֵתִים	עֵד	עֵדִים
const.	פִּי	—	מֵת	מֵתֵי	עֵד	עֵדֵי
+1cs	פִּי	—	מֵתִי	*מֵתַי	עֵדִי	עֵדַי
+2ms	פִּ֫יךָ	—	מֵתְךָ	מֵתֶ֫יךָ	*עֵדְךָ	עֵדֶ֫יךָ
+2fs	פִּיךְ	—	*מֵתֵךְ	*מֵתַ֫יִךְ	*עֵדֵךְ	*עֵדַ֫יִךְ
+3ms	פִּיו/פִּ֫יהוּ	—	מֵתוֹ	*מֵתָיו	*עֵדוֹ	*עֵדָיו
+3fs	פִּ֫יהָ	—	*מֵתָהּ	*מֵתֶ֫יהָ	*עֵדָהּ	*עֵדֶ֫יהָ

10. The table is supplemented by the following forms: גֵּרְךָ "your stranger"; גֵּרוֹ "his stranger"; נֵרָהּ "her lamp." On פֶּה and its classification, see Huehnergard, "Biblical Hebrew Nominal Patterns," 31 and references. Although שֶׂה "sheep" has a similar abs. sg. form, its const. sg. form (שֵׂה Deut 14:4) and form with suffixes (שֵׂיוֹ Deut 22:1 and שֵׂיֵהוּ in 1 Sam 14:34) suggests it is of the *qal* base. In addition, although the abs. and const. sg. form of words like אִי "coastland" look like the const. sg. of פֶּה, nouns like אִי are classified with the *qill* base, as their pl. forms imply (e.g., אִיִּים).

+1cp	פִּ֫ינוּ	—	*מֵתֵ֫נוּ	*מֵתֵ֫ינוּ	*עֵדֵ֫נוּ	*עֵדֵ֫ינוּ
+2mp	פִּיכֶם	—	—	*מֵתֵיכֶם	—	*עֵדֵיכֶם
+2fp	*פִּיכֶן	—	—	*מֵתֵיכֶן	—	*עֵדֵיכֶן
+3mp	פִּיהֶם[11]	—	*מֵתָם	*מֵתֵיהֶם	*עֵדָם	עֵדֵיהֶם
+3fp	*פִּיהֶן	—	*מֵתָן	*מֵתֵיהֶן	*עֵדָן	*עֵדֵיהֶן

Table 6.6. Biconsonantal Bases with Long Vowel[12]

	*qāl sg./pl. "beloved" *dād/*dādīm		*qīl sg./pl. "song" *šīr/*šīrīm	
abs.	דּוֹד	דּוֹדִים	שִׁיר	שִׁירִים
const.	דּוֹד	*דּוֹדֵי	שִׁיר	שִׁירֵי
+1cs	דּוֹדִי	דּוֹדַי	שִׁירִי	*שִׁירַי
+2ms	דּוֹדְךָ	דּוֹדֶ֫יךָ	*שִׁירְךָ	שִׁירֶ֫יךָ
+2fs	דּוֹדֵךְ	דּוֹדַ֫יִךְ	*שִׁירֵךְ	שִׁירַ֫יִךְ
+3ms	דּוֹדוֹ	*דּוֹדָיו	שִׁירוֹ	*שִׁירָיו
+3fs	דּוֹדָהּ	*דּוֹדֶ֫יהָ	*שִׁירָהּ	*שִׁירֶ֫יהָ
+1cp	*דּוֹדֵ֫נוּ	*דּוֹדֵ֫ינוּ	*שִׁירֵ֫נוּ	*שִׁירֵ֫ינוּ
+2mp	*דּוֹדְכֶם	*דּוֹדֵיכֶם	*שִׁירְכֶם	שִׁירֵיכֶם
+2fp	*דּוֹדְכֶן	*דּוֹדֵיכֶן	*שִׁירְכֶן	*שִׁירֵיכֶן
+3mp	*דּוֹדָם	*דּוֹדֵיהֶם	*שִׁירָם	*שִׁירֵיהֶם
+3fp	*דּוֹדָן	דּוֹדֵיהֶן	*שִׁירָן	*שִׁירֵיהֶן

11. Note also פִּימוֹ "their mouth" Ps 59:13.

12. The table is supplemented by the following forms: קוֹלֵ֫נוּ "our voice"; קוֹלְכֶם "your voice"; קוֹלָם and קוֹלָן "their voice; אִישֵׁךְ "your man"; אִישָׁהּ "her man"; רִיבְכֶם "your dispute"; רִיבָם "their dispute"; בִּינָתִי "my understanding"; בִּינָתְךָ "your understanding"; בִּינַתְכֶם "your understanding"; קִינוֹתֵיהֶם "their laments"; טוּבִי "my goodness"; טוּבְךָ "your goodness"; טוּבוֹ "his goodness"; טוּבָהּ "her goodness"; טוּבָם "their goodness"; רוּחֲכֶם "your spirit."

	qīlat sg./pl. "song" **šīrat/*šīrāt*		**qūl* sg./pl. "horse" **sūs/*sūsīm*	
abs.	שִׁירָה	*שִׁירוֹת	סוּס	סוּסִים
const.	שִׁירַת	שִׁירוֹת	סוּס	סוּסֵי
+1cs	*שִׁירָתִי	*שִׁירוֹתַי	*סוּסִי	סוּסַי
+2ms	*שִׁירָתְךָ	*שִׁירוֹתֶ֫יךָ	*סוּסְךָ	סוּסֶ֫יךָ
+2fs	*שִׁירָתֵךְ	*שִׁירוֹתַ֫יִךְ	*סוּסֵךְ	*סוּסַ֫יִךְ
+3ms	*שִׁירָתוֹ	*שִׁירוֹתָיו	*סוּסוֹ	סוּסָיו
+3fs	*שִׁירָתָהּ	*שִׁירוֹתֶ֫יהָ	*סוּסָהּ	*סוּסֶ֫יהָ
+1cp	*שִׁירָתֵ֫נוּ	*שִׁירוֹתֵ֫ינוּ	*סוּסֵ֫נוּ	*סוּסֵ֫ינוּ
+2mp	*שִׁירַתְכֶם	*שִׁירוֹתֵיכֶם	*סוּסְכֶם	סוּסֵיכֶם
+2fp	*שִׁירַתְכֶן	*שִׁירוֹתֵיכֶן	*סוּסְכֶן	*סוּסֵיכֶן
+3mp	*שִׁירָתָם	*שִׁירוֹתֵיהֶם	*סוּסָם	סוּסֵיהֶם
+3fp	*שִׁירָתָן	*שִׁירוֹתֵיהֶן	*סוּסָן	*סוּסֵיהֶן

More Examples

- **qāl*: חוֹל "sand"; טוֹב "good"; כּוֹס "cup"; קוֹל "voice"
- **qīl*: אִישׁ "man"; גִּיל "rejoicing"; דִּין "judging" (*qal* inf. const.) and "judgment"; עִיר "city"; קִיר "wall"; רִיב "contending" (*qal* inf. const.) and "strife"; רִיק "emptiness"; שִׂים "setting" (*qal* inf. const.); שִׁית "setting" (*qal* inf. const.) and "garment"
- **qīlat*: בִּינָה "understanding"; גִּילָה "rejoicing"; קִינָה "lament"
- **qūl*: אוּר "fire"; טוּב "goodness"; כּוּר "furnace"; לוּחַ "tablet"; נוּן "fish"; קוּם "rising" (*qal* inf. const.); רוּחַ "spirit"; שׁוּק "street"; שׁוּר "row" and "wall"

Notes: Relatively rare feminine forms of **qāl* and **qūl* bases also occur: טוֹבָה "good" and סוּפָה "stormwind."

Table 6.7. Geminate Bases, Part 1[13]

	**qall* sg./pl. "people" *ʿ*amm* /*ʿ*ammīm*		**qallat* sg./pl. "daughter-in-law" **kallat*/**kallāt*	
abs.	עַם	עַמִּים	כַּלָּה	*כַּלּוֹת
const.	עַם	עַמֵּי	*כַּלַּת	*כַּלּוֹת
+1cs	עַמִּי	*עַמַּי	*כַּלָּתִי	*כַּלּוֹתַי
+2ms	עַמְּךָ	עַמֶּ֫יךָ	כַּלָּתְךָ	*כַּלּוֹתֶ֫יךָ
+2fs	עַמֵּךְ	*עַמַּ֫יִךְ	כַּלָּתֵךְ	*כַּלּוֹתַ֫יִךְ
+3ms	עַמּוֹ	עַמָּיו	כַּלָּתוֹ	*כַּלּוֹתָיו
+3fs	עַמָּהּ	עַמֶּ֫יהָ	כַּלָּתָהּ	כַּלּוֹתֶ֫יהָ
+1cp	עַמֵּ֫נוּ	*עַמֵּ֫ינוּ	*כַּלָּתֵ֫נוּ	*כַּלּוֹתֵ֫ינוּ
+2mp	*עַמְּכֶם	*עַמֵּיכֶם	*כַּלַּתְכֶם	כַּלּוֹתֵיכֶם
+2fp	*עַמְּכֶן	*עַמֵּיכֶן	*כַּלַּתְכֶן	*כַּלּוֹתֵיכֶן
+3mp	עַמָּם	*עַמֵּיהֶם	*כַּלָּתָם	*כַּלּוֹתֵיהֶם
+3fp	*עַמָּן	עַמֵּיהֶן	*כַּלָּתָן	*כַּלּוֹתֵיהֶן

	qall* sg./pl. "prince" **śarr*/śarrīm*		**qallat* sg./pl. "distress" **ṣarrat*/**ṣarrāt*	
abs.	שַׂר	שָׂרִים	צָרָה	צָרוֹת
const.	שַׂר	שָׂרֵי	צָרַת	צָרוֹת
+1cs	*שָׂרִי	שָׂרַי	צָרָתִי	*צָרוֹתַי
+2ms	*שָׂרְךָ	*שָׂרֶ֫יךָ	*צָרָתְךָ	*צָרוֹתֶ֫יךָ

13. The chart is supplemented by the following forms: אַפְּכֶם "your nose"; חַגַּ֫יִךְ "your festivals"; חַגֵּיכֶם "your festivals." In some cases gemination does not occur with the masc. sg. form of the word with 2m/fp suffix (e.g., שַׂרְכֶם "your prince" Dan 10:21). The form חַיְתוֹ "its wild animal" (Zech 2:14; Ps 50:10; 79:2; 104:11, 20) is anomalous and is in construct with a following word in each passage.

+2fs	*שָׂרֵךְ	שָׂרַ֫יִךְ	*צָרָתֵךְ	*צָרוֹתַ֫יִךְ
+3ms	*שָׂרוֹ	שָׂרָיו	צָרָתוֹ	צָרוֹתָיו
+3fs	*שָׂרָהּ	שָׂרֶ֫יהָ	*צָרָתָהּ	*צָרוֹתֶ֫יהָ
+1cp	*שָׂרֵ֫נוּ	שָׂרֵ֫ינוּ	צָרָתֵ֫נוּ	*צָרוֹתֵ֫ינוּ
+2mp	שַׂרְכֶם	שָׂרֵיכֶם	צָרַתְכֶם	צָרוֹתֵיכֶם
+2fp	*שַׂרְכֶן	*שָׂרֵיכֶן	*צָרַתְכֶן	*צָרוֹתֵיכֶן
+3mp	*שָׂרָם	שָׂרֵיהֶם	צָרָתָם	צָרוֹתָם
+3fp	*שָׂרָן	*שָׂרֵיהֶן	*צָרָתָן	*צָרוֹתָן

More Examples

- *qall*: אַף "nose" (< *'anp*); גַּן "garden"; דַּל "poor"; חַג "festival"; חַי "alive"; כַּף "palm"; מַר "bitter"; עַז "mighty"; פַּר "male bovine"; צַר "enemy"; רַב "numerous"; רַע "evil"; שַׂר "prince"
- *qallat*: אַמָּה "cubit"; חַיָּה "wild animal"; חַלָּה "circle-shaped bread"; חַמָּה "glow, sun"; צָרָה "distress"; צָרָה "concubine"; קָרָה "cold"; שָׂרָה "princess"

Table 6.8. Geminate Bases, Part 2[14]

	*qill sg./pl. "arrow" *ḥiṯṯ/*ḥiṯṯīm		*qillat sg./pl. "corner" *pinnat/*pinnāt	
abs.	חֵץ	חִצִּים	פִּנָּה	פִּנּוֹת
const.	חֵץ	חִצֵּי	פִּנַּת	פִּנּוֹת
+1cs	חִצִּי	חִצַּי	*פִּנָּתִי	*פִּנּוֹתַי

14. The chart is supplemented by the following forms: צִלְּךָ "your shade"; קִצֵּךְ "your end"; צִלָּהּ "her shade"; אֶשְׁכֶם "your fire"; אִמְּכֶם and אִמְּכֶן "your mother"; קִצֵּ֫ינוּ "our ends"; שִׁנֵּיהֶם "their teeth"; רִנָּתִי "my cry"; רִנָּתָם "their cry"; מִדּוֹתֶ֫יהָ "its measurements"; עֻזִּי "my strength"; עֻזְּךָ "your strength"; עֻזָּהּ "its strength"; and כֻּלָּהּ "all of it"; עֻזְּכֶם "your strength" כֻּלְּכֶם "all of you"; תֻּמָּתִי "my integrity"; תֻּמָּתֶ֫ךָ "your integrity" (pausal); סֻכָּתוֹ "his booth." In some cases gemination does not occur with the masc. sg. form of the word with 2ms and 2m/fp suffix (e.g., חָקְךָ "your statute" Lev 10:13; אֶשְׁכֶם "your fire" Isa 50:11; חָקְכֶם "your statute" Exod 5:14).

+2ms	*חִצְּךָ	חִצֶּ֫יךָ	*פִּנָּתְךָ	*פִּנּוֹתֶ֫יךָ
+2fs	*חִצֵּךְ	*חִצַּ֫יִךְ	*פִּנָּתֵךְ	*פִּנּוֹתַ֫יִךְ
+3ms	חִצּוֹ	חִצָּיו	*פִּנָּתוֹ	פִּנֹּתָיו
+3fs	*חִצָּהּ	*חִצֶּ֫יהָ	פִּנָּתָהּ	*פִּנּוֹתֶ֫יהָ
+1cp	*חִצֵּ֫נוּ	*חִצֵּ֫ינוּ	*פִּנָּתֵ֫נוּ	*פִּנּוֹתֵ֫ינוּ
+2mp	*חֶצְּכֶם / *חִצְּכֶם	*חִצֵּיכֶם	*פִּנַּתְכֶם	*פִּנּוֹתֵיכֶם
+2fp	*חֶצְּכֶן / *חִצְּכֶן	*חִצֵּיכֶן	*פִּנַּתְכֶן	*פִּנּוֹתֵיכֶן
+3mp	חִצָּם	*חִצֵּיהֶם	*פִּנָּתָם	פִּנּוֹתָם
+3fp	*חִצָּן	*חִצֵּיהֶן	*פִּנָּתָן	*פִּנּוֹתָן

	qull sg./pl. "statute" **ḥuqq*/**ḥuqqīm*		*qullat* sg./pl. "statute" **ḥuqqat*/**ḥuqqāt*	
abs.	חֹק	חֻקִּים	חֻקָּה	*חֻקּוֹת
const.	חֹק/חָק־	חֻקֵּי	חֻקַּת	חֻקּוֹת
+1cs	חֻקִּי / *חָקִּי	חֻקַּי	*חֻקָּתִי	חֻקּוֹתַי
+2ms	חָקְךָ / *חֻקְּךָ	חֻקֶּ֫יךָ	*חֻקָּתְךָ	חֻקֹּתֶ֫יךָ
+2fs	חֻקֵּךְ	*חֻקַּ֫יִךְ	*חֻקָּתֵךְ	*חֻקּוֹתַ֫יִךְ
+3ms	חֻקּוֹ	חֻקָּיו	*חֻקָּתוֹ	חֻקֹּתָיו
+3fs	*חֻקָּהּ	*חֻקֶּ֫יהָ	*חֻקָּתָהּ	*חֻקּוֹתֶ֫יהָ
+1cp	*חֻקֵּ֫נוּ	*חֻקֵּ֫ינוּ	*חֻקָּתֵ֫נוּ	*חֻקּוֹתֵ֫ינוּ
+2mp	חָקְכֶם / *חֻקְּכֶם	*חֻקֵּיכֶם	*חֻקַּתְכֶם	*חֻקּוֹתֵיכֶם
+2fp	*חָקְכֶן / *חֻקְּכֶן	*חֻקֵּיכֶן	*חֻקַּתְכֶן	*חֻקּוֹתֵיכֶן
+3mp	חֻקָּם	*חֻקֵּיהֶם	*חֻקָּתָם	חֻקֹּתֵיהֶם / חֻקֹּתָם
+3fp	*חֻקָּן	*חֻקֵּיהֶן	*חֻקָּתָן	*חֻקֹּתֵיהֶן / *חֻקֹּתָן

More Examples

- **qill*: אֵם "mother"; אֵשׁ "fire"; חֵן "grace"; לֵב "heart"; צֵל "shade"; קֵץ "end"; שֵׁן "tooth"
- III-*vav*/*yod*: אִי "coastland"; אִי "hyena"; הִי "lamentation"; עִי "ruin"; צִי "ship"; צִי "desert animal"; רִי "moisture"[15]
- **qillat*: מִדָּה "measure"; רִנָּה "cry, celebration"
- **qull*: דֹּב "bear"; כֹּל "all"; מֹר "myrrh"; עֹז "might"; תֹּם "integrity"; רֹב "multitude"; רֹעַ "evil"
- **qullat*: אֻמָּה "people"; סֻכָּה "booth"; תֻּמָּה "integrity"

Table 6.9. Segolate Bases, Part 1[16]

	**qatl* sg./pl. "king" **malk/*malakīm*		**qatlat* sg./pl. "queen" **malkat/*malakāt*		**qatl* sg./pl. "death" **mawt/*mawtīm*	
abs.	מֶלֶךְ	מְלָכִים	מַלְכָּה	מְלָכוֹת	מָוֶת	*מוֹתִים
const.	מֶלֶךְ	מַלְכֵי	מַלְכַּת	מַלְכוֹת	מוֹת	מוֹתֵי
+1cs	מַלְכִּי	*מְלָכַי	*מַלְכָּתִי	*מַלְכוֹתַי	מוֹתִי	*מוֹתַי
+2ms	מַלְכְּךָ	*מְלָכֶיךָ	*מַלְכָּתְךָ	*מַלְכוֹתֶיךָ	*מוֹתְךָ	*מוֹתֶיךָ
+2fs	מַלְכֵּךְ	*מְלָכַיִךְ	*מַלְכָּתֵךְ	*מַלְכוֹתַיִךְ	*מוֹתֵךְ	*מוֹתַיִךְ
+3ms	מַלְכּוֹ	*מְלָכָיו	*מַלְכָּתוֹ	*מַלְכוֹתָיו	מוֹתוֹ	מֹתָיו
+3fs	מַלְכָּהּ	מְלָכֶיהָ	*מַלְכָּתָהּ	*מַלְכוֹתֶיהָ	מוֹתָהּ	*מוֹתֶיהָ
+1cp	מַלְכֵּנוּ	מְלָכֵינוּ	*מַלְכָּתֵנוּ	*מַלְכוֹתֵינוּ	*מוֹתֵנוּ	*מוֹתֵינוּ

15. III-*vav*/*yod* words like אִי "coastland" have pl. forms revealing a doubled *yod*: אִיִּים. The words are not attested with suffixes. However, these derive ultimately from a **qall* base (see Steiner, "On the Monophthongization," 73–83).

16. The table is supplemented by the following forms: אַהֲבָתִי "my love"; אַהֲבָתְךָ "your love"; אַהֲבָתוֹ "his love"; אַהֲבָתָהּ "her love"; אַהֲבָתָם "their love"; נַעֲרֹתָיו "his young women"; נַעֲרֹתֶיהָ "her young women." Unlike most other Hebrew nouns, the class of segolate nouns has one base pattern for the sg. and another base pattern for the pl. While the sg. pattern has just one vowel, the pl. base pattern almost always has two. There are, however, some exceptional pl. segolate nouns that attest an alternative form with just one historical vowel in the stem: חָכְמוֹת "wisdom"; רַחֲמִים "bowels, compassion"; שִׁקְמִים "sycamores"; פִּשְׁתִּים "flax." These nouns exhibit no medial */ā/ (> THP /å/) with suffixes (e.g., רַחֲמֶיךָ and רַחֲמָיו).

+2mp	מַלְכְּכֶם	מַלְכֵיכֶם	*מַלְכַּתְכֶם	*מַלְכוּתֵיכֶם	*מוּתְכֶם	*מוּתֵיכֶם
+2fp	*מַלְכְּכֶן	*מַלְכֵיכֶן	*מַלְכַּתְכֶן	*מַלְכוּתֵיכֶן	*מוּתְכֶן	*מוּתֵיכֶן
+3mp	מַלְכָּם	מַלְכֵיהֶם	*מַלְכָּתָם	*מַלְכוּתָם	מוּתָם	*מוּתֵיהֶם
+3fp	*מַלְכָּן	*מַלְכֵיהֶן	*מַלְכָּתָן	*מַלְכוּתָן	*מוּתָן	*מוּתֵיהֶן

More Examples

- **qatl*: אֶבֶן "stone"; אֶלֶף "thousand"; אֶרֶז "cedar"; אֶרֶץ "earth"; גֶּבֶר "man"; גֶּפֶן "vine"; דֶּרֶךְ "path"; זֶרַע "seed"; חֶסֶד "kindness"; חֶרֶב "sword"; יֶלֶד "boy"; כֶּסֶף "silver"; כֶּרֶם "vineyard"; לֶחֶם "bread"; נֶפֶשׁ "soul"; עֶבֶד "slave"; עֶצֶם "bone"; עֶרֶב "evening"; צֶלֶם "image"; קֶרֶן "horn"; רֶגֶל "foot"; שֶׁמֶן "oil"
- II-*vav*/*yod* roots: תָּוֶךְ "midst"; בַּיִת "house"; עַיִן "spring, eye" (see table 6.14); אַיִל "ram"
- III-*yod* roots: see below under **qiṭl*
- III-*vav* roots: שָׂחוּ "swimming"; אָחוּ "reeds"
- Aramaic-like forms: בְּעַד "behind" (const.); גְּבַר "man of" (const., vs. גֶּבֶר abs.); הֲבֵל "vanity of" (const., vs. הֶבֶל abs.); הֲדַס "myrtle"; חֲדַר "room of" (const., vs. חֶדֶר abs./const.);[17] זְמָן "time";[18] סְחַר "merchant of" const.; שְׁכֶם "shoulder"[19]
- **qatl* in pause, but with **qiṭl*-base for suffixes: פֶּסֶל "image of divinity"; קֶבֶר "grave"; רֶכֶב "chariotry"; שֶׁבֶר "break"; שֶׁמֶשׁ "sun"
- **qatlat*: אַהֲבָה "love, loving" (*qal* inf. const.); כַּבְשָׂה (vs. כִּבְשָׂה) "young ram"; נַעֲרָה "girl"; עַלְמָה "marriageable girl"; עַוְלָה "injustice"

17. Huehnergard, ("Biblical Hebrew Nominal Patterns," 36) lists this as a **qiṭl* noun, though it appears in most of its suffixed-occurrences (and in the const. pl.) with a *patakh* in the first syllable; only once does it have a *segol* (Joel 2:16).

18. This is an Aramaic loanword; note BA זְמָן (Dan 2:16) but זְמַן (Dan 7:12) and the emphatic form זִמְנָא. The *qamets* in the Hebrew form is presumably an accomodation to Hebrew sound rules. Fox (*Semitic Noun Patterns*, 137) suggests that the form of the Aramaic noun, זְמַן, suggested to Hebrew speakers that the final *nun* was geminated with endings, thus leading to forms like זְמַנָּם (Esth 9:27), akin presumably to עַם and עַמִּים. Similarly, for הֲדַס in the plural הֲדַסִּים.

19. On שְׁכֶם, see Fox, *Semitic Noun Patterns*, 136. Note also חֲסַר "want of" (const., vs. חֶסֶר abs.); שְׁגַר "offspring of" (const., vs. שֶׁגֶר abs.).

Table 6.10. Segolate Bases, Part 2

	qatl sg./pl. "father" **ʾab/*ʾabāt*		*qatl* sg./pl. "brother" **ʾaḫ/*ʾaḫ(ḫ)īm*	
abs.	אָב	אָבוֹת	אָח	אַחִים
const.	אֲבִי	אֲבוֹת	אֲחִי	אַחֵי
+1cs	אָבִי	אֲבוֹתַי	אָחִי	אַחַי
+2ms	אָבִ֫יךָ	אֲבוֹתֶ֫יךָ	אָחִ֫יךָ	אַחֶ֫יךָ
+2fs	אָבִיךְ	*אֲבוֹתַ֫יִךְ	אָחִיךְ	אַחַ֫יִךְ
+3ms	אָבִ֫יהוּ / אָבִיו	אֲבוֹתָיו	אָחִ֫יהוּ / אָחִיו	אֶחָיו
+3fs	אָבִ֫יהָ	*אֲבוֹתֶ֫יהָ	אָחִ֫יהָ	אַחֶ֫יהָ
+1cp	אָבִ֫ינוּ	אֲבוֹתֵ֫ינוּ	אָחִ֫ינוּ	אַחֵ֫ינוּ
+2mp	אֲבִיכֶם	אֲבוֹתֵיכֶם	אֲחִיכֶם	אֲחֵיכֶם
+2fp	אֲבִיכֶן	*אֲבוֹתֵיכֶן	*אֲחִיכֶן	*אֲחֵיכֶן
+3mp	אֲבִיהֶם	אֲבוֹתֵיהֶם / אֲבוֹתָם	אֲחִיהֶם	אֲחֵיהֶם
+3fp	אֲבִיהֶן	*אֲבוֹתֵיהֶן / *אֲבוֹתָן	*אֲחִיהֶן	*אֲחֵיהֶן

Table 6.11. Segolate Bases, Part 3[20]

	qitl sg./pl. "book" **sipr/*siparīm*		*qitlat* sg./pl. "tears" **dimʿat/*dimaʿāt*		*qitl* sg./pl. "ornament" **ʿidy/*ʿidayīm*		*qitl* sg. "captivity" **šiby*
abs.	סֵ֫פֶר	סְפָרִים	דִּמְעָה	דְּמָעוֹת	עֲדִי	עֲדָיִים	שְׁבִי
const.	סֵ֫פֶר	*סִפְרֵי	דִּמְעַת	*דִּמְעוֹת	עֲדִי	*עֲדָיֵי	שְׁבִי

20. The following chart is supplemented by the following forms: זִכְרוֹ "his memory"; עִמְקֵךְ "your valley"; שִׁמְעָהּ "her news"; זִכְרָם "their memory"; אֲמָרַי "my words"; שְׁבָטֶ֫יךָ "your tribes"; אֲמָרָיו "his words"; אֲמָרֶ֫יהָ "her words"; שִׁבְטֵיכֶם "your tribes"; שִׁבְטֵיהֶם "their tribes"; pausal דִּמְעָתֶ֫ךָ "your tears"; מִנְחָתוֹ "his offering"; מִנְחָתָם "their offering"; מִנְחֹתֵיכֶם " their offerings"; פֶּרְיְכֶם "your fruit"; גְּדָיֵי "kids of"; לְחָיַי "my jaws"; לְחָיֶ֫יךָ "your jaws"; לְחָיַ֫יִךְ "your jaws"; לְחָיָו "his jaws"; לְחֵיהֶם "their jaws." The word שְׁבִי shows a peculiar form with the 2mp suffix, what is essentially the const. form + suffix: שְׁבִיכֶם.

+1cs	סִפְרִי	*סְפָרַי	דִּמְעָתִי	*דִּמְעוֹתַי	*עֶדְיִי	*עֲדָיַי	*שִׁבְיִי
+2ms	סִפְרְךָ	*סְפָרֶיךָ	*דִּמְעָתְךָ	*דִּמְעוֹתֶיךָ	עֶדְיְךָ	*עֲדָיֶיךָ	שֶׁבְיְךָ
+2fs	*סִפְרֵךְ	*סְפָרַיִךְ	*דִּמְעָתֵךְ	*דִּמְעוֹתַיִךְ	עֶדְיֵךְ	*עֲדָיַיִךְ	*שִׁבְיֵךְ
+3ms	*סִפְרוֹ	*סְפָרָיו	*דִּמְעָתוֹ	*דִּמְעוֹתָיו	עֶדְיוֹ	*עֲדָיָיו	שִׁבְיוֹ
+3fs	*סִפְרָהּ	*סְפָרֶיהָ	דִּמְעָתָהּ	*דִּמְעוֹתֶיהָ	עֶדְיָהּ	*עֲדָיֶיהָ	שִׁבְיָהּ
+1cp	*סִפְרֵנוּ	*סְפָרֵינוּ	*דִּמְעָתֵנוּ	*דִּמְעוֹתֵינוּ	*עֶדְיֵנוּ	*עֲדָיֵינוּ	*שִׁבְיֵנוּ
+2mp	*סִפְרְכֶם	*סִפְרֵיכֶם	*דִּמְעַתְכֶם	*דִּמְעוֹתֵיכֶם	*עֶדְיְכֶם	*עֲדֵיכֶם	שְׁבִיכֶם
+2fp	*סִפְרְכֶן	*סִפְרֵיכֶן	*דִּמְעַתְכֶן	*דִּמְעוֹתֵיכֶן	*עֶדְיְכֶן	*עֲדֵיכֶן	*שְׁבִיכֶן
+3mp	*סִפְרָם	*סִפְרֵיהֶם	*דִּמְעָתָם	*דִּמְעוֹתָם	עֶדְיָם	*עֲדֵיהֶם	שִׁבְיָם
+3fp	*סִפְרָן	*סִפְרֵיהֶן	*דִּמְעָתָן	*דִּמְעוֹתָן	*עֶדְיָן	*עֲדֵיהֶן	*שִׁבְיָן

More Examples

- **qitl*: זֵכֶר "memory"; שֵׁמַע "news"; אֵמֶר "word"; חֵטְא "sin"; סֵתֶר "hiding place"; עֵמֶק "valley"; שֵׁבֶט "tribe"; עֵדֶר "herd"; חֵלֶב "fat"; חֵלֶק "share"; עֵגֶל "calf"; עֵזֶר "help"; עֵשֶׂב "herbage"; תֵּשַׁע "nine"
- with initial *segol*: זֶבַח "sacrifice"; קֶרֶב "midst"; שֶׁבַע "seven"; שֶׁקֶל "shekel"
- mixed type: נֶדֶר/נֵדֶר "vow"; שֶׁבֶר/שֵׁבֶר "breach"
- III-*yod* roots (some perhaps originally **qatl*): בְּכִי "weeping"; גְּדִי "kid"; לְחִי "jawbone"; פְּרִי "fruit"; צְבִי "beauty"; צְבִי "gazelle"; שְׁבִי "captivity"
- Aramaic-like forms: בְּאֵר "well"; דְּבַשׁ "honey";[21] שְׁבַע "seven of" (const., vs. שֶׁבַע abs.); תְּשַׁע "nine of" (const., vs. תֵּשַׁע abs.)
- **qitlat*: גִּבְעָה "hill"; יִרְאָה "fear, fearing" (*qal* inf. const.); מִנְחָה "gift"; שִׂמְחָה "joy"; שִׂמְלָה "cloak"; שִׁפְחָה "maidservant"

21. See Fox, *Semitic Noun Patterns*, 136; Alexey Yuditsky, "דְּבַשׁ and Similar Forms," *Leshonenu* 71 (2009): 281–86 (Hebrew).

Table 6.12. Segolate Bases, Part 4[22]

	qutl sg./pl. "holiness" *quds* / *qudašīm*			*qutlat* sg./pl. "foreskin" *ġurlat* / *ġuralāt*	
abs.	קֹ֫דֶשׁ	קָדְשִׁים / קֳדָשִׁים / קָדָשִׁים		עָרְלָה	*עֲרָלוֹת
const.	קֹ֫דֶשׁ	קָדְשֵׁי		עָרְלַת	עָרְלוֹת
+1cs	קָדְשִׁי	קָדָשַׁי	*קֳדָשַׁי	*עָרְלָתִי	*עָרְלוֹתַי
+2ms	קָדְשְׁךָ	*קָדָשֶׁ֫יךָ	קֳדָשֶׁ֫יךָ	*עָרְלָתְךָ	*עָרְלוֹתֶ֫יךָ
+2fs	*קָדְשֵׁךְ	*קָדָשַׁ֫יִךְ	*קֳדָשַׁ֫יִךְ	*עָרְלָתֵךְ	*עָרְלוֹתַ֫יִךְ
+3ms	קָדְשׁוֹ	קָדָשָׁיו	קֳדָשָׁיו	עָרְלָתוֹ	*עָרְלוֹתָיו
+3fs	*קָדְשָׁהּ	*קָדָשֶׁ֫יהָ	*קֳדָשֶׁ֫יהָ	*עָרְלָתָהּ	*עָרְלוֹתֶ֫יהָ
+1cp	קָדְשֵׁ֫נוּ	*קָדָשֵׁ֫ינוּ	*קֳדָשֵׁ֫ינוּ	*עָרְלָתֵ֫נוּ	*עָרְלוֹתֵ֫ינוּ
+2mp	*קָדְשְׁכֶם		קָדְשֵׁיכֶם	עָרְלַתְכֶם	*עָרְלוֹתֵיכֶם
+2fp	*קָדְשְׁכֶן		*קָדְשֵׁיכֶן	*עָרְלַתְכֶן	*עָרְלוֹתֵיכֶן
+3mp	*קָדְשָׁם		קָדְשֵׁיהֶם	עָרְלָתָם	עָרְלֹתֵיהֶם
+3fp	*קָדְשָׁן		*קָדְשֵׁיהֶן	*עָרְלָתָן	*עָרְלוֹתֵיהֶן

More Examples

- **qutl*: אֹ֫כֶל "food"; אֹ֫רַח "way"; בֹּ֫קֶר "morning"; גֹּ֫רֶן "threshing floor"; חֹ֫דֶשׁ "month"; חֹ֫רֶב "dryness"; חֹ֫שֶׁךְ "darkness"; עֹ֫רֶף "neck"; שֹׁ֫רֶשׁ "root"; רֹ֫חַב "breadth"
- III-*yod* roots: חֳלִי "sickness"; עֳנִי "affliction" (see table 6.13); צֳרִי "balsam"
- III-*vav* roots: בֹּ֫הוּ "emptiness"; תֹּ֫הוּ "formlessness"
- Aramaic-like forms: בְּאֹשׁ "stench" (see table 6.13); מְאֹד "very much"
- **qutlat*: אָכְלָה "food"; טָהֳרָה "purity"; טֻמְאָה "impurity"; קָרְחָה "bald patch"; חָרְבָּה "ruins"; עָרְמָה "cleverness"

22. The chart is supplemented by the following forms: אָכְלְכֶם "your food"; אָכְלָם "their food"; שָׁרָשֶׁיהָ "her roots"; חָרְבֹתַ֫יִךְ "your ruins"; חָרְבֹתָיו "his ruins"; חָרְבֹתֶ֫יהָ "her ruins."

Table 6.13. Segolate Bases, Part 5

	**qutl* sg./pl. "tent" *ʾ*ahl* / *ʾ*ahalīm*[23]		**qutl* sg. "iniquity" *ʿ*uny*	**qutl* sg. "stench" **buʾš*	**qutl* sg. "fullness" **mulʾ*
abs.	אֹ֫הֶל	אֹהָלִים	עָנִי	*בְּאֹשׁ	*מְלֹא
const.	אֹ֫הֶל	אָהֳלֵי	עֳנִי	בְּאשׁ	מְלֹא
+1cs	אָהֳלִי	אֹהָלַי	עָנְיִי	*בָּאְשִׁי	*מְלֹאִי
+2ms	אָהָלְךָ	אֹהָלֶ֫יךָ	*עָנְיְךָ	*בָּאְשְׁךָ	*מְלֹאֲךָ
+2fs	אָהֳלֵךְ	*אֹהָלַ֫יִךְ	עָנְיֵךְ	*בָּאְשָׁהּ	*מְלֹאֵךְ
+3ms	אָהֳלוֹ	אֹהָלָיו	עָנְיוֹ	בָּאְשׁוֹ	מְלֹאוֹ
+3fs	*אָהֳלָהּ	*אֹהָלֶ֫יהָ	עָנְיָהּ	*בָּאְשָׁהּ	מְלֹאָהּ
+1cp	*אָהֳלֵ֫נוּ	*אֹהָלֵ֫ינוּ	עָנְיֵ֫נוּ	*בָּאְשֵׁ֫נוּ	*מְלֹאֵ֫נוּ
+2mp	—	אָהֳלֵיכֶם	*עָנְיְכֶם	—	—
+2fp	—	*אָהֳלֵיכֶן	*עָנְיְכֶן	—	—
+3mp	*אָהֳלָם	אָהֳלֵיהֶם	עָנְיָם	בָּאְשָׁם	*מְלֹאָם
+3fp	*אָהֳלָן	*אָהֳלֵיהֶן	*עָנְיָן	*בָּאְשָׁן	*מְלֹאָן

Table 6.14. Segolate Bases, Part 6

	**qatl* sg./du./pl. "eye" *ʿ*ayn* / *ʿ*aynaym* / *ʿ*ay*(*a*)*nāt*			**qutl* sg./du. "ear" *ʾ*uḏn* / *ʾ*uḏnaym*	
abs.	עַ֫יִן	עֵינַ֫יִם	עֲיָנוֹת	אֹ֫זֶן	אָזְנַ֫יִם
const.	עֵין	עֵינֵי	עֵינֹת	אֹ֫זֶן	אָזְנֵי
+1cs	עֵינִי	עֵינַי	*עֵינוֹתַי	אָזְנִי	אָזְנַי
+2ms	עֵינְךָ	עֵינֶ֫יךָ	*עֵינוֹתֶ֫יךָ	אָזְנְךָ	אָזְנֶ֫יךָ
+2fs	עֵינֵךְ	עֵינַ֫יִךְ	*עֵינוֹתַ֫יִךְ	אָזְנֵךְ	אָזְנַ֫יִךְ

23. The etymology of "tent" is hard to piece together; perhaps *ʾ*ahl* > *ʾ*āl* > *ʾ*ōl* > *ʾ*ohl* (?) (see Fox, *Semitic Noun Patterns*, 74 and references).

+3ms	עֵינוֹ	עֵינָיו	*עֵינוֹתָיו	אָזְנוֹ	אָזְנָיו
+3fs	עֵינָהּ	עֵינֶ֫יהָ	*עֵינוֹתֶ֫יהָ	*אָזְנָהּ	*אָזְנֶ֫יהָ
+1cp	עֵינֵ֫נוּ	עֵינֵ֫ינוּ	*עֵינוֹתֵ֫ינוּ	*אָזְנֵ֫נוּ	אָזְנֵ֫ינוּ
+2mp	עֵינְכֶם	עֵינֵיכֶם	*עֵינוֹתֵיכֶם	אָזְנֵיכֶם	אָזְנֵיכֶם
+2fp	עֵינְכֶן	*עֵינֵיכֶן	*עֵינוֹתֵיכֶן	*אָזְנֵיכֶן	*אָזְנֵיכֶן
+3mp	עֵינָם	עֵינֵיהֶם	עֵינוֹתָם	אָזְנָם	אָזְנֵ֫יהֶם
+3fp	*עֵינָן	עֵינֵיהֶן	*עֵינוֹתָן	*אָזְנָן	*אָזְנֵיהֶן

Table 6.15. **Qatal* Base[24]

	qatal* sg./pl. "word" **dabar*/dabarīm*		**qatalat* sg./pl. "righteousness" **ṣadaqat*/**ṣadaqāt*		**qatal* sg. "field" **śaday*[25]	**qatal* pl. "face" **panayīm*
abs.	דָּבָר	דְּבָרִים	צְדָקָה	צְדָקוֹת	שָׂדֶה	פָּנִים
const.	דְּבַר	דִּבְרֵי	צִדְקַת	צִדְקוֹת	שְׂדֵה	פְּנֵי
+1cs	דְּבָרִי	דְּבָרַי	צִדְקָתִי	*צִדְקוֹתַי	שָׂדִי	פָּנַי
+2ms	דְּבָרְךָ	דְּבָרֶ֫יךָ	צִדְקָתְךָ	צִדְקֹתֶ֫יךָ	שָׂדְךָ	פָּנֶ֫יךָ
+2fs	דְּבָרֵךְ	דְּבָרַ֫יִךְ	צִדְקָתֵךְ	*צִדְקוֹתַ֫יִךְ	*שָׂדֵךְ	פָּנַ֫יִךְ
+3ms	דְּבָרוֹ	דְּבָרָיו	צִדְקָתוֹ	צִדְקֹתָו	שָׂדֵ֫הוּ	פָּנָיו
+3fs	*דְּבָרָהּ	דְּבָרֶ֫יהָ	*צִדְקָתָהּ	*צִדְקוֹתֶ֫יהָ	שָׂדָהּ	פָּנֶ֫יהָ
+1cp	דְּבָרֵ֫נוּ	*דְּבָרֵ֫ינוּ	*צִדְקָתֵ֫נוּ	צִדְקֹתֵ֫ינוּ	*שָׂדֵ֫ינוּ	פָּנֵ֫ינוּ
+2mp	*דְּבַרְכֶם	דִּבְרֵיכֶם	*צִדְקַתְכֶם	*צִדְקוֹתֵיכֶם	—	פְּנֵיכֶם
+2fp	*דְּבַרְכֶן	*דִּבְרֵיכֶן	*צִדְקַתְכֶן	*צִדְקוֹתֵיכֶן	—	*פְּנֵיכֶן
+3mp	*דְּבָרָם	דִּבְרֵיהֶם	צִדְקָתָם	*צִדְקוֹתָם	*שָׂדָם	פְּנֵיהֶם
+3fp	*דְּבָרָן	*דִּבְרֵיהֶן	*צִדְקָתָן	*צִדְקוֹתָן	*שָׂדָן	*פְּנֵיהֶן

24. The table is supplemented by the following forms: בְּשָׂרָם "their flesh"; בְּשַׂרְכֶם "your flesh"; אַדְמַתְכֶם "your earth."

25. The plural of "field" is usually fem. in form: שָׂדוֹת (pl. abs.), שְׂדוֹת (pl. const.), שְׂדֹתֶ֫יהָ "her fields," though masc. forms also occur: שְׂדֵי (pl. const.), שָׂדֶ֫יךָ "your fields," שָׂדֵ֫ינוּ "our fields."

More Examples

- * *qatal*: אָדָם "human"; בָּשָׂר "flesh"; זָקָן "beard"; חָדָשׁ "new"; חָכָם "wise"; יָשָׁר "straight"; כָּנָף "wing"; מָטָר "rain"; נָהָר "river"; צָמָא "thirst"; רָעָב "hunger"
- III-*vav/yod* roots: פָּנֶה (in pl.) "face"; קָנֶה "reed"; קָצֶה "end"; שָׂדֶה "field"
- **qatalat*: אֲדָמָה "earth"; בְּרָכָה "blessing"; זְעָקָה "screaming"; סְעָרָה "storm"; צְעָקָה "screaming"; קְלָלָה "cursing"; רְבָבָה "many"; שְׁאָגָה "roaring"
- III-*vav/yod* roots, only Aramaic-like forms: מְנָת "portion" and קְצָת "end"

Table 6.16. **Qatil* Base[26]

	qatil* sg./pl. "old" **ḏaqin*/ḏaqinīm*		**qatilat* sg. "corpse" **nabilat*
abs.	זָקֵן	זְקֵנִים	נְבֵלָה
const.	זְקַן	זִקְנֵי	נִבְלַת
+1cs	*זְקֵנִי	זְקֵנַי	נִבְלָתִי
+2ms	—	זְקֵנֶ֫יךָ	נִבְלָתְךָ
+2fs	*זְקֵנֵךְ	*זְקֵנַ֫יִךְ	*נִבְלָתֵךְ
+3ms	*זְקֵנוֹ	זְקֵנָיו	נִבְלָתוֹ
+3fs	*זְקֵנָהּ	זְקֵנֶ֫יהָ	נִבְלָתָהּ
+1cp	*זְקֵנֵ֫נוּ	זְקֵנֵ֫ינוּ	*נִבְלָתֵ֫נוּ
+2mp	—	זִקְנֵיכֶם	*נִבְלַתְכֶם
+2fp	—	*זִקְנֵיכֶן	*נִבְלַתְכֶן
+3mp	*זְקֵנָם	*זִקְנֵיהֶם	נִבְלָתָם
+3fp	*זְקֵנָן	*זִקְנֵיהֶן	*נִבְלָתָן

26. The table is supplemented by the following forms: יְרֵכִי "my thigh"; יְרֵכְךָ "your thigh"; יְרֵכוֹ "his thigh"; יְרֵכָהּ "her thigh"; כְּתֵפָם "their shoulder." Other nouns of the **qatilat* base do not often occur with suffixes.

More Examples

- **qatil*: *qal* participles of stative verbs; אָמֵן "true"; חָסֵר "lacking"; טָמֵא "impure"; יָבֵשׁ "dry"; יָפֵחַ "witness" (Hab 2:3 and וִיפֵחַ "and witness of" [const.] Ps 27:12); יָשֵׁן "old"; כָּבֵד "heavy"; מָלֵא "full"; רָעֵב "hungry"
- Aramaic-like form: יָפִיחַ "witness of" (const.), e.g., Prov 6:19 and passim[27]
- **qatilat*: *qal* participles of stative verbs; בְּרֵכָה "pool"; גְּנֵבָה "theft"

Table 6.17. **Qatul*, **Qital*, *Qutul*, *Qutull* Bases[28]

	qatul* sg./pl. "great" **gadul*/gadulīm*		**qital* sg. "heart" **libab*	**qitalīm* pl. "guts" **miʿayīm*	**qutul* sg. "first born" **bukur*	**qutullat* "greatness" **gudullat*
abs.	גָּדוֹל	גְּדוֹלִים	לֵבָב	*מֵעִים	בְּכֹר	גְּדֻלָּה
const.	גְּדוֹל	גְּדֹלֵי	לְבַב	מְעֵי	בְּכֹר	גְּדֻלַּת
+1cs	*גְּדוֹלִי	*גְּדוֹלַי	לְבָבִי	מֵעַי	בְּכֹרִי	גְּדֻלָּתִי
+2ms	*גְּדוֹלְךָ	*גְּדוֹלֶיךָ	לְבָבְךָ	מֵעֶיךָ	בְּכֹרְךָ	*גְּדֻלָּתְךָ
+2fs	*גְּדוֹלֵךְ	*גְּדוֹלַיִךְ	לְבָבֵךְ	מֵעַיִךְ	*בְּכֹרֵךְ	*גְּדֻלָּתֵךְ
+3ms	*גְּדוֹלוֹ	גְּדוֹלָיו	לְבָבוֹ	מֵעָיו	בְּכֹרוֹ	גְּדֻלָּתוֹ
+3fs	*גְּדוֹלָהּ	גְּדוֹלֶיהָ	לְבָבָהּ	*מֵעֶיהָ	*בְּכֹרָהּ	*גְּדֻלָּתָהּ
+1cp	*גְּדוֹלֵנוּ	*גְּדוֹלֵינוּ	לְבָבֵנוּ	*מֵעֵינוּ	*בְּכֹרֵנוּ	*גְּדֻלָּתֵנוּ
+2mp	*גְּדוֹלְכֶם	*גְּדוֹלֵיכֶם	לְבַבְכֶם	*מֵעֵיכֶם	*בְּכֹרְכֶם	*גְּדֻלַּתְכֶם
+2fp	*גְּדוֹלְכֶן	*גְּדוֹלֵיכֶן	*לְבַבְכֶן	*מֵעֵיכֶן	*בְּכֹרְכֶן	*גְּדֻלַּתְכֶן
+3mp	גְּדוֹלָם	*גְּדוֹלֵיהֶם	לְבָבָם	מֵעֵיהֶם	*בְּכֹרָם	*גְּדֻלָּתָם
+3fp	*גְּדוֹלָן	*גְּדוֹלֵיהֶן	*לְבָבָן	*מֵעֵיהֶן	*בְּכֹרָן	*גְּדֻלָּתָן

27. See Dennis Pardee, "Yph̩ 'Witness' in Hebrew and Ugaritic," *VT* 28 (1978): 204–13. The form in Proverbs is apparently assimilated to the spelling of the *hiphil* imperfect of פוח, found, e.g., in Prov 29:8: יָפִיחוּ "will blow against (a city)."

28. The table is supplemented by the following forms: קְדֹשִׁי "my holy one"; קְרֹבוֹ "his neighbor"; קְדוֹשְׁכֶם "your holy one"; קְרוֹבַי "my neighbors."

More Examples

- **qatul*: טָהוֹר "pure"; קָדוֹשׁ "holy"; קָרוֹב "near"; רָחוֹב "far"; יָתוֹם "orphan"; גָּבֹהַ "high
- **qital*: נֵכָר "foreigner"; צֵלָע "rib"; עֵנָב "grapes"; רֵעֶה "companion"; שֵׂעָר "hair"
- **qutul* (see **qitāl*): *qal* infinitives of strong and guttural roots; חֲלוֹם "dream"[29]
- **qutullat*: אֲחֻזָּה "possession"
- The *qatull* base is similar to *qatul* in the masculine singular: אָדֹם "red"; אָיֹם"terrible"; נָקֹד "speckled."

Table 6.18. **Qātil* Base[30]

	**qātil* sg./pl. "one who creates" **yāṣir/*yāṣirīm*		**qātilt* sg. "one who bears" **yālidt*[31]	**qātil* sg./pl. "one who makes" **ʿāśiy/*ʿāśiyīm*	
abs.	יֹצֵר	*יֹצְרִים	יֹלֶ֫דֶת	עֹשֶׂה	עֹשִׂים
const.	יֹצֵר	יֹצְרֵי	יֹלֶ֫דֶת	עֹשֵׂה	עֹשֵׂי
+1cs	יֹצְרִי	*יֹצְרַי	*יוֹלַ֫דְתִּי	עֹשֵׂ֫נִי	עֹשַׂי
+2ms	יֹצֶרְךָ	*יֹצְרֶ֫יךָ	יוֹלַדְתְּךָ	עֹשֶׂ֫ךָ	*עֹשֶׂ֫יךָ
+2fs	*יֹצְרֵךְ	*יֹצְרַ֫יִךְ	*יוֹלַדְתֵּךְ	*עֹשֵׂךְ	עֹשַׂ֫יִךְ
+3ms	יֹצְרוֹ	*יֹצְרָיו	יוֹלַדְתּוֹ	עֹשֵׂ֫הוּ	עֹשָׂיו
+3fs	יֹצְרָהּ	*יֹצְרֶ֫יהָ	יוֹלַדְתָּהּ	עֹשָׂ֫הּ	*עֹשֶׂ֫יהָ
+1cp	יֹצְרֵ֫נוּ	*יֹצְרֵ֫ינוּ	*יוֹלַדְתֵּ֫נוּ	עֹשֵׂ֫נוּ	*עֹשֵׂ֫ינוּ

29. See Fox, *Semitic Noun Patterns*, 205.

30. The table is supplemented by the following forms: גֹּאַלְכֶם "your (pl.) redeemer" (cf. גֹּאַלְךָ "your [sg.] redeemer"); רֹדְפָם "their pursuer"; רֹדְפַי "my pursuers"; אֹרְרֶ֫יךָ "your cursers"; יֹשְׁבָיו "his dwellers"; יֹשְׁבֶ֫יהָ "her dwellers"; רֹדְפֵ֫ינוּ "our pursuers"; שֹׁפְטֵיכֶם "your judges"; שֹׁפְטֵיהֶם "their judges"; רֹכַלְתֵּךְ "one who traded you"; רֹצָם "one accepting them" (pausal). There is some variety expressed in words of this base with suffix: note also אֹסִפְךָ "your gatherer"; שֹׁלֵ֫חֲךָ "your sender"; רֹאִי "one who sees me"; רֹאָ֫נִי "one who sees me"; עֹטְךָ "one covering you"; רֹדֵם "one ruling them"; רֹאֶ֫יךָ "those seeing you"; רֹאֶ֫יהָ "those seeing her"; שׁוֹסֵ֫ינוּ "our plunderers."

31. Note also the absolute form יוֹלֵדָה, reflecting **qatilat*.

+2mp	*יְצֶרְכֶם	*יְצָרֵיכֶם	יוֹלַדְתְּכֶם	—	*עֲשֵׂיכֶם
+2fp	*יְצֶרְכֶן	*יְצָרֵיכֶן	*יוֹלַדְתְּכֶן	—	*עֲשֵׂיכֶן
+3mp	*יְצָרָם	*יְצָרֵיהֶם	*יוֹלַדְתָּם	*עֲשָׂם	עֲשֵׂיהֶם
+3fp	*יְצָרָן	*יְצָרֵיהֶן	*יוֹלַדְתָּן	*עֲשָׂן	*עֲשֵׂיהֶן

More Examples

- **qātil*: *qal* participles of active verbs; אֹיֵב "enemy"; כֹּהֵן "priest"; שֹׁפֵט "judge"

Table 6.19. **Qatāl* and Aramaic-Like **QVtāl* Bases[32]

	**qatāl* sg./pl. "lord" *ʾadān/*ʾadānīm		**qVtāl* sg. "writing" **katāb*
abs.	אָדוֹן	אֲדֹנִים	כְּתָב
const.	אֲדוֹן	אֲדֹנֵי	כְּתָב
+1cs	אֲדוֹנִי	אֲדֹנַי	*כְּתָבִי
+2ms	*אֲדוֹנְךָ	אֲדֹנֶיךָ	*כְּתָבְךָ
+2fs	*אֲדוֹנֵךְ	אֲדֹנַיִךְ	*כְּתָבֵךְ
+3ms	*אֲדוֹנוֹ	אֲדֹנָיו	*כְּתָבוֹ
+3fs	*אֲדוֹנָהּ	אֲדוֹנֶיהָ	כְּתָבָהּ
+1cp	*אֲדוֹנֵנוּ	אֲדוֹנֵינוּ	*כְּתָבֵנוּ
+2mp	*אֲדוֹנְכֶם	אֲדוֹנֵיכֶם	—
+2fp	*אֲדוֹנְכֶן	*אֲדוֹנֵיכֶן	—
+3mp	*אֲדוֹנָם	אֲדוֹנֵיהֶם	כְּתָבָם
+3fp	*אֲדוֹנָן	*אֲדוֹנֵיהֶן	*כְּתָבָן

32. The table is supplemented by the following forms: לְשׁוֹנִי "my tongue"; לְשׁוֹנְךָ "your tongue"; לְשׁוֹנֵךְ "your tongue"; לְשׁוֹנוֹ "his tongue"; לְשׁוֹנָהּ "her tongue"; לְשֹׁנֵנוּ "our tongue"; לְשׁוֹנְכֶם "your tongue"; לְשׁוֹנָם "their tongue"; יְהָבְךָ "your burden"; יְקָרוֹ "his honor"; note also אֲדֹנָי, a pausal form used also in context, always in reference to God.

More Examples

- *qaṭāl*: שָׁלוֹשׁ "three"; לָשׁוֹן "tongue"; *qal* infinitives absolute (e.g., שָׁמוֹר)
- Aramaic forms: יְהָב "burden"; יְעָף "weariness"; יְקָר "honor"; סְפָר "enumeration"; עֲבָד "deed"; קְרָב "war"; שְׂרָד "plaited work"; שְׁאָר "remainder"
- Aramaic-like *nomen agentis* nouns of the *qāṭōl* type are associated with this base; בָּחוֹן "checker"; חָמוֹץ "oppressor"; עָשׁוֹק "oppressor"; בָּגוֹדָה "treacherous"[33]

Table 6.20. **Qatīl* Bases[34]

	qatīl* sg./pl. "prophet" **nabīʾ*/nabīʾīm*		**qatīl* sg./pl. "afflicted" **ʿanīy*/**ʿanīyīm*	
abs.	נָבִיא	נְבִיאִים	עָנִי	עֲנִיִּים
const.	*נְבִיא	נְבִיאֵי	*עֲנִי	עֲנִיֵּי
+1cs	*נְבִיאִי	נְבִיאַי		
+2ms	נְבִיאֲךָ	נְבִיאֶיךָ		
+2fs	*נְבִיאֵךְ	נְבִיאַיִךְ		עֲנִיַּיִךְ
+3ms	*נְבִיאוֹ	נְבִיאָיו		עֲנִיָּיו
+3fs	*נְבִיאָהּ	נְבִיאֶיהָ		
+1cp	*נְבִיאֵנוּ	נְבִיאֵינוּ		
+2mp	נְבִיאֲכֶם	נְבִיאֵיכֶם		
+2fp	*נְבִיאֲכֶן	*נְבִיאֵיכֶן		
+3mp	*נְבִיאָם	נְבִיאֵיהֶם		
+3fp	*נְבִיאָן	*נְבִיאֵיהֶן		

33. See Fox, *Semitic Noun Patterns*, 184.

34. The table is supplemented by the following forms: יְמִינִי "my right hand"; יְמִינוֹ "his right hand"; יְמִינָהּ "her right hand"; יְמִינָם "their right hand"; נְקִי "innocent of"

More Examples

- **qatīl*: יָמִין "right hand/side"; כָּלִיל "whole"; צָעִיר "small"; אָסִיר "prisoner"; מָשִׁיחַ "anointed"; נָשִׂיא "prince"; נָגִיד "prince"; נָזִיר "one devoted"; פָּקִיד "overseer"; פָּלִיט "fugitive"; סָבִיב "around"
- III-*vav*/*yod* roots: נָקִי "innocent, clean"
- Aramaic-like forms: בְּדִיל "tin, dross"; בְּרִיחַ "bar"; גְּבִיר "lord"; דְּבִיר "holy of holies"; כְּסִיל "fool"; נְצִיב "prefect"; עֲוִיל "young boy"; כְּפִיר "lion"

Table 6.21. **Qatūl*, **Qitāl* Bases[35]

	qatūl* sg./pl. "one numbered" **paqūd*/paqūdīm*		**qatūlat* sg./pl. "strength" **gabūrat*/**gabūrāt*		**qitāl* sg./pl. "arm" **zirāʿ*/**zirāʿāt*	
abs.	*פָּקוּד	*פְּקֻדִים	גְּבוּרָה	גְּבוּרוֹת	זְרוֹעַ	*זְרוֹעוֹת
const.	*פְּקוּד	פְּקֻדֵי	גְּבוּרַת	גְּבֻרוֹת	זְרוֹעַ	זְרוֹעוֹת
+1cs	*פְּקוּדִי	*פְּקֻדַי	גְּבוּרָתִי	*גְּבוּרֹתַי	זְרוֹעִי	זְרוֹעוֹתַי
+2ms	*פְּקוּדְךָ	*פְּקֻדֶיךָ	גְּבוּרָתְךָ	גְּבוּרֹתֶיךָ	זְרוֹעֲךָ	*זְרוֹעוֹתֶיךָ
+2fs	*פְּקוּדֵךְ	*פְּקֻדַיִךְ	גְּבוּרָתֵךְ	*גְּבוּרֹתַיִךְ	*זְרוֹעֵךְ	*זְרוֹעוֹתַיִךְ
+3ms	*פְּקוּדוֹ	פְּקֻדָיו	גְּבוּרָתוֹ	גְּבוּרֹתָיו	זְרוֹעוֹ	זְרוֹעֹתָיו
+3fs	*פְּקוּדָהּ	פְּקֻדֶיהָ	גְּבוּרָתָהּ	*גְּבוּרֹתֶיהָ	*זְרוֹעָהּ	זְרֹעוֹתֶיהָ
+1cp	*פְּקוּדֵנוּ	*פְּקֻדֵינוּ	*גְּבוּרָתֵנוּ	*גְּבוּרֹתֵינוּ	*זְרוֹעֵנוּ	*זְרוֹעוֹתֵינוּ
+2mp	*פְּקוּדְכֶם	פְּקֻדֵיכֶם	גְּבוּרַתְכֶם	*גְּבוּרֹתֵיכֶם	*זְרוֹעֲכֶם	זְרוֹעֹתֵיכֶם
+2fp	*פְּקוּדְכֶן	*פְּקֻדֵיכֶן	*גְּבוּרַתְכֶן	*גְּבוּרֹתֵיכֶן	*זְרוֹעֲכֶן	*זְרוֹעוֹתֵיכֶן
+3mp	*פְּקוּדָם	פְּקֻדֵיהֶם	גְּבוּרָתָם	*גְּבוּרֹתָם	זְרוֹעָם	זְרוֹעֹתָם
+3fp	*פְּקוּדָן	*פְּקֻדֵיהֶן	גְּבוּרָתָן	*גְּבוּרֹתָן	*זְרוֹעָן	*זְרוֹעוֹתָן

35. The table is supplemented by the following forms: בָּרוּךְ "blessed"; בְּרוּךְ "blessed of"; יְצוּעִי "my couch"; זְכוּרְךָ "your male"; זְכוּרָהּ "her male"; עֲלֻמֵנוּ "our secret"; יְצוּעָי "my couches" (pausal); בְּתוּלֹתַי "my young women"; בְּתוּלֹתֶיהָ "her young women"; זְרוֹעֹתָי "my arms" (pausal).

More Examples

- **qatūl*: *qal* passive participles (אָרוּר "cursed" [ms], אֲרוּרָה [fs], אֲרוּרִים [mp], *אֲרוּרוֹת [fp]); זָכוּר "male"; חָרוּץ "gold"; יָצוּעַ "couch"; עָצוּם "mighty"; עָרוּם "clever"; שָׁבוּעַ "week"
- III-*vav*/*yod* roots: *qal* passive participles: בָּנוּי "what is built" (ms), בְּנוּיָה (fs), בְּנוּיִם (mp), *בְּנוּיוֹת (fp)
- **qatūlat*: אֱמוּנָה "faithfulness"; בְּתוּלָה "young woman"; יְשׁוּעָה "salvation"; מְלוּכָה "kingship, royalty"
- **qitāl* (see **qutul*): תְּהוֹם "deep"; אֱלוֹהַּ "God"

Table 6.22. **Qattal* and/or **Qattāl* Base(s)[36]

	qattalt sg./pl. "sabbath" **šabbatt*/**šabbatāt*		*qattalt* sg. "sin" **ḫaṭṭaʾt*/**ḫaṭṭaʾāt*		**qattalat* or **qattālat* sg. "request" **baqqašat* or **baqqāšat*
abs.	שַׁבָּת	שַׁבָּתוֹת	חַטָּאת	חַטָּאוֹת	*בַּקָּשָׁה
const.	שַׁבַּת	שַׁבְּתוֹת	חַטַּאת	חַטֹּאות	*בַּקָּשַׁת
+1cs	*שַׁבַּתִּי	שַׁבְּתוֹתַי	חַטָּאתִי	חַטֹּאותַי	בַּקָּשָׁתִי
+2ms	*שַׁבַּתְּךָ	*שַׁבְּתוֹתֶיךָ	חַטָּאתְךָ	חַטֹּאותֶיךָ	—
+2fs	*שַׁבַּתֵּךְ	*שַׁבְּתוֹתַיִךְ	*חַטָּאתֵךְ	חַטֹּאתַיִךְ	בַּקָּשָׁתֵךְ
+3ms	שַׁבַּתּוֹ	*שַׁבְּתוֹתָיו	חַטָּאתוֹ	חַטֹּאתָו	בַּקָּשָׁתוֹ
+3fs	שַׁבַּתָּהּ	שַׁבְּתוֹתֶיהָ	*חַטָּאתָהּ	חַטֹּאותֶיהָ	*בַּקָּשָׁתָהּ
+1cp	*שַׁבַּתֵּנוּ	*שַׁבְּתוֹתֵינוּ	חַטָּאתֵנוּ	חַטֹּאותֵינוּ	*בַּקָּשָׁתֵנוּ
+2mp	שַׁבַּתְּכֶם	שַׁבְּתֹתֵיכֶם	חַטַּאתְכֶם	חַטֹּאותֵיכֶם	—
+2fp	*שַׁבַּתְּכֶן	*שַׁבְּתֹתֵיכֶן	*חַטַּאתְכֶן	*חַטֹּאותֵיכֶן	—
+3mp	*שַׁבַּתָּם	*שַׁבְּתוֹתָם	חַטָּאתָם	חַטֹּאותָם	*בַּקָּשָׁתָם
+3fp	*שַׁבַּתָּן	*שַׁבְּתוֹתָן	*חַטָּאתָן	*חַטֹּאותָן	*בַּקָּשָׁתָן

More Examples

- **qattalt*: יַבֶּלֶת "wart"; יַלֶּפֶת "scabs"; צָרַעַת "leprosy"
- **qattalat*: בַּלָּהָה "terror"; בַּצָּרָה "drought"; חַטָּאָה "sin"

36. The table is supplemented by the following forms: בַּקָּרַת "care of."

Table 6.23. *Qal*, *Piel*, *Hiphil*, *Niphal*, *Pual*, and *Hophal* of Strong Roots

שׁמר

qåṭal

	qal	*piel*[37]	*hiphil*	*niphal*	*pual*	*hophal*
3ms	שָׁמַר	*שִׁמֵּר	*הִשְׁמִיר	נִשְׁמַר	*שֻׁמַּר	*הָשְׁמַר
3fs	שָׁמְרָה	*שִׁמְּרָה	*הִשְׁמִ֫ירָה	*נִשְׁמְרָה	*שֻׁמְּרָה	*הָשְׁמְרָה
2ms	שָׁמַ֫רְתָּ	*שִׁמַּ֫רְתָּ	*הִשְׁמַ֫רְתָּ	נִשְׁמַ֫רְתָּ	*שֻׁמַּ֫רְתָּ	*הָשְׁמַ֫רְתָּ
2fs	*שָׁמַרְתְּ	*שִׁמַּרְתְּ	*הִשְׁמַ֫רְתְּ	*נִשְׁמַרְתְּ	*שֻׁמַּרְתְּ	*הָשְׁמַרְתְּ
1cs	שָׁמַ֫רְתִּי	*שִׁמַּ֫רְתִּי	*הִשְׁמַ֫רְתִּי	*נִשְׁמַ֫רְתִּי	*שֻׁמַּ֫רְתִּי	*הָשְׁמַ֫רְתִּי
3cp	שָׁמְרוּ	*שִׁמְּרוּ	*הִשְׁמִ֫ירוּ	נִשְׁמְרוּ	*שֻׁמְּרוּ	*הָשְׁמְרוּ
2mp	שְׁמַרְתֶּם	*שִׁמַּרְתֶּם	*הִשְׁמַרְתֶּם	נִשְׁמַרְתֶּם	*שֻׁמַּרְתֶּם	*הָשְׁמַרְתֶּם
2fp	*שְׁמַרְתֶּן	*שִׁמַּרְתֶּן	*הִשְׁמַרְתֶּן	*נִשְׁמַרְתֶּן	*שֻׁמַּרְתֶּן	*הָשְׁמַרְתֶּן
1cp	שָׁמַ֫רְנוּ	*שִׁמַּ֫רְנוּ	*הִשְׁמַ֫רְנוּ	*נִשְׁמַ֫רְנוּ	*שֻׁמַּ֫רְנוּ	*הָשְׁמַ֫רְנוּ

yiqṭol

	qal	*piel*	*hiphil*	*niphal*	*pual*	*hophal*
3ms	יִשְׁמֹר	*יְשַׁמֵּר	*יַשְׁמִיר	*יִשָּׁמֵר	*יְשֻׁמַּר	*יָשְׁמַר
3fs	תִּשְׁמֹר	*תְּשַׁמֵּר	*תַּשְׁמִיר	תִּשָּׁמֵר	*תְּשֻׁמַּר	*תָּשְׁמַר
2ms	תִּשְׁמֹר	*תְּשַׁמֵּר	*תַּשְׁמִיר	*תִּשָּׁמֵר	*תְּשֻׁמַּר	*תָּשְׁמַר
2fs	*תִּשְׁמְרִי	*תְּשַׁמְּרִי	*תַּשְׁמִ֫ירִי	*תִּשָּׁמְרִי	*תְּשֻׁמְּרִי	*תָּשְׁמְרִי
1cs	אֶשְׁמֹר	*אֲשַׁמֵּר	*אַשְׁמִיר	*אִשָּׁמֵר	*אֲשֻׁמַּר	*אָשְׁמַר
3mp	יִשְׁמְרוּ	*יְשַׁמְּרוּ	*יַשְׁמִ֫ירוּ	*יִשָּׁמְרוּ	*יְשֻׁמְּרוּ	*יָשְׁמְרוּ
3fp	*תִּשְׁמֹ֫רְנָה	*תְּשַׁמֵּ֫רְנָה[38]	—	*תִּשָּׁמַ֫רְנָה	*תְּשֻׁמַּ֫רְנָה	—
2mp	תִּשְׁמְרוּ	*תְּשַׁמְּרוּ	*תַּשְׁמִ֫ירוּ	תִּשָּׁמְרוּ	*תְּשֻׁמְּרוּ	*תָּשְׁמְרוּ
2fp	*תִּשְׁמֹ֫רְנָה	*תְּשַׁמֵּ֫רְנָה	—	*תִּשָּׁמַ֫רְנָה	*תְּשֻׁמַּ֫רְנָה	—
1cp	נִשְׁמֹר	*נְשַׁמֵּר	*נַשְׁמִיר	*נִשָּׁמֵר	*נְשֻׁמַּר	*נָשְׁמַר

37. In the *piel*, only a few roots evidence the elision of one of the geminated continuant consonants and shewa: מִלְאוּ "they filled"; קִנְנוּ "they made nests"; בִּקְשׁוּ "they sought." The unattested forms of the verb are based on the relatively well-attested forms of other verbs. In particular, note לַמֵּ֫דְנָה "teach!"; הַאְזֵ֫נָּה "give ear!"; note also the two alternative forms of the *niphal* inf. const. הִלָּחֵם and הִלָּ֫חֶם "to fight."

38. Pausal forms often evidence a *patakh* in the accented syllable (e.g., תְּרַטַּשְׁנָה "they will crush" Isa 13:18).

Short-*yiqṭol and wayyiqṭol*[39]

	qal	*piel*	*hiphil*	*niphal*
3ms			*יַשְׁמֵר	*וַיִּשָּׁמֶר
3fs			*תַּשְׁמֵר	
2ms			*תַּשְׁמֵר	
1cs			*וָאַשְׁמִיר	
1cp			*נַשְׁמֵר	

Imperative

	qal	*piel*	*hiphil*	*niphal*	*pual*	*hophal*
ms	שְׁמֹר	*שַׁמֵּר	*הַשְׁמֵר	הִשָּׁמֶר	—	—
fs	*שִׁמְרִי	*שַׁמְּרִי	*הַשְׁמִירִי	הִשָּׁמְרִי	—	—
mp	שִׁמְרוּ	*שַׁמְּרוּ	*הַשְׁמִירוּ	הִשָּׁמְרוּ	—	—
fp	*שְׁמֹרְנָה	*שַׁמֵּרְנָה	*הַשְׁמֵרְנָה	—	—	—

Infinitives

const.	שְׁמֹר	*שַׁמֵּר	*הַשְׁמִיר	*הִשָּׁמֶר	—	*הָשְׁמַר
abs.	שָׁמוֹר	*שַׁמֵּר	*הַשְׁמֵר	הִשָּׁמֵר[40]	*שֻׁמֹּר	*הָשְׁמֵר

Participles

ms	שֹׁמֵר	*מְשַׁמֵּר	*מַשְׁמִיר	*נִשְׁמָר	*מְשֻׁמָּר	*מָשְׁמָר
fs	*שֹׁמֶרֶת	*מְשַׁמֶּרֶת	*מַשְׁמֶרֶת	*נִשְׁמָרָה	*מְשֻׁמָּרָה	*מָשְׁמֶרֶת
mp	שֹׁמְרִים	מְשַׁמְּרִים	*מַשְׁמִירִים	*נִשְׁמָרִים	*מְשֻׁמָּרִים	*מָשְׁמָרִים
fp	*שֹׁמְרוֹת	*מְשַׁמְּרוֹת	*מַשְׁמִירוֹת	*נִשְׁמָרוֹת	*מְשֻׁמָּרוֹת	*מָשְׁמָרוֹת

39. This portion of the table is supplemented by the following forms: וָאַשְׁמִיד "I destroyed" (Amos 2:9); נַשְׁאֵר "let us leave over" (1 Sam 14:36) and וַנַּקְרֵב "we brought near" (Num 31:50); וַיִּלָּחֶם "he fought" (Exod 17:8). In relation to the following categories, note the alternative forms to the feminine singular *niphal* (*נִשְׁמֶרֶת), *pual* (*מְשֻׁמֶּרֶת) participles.

40. Also הִשָּׁמֹר and נִשְׁמֹר.

Table 6.24. *Qal*, *Piel*, and *Niphal* of III-Guttural and III-*Aleph* Roots[41]

qåṭal

	שלח		מצא		מלא	
	qal	*piel*	*qal*	*niphal*	*qal*	*piel*
3ms	שָׁלַח	שִׁלַּח	מָצָא	נִמְצָא	מָלֵא	מִלֵּא
3fs	שָׁלְחָה	שִׁלְּחָה	מָצְאָה	נִמְצְאָה	מָלְאָה	*מִלְּאָה
2ms	שָׁלַ֫חְתָּ	שִׁלַּ֫חְתָּ	מָצָ֫אתָ	*נִמְצֵ֫אתָ	מָלֵ֫אתָ	מִלֵּ֫אתָ
2fs	*שָׁלַ֫חַתְּ	*שִׁלַּ֫חַתְּ	מָצָאת	נִמְצֵאת	*מָלֵאת	*מִלֵּאת
1cs	שָׁלַ֫חְתִּי	שִׁלַּ֫חְתִּי	מָצָ֫אתִי	נִמְצֵ֫אתִי	מָלֵ֫אתִי	מִלֵּ֫אתִי
3cp	שָׁלְחוּ	שִׁלְּחוּ	מָצְאוּ	נִמְצְאוּ	מָלְאוּ	מִלְּאוּ
2mp	שְׁלַחְתֶּם	שִׁלַּחְתֶּם	מְצָאתֶם	*נִמְצֵאתֶם	*מְלֵאתֶם	מִלֵּאתֶם
2fp	*שְׁלַחְתֶּן	*שִׁלַּחְתֶּן	מְצָאתֶן	*נִמְצֵאתֶן	*מְלֵאתֶן	*מִלֵּאתֶן
1cp	שָׁלַ֫חְנוּ	שִׁלַּ֫חְנוּ	מָצָ֫אנוּ	*נִמְצֵ֫אנוּ	*מָלֵ֫אנוּ	מִלֵּ֫אנוּ

yiqṭol

	qal	*piel*	*qal*	*niphal*	*qal*	*piel*
3ms	יִשְׁלַח	יְשַׁלַּח	יִמְצָא	יִמָּצֵא	*יִמְלָא	יְמַלֵּא
3fs	*תִּשְׁלַח	תְּשַׁלַּח	תִּמְצָא	תִּמָּצֵא	*תִּמְלָא	תְּמַלֵּא
2ms	תִּשְׁלַח	תְּשַׁלַּח	תִּמְצָא	*תִּמָּצֵא	*תִּמְלָא	תְּמַלֵּא
2fs	*תִּשְׁלְחִי	*תְּשַׁלְּחִי	*תִּמְצְאִי	תִּמָּצְאִי	*תִּמְלְאִי	*תְּמַלְּאִי
1cs	אֶשְׁלַח	אֲשַׁלַּח	אֶמְצָא	*אִמָּצֵא	*אֶמְלָא	אֲמַלֵּא
3mp	יִשְׁלְחוּ	יְשַׁלְּחוּ	יִמְצְאוּ	יִמָּצְאוּ	יִמְלְאוּ	יְמַלְּאוּ
3fp	תִּשְׁלַ֫חְנָה	תְּשַׁלַּ֫חְנָה	תִּמְצֶ֫אןָ	תִּמָּצֶ֫אינָה	*תִּמְלֶ֫אנָה	תְּמַלֶּ֫אנָה
2mp	תִּשְׁלְחוּ	תְּשַׁלְּחוּ	תִּמְצְאוּ	*תִּמָּצְאוּ	*תִּמְלְאוּ	*תְּמַלְּאוּ
2fp	תִּשְׁלַ֫חְנָה	*תְּשַׁלַּ֫חְנָה	*תִּמְצֶ֫אןָ	*תִּמָּצֶ֫אינָה	*תִּמְלֶ֫אנָה	*תְּמַלֶּ֫אנָה
1cp	נִשְׁלַח	*נְשַׁלַּח	נִמְצָא	*נִמָּצֵא	*נִמְלָא	נְמַלֵּא

41. The table is supplemented by this form: שָׁכַ֫חַתְּ "you forgot" (Isa 17:10).

Imperative

	qal	*piel*	*qal*	*niphal*	*qal*	*piel*
ms	שְׁלַח	שַׁלַּח	מְצָא	*הִמָּצֵא	*מְלָא	מַלֵּא
fs	*שִׁלְחִי	*שַׁלְּחִי	*מִצְאִי	*הִמָּצְאִי	*מִלְאִי	*מַלְּאִי
mp	שִׁלְחוּ	שַׁלְּחוּ	מִצְאוּ	*הִמָּצְאוּ	מִלְאוּ	מַלְּאוּ
fp	*שְׁלַחְנָה	*שַׁלַּחְנָה	מְצֶאןָ	*הִמָּצֶאנָה	*מְלֶאנָה	—

Infinitives

const.	שְׁלֹחַ	שַׁלַּח	מְצֹא	הִמָּצֵא	מְלֹאת	מַלְּאוֹת and מַלֵּא
abs.	שָׁלֹחַ	שַׁלַּח	*מָצֹא	*הִמָּצֵא	*מָלֹא	*מַלֵּא

Participles

	qal	*piel*	*qal*	*niphal*	*qal*	*piel*
ms	שֹׁלֵחַ	מְשַׁלֵּחַ	מוֹצֵא	נִמְצָא	מָלֵא	מְמַלֵּא
fs	*שֹׁלַחַת	*מְשַׁלַּחַת	מֹצֵאת	נִמְצָאָה	*מְלֵאת	*מְמַלֵּאת
mp	שֹׁלְחִים	מְשַׁלְּחִים	מֹצְאִים	נִמְצָאִים	מְלֵאִים	מְמַלְּאִים
fp	*שֹׁלְחוֹת	*מְשַׁלְּחוֹת	מֹצְאוֹת	נִמְצָאוֹת	*מְלֵאוֹת	מְמַלְּאוֹת

Table 6.25. *Qal*, *Hiphil*, *Niphal*, and *Hophal* of II-*Vav* Roots[42]

	II-*vav*: קום "to rise"			II-*vav*: בוא "to enter"	II-*vav*: כון "to establish"
			qåṭal		
	qal	*hiphil*	*hophal*	*hiphil*	*niphal*
3ms	קָם	הֵקִים	הוּקַם	הֵבִיא	נָכוֹן
3fs	קָ֫מָה	הֵקִ֫ימָה	—	הֵבִ֫יאָה	נָכֹ֫ונָה
2ms	קַ֫מְתָּ	הֲקִמֹ֫תָ	—	הֵבֵ֫אתָ	—
2fs	*קַמְתְּ	*הֲקֵמֹת	—	*הֵבֵאת	—
1cs	קַ֫מְתִּי	הֲקִמֹ֫תִי	—	הֵבֵ֫אתִי	—
3cp	קָ֫מוּ	הֵקִ֫ימוּ	*הוּקְמוּ	הֵבִ֫יאוּ	נָכֹ֫ונוּ
2mp	קַמְתֶּם	*הֲקֵמֹתֶם	—	הֲבֵאתֶם	—
2fp	*קַמְתֶּן	*הֲקֵמֹתֶן	—	*הֲבֵאתֶן	—
1cp	*קַ֫מְנוּ	הֲקֵמֹ֫נוּ	—	*הֵבֵ֫אנוּ	—
			yiqṭol		
	qal	*hiphil*	*hophal*	*hiphil*	*niphal*
3ms	יָקוּם	יָקִים	*יוּקַם	יָבִיא	יִכּוֹן
3fs	תָּקוּם	*תָּקִים	*תּוּקַם	תָּבִיא	תִּכּוֹן
2ms	תָּקוּם	תָּקִים	—	תָּבִיא	תִּכּוֹן
2fs	תָּק֫וּמִי	תָּקִ֫ימִי	—	*תָּבִ֫יאִי	*תִּכֹּ֫נִי
1cs	אָקוּם	אָקִים	—	אָבִיא	*אִכּוֹן
3mp	יָק֫וּמוּ	יָקִ֫ימוּ	יוּקְמוּ*	יָבִ֫יאוּ	יִכֹּ֫נוּ
3fp	*תָּקֹ֫מְנָה	*תָּקִ֫ימְנָה	—	תְּבִיאֶ֫ינָה	—
2mp	תָּק֫וּמוּ	תָּקִ֫ימוּ	—	תָּבִ֫יאוּ	*תִּכֹּ֫נוּ
2fp	*תָּקֹ֫מְנָה	תָּקִ֫ימְנָה	—	*תְּבִיאֶ֫ינָה	—
1cp	נָקוּם	*נָקִים	—	נָבִיא	*נִכּוֹן

42. The table is supplemented by the following forms: תָּשֹׁ֫בְןָ "they will return" (Ezek 16:55); יָשֹׁב "let it return" (Num 25:4); הֲשֵׁבֹתֶם "you returned" (1 Sam 6:8); הוּטְלוּ "they were hurled" (Jer 22:28); יוּמַת "he will [not] be put to death" (1 Sam 11:13); יוּמְתוּ "they will [not] be put to death" (2 Kgs 14:6); וַיּוּשַׁב "he was returned" (Exod 10:8); מוּמָת "one to be put to death" (1 Sam 19:11); מוּשָׁבִים "those brought back" (Jer 27:16); הִמֹּלוּ "circumcise yourself!" (Jer 4:4); הִמּוֹל "to circumcise yourself" (Gen 34:17); הִמּוֹל "circumcising oneself" (Gen 17:13 [*niph*. inf. abs.]).

Short-*yiqṭol*

	qal	*hiphil*	*hophal*	*hiphil*	*niphal*
3ms	*יָקֹם	יָקֵם		—	—
3fs	*תָּקֹם	*תָּקֵם		—	—
2ms	*תָּקֹם	*תָּקֵם		—	—

wayyiqṭol

3ms	וַיָּ֫קָם	וַיָּ֫קֶם	*וַיּוּקַם	וַיָּבֵא	וַיִּכּוֹן

Imperative

	qal	*hiphil*	*hophal*	*hiphil*	*niphal*
ms	קוּם	הָקֵם		הָבֵא	הִכּוֹן
fs	ק֫וּמִי	*הָקִ֫ימִי		הָבִ֫יאִי	—
mp	ק֫וּמוּ	הָקִ֫ימוּ		הָבִ֫יאוּ	*הִכֹּנוּ
fp	קֹמְנָה	—		—	—

Infinitives

	qal	*hiphil*	*hophal*	*hiphil*	*niphal*
const.	קוּם	הוֹשִׁיב		הָבִיא	*הִכּוֹן
abs.	קוֹם	*הוֹשֵׁב		הָבֵא	*הִכּוֹן

Participles

ms	*קָם	מוֹשִׁיב	*מוּקָם	מֵבִיא	נָכוֹן
fs	קָמָה	*מוֹשֶׁ֫בֶת	—	—	נְכוֹנָה
mp	קָמִים	*מוֹשִׁיבִים	*מוּקָמִים	מְבִיאִים	נְכֹנִים
fp	*קָמוֹת	*מוֹשִׁיבוֹת	*מוּקָמוֹת	—	*נְכֹנוֹת

Table 6.26. Verb Forms of III-*Vav*/*Yod* Roots[43]

גלה

qåṭal

	qal	*piel*	*hiphil*	*niphal*	*pual*	*hophal*
3ms	גָּלָה	גִּלָּה	הֶגְלָה	נִגְלָה	*גֻּלָּה	הָגְלָה
3fs	גָּלְתָה	גִּלְּתָה	*הֶגְלְתָה	נִגְלְתָה	גֻּלְּתָה	הָגְלְתָה[44]
2ms	גָּלִ֫יתָ	*גִּלִּ֫יתָ	הִגְלִ֫יתָ	*נִגְלֵ֫יתָ	*גֻּלֵּ֫יתָ	*הָגְלֵ֫יתָ
2fs	*גָּלִית	גִּלִּית	*הִגְלִית	*נִגְלֵית	*גֻּלֵּית	*הָגְלֵית
1cs	גָּלִ֫יתִי	גִּלִּ֫יתִי	הִגְלֵ֫יתִי	נִגְלֵ֫יתִי	*גֻּלֵּ֫יתִי	*הָגְלֵ֫יתִי
3cp	גָּלוּ	גִּלּוּ	הִגְלוּ	נִגְלוּ	*גֻּלּוּ	הָגְלוּ
2mp	*גְּלִיתֶם	*גִּלִּיתֶם	הִגְלִיתֶם	*נִגְלֵיתֶם	*גֻּלֵּיתֶם	*הָגְלֵיתֶם
2fp	*גְּלִיתֶן	*גִּלִּיתֶן	*הִגְלִיתֶן	*נִגְלֵיתֶן	*גֻּלֵּיתֶן	*הָגְלֵיתֶן
1cp	*גָּלִ֫ינוּ	*גִּלִּ֫ינוּ	*הִגְלִ֫ינוּ	נִגְלֵ֫ינוּ	*גֻּלֵּ֫ינוּ	*הָגְלֵ֫ינוּ

yiqṭol

	qal	*piel*	*hiphil*	*niphal*	*pual*	*hophal*
3ms	יִגְלֶה	יְגַלֶּה	*יַגְלֶה	יִגָּלֶה	*יְגֻלֶּה	*יָגְלֶה
3fs	*תִּגְלֶה	*תְּגַלֶּה	*תַּגְלֶה	תִּגָּלֶה	*תְּגֻלֶּה	*תָּגְלֶה
2ms	*תִּגְלֶה	תְּגַלֶּה	*תַּגְלֶה	*תִּגָּלֶה	*תְּגֻלֶּה	*תָּגְלֶה
2fs	*תִּגְלִי	תְּגַלִּי	*תַּגְלִי	*תִּגָּלִי	*תְּגֻלִּי	*תָּגְלִי
1cs	אֶגְלֶה	אֲגַלֶּה	*אַגְלֶה	*אִגָּלֶה	*אֲגֻלֶּה	*אָגְלֶה
3mp	יִגְלוּ	יְגַלּוּ	*יַגְלוּ	יִגָּלוּ	*יְגֻלּוּ	*יָגְלוּ
3fp	*תִּגְלֶ֫ינָה	*תְּגַלֶּ֫ינָה	*תַּגְלֶ֫ינָה	*תִּגָּלֶ֫ינָה	*תְּגֻלֶּ֫ינָה	*תָּגְלֶ֫ינָה
2mp	*תִּגְלוּ	*תְּגַלּוּ	*תַּגְלוּ	*תִּגָּלוּ	*תְּגֻלּוּ	*תָּגְלוּ
2fp	*תִּגְלֶ֫ינָה	*תְּגַלֶּ֫ינָה	*תַּגְלֶ֫ינָה	*תִּגָּלֶ֫ינָה	*תְּגֻלֶּ֫ינָה	*תָּגְלֶ֫ינָה
1cp	*נִגְלֶה	*נְגַלֶּה	*נַגְלֶה	*נִגָּלֶה	*נְגֻלֶּה	*נָגְלֶה

43. The table is supplemented by these forms: וָאֵ֫פֶן "I turned"; וַנֵּ֫פֶן "we turned."
44. Note also הָגְלָת.

Short-*yiqṭol and wayyiqṭol*

	qal	*piel*	*hiphil*	*niphal*	*pual*	*hophal*
3ms	יִ֫גֶל	יְגַל	יֶ֫גֶל	*יִגָּל		
3fs	*תִּ֫גֶל	וַתְּגַל	*תֶּ֫גֶל	תִּגָּל		
2ms	*תִּ֫גֶל	תְּגַל	*תֶּ֫גֶל	*תִּגָּל		
1cs	*וָאֵ֫גֶל	—	—	—		
1cp	*וַנֵּ֫גֶל	—	—	—		

Imperative

	qal	*piel*	*hiphil*	*niphal*	*pual*	*hophal*
ms	גְּלֵה	*גַּלֵּה / גַּל	*הַגְלֵה	הִגָּלֵה		
fs	*גְּלִי	גַּלִּי	*הַגְלִי	*הִגָּלִי		
mp	*גְּלוּ	*גַּלּוּ	*הַגְלוּ	הִגָּלוּ		
fp	*גְּלֶ֫ינָה	*גַּלֶּ֫ינָה	*הַגְלֶ֫ינָה	*הִגָּלֶ֫ינָה		

Infinitives

	qal	*piel*	*hiphil*	*niphal*	*pual*	*hophal*
const.	גְּלוֹת	גַּלּוֹת	הַגְלוֹת	הִגָּלוֹת		
abs.	גָּלֹה	*גַּלֹּה	*הַגְלֵה	נִגְלֹה		

Participles

ms	גֹּלֶה	מְגַלֶּה	*מַגְלֶה	*נִגְלֶה	*מְגֻלֶּה	*מָגְלֶה
fs	*גֹּלָה	*מְגַלָּה	*מַגְלָה	*נִגְלָה	מְגֻלָּה	*מָגְלָה
mp	גֹּלִים	*מְגַלִּים	*מַגְלִים	*נִגְלִים	*מְגֻלִּים	מָגְלִים
fp	*גֹּלוֹת	*מְגַלּוֹת	*מַגְלוֹת	נִגְלֹת	*מְגֻלּוֹת	*מָגְלוֹת

Table 6.27. Verb Forms of I-Guttural and III-*Vav*/*Yod* Roots[45]

עשה

qåṭal

	qal	*piel*	*hiphil*	*niphal*	*pual*	*hophal*
3ms	עָשָׂה	*עִשָּׂה	*הֶעֱשָׂה	נַעֲשָׂה	*עֻשָּׂה	*הָעֳשָׂה
3fs	עָשְׂתָה	*עִשְּׂתָה	*הֶעֶשְׂתָה	נֶעֶשְׂתָה	*עֻשְּׂתָה	*הָעָשְׂתָה
2ms	עָשִׂיתָ	*עִשִּׂיתָ	*הֶעֱשִׂיתָ	*נַעֲשֵׂיתָ	*עֻשֵּׂיתָ	*הָעֳשֵׂיתָ
2fs	עָשִׂית	*עִשִּׂית	*הֶעֱשִׂית	*נַעֲשֵׂית	*עֻשֵּׂית	*הָעֳשֵׂית
1cs	עָשִׂיתִי	*עִשִּׂיתִי	*הֶעֱשִׂיתִי	*נַעֲשֵׂיתִי	עֻשֵּׂיתִי	*הָעֳשֵׂיתִי
3cp	עָשׂוּ	עִשּׂוּ	*הֶעֱשׂוּ	נַעֲשׂוּ	*עֻשּׂוּ	*הָעֳשׂוּ
2mp	עֲשִׂיתֶם	*עִשִּׂיתֶם	*הֶעֱשִׂיתֶם		*עֻשֵּׂיתֶם	*הָעֳשֵׂיתֶם
2fp	עֲשִׂיתֶן	*עִשִּׂיתֶן	*הֶעֱשִׂיתֶן		*עֻשֵּׂיתֶן	*הָעֳשֵׂיתֶן
1cp	עָשִׂינוּ	*עִשִּׂינוּ	*הֶעֱשִׂינוּ	*נַעֲשֵׂינוּ	*עֻשֵּׂינוּ	*הָעֳשֵׂינוּ

yiqṭol

	qal	*piel*	*hiphil*	*niphal*	*pual*	*hophal*
3ms	יַעֲשֶׂה	*יְעַשֶּׂה	*יַעֲשֶׂה	יֵעָשֶׂה	*יְעֻשֶּׂה	*יָעֳשֶׂה
3fs	תַּעֲשֶׂה	*תְּעַשֶּׂה	*תַּעֲשֶׂה	תֵּעָשֶׂה	*תְּעֻשֶּׂה	*תָּעֳשֶׂה
2ms	תַּעֲשֶׂה	*תְּעַשֶּׂה	*תַּעֲשֶׂה	*תֵּעָשֶׂה	*תְּעֻשֶּׂה	*תָּעֳשֶׂה
2fs	תַּעֲשִׂי	*תְּעַשִּׂי	*תַּעֲשִׂי	*תֵּעָשִׂי	*תְּעֻשִּׂי	*תָּעֳשִׂי
1cs	אֶעֱשֶׂה	*אֲעַשֶּׂה	*אַעֲשֶׂה	*אֵעָשֶׂה	*אֲעֻשֶּׂה	*אָעֳשֶׂה
3mp	יַעֲשׂוּ	*יְעַשּׂוּ	*יַעֲשׂוּ	יֵעָשׂוּ	*יְעֻשּׂוּ	*יָעֳשׂוּ

45. The unattested forms of the verb are based on the relatively well-attested forms of other verbs like עלה "to go up." In addition, the following rare forms help to complete the table: אָ֫חַז "I saw" (pausal from חזה "to see"); בְּכֶ֫ינָה "weep!"; אֲעַנֵּךְ "I will afflict you"; תְּעַר "do (not) strip." Note also the appocopated form of the *piel* and *hiphil* masc. sg. impv.: צַו "command"; גַּל "uncover"; הַ֫עַל "bring up"; the alternative forms of the *hiphil* perfect of עלה "to go up": הֶעֱלִ֫יתָ vs. הֶעֱלֵיתָ and הַעֲלִ֫יתָ vs. הַעֲלֵיתָ; and the *wayyiqṭol* forms: וָאֲצַו "I commanded" (Deut 3:18) vs. וָאֲצַוֶּה (Deut 1:18); וָאַ֫עַל "I offered up" (Num 23:4) vs. וָאַעֲלֶה "I offered up" (1 Sam 13:12); וָאֵרָא "I was seen" (Exod 6:3).

3fp	תַּעֲשֶׂינָה	*תְּעַשֶּׂינָה	*תַּעֲשֶׂינָה	תֵּעָשֶׂינָה	*תְּעֻשֶּׂינָה	*תָּעֳשֶׂינָה
2mp	תַּעֲשׂוּ	*תְּעַשּׂוּ	*תַּעֲשׂוּ	*תֵּעָשׂוּ	*תְּעֻשּׂוּ	*תָּעֳשׂוּ
2fp	תַּעֲשֶׂינָה	*תְּעַשֶּׂינָה	*תַּעֲשֶׂינָה	*תֵּעָשֶׂינָה	*תְּעֻשֶּׂינָה	*תָּעֳשֶׂינָה
1cp	נַעֲשֶׂה	*נְעַשֶּׂה	*נַעֲשֶׂה	*נֵעָשֶׂה	*נְעֻשֶּׂה	*נָעֳשֶׂה

Short-*yiqṭol and wayyiqṭol*

3ms	יַ֫עַשׂ	*יְעַשׂ	*יַ֫עַשׂ	*יֵעָשׂ
3fs	*תַּ֫עַשׂ	*תְּעַשׂ	*תַּ֫עַשׂ	תֵּעָשׂ
2ms	תַּ֫עַשׂ	*תְּעַשׂ	*תַּ֫עַשׂ	*תֵּעָשׂ
1cs	וָאַ֫עַשׂ	וָאֲעַשׂ	*וָאַ֫עַשׂ	*וָאֵעָשׂ
1cp	וַנַּ֫עַשׂ	*נְעַשׂ	*נַ֫עַשׂ	*וַנֵּעָשׂ

Imperative

	qal	*piel*	*hiphil*	*niphal*	*pual*	*hophal*
ms	עֲשֵׂה	*עַשֵּׂה	*הַעֲשֵׂה	*הֵעָשֶׂה		
fs	עֲשִׂי	*עַשִּׂי	*הַעֲשִׂי	*הֵעָשִׂי		
mp	עֲשׂוּ	*עַשּׂוּ	*הַעֲשׂוּ	*הֵעָשׂוּ		
fp	*עֲשֶׂינָה	*עַשֶּׂינָה	*הַעֲשֶׂינָה	*הֵעָשֶׂינָה		

Infinitives

	qal	*piel*	*hiphil*	*niphal*	*pual*	*hophal*
const.	עֲשׂוֹת	*עַשּׂוֹת	*הַעֲשׂוֹת	הֵעָשׂוֹת	*עֻשּׂוֹת	
abs.	עָשֹׂה	*עַשֵּׂה	*הַעֲשֵׂה	*הֵעָשֹׂה		

Participles

ms	עֹשֶׂה	*מְעַשֶּׂה	*מַעֲשֶׂה	נַעֲשֶׂה	*מְעֻשֶּׂה	*מָעֳשֶׂה
fs	עֹשָׂה	*מְעַשָּׂה	*מַעֲשָׂה	*נַעֲשָׂה	*מְעֻשָּׂה	*מָעֳשָׂה
mp	עֹשִׂים	*מְעַשִּׂים	*מַעֲשִׂים	נַעֲשִׂים	*מְעֻשִּׂים	*מָעֳשִׂים
fp	עֹשׂוֹת	*מְעַשּׂוֹת	*מַעֲשׂוֹת	נַעֲשׂוֹת	*מְעֻשּׂוֹת	*מָעֳשׂוֹת

Table 6.28. *Qal*, *Hiphil*, and *Niphal* of I-, II-, and III-*Vav*/*Yod* Roots[46]

	I-*vav*/*yod*: ישב "to dwell"			II-*vav*: שוב "to return"		III-*vav*/*yod*: שבה "to capture"	
				qåṭal			
	qal	*hiphil*	*niphal*	*qal*	*hiphil*	*qal*	*niphal*
3ms	יָשַׁב	הֹשִׁיב	*נוֹשַׁב	שָׁב	הֵשִׁיב	שָׁבָה	נִשְׁבָּה
3fs	יָשְׁבָה	*הוֹשִׁ֫יבָה	נוֹשְׁבָה	שָׁ֫בָה	*הֵשִׁ֫יבָה	*שָׁבְתָה	*נִשְׁבְּתָה
2ms	יָשַׁ֫בְתָּ	*הוֹשַׁ֫בְתָּ	*נוֹשַׁ֫בְתָּ	שַׁ֫בְתָּ	הֲשִׁבֹ֫תָ	שָׁבִ֫יתָ	*נִשְׁבֵּ֫יתָ
2fs	יָשַׁבְתְּ	*הוֹשַׁבְתְּ	*נוֹשַׁבְתְּ	*שַׁ֫בְתְּ	—	*שָׁבִית	*נִשְׁבֵּית
1cs	יָשַׁ֫בְתִּי	הוֹשַׁ֫בְתִּי	*נוֹשַׁ֫בְתִּי	שַׁ֫בְתִּי	הֲשִׁבֹ֫תִי	*שָׁבִ֫יתִי	*נִשְׁבֵּ֫יתִי
3cp	יָשְׁבוּ	הֹשִׁ֫יבוּ	נוֹשְׁבוּ	שָׁ֫בוּ	הֵשִׁ֫יבוּ	שָׁבוּ	נִשְׁבּוּ
2mp	יְשַׁבְתֶּם	*הוֹשַׁבְתֶּם	*נוֹשַׁבְתֶּם	שַׁבְתֶּם	הֲשֵׁבֹתֶם	שְׁבִיתֶם	*נִשְׁבֵּיתֶם
2fp	*יְשַׁבְתֶּן	*הוֹשַׁבְתֶּן	*נוֹשַׁבְתֶּן	*שַׁבְתֶּן	*הֲשֵׁבֹתֶן	*שְׁבִיתֶן	*נִשְׁבֵּיתֶן
1cp	יָשַׁ֫בְנוּ	*הוֹשַׁ֫בְנוּ	*נוֹשַׁ֫בְנוּ	שַׁ֫בְנוּ	הֱשִׁיבֹ֫נוּ	*שָׁבִ֫ינוּ	*נִשְׁבֵּ֫ינוּ

				yiqṭol			
	qal	*hiphil*	*niphal*	*qal*	*hiphil*	*qal*	*niphal*
3ms	יֵשֵׁב	*יוֹשִׁיב	*יִוָּשֵׁב	יָשׁוּב	יָשִׁיב	*יִשְׁבֶּה	*יִשָּׁבֶה
3fs	תֵּשֵׁב	*תּוֹשִׁיב	*תִּוָּשֵׁב	תָּשׁוּב	תָּשִׁיב	*תִּשְׁבֶּה	*תִּשָּׁבֶה
2ms	תֵּשֵׁב	תּוֹשִׁיב	*תִּוָּשֵׁב	תָּשׁוּב	תָּשִׁיב	*תִּשְׁבֶּה	*תִּשָּׁבֶה
2fs	תֵּשְׁבִי	*תּוֹשִׁ֫יבִי	*תִּוָּשְׁבִי	*תָּשׁ֫וּבִי	תָּשִׁ֫בִי	*תִּשְׁבִּי	*תִּשָּׁבִי
1cs	אֵשֵׁב	*אוֹשִׁיב	*אִוָּשֵׁב	אָשׁוּב	אָשִׁיב	*אֶשְׁבֶּה	*אִשָּׁבֶה
3mp	יֵשְׁבוּ	יוֹשִׁ֫יבוּ	*יִוָּשְׁבוּ	יָשׁ֫וּבוּ	יָשִׁ֫יבוּ	*יִשְׁבּוּ	*יִשָּׁבוּ
3fp	תֵּשַׁ֫בְנָה	—	—	תָּשֹׁ֫בְןָ	תָּשֵׁבְנָה	*תִּשְׁבֶּ֫ינָה	*תִּשָּׁבֶ֫ינָה
2mp	תֵּשְׁבוּ	*תּוֹשִׁ֫יבוּ	*תִּוָּשְׁבוּ	תָּשׁ֫וּבוּ	תָּשִׁ֫יבוּ	*תִּשְׁבּוּ	*תִּשָּׁבוּ

46. The table is supplemented by the following forms: צְאֶ֫ינָה "go forth" (Song 3:11); יֹסֵף "may he do it again" (Gen 30:24); אֹסֵף "I will do it again" (Deut 18:16); הוֹכֵחַ "reproving" (Lev 19:17); יִוָּלֵד "it will be born" (Lev 22:27); הִוָּשְׁעוּ "be saved!" (Isa 45:22); בְּהִוָּלֶד לוֹ "when he was born to him" (Gen 21:5); אָסֵף "I bring to an end" (Zeph 1:2); וַיִּשְׁבּוּ "they captured" (Num 31:9); וּשֲׁבֵה "and capture!" (Judg 5:12).

2fp	*תֵּשַׁבְנָה	—	—	תְּשֻׁבֶ֫ינָה	*תָּשֵׁבְנָה	*תִּשְׁבֶ֫ינָה	*תִּשָּׁבֶ֫ינָה
1cp	נֵשֵׁב	*נוֹשִׁיב	*נִוָּשֵׁב	נָשׁוּב	נָשִׁיב	*נִשְׁבֶּה	*נִשָּׁבֶה

Short-*yiqṭol*

	qal	*hiphil*	*niphal*	*qal*	*hiphil*	*qal*	*niphal*
3ms		*יֹשֵׁב		יָשֹׁב	יָשֵׁב	—	*יִשָּׁב
3fs		*תֹּשֵׁב		תָּשֹׁב	*תָּשֵׁב	—	*תִּשָּׁב
2ms		*תֹּשֵׁב		תָּשֹׁב	תָּשֵׁב	—	*תִּשָּׁב
1cs		*אֹשֵׁב				—	*אִשָּׁב
1cp		*נֹשֵׁב				—	*נִשָּׁב

wayyiqṭol

3ms	וַיֵּ֫שֶׁב	וַיּ֫וֹשֶׁב		וַיָּ֫שָׁב	וַיָּ֫שֶׁב	וַיִּ֫שְׁבְּ	*וַיִּשָּׁב

Imperative

	qal	*hiphil*	*niphal*	*qal*	*hiphil*	*qal*	*niphal*
ms	שֵׁב	הוֹשֵׁב	*הִוָּשֵׁב	שׁוּב	הָשֵׁב	*שְׁבֵה	*הִשָּׁבֵה
fs	שְׁבִי	*הוֹשִׁ֫יבִי	*הִוָּשְׁבִי	שׁ֫וּבִי	*הָשִׁ֫יבִי	*שְׁבִי	*הִשָּׁבִי
mp	שְׁבוּ	הוֹשִׁ֫יבוּ	הִוָּשְׁבוּ	שׁ֫וּבוּ	הָשִׁ֫יבוּ	*שְׁבוּ	*הִשָּׁבוּ
fp	*שֵׁ֫בְנָה	—	—	שֹׁ֫בְנָה	—	*שְׁבֶ֫ינָה	*הִשָּׁבֶ֫ינָה

Infinitives

	qal	*hiphil*	*niphal*	*qal*	*hiphil*	*qal*	*niphal*
const.	שֶׁ֫בֶת	הוֹשִׁיב	*הִוָּ֫שֵׁב	שׁוּב	הָשִׁיב	שְׁבוֹת	*הִשָּׁבוֹת
abs.	יָשֹׁב	*הוֹשֵׁב	—	שׁוֹב	הָשֵׁב	*שָׁבֹה	*הִשָּׁבֵה

Participles

ms	יֹשֵׁב	מוֹשִׁיב	*נוֹשָׁב	שָׁב	מֵשִׁיב	*שֹׁבֶה	*נִשְׁבֶּה
fs	יֹשֶׁ֫בֶת	*מוֹשֶׁ֫בֶת	נוֹשֶׁ֫בֶת	שָׁבָה	מְשִׁיבָה	*שֹׁבָה	*נִשְׁבָּה
mp	יֹשְׁבִים	*מוֹשִׁבִים	*נוֹשָׁבִים	שָׁבִים	מְשִׁבִים	שֹׁבִים	*נִשְׁבִּים
fp	יֹשְׁבוֹת	*מוֹשִׁיבוֹת	נוֹשָׁבוֹת	*שָׁבוֹת	*מְשִׁיבוֹת	*שֹׁבוֹת	*נִשְׁבּוֹת

Table 6.29. Verb Forms of Geminate Roots: סבב "to Go Around" and חמם "to Be Hot"[47]

	סבב	חמם	סבב		
			qåṭal		
	qal	*qal*-stative	*niphal*	*hiphil*	*hophal*
3ms	סָבָב	חַם	נָסַב	הֵסֵב	*הוּסַב
3fs	סָבְבָה	*חַמָּה	נָסֵ֫בָּה	*הֵסַ֫בָּה	*הוּסַ֫בָּה
2ms	*סַבֹּ֫תָ	*חַמֹּ֫תָ	—	הֲסִבֹּ֫תָ	—
2fs	*סַבֹּ֫ת	*חַמֹּת	—	*הֲסִבֹּת	—
1cs	סַבֹּ֫תִי	חַמֹּ֫וֹתִי	—	הֲסִבֹּ֫תִי	—
3cp	סָבְבוּ	*חַמּוּ	נָסַ֫בּוּ	הֵסַ֫בּוּ	הוּסַ֫בּוּ
2mp	סַבֹּתֶם	*חַמֹּתֶם	*נְסַבֹּתֶם	*הֲסִבֹּתֶם	—
2fp	*סַבֹּתֶן	*חַמֹּתֶן	*נְסַבֹּתֶן	*הֲסִבֹּתֶן	—
1cp	*סַבֹּ֫נוּ	*חַמֹּ֫נוּ	—	—	—

47. The table is supplemented by the following forms: דַּ֫לּוֹנוּ "we are brought low" (Ps 79:8); קֹב "cursing" (Num 23:25 [*qal* inf. abs.]); שָׁדוֹד "destroying" (Mic 2:4); שֹׁגֶ֫גֶת "one who errs" (Num 15:28); קַ֫לּוֹתָ "you are insignificant" (Nah 1:14); יִדְּמוּ "they will be silent" (Ps 31:18); וַיִּתְּמוּ "they were complete" (Deut 34:8); וַיֵּ֫צֶר "it was distressing" (Judg 2:15); וּנְמַקֹּתֶם "and you will pine away" (Ezek 24:23); תִּמַּק "it will rot" (Zech 14:12 [*niph.*]); תִּמַּקְנָה "they will rot" (Zech 14:12); הִבּוֹק "being destroyed"(Isa 24:3 [*niph*. inf. abs.]); נָבָר "one pure" (2 Sam 22:27 [*niph*. ptc.]); נְשַׁ֫מָּה "that which is desolate" (Ezek 36:34); נְמַקִּים "rotten" (Ezek 33:10); נְשַׁמּוֹת "desolated" (Ezek 30:7); וַהֲדִקּוֹת "you will crush" (Mic 4:13); הֲרֵעֹתֶם "you have done bad" (Jer 16:12); תָּסֵךְ "you will cover" (Ps 5:12 [*hiphil yiqṭol*]); אָחֵל "I will begin" (Josh 3:7); יָהֵ֫לּוּ "they will make shine" (Isa 13:10); יָ֫סֶךְ "it covered" (Ps 91:4 [*hiphil* short-*yiqṭol*]); תָּ֫הֶל "it shone" (Job 41:10); הָבֵ֫רוּ "sharpen!" (Jer 51:11); הָתֵם "completing" (Ezek 24:10 [*hiphil* inf. abs.]); מְסִבָּי "those surrounding me" (Ps 140:10); מְצֵרָה "who is in labor" (Jer 49:22); מְרֵעִים "those doing evil" (Isa 1:4); יָתֵם "he will complete" (2 Kgs 22:4); וַיַּכְּתוּ "they thrashed" (Deut 1:44); הוּתַל "it was deceived" (Isa 44:20); הוּחַ֫דָּה "it was sharpened" (Ezek 21:14).

yiqṭol

	qal active	*qal* active Aramaic-like	*qal* stative	*qal* stative Aramaic-like	*niphal*	*hiphil*	*hiphil* Aramaic-like	*hophal*
3ms	יָסֹב	יִסֹּב	יֵחַם	יִחַם	*יִסַּב	*יָסֵב	*יַסֵּב	יוּסַב
3fs	*תָּסֹב	תִּסֹּב	—	—	*תִּסַּב	*תָּסֵב	*תַּסֵּב	*תּוּסַב
2ms	*תָּסֹב	תִּסֹּב	—	—	*תִּסַּב	*תָּסֵב	*תַּסֵּב	*תּוּסַב
2fs	*תָּסֹבִּי	*תִּסְּבִי	—	—	—	—	—	—
1cs	*אָסֹב	*אֶסֹּב	—	—	—	—	—	—
3mp	יָסֹבּוּ	*יִסְּבוּ	יֵחַמּוּ	*יִחֲמוּ	יִסַּבּוּ	*יָסֵבּוּ[48]	*יַסְּבוּ	—[49]
3fp	תְּסֻבֶּינָה	—	—	—	*תִּסַּבְנָה	—	—	—
2mp	תָּסֹבּוּ	*תִּסְּבוּ	—	—	*תִּסַּבּוּ	*תָּסֵבּוּ	*תַּסְּבוּ	—
2fp	*תְּסֻבֶּינָה	—	—	—	*תִּסַּבְנָה	—	—	—
1cp	*נָסֹב	*נִסֹּב	—	—	—	נָסֵב	—	—

Short-*yiqṭol and wayyiqṭol*

	qal	*qal*	*hiphil*
3ms	וַיָּסָב	*וַיֵּחַם	*יָסֵב
3fs	*וַתָּסָב	—	*תָּסֵב
2ms	*וַתָּסָב	—	*תָּסֵב
1cs	—	—	—
1cp	וַנָּסָב	—	—

48. Note also the combination of Hebrew and Aramaic patterns: וַיַּסֵּבּוּ "they made go around" (1 Sam 5:8).

49. Note again the combination of Hebrew and Aramaic patterns: יֻכַּתּוּ "they were beaten" (Mic 1:7).

Imperative

	qal	*niphal*	*hiphil*
ms	סֹב		הָסֵב
fs	סֹ֫בִּי		הָסֵ֫בִּי
mp	סֹ֫בּוּ		*הָסֵ֫בּוּ
fp	—		—

Infinitives

const.	סֹב and סְבֹב	—	הָסֵב
abs.	*סֹב and *סָבֹב	הִסֹּב	*הָסֵב

Participles

	qal	*niphal*	*hiphil*	*hophal*
ms	סֹבֵב	*נָסָב	מֵסֵב	*מוּסָב
fs	*סֹבֶ֫בֶת	*נְסַבָּה	*מְסִבָּה	*מוּסַבָּה
mp	סֹבְבִים	*נְסַבִּים	*מְסִבִּים	*מוּסַבִּים
fp	*סֹבְבוֹת	*נְסַבּוֹת	*מְסִבּוֹת	מוּסַבּוֹת

Table 6.30. Third Masculine Singular or Unconjugated *Qal* Verb Forms with Possessive Suffixes[50]

	qåṭal 3ms	inf. cons.	impv. ms	ptc.	*qåṭal* 3ms	inf. cons.	impv. ms
	**šamara*	**šumur*	**š[u]mur*	**šāmir*	**šamaʿa*	**š[u]muʿ*	**š[a]maʿ*
suffix	שָׁמַר	שְׁמֹר	שְׁמֹר	שֹׁמֵר	שָׁמַע	שְׁמֹע	שְׁמַע
+1cs	שְׁמָרַ֫נִי	שָׁמְרִי	שָׁמְרֵ֫נִי	*שֹׁמְרִי	*שְׁמָעַ֫נִי	שָׁמְעִי	שְׁמָעֵ֫נִי
+2ms	*שְׁמָרְךָ	שָׁמְרְךָ		*שֹׁמֶרְךָ	*שְׁמָעֲךָ	שָׁמְעֲךָ	
+2fs	*שְׁמָרֵךְ	*שָׁמְרֵךְ		*שֹׁמְרֵךְ	*שְׁמָעֵךְ	*שָׁמְעֵךְ	
+3ms	שְׁמָרוֹ	שָׁמְרוֹ	*שָׁמְרֵ֫הוּ	*שֹׁמְרוֹ	*שְׁמָעוֹ	שָׁמְעוֹ	*שְׁמָעֵ֫הוּ
+3fs	שְׁמָרָהּ	שָׁמְרָהּ	*שָׁמְרָהּ	*שֹׁמְרָהּ	*שְׁמָעָהּ	*שָׁמְעָהּ	
+1cp	*שְׁמָרָ֫נוּ	*שָׁמְרֵ֫נוּ	*שָׁמְרֵ֫נוּ	*שֹׁמְרֵ֫נוּ	*שְׁמָעָ֫נוּ	*שָׁמְעֵ֫נוּ	שְׁמָעֵ֫נוּ
+2mp	—	*שָׁמְרְכֶם		*שֹׁמֶרְכֶם	—	שָׁמְעֲכֶם	
+2fp	—	*שָׁמְרְכֶן		*שֹׁמֶרְכֶן	—	*שָׁמְעֲכֶן	
+3mp	*שְׁמָרָם	שָׁמְרָם	שָׁמְרֵם	*שֹׁמְרָם	*שְׁמָעָם	שָׁמְעָם	*שְׁמָעֵם
+3fp	*שְׁמָרָן	*שָׁמְרָן	*שָׁמְרֵן	*שֹׁמְרָן	*שְׁמָעָן	*שָׁמְעָן	*שְׁמָעֵן
cf. long impv., ms only			שָׁמְרָה				שִׁמְעָה

50. The table is supplemented by the following forms: שְׁפָטְךָ "he judged you"; שְׁבָרֵךְ "he broke you"; נְטָשָׁ֫נוּ "he forsook us"; מְכָרָם "he sold them"; עָזְבֵךְ "your leaving"; אֲכָלְכֶם "your eating"; עָבְדֵ֫הוּ "serve him!"; לָכְדָהּ "capture her!"; עָזְרֵ֫נוּ "help us!"; מֹצְאִי "one finding me"; נֹתֶנְךָ "one who gives you"; גֹּאֲלֵ֫ךְ "one redeeming you"; מֹשְׁלוֹ "his ruler"; שֹׁמְעָהּ "one hearing her"; יֹצְרֵ֫נוּ "our creator"; גֹּאַלְכֶם "one redeeming you"; נֹתְשָׁם "one who uproots them"; מְנָעַ֫נִי "he withheld me"; מְנָעֲךָ "he withheld you"; שְׁלָחֵךְ "he sent you"; יְדָעוֹ "he knew him"; יְדָעָהּ "he knew her"; יְדָעָ֫נוּ "he knew us"; לְקָחָ֫ם "he took them"; בְּקָעֵ֫הוּ "split it!"; קְרָאֶ֫נָה "call her!"; כְּלָאֵם "restrain them!" Note also these unusual forms of the inf. const. with 2ms/p suffix: אָסְפְּךָ "your gathering"; אָסְפְּכֶם "your gathering"; קֻצְרְכֶם "your reaping"; מֹצַאֲכֶם "your finding."

Table 6.31. Third Masculine Plural *Qal* with Possessive Suffixes[51]

	qåṭal 3cp	impv. mp	*qåṭal* 3cp	impv. mp
	**šamarū*	**š[u]murū*	**šamaʿū*	**š[u]murū*
	שָׁמְרוּ	שִׁמְרוּ	שָׁמְעוּ	שִׁמְעוּ
+1cs	*שְׁמָר֫וּנִי	*שִׁמְר֫וּנִי	*שְׁמָע֫וּנִי	שְׁמָע֫וּנִי
+2ms	*שְׁמָר֫וּךָ		*שְׁמָע֫וּךָ	
+2fs	*שְׁמָרוּךְ		*שְׁמָעוּךְ	
+3ms	*שְׁמָר֫וּהוּ	*שִׁמְר֫וּהוּ	*שְׁמָע֫וּהוּ	*שְׁמָע֫וּהוּ
+3fs	*שְׁמָר֫וּהָ	*שִׁמְר֫וּהָ	*שְׁמָע֫וּהָ	*שְׁמָע֫וּהָ
+1cp	*שְׁמָר֫וּנוּ	*שִׁמְר֫וּנוּ	*שְׁמָע֫וּנוּ	שְׁמָע֫וּנוּ
+2mp	—		—	
+2fp	—		—	
+3mp	*שְׁמָרוּם	*שִׁמְרוּם	*שְׁמָעוּם	—
+3fp	*שְׁמָרוּן	*שִׁמְרוּן	*שְׁמָעוּן	—

Table 6.32. Third Masculine Singular or Unconjugated *Qal* of עשׂה with Possessive Suffixes[52]

	qåṭal 3ms	inf. cons./*qal*-impv. ms		ptc.
	עָשָׂה	עֲשׂוֹת	עֲשֵׂה	עֹשֶׂה
+1cs	עָשָׂ֫נִי	עֲשֹׂתִי	*עֲשֵׂ֫נִי	עֹשֵׂ֫נִי
+2ms	עָשְׂךָ	עֲשׂוֹתְךָ		עֹשֶׂ֫ךָ
+2fs	—	עֲשׂוֹתֵךְ		*עֹשֵׂךְ

51. The table is supplemented by the following forms: הֲרָג֫וּנִי "they killed me"; עֲבָד֫וּךָ "they serve you"; שְׁפָטוּךְ "they judged you"; עֲבָד֫וּהוּ "they served him"; חֲפָר֫וּהָ "they dug it"; עֲבָדוּם "they served them"; עִזְרֻ֫נִי "help me!"; אִכְל֫וּהוּ "eat it!"; אִכְל֫וּהָ "eat it!"; תִּפְשׂוּם "seize them!"; יְדָעוּךְ "they knew you"; יְדָעוּם "they knew them"; בְּלָע֫וּנוּ "they swallowed us"; קְרָאֻ֫הוּ "call him!"; סְחָר֫וּהָ "trade it!"

52. The historical reconstruction of the verb is complex. The table is supplemented by the following forms: רָאָהּ "he saw her"; חֲנֹתֵ֫נוּ "our camping"; עֲנֵ֫נִי "answer me!"; עֲנֵ֫נוּ "answer us!"; רְעֵם "shepherd them!"; for the forms of עֹשֶׂה see table 6.27 above.

+3ms	עָשָׂהוּ	עֲשׂתוֹ	—	עֹשֵׂהוּ
+3fs	*עָשָׂהּ	עֲשׂתָהּ	—	עֹשָׂהּ
+1cp	עָשָׂנוּ	*עֲשׂוֹתֵנוּ	*עֲשֵׂנוּ	עֹשֵׂנוּ
+2mp	—	עֲשׂתְכֶם		—
+2fp	—	*עֲשׂתְכֶן		—
+3mp	עָשָׂם	עֲשׂתָם	—	*עֹשָׂם
+3fp	*עָשָׂן	*עֲשׂתָן	—	*עֹשָׂן

Table 6.33. Third Feminine Singular, Second Masculine Singular, Second Feminine Singular, and First Common Singular *Qal* with Possessive Suffixes[53]

	3fs	2ms	2fs	1cs
	**šamarat*	**šamarta*	**šamarti*	**šamartu*
	שָׁמְרָה	שָׁמַרְתָּ	*שָׁמַרְתְּ	שָׁמַרְתִּי
+1cs	*שְׁמָרַתְנִי	שְׁמַרְתַּנִי	*שְׁמַרְתִּנִי	*שְׁמַרְתִּנִי
+2ms	*שְׁמָרַתְךָ	*שְׁמַרְתְּךָ	*שְׁמַרְתִּיךָ	שְׁמַרְתִּיךָ
+2fs	*שְׁמָרַתֶךְ	*שְׁמַרְתֵּךְ	*שְׁמַרְתִּיךְ	*שְׁמַרְתִּיךְ
+3ms	*שְׁמָרַתְהוּ / *שְׁמָרַתּוּ	*שְׁמַרְתּוֹ	*שְׁמַרְתִּיהוּ	*שְׁמַרְתִּיהוּ
+3fs	*שְׁמָרַתָה	*שְׁמַרְתָּהּ	*שְׁמַרְתִּיהָ	*שְׁמַרְתִּיהָ
+1cp	*שְׁמָרַתְנוּ	*שְׁמַרְתָּנוּ	—	—
+2mp	—	—	—	—
+2fp	—	—	—	—
+3mp	*שְׁמָרַתַם	*שְׁמַרְתָּם	*שְׁמַרְתִּים	*שְׁמַרְתִּים
+3fp	*שְׁמָרַתַן	*שְׁמַרְתָּן	*שְׁמַרְתִּין	*שְׁמַרְתִּין

53. The table is supplemented by the following forms: יְלָדַתְנִי "she bore me"; יְלָדַתְךָ "she bore you"; אֲהֵבַתֶךְ "she loves you"; יְלָדַתּוּ "she bore him" and אֲכָלַתְהוּ "she ate him"; אֲחָזַתָּה "she held her"; מְצָאַתְנוּ "she found us"; אֲכָלָתַם "she ate them"; יְדַעְתּוֹ "you know him"; נְטַשְׁתָּהּ "you abandoned her"; עֲבַדְתָּם "you served them"; יְלִדְתִּנִי "you bore me"; נְתַתִּיהוּ "you gave him"; מְצָאתִים "you found them"; עֲזַרְתִּיךָ "I helped you"; נְתַתִּיו "I gave him"; נְתַתִּיהָ "I gave her"; עֲזַבְתִּים "I abandoned them."

Table 6.34. Third Masculine Singular *Qal Yiqṭol* Energic and Nonenergic Verb Forms[54]

	3ms **yašmuru*	3ms **yašmuran*	3ms **yišmaʿu*	3ms **yišmaʿan*	3ms **yantinu*	3ms **yantinan*
	יִשְׁמֹר	—	יִשְׁמַע	—	יִתֵּן	—
+1cs	יִשְׁמְרֵ֫נִי	*יִשְׁמְרַ֫נִּי	יִשְׁמָעֵ֫נִי	*יִשְׁמָעַ֫נִּי	יִתְּנֵ֫נִי	—
+2ms	יִשְׁמָרְךָ	*יִשְׁמְרֶ֫ךָּ	*יִשְׁמָעֲךָ	יִשְׁמָעֶ֫ךָּ	יִתֶּנְךָ	—
+2fs	*יִשְׁמְרֵךְ	—	*יִשְׁמָעֵךְ	—	*יִתְּנֵךְ	—
+3ms	יִשְׁמְרֵ֫הוּ	יִשְׁמְרֶ֫נּוּ	*יִשְׁמָעֵ֫הוּ	*יִשְׁמָעֶ֫נּוּ	*יִתְּנֵ֫הוּ	יִתְּנֶ֫נּוּ
+3fs	*יִשְׁמְרֶ֫הָ	*יִשְׁמְרֶ֫נָּה	*יִשְׁמָעֶ֫הָ	*יִשְׁמָעֶ֫נָּה	*יִתְּנָהּ	יִתְּנֶ֫נָּה
+1cp	יִשְׁמְרֵ֫נוּ	—	*יִשְׁמָעֵ֫נוּ	—	*יִתְּנֵ֫נוּ	—
+2mp	—	—	—	—	—	—
+2fp	—	—	—	—	—	—
+3mp	*יִשְׁמְרֵם	—	*יִשְׁמָעֵם	—	יִתְּנֵם	—
+3fp	*יִשְׁמְרֵן	—	*יִשְׁמָעֵן	—	*יִתְּנֵן	—

54. For the verbs שמר and שמע, I cite the *wayyiqṭol* form (without conjunction) when the *yiqṭol* form is lacking. Some forms listed that are nonenergic may, in fact, be short-*yiqṭol* forms (as in יִשְׁמְרֵ֫נִי Job 29:2). The table is further supplemented by the following forms: תֹּאכְלֵךְ "she will eat you"; יַעְזְרֶ֫הָ "he will help her"; תִּשְׁמְרֵם "you will guard them"; תְּבָרֲכֵ֫נִי "she will bless me" (*piel*); תִּשְׁמְרֶ֫ךָּ "she will guard you"; אֶשְׁמְרֶ֫נָּה "I will guard her"; יִשְׂבָּעֶךָּ "he will weary you"; יִגְאָלֵ֫ךְ "he will redeem you"; יִמְצָאֵ֫הוּ "he will find him"; יִקְרָעֶ֫הָ "he will tear her"; יִפְגָּעֵ֫נוּ "he will meet us"; יִרְפָּאֵם "he will heal them"; יִקְרָאֶ֫נּוּ "he will call him"; נִשְׁמָעֶ֫נָּה "we will hear her"; תִּתְּנֵ֫הוּ "may you [not] give him"; תִּתְּנֵ֫נוּ "you gave us"; וַתִּתְּנָהּ "you gave it"; תִּשְׁבֵּ֫ךָ "she will capture you"; תַּעֲשֶׂ֫נּוּ "you will make it." Note also: יִשְׁמְרֶ֫ךָּ "he will guard you" (pausal); יַעְכָּרְךָ "he will trouble you"; אֶזְכְּרֵ֫כִי "I will remember you"; תִּשְׁמוּרֵם "she will guard them."

Table 6.35. The Verbs ראה "to See" and ירא "to Fear"

	ראה			ירא	
			qåṭal		
	qal	*hiphil*	*niphal*	*qal*	*niphal*
3ms	רָאָה	הֶרְאָה	נִרְאָה	יָרֵא	—
3fs	רָאֲתָה	—	נִרְאֲתָה	יָרְאָה	—
2ms	רָאִ֫יתָ	הִרְאִ֫יתָה	—	יָרֵ֫אתָ	—
			yiqṭol		
3ms	יִרְאֶה	יַרְאֶה	יֵרָאֶה	יִירָא	יִוָּרֵא
3mp	יִרְאוּ	יַרְאוּ	יֵרָאוּ	יִירְאוּ/יָֽרְאוּ	יִוָּרְאוּ
			short-*yiqṭol*		
3ms	יֵ֫רֶא	—	יֵרָא	—	—
			wayyiqṭol		
3ms	וַיַּרְא	וַיַּרְא	וַיֵּרָא	וַיִּירָא	—
			Imperative		
ms	רְאֵה	הַרְאֵה	הֵרָאֵה	יְרָא	—
			Infinitives		
const.	רְאוֹת	הַרְאוֹת	הֵרָאוֹת	יִרְאָה	—
abs.	רָאֹה	—	—	—	—
			Participles		
ms	רֹאֶה	מַרְאֶה	נִרְאֶה	יָרֵא	נוֹרָא

Table 6.36. The Verbs רעע "to Be Evil"; רעה "to Graze, Shepherd"; and רוע "to Shout"[55]

	רעע		רעה	רוע
		qåṭal		
	qal	*hiphil*	*qal*	*hiphil*
3ms	רַע	הֵרַע	רָעָה	*הֵרִיעַ
3fs	רָעָה	*הֵרֵ֫עָה	*רָעֲתָה	*הֵרִ֫יעָה
2ms	—	הֲרֵעֹ֫תָ	*רָעִ֫יתָ	*הֲרִיעֹ֫תָ
		yiqṭol		
3ms	יֵרַע	יָרֵעַ	יִרְעֶה	יָרִיעַ
3mp	יֵרְעוּ	יָרֵ֫עוּ	יִרְעוּ	יָרִ֫יעוּ
		Short-*yiqṭol*		
3ms	—	—	יֵ֫רַע	—
		wayyiqṭol		
3ms	וַיֵּ֫רַע	וַיָּ֫רַע	*וַיֵּ֫רַע	וַיָּ֫רַע
		Imperative		
ms	—	*הָרַע	רְעֵה	הָרֵעַ
		Infinitives		
const.	—	הָרַע	רְעוֹת	הָרִיעַ
abs.	—	הָרֵעַ	*רָעֹה	—
		Participles		
ms	—	מֵרַע	רֹעֶה	*מֵרִיעַ

55. The table is supplemented by these forms: הֵחֵ֫לָּה "she began"; הָשַׁע "smear over!"; רָאֲתָה "she saw"; רָאִ֫יתָ "you saw"; רָאֹה "seeing"; הֵנִיחַ "he caused to rest"; הֵרִ֫יעוּ "they shouted"; הֲנִעֹ֫ותִי "I shook"; הָסֵר "turn back!"; מֵסִיר "one who turns back."

Table 6.37. The Verbs חלל "to Defile, Begin"; חלה "to Be Sick"; חיל and חול "to Writhe"; and נחל "to Inherit"[56]

	חלל			חלה			חיל / חול	נחל	
					qåṭal				
	piel	*hiphil*	*niphal*	*qal*	*piel*	*niphal*	*qal*	*qal*	*piel*
3ms	חִלֵּל	הֵחֵל	נִחַל	חָלָה	חִלָּה	*נַחְלָה	*חָל	נָחַל	נִחַל
3fs	חִלְּלָה	הֵחֵ֫לָּה	*נִחֲלָה	*חָלְתָה	*חִלְּתָה	—	חָ֫לָה	*נָחֲלָה	*נִחֲלָה
2ms	חִלַּ֫לְתָּ	הַחִלֹּ֫תָ	*נִחַ֫לְתָּ	*חָלִ֫יתָ	*חִלִּ֫יתָ	נֶחֱלֵ֫יתָ	*חַ֫לְתָּ	נָחַ֫לְתָּ	—
					yiqṭol				
3ms	יְחַלֵּל	יָחֵל	*יֵחַל	—	*יְחַלֶּה	—	יָחוּל / יָחִיל	יִנְחַל	—
3mp	יְחַלְּלוּ	יָחֵ֫לּוּ	*יֵחַ֫לּוּ	—	יְחַלּוּ	—	יָחֻ֫לוּ / יָחִילוּ	יִנְחֲלוּ	—
					wayyiqṭol				
3ms		וַיָּ֫חֶל	*וַיֵּחַל	וַיָּ֫חַל	וַיְחַל	—	*וַיָּ֫חָל / וַיָּ֫חֶל	—	—
					Imperative				
ms	—	הָחֵל	—	—	חַל	—	*חִיל	—	—
					Infinitives				
const.	חַלֵּל	הָחֵל	הֵחֵל	*חֲלוֹת	חַלּוֹת	—	חוּל	נְחֹל	נַחֵל
abs.	—	הָחֵל	—	—	—	—	—	—	—
					Participles				
ms	מְחַלֵּל	מֵחֵל	—	חֹלֶה	—	*נַחְלֶה	—	—	—

56. The table is supplemented by the following forms: חִלְּלוּ "they profaned"; נִחָל "it was profaned" (pausal); נִחֲלוּ "they were profaned"; נִחַלְתְּ "you were profaned"; יֵחָל "it will be profaned" (pausal); יִשַּׁסוּ "they will be plundered"; וְאֵחַל "I am profaned"; חָלִית "you were sick"; חֲלֹתוֹ "his being sick"; חִלִּ֫יתִי "I entreat"; נַחְלָה "what is sick" [*niphal* ptc. fem. sg.]; נֶחֱלֵ֫יתִי "I was sick"; חַ֫לְתִּי "I writhed"; וַתָּחֹל "it writhed" (pausal); חִ֫ילוּ "writhe"; נָחֲלוּ "they inherited"; נִחֲלוּ "they distributed."

Appendix
Producing Nominal and Verbal Forms

Producing Nominal Forms

The noun has four basic forms, differentiated based on endings and the sequence of vowels in the noun's stem: absolute singular, absolute plural, construct singular, and construct plural. The sequence of vowels in nouns with pronominal suffixes follows one of these four forms.

In the following, I first address masculine nouns (i.e., those that inflect as masc. nouns). Furthermore, I distinguish between nonexceptional and exceptional nouns. Exceptional nouns are the geminate nouns (e.g., עַם "people"), the segolate nouns (e.g., מֶ֫לֶךְ "king"), one variety of which is middle-weak nouns with a diphthong (e.g., זַ֫יִת "olive"), and etymological III-*vav*/*yod* nouns, also commonly called III-*he* nouns (e.g., חֹזֶה "seer"). Nonexceptional nouns are all the other types. For each category, we first address the nonexceptional nouns. The nouns are described in terms of their number of syllables in THT. All forms occur in the Hebrew Bible, unless preceded by an asterisk. An attempt has been made to cite nouns that appear relatively frequently.

Producing Plural Nouns

The following is a self-consciously simplified description of how to produce particular nominal and verbal forms. The underlying historical changes that led to these forms are described in greater detail in chapters 2–5. I refer in this section only to the Tiberian vowels and symbols.

Due to the manner of our pronunciation, it is often the case that students find it difficult to predict where a word should exhibit a *patakh* and where it should exhibit a *qamets*. Keep these general rules in mind:

1. A tonic syllable in a noun will often have a *qamets* (e.g., the second syllable of דָּבָר "word"), while a tonic syllable in a verb will often have a *patakh* (e.g., the second syllable of שָׁמַע "he heard").
2. An open pretonic syllable in both a noun and verb will often have a *qamets* (e.g., the first syllable of דָּבָר "word" and שָׁמַע "he heard").

When one adds the masculine plural morpheme ִים- to a nonexceptional noun that has only one syllable, usually no other change takes place in the word:

"good"	טוֹבִים	=	ִים -	+	טוֹב
"light"	אוֹרִים	=	ִים -	+	אוֹר
"one who arises"	קָמִים	=	ִים -	+	קָם*
"song"	שִׁירִים	=	ִים -	+	שִׁיר
"flame, Urim"	אוּרִים	=	ִים -	+	אוּר
"blood, spilled blood"	דָּמִים	=	ִים -	+	דָּם

Exceptional nouns of one syllable include the geminates, which, when a syllable is added to their end, reveal their etymological vowel and their etymological gemination (that is, the doubling of their second consonant). To produce the plural form of such words, one must first know that they are from a geminate base. Most nouns of two consonants with *patakh*, *tsere*, or *holem* are geminate nouns (the *patakh* reflecting historical /*a/, *tsere* /*i/, and *holem* /*u/).

"people"	עַמִּים	=	ִים -	+	עַמּ-	←	עַם
"prince"[1]	שָׂרִים	=	ִים -	+	שָׂר-	←	שַׂר
"arrow"	חִצִּים	=	ִים -	+	חִצּ-	←	חֵץ
"statute"	חֻקִּים	=	ִים -	+	חֻקּ-	←	חֹק

Nonexceptional masculine nouns that contain two syllables in their stem often exhibit further changes in their vowel patterns when pluralized. This

1. Note the compensatory lengthening in the word שַׂר; the *resh* cannot double and, as if in place of this, the preceding vowel appears as *qamets*, not *patakh*.

is due to the fact that one is usually adding an extra syllable to the end of the word and thus causing a preceding syllable to shorten, if possible. After applying the plural morpheme (-ִים), if the propretonic syllable contains a *qamets* or *tsere*, this vowel reduces to *shewa* or a muttered vowel:

	qamets > ə//tsere > ə						
"word"	דְּבָרִים	←	*דָּבָרִים	=	-ִים	+	דָּבָר
"elder"	זְקֵנִים	←	*זָקֵנִים	=	-ִים	+	זָקֵן
"full"	מְלֵאִים	←	*מָלֵאִים	=	-ִים	+	מָלֵא
"pious"	חֲסִידִים	←	*חָסִידִים	=	-ִים	+	חָסִיד
"written"	כְּתוּבִים	←	*כָּתוּבִים	=	-ִים	+	כָּתוּב
"grape"	עֲנָבִים	←	*עֵנָבִים	=	-ִים	+	עֵנָב

If a noun does not contain a *qamets* or *tsere* in its propretonic syllable, but it does contain a *tsere* in its pretonic syllable, then, this *tsere* reduces to *shewa* or a muttered vowel:

"judge"	שֹׁפְטִים	←	*שֹׁפֵטִים	=	-ִים	+	שֹׁפֵט
"blind"	עִוְרִים	←	*עִוֵּרִים	=	-ִים	+	עִוֵּר

A *tsere* does not reduce in the pretonic syllable if a vowel has reduced in the propretonic (cf. מְלֵאִים "full"). Most other nouns of this category do not exhibit any change in their stem vowels.

"eternity"	עוֹלָמִים	=	-ִים	+	עוֹלָם
"thief"	גַּנָּבִים	=	-ִים	+	גַּנָּב
"righteous"	צַדִּיקִים	=	-ִים	+	צַדִּיק
"God"[2]	אֱלֹהִים	=	-ִים	+	אֱלוֹהַּ
"cherub"	כְּרוּבִים	=	-ִים	+	כְּרוּב
"border"[3]	*גְּבוּלִים	=	-ִים	+	גְּבוּל
"judgment, justice"	מִשְׁפָּטִים		-ִים		מִשְׁפָּט

2. The plural is spelled defectively.

3. The plural absolute is not attested.

Among exceptional nouns, those with an etymological III-*vav/yod* often have a *segol* in the masculine singular form as a final vowel. To pluralize such nouns, one subtracts this ending and supplies the masculine plural morpheme ִים -. Since one has not added another syllable, the vowels of the singular stem are usually the vowels of the plural stem too.

"beautiful"	יָפִים	=	ִים -	+	יָפ-	←	יָפֶה
"one making"	עֹשִׂים	=	ִים -	+	עֹשׂ-	←	עֹשֶׂה
"seer"	חֹזִים	=	ִים -	+	חֹז-	←	חֹזֶה
"deed"	מַעֲשִׂים	=	ִים -	+	מַעֲשׂ-	←	מַעֲשֶׂה

Sometimes the noun ends with an etymological *vav* or *yod*; in these cases, the noun inflects like any other noun of this category.

	qamets > ə//tsere > ə						
"built"[4]	בְּנוּיִם	←	*בָּנוּיִם	=	ִים -	+	בָּנוּי

The other major category of exceptional noun is the segolates. Almost universally, to pluralize segolates one supplies the vowel symbols *shewa-qamets* to the stem consonants and then adds the plural morpheme ִים -.

"king"	מְלָכִים	=	ִים	-	+	*מְלָךְ-	=	ְ ָ	+	מלך	←	מֶ֫לֶךְ
"masters"	בְּעָלִים	=	ִים	-	+	*בְּעָל-	=	ְ ָ	+	בעל	←	בַּ֫עַל
"book"	סְפָרִים	=	ִים	-	+	*סְפָר-	=	ְ ָ	+	ספר	←	סֵ֫פֶר
"morning"	בְּקָרִים	=	ִים	-	+	*בְּקָר-	=	ְ ָ	+	בקר	←	בֹּ֫קֶר
"holy"[5]	קֳדָשִׁים	=	ִים	-	+	*קֳדָשׁ-	=	ְ ָ	+	קדשׁ	←	קֹ֫דֶשׁ
"ornament"	עֲדָיִים	=	ִים	-	+	*עֲדָי-	=	ְ ָ	+	עדי	←	עֲדִי

4. By convention, a *mater yod* is not written after a consonantal *yod* at the end of a word.

5. The *hatef-qamets* appears in place of a regular *shewa* due to the guttural pronunciation of the *qoph* as well as the underlying historical /u/ vowel, as explained above. This plural form of "holiness" is found especially where the word bears the definite article. Without the article the plural form is קְדָשִׁים.

"sickness"[6]	חֳלָיִם	=	ִים-	+	*חֳלָיְ-	=	ָ ְ	+	חלי	←	חֳלִי

Among the larger category of segolate nouns, there are a limited number that exhibit in their singular absolute form a *patakh* or *qamets* followed by a *yod* or *vav* as a second root consonant (i.e., not a *mater*). An extra *hireq* or *segol* is also present after the *yod* or *vav*. The historical diphthong (**ay* or **aw*) resolves when it is not accented, or, in other words, in almost every case when an ending is added.

	**ay* > *tsere*, **aw* > *holem*						
"olive"	זֵיתִים	←	*זַ֫יִתִים	=	ִים-	+	זַ֫יִת
"death"	מוֹתִים	←	*מָ֫וֶתִים	=	ִים-	+	מָ֫וֶת

Generally, when one inflects feminine nouns (i.e., those marked as feminine) for plurality, one subtracts the morpheme ָה- and supplies the ending וֹת-. Since, in essence, one syllable is exchanged for another, the accent does not shift and the vowels of the singular stem are usually the vowels of the plural stem too:

"good"	טוֹבוֹת	=	וֹת-	+	טוֹב-	←	טוֹבָה
"one who arises"	קָמוֹת	=	וֹת-	+	קָמ-	←	קָמָה
"song"	שִׁירוֹת	=	וֹת-	+	שִׁיר-	←	שִׁירָה
"counsel"	עֵצוֹת	=	וֹת-	+	עֵצ-	←	עֵצָה
"cubit"	אַמּוֹת	=	וֹת-	+	אַמּ-	←	אַמָּה
"princess"	שָׂרוֹת	=	וֹת-	+	שָׂר-	←	שָׂרָה
"corner"	פִּנּוֹת	=	וֹת-	+	פִּנּ-	←	פִּנָּה
"statute"	חֻקּוֹת	=	וֹת-	+	חֻקּ-	←	חֻקָּה
"blessing"	בְּרָכוֹת	=	וֹת-	+	בְּרָכ-	←	בְּרָכָה
"full"	מְלֵאוֹת	=	וֹת-	+	מְלֵא-	←	מְלֵאָה

6. The *hatef-qamets* appears in place of a regular *shewa* due to the guttural pronunciation of the *khet* as well as the underlying historical /u/ vowel.

"war"	מִלְחָמוֹת	=	-וֹת	+	מִלְחָמ-	←	מִלְחָמָה
"beautiful"	יָפוֹת	=	-וֹת	+	יָפ-	←	יָפָה
"one who goes up"	עֹלוֹת	=	-וֹת	+	עֹל-	←	עֹלָה

The most common exception to this rule is the feminine segolate nouns. As with the masculine segolate nouns, one supplies the vowel symbols *shewa-qamets* to the stem consonants and then adds the plural morpheme (in this case -וֹת).

"queen"	מְלָכוֹת	=	-וֹת	+	*מְלָכ-	=	ְ ָ	+	מלכ-	←	מַלְכָּה
"tears"	דְּמָעוֹת	=	-וֹת	+	*דְּמָע-	=	ְ ָ	+	דמע-	←	דִּמְעָה
"waste"	חֳרָבוֹת	=	-וֹת	+	*חֳרָב-	=	ְ ָ	+	חרב-	←	חָרְבָּה

Producing Masculine Nouns with (Most) Suffixes

The pronominal suffixes on singular nouns are most commonly the following, listed as attached to the word קוֹל "voice": קֹלִי "my voice"; קֹלְךָ "your (ms) voice"; קוֹלֵךְ "your (fs) voice"; קֹלוֹ "his voice"; קֹלָהּ "her voice"; קוֹלֵנוּ "our voice"; קוֹלְכֶם "your (mp) voice"; *קוֹלְכֶן "your (fp) voice"; קוֹלָם "their (mp) voice"; קוֹלָן "their (fp) voice."[7] Pronominal suffixes on plural nouns are actually composed of a historical dual ending *-*ay*- plus a pronominal element (as explained in ch. 4): סוּסַי "my horses"; סוּסֶיךָ "your (ms) horses"; *סוּסַיִךְ "your (fs) horses"; סוּסָיו "his horses"; *סוּסֶיהָ "her horses"; *סוּסֵינוּ "our horses"; סוּסֵיכֶם "your (mp) horses"; *סוּסֵיכֶן "your (fp) horses"; סוּסֵיהֶם "their (mp) horses"; *סוּסֵיהֶן "their (fp) horses." All these suffixes can be broken apart into two categories: those that are "heavy" and those that are not. Heavy suffixes are those having a sequence of consonant + vowel + consonant = the second masculine/feminine plural on the singular noun (-כֶם and -כֶן) and the second masculine/feminine plural (-כֶם and -כֶן) and third masculine/feminine plural (-הֶם ,-הֶן)

7. The forms are listed as they appear in the Hebrew Bible, though there is sometimes variation in spelling. Only the form of the noun "voice" with 2fp suffix is unattested. Note that it is common to find a word in the absolute with an internal *mater*, but the same word with no internal *mater* when it has a suffix. In general, the scribes seemed reluctant to use more than one *mater* per word.

on plural nouns.[8] This section deals only with the forms of the masculine noun without heavy suffixes; a subsequent section treats the masculine noun with heavy suffixes.

For most masculine nouns, the stem vowels of the absolute plural are the same as the stem vowels of the noun with nonheavy possessive suffixes. Thus, the production of the noun plus suffix is normally no more complicated than taking the stem and stem vowels of the plural absolute and then adding the correct suffix. Or, in other words, one subtracts ִים- and adds the appropriate suffix. By using this shortcut, one can produce both the masculine singular noun plus suffix and the masculine plural noun plus suffix (including for geminate nouns, II-*vav*/*yod* nouns with diphthongs, and III-*vav*/*yod* nouns). In essence, the only difference between a singular noun + suffix and a plural noun + suffix lies in the form of the suffix, not in the stem vowels of the noun (i.e., the suffix וֹ- "his" indicates a singular noun, but the suffix ָיו- "his" indicates a plural noun).

To Produce the Masculine Singular Noun + Suffix

"his light"	אוֹרוֹ	=	וֹ-	+	אוֹר-	←	אוֹרִים
"your (fs) light"	אוֹרֵךְ	=	ֵךְ-	+			
"his song"	שִׁירוֹ	=	וֹ-	+	שִׁיר-	←	שִׁירִים
"my song"	שִׁירִי	=	ִי-	+			
"his blood"	דָּמוֹ	=	וֹ-	+	דָּם-	←	דָּמִים
"her blood"	דָּמָהּ	=	ָהּ-	+			
"his people"	עַמּוֹ	=	וֹ-	+	עַמ-	←	עַמִּים
"your (ms) people"	עַמְּךָ	=	ְךָ-	+			
"his arrow"	חִצּוֹ	=	וֹ-	+	חִצ-	←	חִצִּים
"their arrow"	חִצָּם	=	ָם-	+			
"his statute"	חֻקּוֹ	=	וֹ-	+	חֻק-	←	חֻקִּים
"their statute"	חֻקָּם	=	ָם-	+			

8. The term "heavy" reflects the fact that these suffixes attract the tone, unlike the other suffixes which are often penultimately stressed. The term is used by many grammars, e.g., Thomas O. Lambdin's (*Introduction to Biblical Hebrew* [New York: Scribners, 1971], 87).

"his word"	דְּבָרוֹ	=	-וֹ	+	דְּבַר-	←	דְּבָרִים
"your (ms) word"	דְּבָרְךָ	=	-ְךָ	+			
"his pious one"	חֲסִידוֹ	=	-וֹ	+	חֲסִיד-	←	חֲסִידִים
"your (ms) pious one"	חֲסִידְךָ	=	-ְךָ	+			
"my judge"	שֹׁפְטִי	=	-ִי	+	שֹׁפְט-	←	שֹׁפְטִים
"our judge"	שֹׁפְטֵ֫נוּ	=	-ֵ֫נוּ	+			
"his eternity"	עוֹלָמוֹ	=	-וֹ	+	עוֹלָמ-	←	עוֹלָמִים
"his God"	אֱלֹהוֹ	=	-וֹ	+	אֱלֹה-	←	אֱלֹהִים
"its border"	גְּבוּלוֹ	=	-וֹ	+	גְּבוּל-	←	*גְּבוּלִים
"your (fs) border"	גְּבוּלֵךְ	=	-ֵךְ	+			
"his judgment"	מִשְׁפָּטוֹ	=	-וֹ	+	מִשְׁפָּט-	←	מִשְׁפָּטִים
"my judgment"	מִשְׁפָּטִי	=	-ִי	+			
"your (ms) olive"	זֵיתְךָ	=	-ְךָ	+	זֵית-	←	זֵיתִים
"his death"	מוֹתוֹ	=	-וֹ	+	מוֹת-	←	מוֹתִים
"her death"	מוֹתָהּ	=	-ָהּ	+			
"one making it (ms)"[9]	עֹשׂוֹ	=	-וֹ	+	עֹשׂ-	←	עֹשִׂים
"one making it (fs)"	עֹשָׂהּ	=	-ָהּ	+			
"our deed"	מַעֲשֵׂ֫נוּ	=	-ֵ֫נוּ	+	מַעֲשׂ-	←	מַעֲשִׂים

To Produce the Masculine Plural Noun + Suffix

"your (ms) songs"	שִׁירֶ֫יךָ	=	-ֶ֫יךָ	+	שִׁיר-	←	שִׁירִים
"his enemies"	קָמָיו	=	-ָיו	+	קָמ-	←	קָמִים
"our enemies"	קָמֵ֫ינוּ	=	-ֵ֫ינוּ	+			
"his spilled blood"	דָּמָיו	=	-ָיו	+	דָּמ-	←	דָּמִים
"her spilled blood"	דָּמֶ֫יהָ	=	-ֶ֫יהָ	+			

9. For this form, see Job 40:19. Usually, however, the 3ms suffix on singular III-*vav/yod* nouns/participles is -ֵהוּ (e.g., עֹשֵׂהוּ).

"his peoples"	עַמָּיו	=	-ָיו	+	עַמּ-	←	עַמִּים
"your (ms) peoples"	עַמֶּ֫יךָ	=	-ֶ֫יךָ	+			
"my princes"	שָׂרַי	=	-ַי	+	שָׂר-	←	שָׂרִים
"your (ms) arrows"	חִצֶּ֫יךָ	=	-ֶ֫יךָ	+	חִצ-	←	חִצִּים
"your (ms) statutes"	חֻקֶּ֫יךָ	=	-ֶ֫יךָ	+	חֻק-	←	חֻקִּים
"his words"	דְּבָרָיו	=	-ָיו	+	דְּבָר-	←	דְּבָרִים
"your (ms) words"	דְּבָרֶ֫יךָ	=	-ֶ֫יךָ	+			
"your (ms) pious ones"	חֲסִידֶ֫יךָ	=	-ֶ֫יךָ	+	חֲסִיד-	←	חֲסִידִים
"his judges"	שֹׁפְטָיו	=	-ָיו	+	שֹׁפְט-	←	שֹׁפְטִים
"your (fs) judges"	שֹׁפְטַ֫יִךְ	=	-ַ֫יִךְ	+			
"your (fs) sailors"	מַלָּחַ֫יִךְ	=	-ַ֫יִךְ	+	מַלָּח-	←	מַלָּחִים
"his gods"	אֱלֹהָיו	=	-ָיו	+	אֱלֹה-	←	אֱלֹהִים
"your (ms) gods"	אֱלֹהֶ֫יךָ	=	-ֶ֫יךָ	+			
"its borders"	גְּבוּלֶ֫יהָ	=	-ֶ֫יהָ	+	גְּבוּל-	←	*גְּבוּלִים
"your (ms) borders"	גְּבוּלֶ֫יךָ	=	-ֶ֫יךָ	+			
"his judgments"	מִשְׁפָּטָיו	=	-ָיו	+	מִשְׁפָּט-	←	מִשְׁפָּטִים
"my judgments"	מִשְׁפָּטַי	=	-ַי	+			
"his deaths"	מוֹתָיו	=	-ָיו	+	מוֹת-	←	מוֹתִים
"ones making it"	עֹשָׂיו	=	-ָיו	+	עֹשׂ-	←	עֹשִׂים
"ones making you"	עֹשַׂ֫יִךְ	=	-ַ֫יִךְ	+			
"his deeds"	מַעֲשָׂיו	=	-ָיו	+	מַעֲשׂ-	←	מַעֲשִׂים
"our deeds"	מַעֲשֵׂ֫ינוּ	=	-ֵ֫ינוּ	+			

The only group of exceptional nouns not included in the above lists are the segolates. Because the segolates have one base for their singular forms (**qatl*, **qitl*, **qutl*) and another base for their plural forms (**qatalīm*, **qitalīm*, **qutalīm*), the kind of correspondences one sees in the above words is not found in this group of nouns. Instead, the singular + suffix is formed by taking the base form and adding a suffix to it. In essence, **malk* + *ī* = **malkī* (> מַלְכִּי) "my king"; **sipr* + *ī* = **siprī* (> סִפְרִי) "my book"; **qudš* + *ī* = **qudšī* > **qodšī* (> קָדְשִׁי) "my holiness." Due to this, it is essential to know first the base of a segolate noun before producing its form plus a suffix. The historical vowel is often implicit in the absolute singular (an initial *patakh* signals a historical */a/, *tsere* */i/, and *holem* */u/; a *segol* may reflect a historical */a/ or */i/; a *shewa* usually reflects historical */i/).

"my king"	מַלְכִּי	=	-ִי	+	*מַלְךְּ	←	מֶ֫לֶךְ
"our king"	מַלְכֵּ֫נוּ	=	-ֵ֫נוּ	+			
"his master"	בַּעְלוֹ	=	-וֹ	+	*בַּעְל	←	בַּ֫עַל
"her master"	בַּעְלָהּ	=	-ָהּ	+			
"her midst"	קִרְבָּהּ	=	-ָהּ	+	*קִרְבּ	←	קֶ֫רֶב
"your (ms) midst"	קִרְבְּךָ	=	-ְךָ	+			
"my book"	סִפְרִי	=	-ִי	+	*סִפְר	←	סֵ֫פֶר
"your (ms) book"	סִפְרְךָ	=	-ְךָ	+			
"his rod, tribe"	שִׁבְטוֹ	=	-וֹ	+	*שִׁבְט	←	שֵׁ֫בֶט
"your (ms) rod, tribe"	שִׁבְטְךָ	=	-ְךָ	+			
"my holy thing"	קָדְשִׁי	=	-ִי	+	*קָדְשׁ	←	קֹ֫דֶשׁ
"your holy thing"	קָדְשְׁךָ	=	-ְךָ	+			
"his captivity"	שִׁבְיוֹ	=	-וֹ	+	*שִׁבְי	←	שְׁבִי
"her captivity"	שִׁבְיָהּ	=	-ָהּ	+			
"sickness"	חָלְיוֹ	=	-וֹ	+	*חָלְי	←	חֳלִי

The plural forms of the segolates with suffixes look, for the most part, like the plural forms of words like דָּבָר "word"; recall that similar vowel patterns appear in the absolute plural forms of both types of nouns: דְּבָרִים "words" and מְלָכִים "kings." Thus, to produce the proper form of the masculine plural segolate plus suffix, one can (in most cases) simply add the appropriate suffix to the plural stem.

"her kings"	מְלָכֶ֫יהָ	=	-ֶ֫יהָ	+	מְלָכ-	←	מְלָכִים
"our kings"	מְלָכֵ֫ינוּ	=	-ֵ֫ינוּ	+			
"his masters"	בְּעָלָיו	=	-ָיו	+	בְּעָל-	←	*בְּעָלִים
"her masters"	בְּעָלֶ֫יהָ	=	-ֶ֫יהָ	+			

"his rods, tribes"	שְׁבָטָיו	=	־ָיו	+	שְׁבָט־	←	שְׁבָטִים
"your (ms) rods, tribes"	שְׁבָטֶיךָ	=	־ֶיךָ	+			
"his holy things"	קֳדָשָׁיו	=	־ָיו	+	קֳדָשׁ־	←	קֳדָשִׁים
"my holy things"	קֳדָשַׁי	=	־ַי	+			
"our sicknesses"	חֳלָיֵנוּ	=	־ֵינוּ	+	חֳלָי־	←	חֳלָיִם

The preceding correspondences, it should be emphasized again, do not pertain to the noun with heavy pronominal suffixes (i.e., for singular nouns with ־כֶם and ־כֶן; and for plural nouns with ־כֶם and ־כֶן and ־הֶם, ־הֶן). In each case, where these suffixes are used, they appear on the construct form of the noun. Thus, to produce such forms, one can simply add the suffix to the construct form. Before addressing the form of nouns with heavy suffixes, we will look at producing the construct form of nouns. The inflection of feminine nouns with suffixes also reflects the construct form of nouns and is treated after the following section.

Producing the Construct Form of Nouns

The construct is the shortest form of a Hebrew noun. Its brevity reflects the fact that it is pronounced together with a following word, as essentially one long word. In general, in an open syllable, a *qamets* or *tsere* in the absolute is turned to *shewa* in the construct. In closed syllables, these same vowels are turned to *patakh*. In the list below, the absolute is found in the far right column and to the left of this is the form of the word with vowels reduced and to the left of this, the form of the word with shortened vowels.

	construct		closed syllable $\bar{a} > a, \bar{e} > a$	open syllable $\bar{a} > ə, \bar{e} > ə$		absolute
"blood of"	דַּם	=	דַּם		←	דָּם
"word of"	דְּבַר	=	דְּבַר	*דְּבָר	←	דָּבָר
"elder of"	זְקַן	=	זְקַן	*זְקֵן	←	זָקֵן
"heart of"	לְבַב	=	לְבַב	*לְבָב	←	לֵבָב
"ruler of"	נְגִיד	=		נְגִיד	←	נָגִיד
"blessed of"	בְּרוּךְ	=		בְּרוּךְ	←	בָּרוּךְ

No shift in the *tsere* takes place in the *qal* masculine singular participle (as well as in similarly formed nouns). For these nouns, the absolute and the construct are identical in the singular: שֹׁפֵט "judge" or "judge of," and שֹׁמֵר "guard" or "guard of."

Nonexceptional masculine singular nouns that lack *qamets* or *tsere* usually have construct forms identical to their absolute forms, such as טוֹב "good" and "good of," אוֹר "light (of)," שִׁיר "song (of)," אַדִּיר "majestic (of)," גְּבוּל "boundary (of)." In addition, most masculine singular exceptional nouns have construct forms also identical to their absolute forms, even when they contain a *tsere*: עַם "people" and "people of," שַׂר "prince (of)," חֵץ "arrow (of)," חֹק "statute (of)," מֶ֫לֶךְ "king (of)," בַּ֫עַל "master (of)," סֵ֫פֶר "book (of)," קֹ֫דֶשׁ "holy thing (of)," גְּדִי "kid (of)," עֳנִי "affliction (of)."[10] II-*vav*/*yod* nouns with a diphthong show resolution of the diphthong: בַּ֫יִת "house" versus בֵּית "house of" and מָ֫וֶת "death" versus מוֹת "death of." In III-*vav*/*yod* masculine singular nouns (and participles), the absolute contains a *segol* and the construct a *tsere*: עֹשֶׂה "maker" versus עֹשֵׂה "maker of" and מַעֲשֶׂה "deed" versus מַעֲשֵׂה "deed of."

In the masculine plural construct, one applies the same rules of vowel reduction (*qamets* and *tsere* in open syllables reduce to *shewa*). In addition, one replaces the plural absolute ending, ־ִים, with ־ֵי (which does not reduce). Occasionally, after the reduction of vowels, two consecutive syllables would each contain a *shewa*; in these cases, the first *shewa* is changed to *hireq*. Segolate nouns, on the other hand, reveal their historical first vowel (מַלְכֵי [< **malakay*] "kings of"; אִמְרֵי [< *ʾ*imaray*] "words of"; חָדְשֵׁי [< **ḥodašay* < **ḥudaṯay*] "months of").

	construct	ə + ə > i, a, or o	open syllable ā > ə, ē > ə								absolute
"blood of"	דְּמֵי		דְּמֵי	←	*דָּמֵי	=	־ֵי	+	דָּם־	←	דָּמִים
"words of"	דִּבְרֵי	דִּבְרֵי	*דְּבְרֵי	←	*דְּבָרֵי	=	־ֵי	+	דְּבָר־	←	דְּבָרִים
"elders of"	זִקְנֵי	זִקְנֵי	*זְקְנֵי	←	*זְקֵנֵי	=	־ֵי	+	זְקֵן־	←	זְקֵנִים
"kings of"	מַלְכֵי	מַלְכֵי	*מְלְכֵי	←	*מְלָכֵי	=	־ֵי	+	מְלָכ־	←	מְלָכִים
"words of"	אִמְרֵי	אִמְרֵי	*אֲמְרֵי	←	*אֲמָרֵי	=	־ֵי	+	אֲמָר־	←	אֲמָרִים
"months of"	חָדְשֵׁי	חָדְשֵׁי	*חֳדְשֵׁי	←	*חֳדָשֵׁי	=	־ֵי	+	חֳדָשׁ־	←	חֳדָשִׁים

10. In the case of geminate nouns with *maqqep*, the vowel will sometimes be short, as with לֵב versus לֶב־ "heart of" and חֹק versus חָק־ "statute of."

Many other nouns are identical in their absolute and construct forms, except for the ending ֵי-. For example, note שֹׁפְטִים versus שֹׁפְטֵי "judges of"; עַמִּים versus עַמֵּי "peoples of"; חֻקִּים versus חֻקֵּי "statutes of"; נְגִידִים versus נְגִידֵי "leaders of"; עֹשִׂים versus עֹשֵׂי "makers of"; מַעֲשִׂים versus מַעֲשֵׂי "deeds of."

For feminine singular nouns in the construct state, one replaces the absolute ending ָה- with word-final ַת-. One applies the same rules of vowel reduction: *qamets* and *tsere* in open syllables are reduced to *shewa*. As with the masculine plural, where two consecutive syllables would attest *shewas*, the first changes to *hireq*.

	construct	ə + ə > i	ā > ə, ē > ə									absolute
"sleep of"	שְׁנַת		שְׁנַת	←	*שֵׁנַת	=	ַת-	+	שֵׁנ-	←		שֵׁנָה
"year of"	שְׁנַת		שְׁנַת	←	*שָׁנַת	=	ַת-	+	שָׁנ-	←		שָׁנָה
"blessing of"	בִּרְכַת	בִּרְכַת	*בְּרְכַת	←	*בְּרָכַת	=	ַת-	+	בְּרָכ-	←		בְּרָכָה

Most other nouns (including exceptional nouns) show only the shift from ָה- to ַת-, as with טוֹבָה versus טוֹבַת "good of"; שִׁירָה versus שִׁירַת "song of"; אַמָּה versus אַמַּת "cubit of"; פִּנָּה versus פִּנַּת "corner of"; חֻקָּה versus חֻקַּת "statute of"; מַלְכָּה versus מַלְכַּת "queen of"; דִּמְעָה versus דִּמְעַת "tears of"; חָכְמָה versus חָכְמַת "wisdom of"; מְגִלָּה versus מְגִלַּת "scroll of"; עֲבוֹדָה versus עֲבוֹדַת "labor of"; עֹלָה versus עֹלַת "burnt offering of." Nouns with a prefix *mem* often exhibit a segolate pattern in the singular construct: מַמְלָכָה versus מַמְלֶכֶת "kingdom of."

For feminine plural nouns, one again reduces *qamets* and *tsere* in open syllables to *shewa*; when two *shewas* would appear in adjacent syllables, the first is changed to *hireq*. No other changes are made. These nouns exhibit the same ending in the absolute and construct: וֹת-.

	construct		ə + ə > i	open syllable ā > ə, ē > ə		
"years of"	שְׁנוֹת	=		שְׁנוֹת	←	*שָׁנוֹת
"kingdoms of"	מַמְלְכוֹת	=		מַמְלְכוֹת		מַמְלָכוֹת
"blessings of"	בִּרְכוֹת	=	בִּרְכוֹת	*בְּרְכוֹת	←	בְּרָכוֹת
"tears of"	דִּמְעוֹת	=	דִּמְעוֹת	*דְּמְעוֹת		דְּמָעוֹת

Again, other nouns show no distinction between construct and absolute: אַמּוֹת "cubits (of)"; פִּנּוֹת "corners (of)"; מִצְוֹת "commandments (of)."

Producing Masculine Singular Nouns with כֶם- and כֶן- and Masculine Plural Nouns with כֶם-, כֶן- and הֶם-, הֶן-

To form masculine singular nouns with the second masculine/feminine plural suffixes (כֶם- and כֶן-), one takes the construct form of the singular noun and adds the appropriate suffix. To form the masculine plural with the second masculine/feminine plural or third masculine/feminine plural suffixes (כֶם-, כֶן- and הֶם-, הֶן-), one takes the construct form of the plural noun and adds the appropriate suffix.

Singular Noun with Second Masculine/Feminine Plural Suffix

					construct	absolute
"your voice"	קוֹלְכֶם	=	כֶם-	+	קוֹל	קוֹל
"your dispute"	רִיבְכֶם	=	כֶם-	+	רִיב	רִיב
"your flesh"	בְּשַׂרְכֶם	=	כֶם-	+	בְּשַׂר	בָּשָׂר
"your heart"	לְבַבְכֶם	=	כֶם-	+	לְבַב	לֵבָב
"your glory"	כְּבוֹדְכֶם	=	כֶם-	+	כְּבוֹד	כָּבוֹד
"your dwelling"	מִשְׁכַּבְכֶם	=	כֶם-	+	מִשְׁכַּב	מִשְׁכָּב
"your house"	בֵּיתְכֶם	=	כֶם-	+	בֵּית	בַּ֫יִת
"your midst"	תּוֹכְכֶם	=	כֶם-	+	תּוֹךְ	תָּ֫וֶךְ

Plural Noun with Second Masculine/Feminine Plural, Third Masculine/Feminine Plural Suffix

					construct	absolute
"your songs"	שִׁירֵיכֶם	=	כֶם-	+	*שִׁירֵי	שִׁירִים
"your words"	דִּבְרֵיכֶם	=	כֶם-	+	דִּבְרֵי	דְּבָרִים
"their words"	דִּבְרֵיהֶם	=	הֶם-	+		
"your enemies"	אֹיְבֵיכֶם	=	כֶם-	+	אֹיְבֵי	אֹיְבִים
"their enemies"	אֹיְבֵיהֶם	=	הֶם-	+		

"your God"	אֱלֹהֵיכֶם	=	-כֶם	+	אֱלֹהֵי	אֱלֹהִים
"their God"	אֱלֹהֵיהֶם	=	-הֶם	+		
"their makers"	עֹשֵׂיהֶם	=	-הֶם	+	עֹשֵׂי	עֹשִׂים
"your deeds"	מַעֲשֵׂיכֶם	=	-כֶם	+	מַעֲשֵׂי	מַעֲשִׂים
"their deeds"	מַעֲשֵׂיהֶם	=	-הֶם	+		
"your olives"	זֵיתֵיכֶם	=	-כֶם	+	*זֵיתֵי	זֵיתִים
"their olives"	זֵיתֵיהֶם	=	-הֶם	+		
"your kings"	מַלְכֵיכֶם	=	-כֶם	+	מַלְכֵי	מְלָכִים
"their kings"	מַלְכֵיהֶם	=	-הֶם	+		
"your tribes"	שִׁבְטֵיכֶם	=	-כֶם	+	שִׁבְטֵי	שְׁבָטִים
"their tribes"	שִׁבְטֵיהֶם	=	-הֶם	+		
"your months"	חָדְשֵׁיכֶם	=	-כֶם	+	חָדְשֵׁי	חֳדָשִׁים

Exceptional nouns in the above lists include those with II-*vav/yod* consonants (בַּ֫יִת, תָּ֫וֶךְ, זֵיתִים); those with etymological III-*vav/yod* consonants (עֹשִׂים, מַעֲשִׂים); and the plural segolate nouns. Those not yet mentioned include the geminates and the singular segolates. The geminates exhibit gemination and retention of their historical vowel, as when other suffixes are attached to them (e.g., טַפְּכֶם "your children," חַיֵּיכֶם "your life"; לְבַבְכֶם "your heart"; כֻּלְּכֶם "all of you"). The segolates exhibit their historical vowel, revealing their historical base, as when other suffixes are attached to them (**qatl* [e.g., מַלְכְּכֶם "your king"] **qitl* [e.g., קִרְבְּכֶם "your midst], **qutl* [e.g., אָכְלְכֶם "your food"]).

Producing Feminine Nouns with Suffixes

To form the feminine singular noun with (non-"heavy") suffixes, begin with the construct singular form. Change the final תַ- to תָ- and add the appropriate suffix.

							construct	absolute
"my sleep"	שְׁנָתִי	=	-ִי	+	*שְׁנָת-	←	שְׁנַת	*שֵׁנָה
"their sleep"	שְׁנָתָם	=	-ָם	+	*שְׁנָת-	←		
"her year"	שְׁנָתָהּ	=	-ָהּ	+	*שְׁנָת-	←	שְׁנַת	שָׁנָה
"his year"	שְׁנָתוֹ	=	-וֹ	+	*שְׁנָת-	←		
"my blessing"	בִּרְכָתִי	=	-ִי	+	*בִּרְכָת-	←	בִּרְכַת	בְּרָכָה
"your (ms) blessing"	בִּרְכָתְךָ	=	-ְךָ	+	*בִּרְכָת-	←		
"my labor"	עֲבֹדָתִי	=	-ִי	+	*עֲבֹדָת-	←	עֲבֹדַת	עֲבֹדָה
"their labor"	עֲבֹדָתָם	=	-ָם	+	*עֲבֹדָת-	←		
"my tears"	דִּמְעָתִי	=	-ִי	+	*דִּמְעָת-	←	דִּמְעַת	דִּמְעָה
"her tears"	דִּמְעָתָהּ	=	-ָהּ	+	*דִּמְעָת-	←		
"his burnt offering"	עֹלָתוֹ	=	-וֹ	+	*עֹלָת-	←	עֹלַת	*עֹלָה

Mem-prefix nouns have a segolate-like ending in the construct (abs. מַמְלָכָה "kingdom," const. מַמְלֶכֶת "kingdom [of]") and the form with suffixes also has a segolate-like ending (מַמְלַכְתּוֹ). To form the feminine noun with heavy suffixes, begin with the construct singular form and add the second masculine/feminine plural suffix: עֲבֹדַת → עֲבֹדַתְכֶם "your (mp) labor."

To form feminine plural nouns with suffixes (whether heavy or not), take the construct form of the plural noun and simply add the suffixes that occur on the masculine plural noun (including the reflex of the historical *-*ay*- dual ending): *דִּמְעוֹת "tears of" → *דִּמְעוֹתֶיךָ "your (ms) tears"; *עֹלֹת "burnt offerings of" → עֹלֹתֶיךָ "your (ms) burnt offerings"; בִּרְכוֹת "blessings of" → בִּרְכוֹתֵיכֶם "your blessings."

Producing the *Qåṭal* Verb Form

Usually, producing verbal forms is much easier than producing nominal forms. The finite verbs are inflected for person, number, and gender through suffixal and prefixal components on the verbal stem that are consistent across different verb classes and conjugations (or, *binyanim*).

The paradigm of the *qåṭal* (or, perfect) can be divided into two basic parts: third-person forms and everything else (i.e., second- and first-person forms). The third-person forms are also divisible into two parts: the third masculine singular, on the one hand, and the third feminine singular/third common plural on the other. The third masculine singular form is the "dictionary form" of the word (i.e., the form that is listed in the dictionary and which is memorized in vocabulary lessons [e.g., שָׁמַר "he guarded"]); the third masculine singular, therefore, often constitutes the point of comparison for the other forms. The third feminine singular and third common plural of any given verb differ only in their ending (*qamets*[he] for 3fs and *shureq* for 3cp). In other respects they are almost always identical and can be thought of as a pair. They almost always exhibit the same vowel sequence within the verbal stem. If one knows the form of the third feminine singular, one will be able to predict the form of the third common plural and vice versa. In most cases, the last syllable of these forms bears the tone/stress and the vowel of the penultimate and pretonic syllable reduces (e.g., שָׁמְרָה "she guarded" and שָׁמְרוּ "they guarded").

The other major category of the *qåṭal* is represented by the second- and first-person forms. Most second- and first-person forms attest the same vowel sequences within the verbal stem. The forms are usually penultimately accented and exhibit a *patakh* in the last syllable of the stem (e.g., שָׁמַ֫רְתָּ). This is incredibly regular, across all the different conjugations (e.g., שָׁמַ֫רְתָּ "you guarded" [*qal*]; דִּבַּ֫רְתָּ "you spoke" [*piel*]; הִקְרַ֫בְתָּ "you brought near" [*hiphil*]; נִשְׁמַ֫רְתָּ "you were on guard" [*niphal*]; שֻׁלַּ֫חְתִּי "I was sent away" [*pual*]; הָכְלַ֫מְנוּ "we were humiliated" [*hophal*]; וְהִתְחַזַּ֫קְתֶּם "you should take courage" [*hithpael*]). The same regularity is found in the other second- and first-person forms. The one exception to this regularity is the pair of second plural forms (2mp/2fp), which are accented on the final, suffixal element (תֶּם- and תֶּן-). In these forms (e.g., שְׁמַרְתֶּם), the initial syllable of the word will contain a *shewa* (unless it is a closed syllable, as in the *piel*, e.g., שִׁמַּרְתֶּם). The reason that the verbal suffixes תֶּם- and תֶּן- attract the tone or stress is that they are heavy suffixes, composed of the sequence consonant-vowel-consonant, just like the suffixes כֶם- and כֶן- on nouns.

The predictability of the paradigms means that often it is enough to memorize the first three forms of any *qåṭal* paradigm (i.e., the 3ms, 3fs, 2ms).[11] The third masculine singular is important because it is the "dictionary form" and will sometimes exhibit a vowel different from the

11. Although organizing the verbal paradigm so that it begins with the 1cs form and then continues to the 2ms, 2fs, 3ms and 3fs has become more popular in recent grammars due to the familiarity of this sequence in other modern languages (as well as

second- and first-person forms (e.g., כָּבֵד and שִׁמֵּר). From the third feminine singular one can predict the third common plural (from שָׁמְרָה one can predict שָׁמְרוּ and from שִׁמְּרָה one can predict שִׁמְּרוּ); the second masculine singular will demonstrate the vowel sequence for most of the other forms (from שָׁמַ֫רְתָּ one can predict שָׁמַ֫רְתִּי and from שִׁמַּ֫רְתָּ one can predict שִׁמַּ֫רְתִּי, etc.).

The vowel patterns of the different conjugations or *binyanim* are also important to memorize. Since the Hebrew conjugations or *binyanim* (aside from the *qal* = "simple [conjugation]") are named after the form of the verb פעל "to do, make" in the third masculine singular *qåṭal*, these names (*piel*, *hiphil*, etc.) can serve as ready mnemonic devices for recalling the vowels of the *qåṭal* third masculine singular (as well as sometimes the *yiqṭol* and related forms). Thus, the *piel* (פִּעֵל) exhibits the sequence *hireq-tsere* in the *qåṭal*; the *hiphil* (הִפְעִיל) the sequence *he-hireq-hireq*[yod]; the *niphal* (נִפְעַל) the sequence *nun-hireq-patakh*; the *pual* (פֻּעַל) the sequence *qibbuts-patakh*; the *hophal* (הָפְעַל) the sequence *he-qamets khatuf-patakh*; the *hithpael* (הִתְפַּעֵל) the sequence *he-hireq-tav-patakh-tsere*. Other common features, include the following.

1. The conjugations associated with an active sense (*piel*, *hiphil*, *hithpael*) are characterized by an /i/ class vowel in the last syllable of the third masculine singular *qåṭal*, whereas those associated with passivity (*niphal*, *pual*, and *hophal*) have a *patakh* in the last syllable.
2. In the *qåṭal*, the /i/ class vowel associated with "active" stems appears only in the third masculine singular.
   2.1. In the third feminine singular and third common plural one usually finds a *shewa* (e.g., דִּבְּרָה and דִּבְּרוּ).
   2.2. In the second- and first-person forms, a *patakh* appears in this same slot (e.g., דִּבֵּר vs. דִּבַּ֫רְתִּי, etc.).

Furthermore, it should be noted that the vowel sequences for the *pual*, *hophal*, and *hithpael* are the same in all verbal forms (not only *qåṭal* and *yiqṭol*, but also the impv., infs., and ptc.). In essence, if you can remember the name of the stem, you have a good chance of being able to produce the vowels of the verbal form.

---

for other reasons), the above observation suggests that organizing the verbal paradigm beginning with the 3ms also has its pedagogical benefits.

Producing the *Wəqåṭal* Verb Form

This verb form is identical to that of the *qåṭal*, with one slight exception. In the second masculine singular and first common singular forms, the accent falls on the final syllable (not the penultimate syllable). This usually has no effect on the vowels. That is, the initial vowel does not reduce, as one might expect. Thus, we find וְאָמַרְתָּ֫ "you will say." Rarely one does see a slightly different form, as with the *wəqåṭal* form וְיָכָלְתָּ֫ (Exod 18:23) versus the comparable first-person regular *qåṭal* form יָכֹ֫לְתִּי (e.g., Ps 40:13).

Producing the *Yiqṭol* Verb Form

The inflection of the imperfect or *yiqṭol* forms is even more straightforward than that of the *qåṭal*. Only the final stem vowel of the *yiqṭol* reduces to *shewa* and then only where the suffixal element of the verb form consists exclusively of a vowel. This applies to all the conjugations except the *hiphil*. For example, note the *qal* forms: יִכְתֹּב "he will write" (the 3ms), versus תִּכְתְּבִי (the 2fs), יִכְתְּבוּ (the 3mp), and תִּכְתְּבוּ (the 2mp); the *niphal* forms: יִכָּתֵב "it will be written" (the 3ms) versus תִּכָּתְבִי, יִכָּתְבוּ and תִּכָּתְבוּ; and the *piel* forms: יְכַתֵּב versus תְּכַתְּבִי, יְכַתְּבוּ, and תְּכַתְּבוּ. In the *hiphil*, even this vowel does not reduce: יַכְתִּיב and compare תַּכְתִּ֫יבִי, יַכְתִּ֫יבוּ, and תַּכְתִּ֫יבוּ. Where this vowel reduction occurs, it is the same for all three forms and it is often sufficient to memorize just two forms of the paradigm (the 3ms and the 3mp). From these, one can predict the vowel sequences of the other forms.

The *piel*, *hiphil*, and *niphal* all attest a sequence of vowels in the *yiqṭol* and related forms that is distinct from that of the *qåṭal*. The *piel* attests (*shewa*)-*patakh*-*tsere* (e.g., יְשַׁמֵּר); the *hiphil patakh-hireq*^yod^ (e.g., יַשְׁמִיר); and the *niphal hireq-qamets-tsere* (e.g., יִשָּׁמֵר). In the graphic realization of the first syllables in the *yiqṭol*, the *piel* appears to be the reverse of the *hiphil*: while the *piel* has a *shewa* followed by a *patakh*, the *hiphil* has a *patakh* followed by a silent *shewa*.

Producing the Short-*Yiqṭol* and *Wayyiqṭol* Verb Forms

For most strong roots (and roots with gutturals) in the *qal*, the short-*yiqṭol* (used primarily in its jussive function and seldom in its preterite function) and the *wayyiqṭol* (or *vav*-consecutive imperfect) are identical to the form of the regular *yiqṭol* (e.g., יִשְׁמֹר, יִשְׁמֹר, וַיִּשְׁמֹר; "he will guard," "let him guard," and "he guarded."). In weak roots (especially II- and III-*vav*/*yod* roots) and throughout the *hiphil*, however, the short-*yiqṭol* and *wayyiqṭol* are graphically and phonetically shorter than the *yiqṭol* (יָקוּם, יָקֹם, וַיָּקָם; "he will arise," "let him arise," and "he arose" [**wayyāqom*] and יַעֲשֶׂה, יַעַשׂ, וַיַּעַשׂ "he will do," "let him do," and "he did").

Producing the Imperative

The BH imperative is based on the second-person forms of the (short-) *yiqṭol*. Essentially, the imperative is the *yiqṭol* minus the prefix. Thus, if one starts with תִּשְׁמֹר "you will guard," to form the imperative one simply subtracts the prefix, resulting in שְׁמֹר "guard!" Similarly, the feminine plural תִּשְׁמֹרְנָה becomes שְׁמֹרְנָה. Following this method, in the *qal* the feminine singular and masculine plural result in a sequence of two *shewas* that reduce according to the "rule of *shewa*" (i.e., *ə-ə* > *i*): תִּשְׁמְרִי "you will guard" minus the prefix results in שְׁמְרִי* which resolves into שִׁמְרִי "guard!"; similarly the masculine plural: תִּשְׁמְרוּ minus the prefix results in שְׁמְרוּ* which resolves into שִׁמְרוּ "guard!" These will sometimes resemble the *piel* perfect (e.g., שִׁלְחוּ); the context usually implies the proper form.

The same patterns are found for *yiqṭol* verbs with *patakh* and *tsere* theme vowels in the *qal*. With *patakh*: תִּשְׂמַח "you will rejoice" and the imperative שְׂמַח "rejoice!"; תִּשְׂמְחוּ and שִׂמְחוּ. With *tsere*: תִּתֵּן "you will give" and the imperative תֵּן "give!"; תִּתְּנוּ and תְּנוּ. In the latter case, the *yiqṭol* form attests the assimilation of the *nun*, though in the imperative the *nun* is lost altogether. The same principle, however, seems to be at work: the prefix component of the *yiqṭol* is subtracted to form the imperative.

These patterns are consistent for most derived conjugations, including the *niphal*, the *piel*, and *hithpael*. Note, for example, the *piel yiqṭol* and imperative: תְּדַבֵּר "you will speak" and דַּבֵּר "speak!" In the case of the *niphal* and *hithpael*, the imperative loses the consonantal component of the prefix, but retains its vowel by means of an initial *he*. Thus, the *niphal yiqṭol* and imperative: תִּשָּׁמֵר* "you will be on your guard" and הִשָּׁמֵר "be on guard!"; the *hithpael* יִתְהַלֵּךְ "it will go" and הִתְהַלֵּךְ "go!" The *niphal* imperative is also frequently attested with penultimate accent הִשָּׁ֫מֶר "be on guard" (Deut 24:8 and passim), probably related to the accentuation found sometimes in the *wayyiqṭol*. Compare, for example, הִלָּ֫חֶם "fight" (Judg 9:38) and וַיִּלָּ֫חֶם "he fought" (Josh 10:38).

In essence, since the third masculine singular/plural *yiqṭol* forms are similar to the corresponding second-person forms in all but the consonantal prefix element (e.g., יִשְׁמֹר [3ms] vs. תִּשְׁמֹר [2ms]; יִשְׁמְרוּ [3mp] vs. תִּשְׁמְרוּ [2mp]), one can simply remember the third masculine singular/plural forms and derive from these the basic forms of the imperative (e.g., יִשְׁמֹר and שְׁמֹר; as well as יִשְׁמְרוּ and שִׁמְרוּ).

Summary for Producing Verbal Forms

The following chart summarizes the basic correspondences discussed in the preceding paragraphs.

Qåṭal			
2ms (+ other forms)	3fs and 3cp	3ms	conjugation
			qal
שָׁמַ֫רְתָּ	שָֽׁמְרָה	שָׁמַר	
שָׁמַרְתְּ	שָֽׁמְרוּ		
שָׁמַ֫רְתִּי			
שָׁמַ֫רְנוּ			
שְׁמַרְתֶּם // שְׁמַרְתֶּן			
			piel
שִׁמַּ֫רְתָּ	שִׁמְּרָה	שִׁמֵּר	
שִׁמַּרְתְּ	שִׁמְּרוּ		
שִׁמַּ֫רְתִּי			
שִׁמַּ֫רְנוּ			
שִׁמַּרְתֶּם // שִׁמַּרְתֶּן			
			hiphil
הִשְׁמַ֫רְתָּ	הִשְׁמִ֫ירָה	הִשְׁמִיר	
הִשְׁמַרְתְּ	הִשְׁמִ֫ירוּ		
הִשְׁמַ֫רְתִּי			
הִשְׁמַ֫רְנוּ			
הִשְׁמַרְתֶּם // הִשְׁמַרְתֶּן			

Qal Yiqṭol, Imperative, Infinitive Construct

Forms Ending with -*ū* or -*ī*	Forms ending with Consonant or -*nā*	
יִשְׁמְרוּ	יִשְׁמֹר	*yiqṭol*
תִּשְׁמְרִי	תִּשְׁמֹר	
תִּשְׁמְרוּ	אֶשְׁמֹר	
	תִּשְׁמֹ֫רְנָה	
	נִשְׁמֹר	
	יִשְׁמֹר	short-*yiqṭol*
	תִּשְׁמֹר	
שִׁמְרִי	שְׁמֹר	imperative
שִׁמְרוּ	שְׁמֹ֫רְנָה	
	שְׁמֹר	infinitive construct

Piel Yiqṭol, Imperative, Infinitive Construct

Forms Ending with -*ū* or -*ī*	Forms ending with Consonant or -*nā*	
יְשַׁמְּרוּ	יְשַׁמֵּר	*yiqṭol*
תְּשַׁמְּרִי	תְּשַׁמֵּר	
תְּשַׁמְּרוּ	אֲשַׁמֵּר	
	תְּשַׁמֵּ֫רְנָה	
	נְשַׁמֵּר	
	יְשַׁמֵּר	short-*yiqṭol*
	תְּשַׁמֵּר	
שַׁמְּרִי	שַׁמֵּר	imperative
שַׁמְּרוּ	שַׁמֵּ֫רְנָה	
	שַׁמֵּר	infinitive construct
	שַׁמֵּר	infinitive absolute
	מְשַׁמֵּר	participle

Hiphil Yiqṭol, Imperative, Infinitive Construct				
Forms Ending with -*ū* or -*ī*		Forms ending with Consonant or -*nā*		
	יַשְׁמִ֫ירוּ		יַשְׁמִיר	*yiqṭol*
תַּשְׁמִ֫ירִי		תַּשְׁמִיר		
תַּשְׁמִ֫ירוּ		אַשְׁמִיר		
		נַשְׁמִיר		
			יַשְׁמֵר	short-*yiqṭol*
		תַּשְׁמֵר		
	הַשְׁמִ֫ירִי		הַשְׁמֵר	imperative
הַשְׁמִ֫ירוּ		הַשְׁמֵ֫רְנָה		
			הַשְׁמִיר	infinitive construct
			הַשְׁמֵר	infinitive absolute
			מַשְׁמִיר	participle

Bibliography

Abraham, Kathleen, and Michael Sokoloff. "Aramaic Loanwords in Akkadian—A Reassessment of the Proposals." *AfO* 52 (2011): 22–76.

Aḥituv, Shmuel. *Echoes from the Past: Hebrew and Cognate Inscriptions from the Biblical Period*. Translated by Anson Rainey. Carta Handbook. Jerusalem: Carta, 2008.

Allen, W. Sidney. *Vox Graeca*. 3rd ed. Cambridge: Cambridge University Press, 1987.

Avestad, Silje, and Lutz Edzard. *la-ḥšōḇ, but la-ḥăzōr? Sonority, Optimality, and the Hebrew פ"ח Forms*. AKM 66. Wiesbaden: Harrassowitz, 2009.

Baranowski, Kryzstoff. "The Biblical Hebrew *wayyiqtol* and the Evidence of the Amarna Letters from Canaan." *JHS* 16 (2016). https://doi.org/10.5508/jhs.2015.v15.a12.

Ben-Ḥayyim, Ze'ev. *A Grammar of Samaritan Hebrew: Based on the Recitation of the Law in Comparison with the Tiberian and Other Jewish Traditions*. Jerusalem: Magnes; Winona Lake, IN: Eisenbrauns, 2000.

Bergsträsser, Gotthelf. *Hebräische Grammatik*. 2 vols. Leipzig: Hinrichs, 1918–1929.

———. *Introduction to the Semitic Languages: Text Specimens and Grammatical Sketches*. Translated by Peter T. Daniels. Winona Lake, IN: Eisenbrauns, 1983. Originally published as *Einführung in die semitischen Sprachen*. 3rd ed. Munich: Hueber, 1928.

Beyer, Klaus. *Die aramäischen Texte vom Toten Meer*. 2 vols. Göttingen: Vandenhoeck & Ruprecht, 1984–1994.

Blau, Joshua. *A Grammar of Biblical Hebrew*. 2nd ed. PLO 12. Wiesbaden: Harrassowitz, 1993.

———. *On Polyphony in Biblical Hebrew*. PIASH 6/2. Jerusalem: Israel Academy of Sciences and Humanities, 1982.

———. *On Pseudo-Corrections in Some Semitic Languages*. Jerusalem: Israel Academy of Sciences and Humanities, 1970.

———. *Phonology and Morphology of Biblical Hebrew*. LSAWS 2. Winona Lake, IN: Eisenbrauns, 2010.

———. "Stress: Biblical Hebrew." *EHLL* 3:623–25.

———. "'Weak' Phonetic Change and the Hebrew *śîn*." *HAR* 1 (1977): 67–119.

Bordreuil, Pierre, and Dennis Pardee. *A Manual of Ugaritic*. LSAWS 3. Winona Lake, IN: Eisenbrauns, 2009.

Boyd, J. "The Etymological Relationship between *ndr* and *nzr* Reconsidered." *UF* 17 (1986): 61–75.

Brockelmann, Carl. *A Syriac Lexicon: A Translation from the Latin, Correction, Expansion, and Update of C. Brockelmann's Lexicon Syriacum*. Translated by Michael Sokoloff. Winona Lake, IN: Eisenbrauns; Piscataway, NJ: Gorgias, 2009.

Brønno, Einar. *Studien über Hebräische Morphologie und Vokalismus auf Grundlage der mercatischen Fragmente der zweiten Kolumne der Hexapla des Origenes*. AKM 28. Leipzig: Brockhaus, 1943.

Cohen, David. *Dictionnaire des racines sémitiques, ou attestées dans les langues sémitiques*. 10 vols. Leuven: Peeters, 1994–.

Coogan, Michael D. *West Semitic Personal Names in the Murašû Documents*. HSM 7. Missoula, MT: Scholars Press, 1976.

Cook, John A. "The Hebrew Verb: A Grammaticalization Approach." *ZAH* 14 (2001): 117–43.

———. *Time and the Biblical Hebrew Verb*. LSAWS 7. Winona Lake, IN: Eisenbrauns, 2012.

Creason, Stuart. "Aramaic." *CEWAL*, 391–426.

Crystal, David. *A Dictionary of Linguistics and Phonetics*. 6th ed. Oxford: Blackwell, 2008. https://doi.org/10.1002/9781444302776.

Dallaire, Hélène. *Syntax of Volitives in Biblical Hebrew and Amarna Canaanite Prose*. LSAWS 9. Winona Lake, IN: Eisenbrauns, 2014.

Dat, Florin-Mihai. "Métathèse et homonymie en hébreu biblique." *Suvremena lingvistika* 67 (2009): 1–21.

De Caen, V. "Moveable *Nun* and Intrusive *Nun*: The Nature and Distribution of Verbal Nunation in Joel and Job." *JNSL* 29 (2003): 121–32.

Delitzsch, Friedrich. *Die Lese- und Schreibfehler im Alten Testament*. Berlin: de Gruyter, 1920.

Dobbs-Allsopp, F. W., J. J. M. Roberts, C. L. Seow, and Richard E. Whitaker. *Hebrew Inscriptions: Texts from the Biblical Period of the Monarchy with Concordance*. New Haven: Yale University Press, 2005.

Dolgopolsky, Aron. *From Proto-Semitic to Hebrew: Phonology, Etymological Approach in a Hamito-Semitic Perspective*. Studi Camito-Semitici 2. Milan: Centro Studi Camito-Semitici, 1999.

Eddington, David, and Michael Taylor. "T-Glottalization in American English." *American Speech* 84 (2009): 298–314.

Edzard, Lutz. "Biblical Hebrew." *SLIH*, 480–514.

———. "Phonology, Optimality Theory: Biblical Hebrew." *EHLL* 3:134–38.

Eldar, Ilan. "Ashkenazi Pronunciation Tradition: Medieval." *EHLL* 1:185–92.

Fabry, H. J., and U. Dahmen. "פשר." *TDOT* 12:152–58.

Fales, Frederick Mario. "Old Aramaic." *SLIH*, 555–73.

Fassberg, Steven E. "Cohortative." *EHLL* 1:476–77.

———. "Dead Sea Scrolls: Linguistic Features." *EHLL* 1:663–69.

———. "Dissimilation." *EHLL* 1:766–67.

———. "Pausal Forms." *EHLL* 3:54–55.

———. "Two Biblical Hebrew Sound Laws in the Light of Modern Spoken Semitic." Pages 95–100 in *Nicht nur mit Engelszungen: Beiträge zur semitischen Dialektologie; Festschrift für Werner Arnold zum 60. Geburtstag*. Edited by Renaud Kuty, Ulrich Seeger, and Shabo Talay. Wiesbaden: Harrassowitz, 2013.

———. "Why Doesn't *Melex* Appear as *Ma:lex* in Pause in Tiberian Hebrew?" [Hebrew] *Leshonenu* 64 (2002): 207–19.

Fitzgerald, Aloysius. "The Interchange of *L*, *N*, and *R* in Biblical Hebrew." *JBL* 97 (1978): 481–88.

Florentin, Moshe. "Samaritan Hebrew: Biblical." *EHLL* 3:445–52.

———. "Samaritan Tradition." *HBH* 1:117–32; 2:71–89.

Fox, Joshua. *Semitic Noun Patterns*. HSS 52. Winona Lake, IN: Eisenbrauns, 2003.

Gai, Amikam. "The Connection between Past and Optative in the Classical Semitic Languages." *ZDMG* 150 (2000): 17–28.

Garr, W. Randall. *Dialect Geography of Syria-Palestine, 1000–586 B.C.E.* Philadelphia: University of Pennsylvania Press, 1985.

———. "The Paragogic *nun* in Rhetorical Perspective." Pages 65–74 in *Biblical Hebrew in Its Northwest Semitic Setting: Typological and Historical Perspectives*. Edited by Steven E. Fassberg and Avi Hurvitz. Winona Lake, IN: Eisenbrauns, 2006.

———. "Pretonic Vowels in Hebrew." *VT* 37 (1987): 129–53.

———. "The *Seghol* and Segholation in Hebrew." *JNES* 48 (1989): 109–16.

Getz, Rob, and Stephen Pelle. *The Dictionary of Old English*. Toronto: University of Toronto, 2007–.

Gianto, Agustinus. "Archaic Biblical Hebrew." *HBH* 1:19–29.

Gogel, Sandra L. *A Grammar of Epigraphic Hebrew*. RBS 23. Atlanta: Scholars Press, 1998.

Goldsmith, John. "Two Kinds of Phonology." http://tinyurl.com/SBL0395b.

Gzella, Holger. *A Cultural History of Aramaic: From the Beginnings to the Advent of Islam*. HdO 111. Leiden: Brill, 2015.

———. "Deir ʿAllā." *EHLL* 1:691–93.

———. "Imperial Aramaic." *SLIH*, 574–86.

———. "Tiberian-Palestinian Tradition." *HBH* 1:175–85.

———. "מחה." *ThWQ* 2:638–41.

Hackett, Jo Ann. "Phoenician and Punic." *CEWAL*, 365–85.

Harviainen, Tapani. "Transcription into Latin Script: Jerome." *EHLL* 3:822–24.

Hasselbach, Rebecca. "Barth-Ginsberg Law." *EHLL* 1:258–59.

Heijmans, Shai. "Babylonian Tradition." *HBH* 1:133–45; 2:90–99.

Hornkohl, Aaron D. *Ancient Hebrew Periodization and the Language of the Book of Jeremiah: The Case for a Sixth-Century Date of Composition*. SSLL 74. Leiden: Brill, 2014.

———. "Biblical Hebrew: Periodization." *EHLL* 1:315–25.

———. "Transitional Biblical Hebrew." *HBH* 1:31–42.

Huart, C. *Littérature arabe*. Paris: Colin, 1902.

Huehnergard, John. "Afro-Asiatic." *CEWAL*, 138–59.

———. "Akkadian ḫ and West Semitic *ḥ." Pages 102–19 in *Studia Semitica*. Edited by Leonid Kogan. Orientalia 3. Moscow: Russian State University Press, 2003.

———. "Biblical Hebrew Nominal Patterns." Pages 25–64 in *Epigraphy, Philology, and the Hebrew Bible: Methodological Perspectives on Philological and Comparative Study of the Hebrew Bible in Honor of Jo Ann Hackett*. Edited by Jeremy M. Hutton and Aaron D. Rubin. ANEM 12. Atlanta: SBL Press, 2015.

———. "Features of Central Semitic." Pages 155–203 in *Biblical and Oriental Essays in Memory of William L. Moran*. Edited by Agustinus Gianto. BibOr 48. Rome: Pontifical Biblical Institute, 2005.

———. "Philippi's Law." *EHLL* 3:70–71.

———. "*Qātîl* and *Qətîl* Nouns in Biblical Hebrew." Pages *3–*45 in *Shaʿarei Lashon: Studies in Hebrew, Aramaic, and Jewish Languages Presented to Moshe Bar-Asher; Vol I: Biblical Hebrew, Masorah, and Medieval*

Hebrew. Edited by A. Maman, S. E. Fassberg, and Y. Breuer. Jerusalem: Bialik Institute, 2007.

———. "Remarks on the Classification of the Northwest Semitic Languages." Pp 282–93 in *The Balaam Text from Deir ʿAlla Re-Evaluated: Proceedings of the International Symposium Held at Leiden, 21–24 August 1989*. Edited by J. Hoftijzer and G. van der Kooij. Leiden: Brill, 1991.

———. "Segholates: Pre-Modern Hebrew." *EHLL* 3:520–22.

———. *Ugaritic Vocabulary in Syllabic Transcription*. 2nd ed. HSS 32. Winona Lake, IN: Eisenbrauns, 2008.

Huehnergard, John, and Christopher Woods. "Akkadian and Eblaite." *CEWAL*, 218–87.

Huehnergard, John, and Saul Olyan. "The Etymology of Hebrew and Aramaic *ykl* 'To Be Able.'" *JSS* 58 (2013): 13–19.

Hurvitz, Avi. "Biblical Hebrew, Late." *EHLL* 1:329–38.

Hutton, Jeremy. "Epigraphic Hebrew: Pre-Roman Period." *EHLL* 1:835–42.

IPA Chart. University of Victoria, British Columbia. https://web.uvic.ca/ling/resources/ipa/charts/IPAlab/IPAlab.htm.

Janssens, Gerard. *Studies in Hebrew Historical Linguistics Based on Origen's Secunda*. OrGand 9. Leuven: Peeters, 1982.

Joosten, Jan. "The Hebrew of the Dead Sea Scrolls." *HBH* 1:83–97.

———. "Verbal System: Biblical Hebrew." *EHLL* 3:921–25.

———. *The Verbal System of Biblical Hebrew: A New Synthesis Elaborated on the Basis of Classical Prose*. JBS 10. Jerusalem: Simor, 2012.

Kaufman, Stephen A. "On Vowel Reduction in Aramaic." *JAOS* 104 (1984): 87–95.

———. "Paragogic *Nun* in Biblical Hebrew: Hypercorrection as a Clue to a Lost Scribal Practice." Pages 95–99 in *Solving Riddles, Untying Knots: Biblical, Epigraphic, and Semitic Studies in Honor of Jonas C. Greenfield*. Edited by Ziony Zevit, Seymour Gitin, and Michael Sokoloff. Winona Lake, IN: Eisenbrauns, 1995.

Khan, Geoffrey. "Biblical Hebrew: Linguistic Background of the Masoretic Text." *EHLL* 1:304–15.

———. "Biblical Hebrew: Pronunciation Traditions." *EHLL* 1:341–52.

———. "Compensatory Lengthening." *EHLL* 3:500–504.

———. "Epenthesis: Biblical Hebrew." *EHLL* 1:831–33.

———. "The Historical Background of the Vowel *ṣere* in Some Hebrew Verbal and Nominal Forms." *BSOAS* 57 (1994): 133–44.

———. "Karaite Transcriptions of Biblical Hebrew." *HBH* 1:147–60.

———. "Pretonic Lengthening: Biblical Hebrew." *EHLL* 3:224–29.
———. "Shewa: Pre-modern Hebrew." *EHLL* 3:543–54.
———. "Some Parallels in Linguistic Development between Biblical Hebrew and Neo-Aramaic." Pages 84–108 in *Semitic Studies in Honour of Edward Ullendorff*. Edited by Geoffrey Khan. SSLL 47. Leiden: Brill, 2005.
———. Syllable Structure: Biblical Hebrew." *EHLL* 3:666–76.
———. "The Tiberian Pronunciation Tradition of Biblical Hebrew." *ZAH* 9 (1996): 1–23.
———. "Tiberian Reading Tradition." *EHLL* 3:769–78.
———. "Vowel Length: Biblical Hebrew," *EHLL* 3:981–85.
Kogan, Leonid. "Proto-Semitic Phonetics and Phonology." *SLIH*, 54–151.
———. "Proto-Semitic Lexicon." *SLIH*, 179–258.
Koller, Aaron. "Attenuation." *EHLL* 1:231–232.
Kuryłowicz, Jerzy. *Studies in Semitic Grammar and Metrics*. Prace Językoznawcze 67. Wrocław: Zakład Narodowy imienia Ossolińskich, 1973.
Kutscher, E. Y. *The Language and Linguistic Background of the Complete Isaiah Scroll*. STDJ 6. Leiden: Brill, 1974.
Labrune, Laurence. *The Phonology of Japanese*. Phonology of the World's Languages. Oxford: Oxford University Press, 2012.
Labuschagne, C. J. "Original Shaphʿel Forms in Biblical Hebrew." *OTWSA* 13 (1971): 51–64.
Lam, Joseph, and Dennis Pardee. "Standard/Classical Biblical Hebrew." *HBH* 1:1–18.
Lambdin, Thomas O. *Introduction to Biblical Hebrew*. New York: Scribners, 1971.
———. "Philippi's Law Reconsidered." Pages 135–45 in *Biblical Studies Presented to Samuel Iwry*. Edited by Ann Kort and Samuel Morschauser. Winona Lake, IN: Eisenbrauns, 1985.
Lambdin, Thomas O., and John Huehnergard. "The Historical Grammar of Classical Hebrew: An Outline." Unpublished manuscript, last modified 2000.
Landes, George M. *Building Your Biblical Hebrew Vocabulary: Learning Words by Frequency and Cognate*. RBS 41. Atlanta: Society of Biblical Literature, 2001.
Malkiel, Yakov. "Weak Phonetic Change, Spontaneous Sound Shift, Lexical Contamination." *Lingua* 11 (1962): 263–75.
Mandell, Alice. "Biblical Hebrew, Archaic." *EHLL* 1:325–29.

McCarter, P. Kyle. "Hebrew." *CEWAL*, 319–64.

Mercati, G. *Psalterii Hexapli Religuiqae, pars, prima, Codex rescriptus Bybliothecae Ambrosianae O. 39 SVP: Phototypice expressus et transcriptus*. Rome: Pontifical Biblical Institute, 1958.

Militarev, Alexander, and Leonid Kogan, *Semitic Etymological Dictionary*. 2 vols. AOAT 278. Münster: Ugarit-Verlag, 2000–2005.

Millard, Alan. "Transcriptions into Cuneiform." *EHLL* 3:838–47.

Mitchel, Larry A. *A Student's Vocabulary for Biblical Hebrew and Aramaic*. Grand Rapids: Zondervan, 1984.

Mor, Uri. "Bar Kokhba Documents." *EHLL* 1:254–58.

———. *Judean Hebrew: The Language of the Hebrew Documents from Judea between the First and Second Revolts* [Hebrew]. Jerusalem: Academy of the Hebrew Language, 2016.

Morgenstern, Matthew. "Late Biblical Hebrew." *HBH* 1:43–54.

Muraoka, T. *A Grammar of Qumran Aramaic*. ANESSupp 38. Leuven: Peeters, 2011.

Ofer, Yosef. "The Tiberian Tradition of Reading the Bible and the Masoretic System." *HBH* 1:187–202.

Pardee, Dennis. "Ugaritic." *CEWAL*, 288–318.

———. "Ypḥ 'Witness' in Hebrew and Ugaritic." *VT* 28 (1978): 204–13.

Pat-El, Naʿama. "Israelian Hebrew: A Re-Evaluation." *VT* 67 (2017): 227–63.

Pat-El, Naʿama, and Aren Wilson-Wright. "Deir ʿAllā as a Canaanite Dialect: A Vindication of Hackett." Pages 13–23 in *Epigraphy, Philology, and the Hebrew Bible: Methodological Perspectives on Philological and Comparative Study of the Hebrew Bible in Honor of Jo Ann Hackett*. Edited by Jeremy M. Hutton and Aaron D. Rubin. ANEM 12. Atlanta: SBL Press, 2015.

Qimron, Elisha. *Hebrew of the Dead Sea Scrolls*. HSS 29. Atlanta: Scholars Press, 1986.

Rainey, Anson. *Canaanite in the Amarna Tablets: A Linguistic Analysis of the Mixed Dialect Used by Scribes from Canaan*. 4 vols. HdO 1.25. Leiden: Brill, 1996.

Rendsburg, Gary A. "Ancient Hebrew Phonology." Pages 1:65–83 in *Phonologies of Asia and Africa*. Edited by Alan S. Kaye. Winona Lake, IN: Eisenbrauns, 1997.

———.Biblical Hebrew: Dialects and Linguistic Variation." *EHLL* 3:338–41.

———. "A Comprehensive Guide to Israelian Hebrew." *Or* 38 (2003): 5–35.

Retsö, Jan. "Aramaic/Syriac Loanwords." Pages 1:178–82 in *Encyclopedia of Arabic Language and Linguistics*. Edited by K. Versteegh et al. Leiden: Brill, 2006–2009.

Reymond, Eric D. "The 3ms Suffix on Nouns Written with *Heh* Mater." In *"Like 'Ilu Are You Wise": Studies in Northwest Semitic Languages and Literatures in Honor of Dennis G. Pardee*. Edited by H. Hardy, Joseph Lam, and Eric D. Reymond. Chicago: Oriental Institute of the University of Chicago, forthcoming.

———. "The Passive *Qal* in the Hebrew of the Second Temple Period, Especially as Found in the Wisdom of Ben Sira." Pages 2:1110–27 in *Sibyls, Scriptures, and Scrolls: John Collins at Seventy*. Edited by Joel Baden, Hindy Najman, and Eibert Tigchelaar. 2 vols. JSJSup 175. Leiden: Brill, 2016.

———. *Qumran Hebrew: An Overview of Orthography, Phonology, and Morphology*. RBS 76. Atlanta: Society of Biblical Literature, 2014.

Rubin, Aaron D. "Sumerian Loanwords." *EHLL* 3:665–66.

Schott, Ben. *Schott's Original Miscellany*. New York: Bloomsbury, 2002.

Segert, Stanislav. *A Grammar of Phoenician and Punic*. Munich: Beck, 1976.

Seow, Choon-Leong. *A Grammar for Biblical Hebrew*. Rev. ed. Nashville: Abingdon, 1995.

Shatil, Nimrod. "Guttural Consonants: Modern Hebrew." *EHLL* 2:169–72.

Sivan, Daniel. *Grammatical Analysis and Glossary of the Northwest Semitic Vocables in Akkadian Texts of the 15th–13th c.B.C. from Canaan and Syria*. AOAT 214. Kevelaer: Butzon & Bercker; Neukirchen-Vluyn: Neukirchener Verlag, 1984.

Sperber , Alexander. *A Historical Grammar of Biblical Hebrew: A Presentation of Problems with Suggestions to Their Solutions*. Leiden: Brill, 1966.

Stadel, Christian. "Aramaic Influence on Biblical Hebrew." *EHLL* 1:162–65.

Steiner, Richard C. "Addenda to *The Case for Fricative-Laterals in Proto-Semitic*." Pages 1499–1513 in *Semitic Studies in Honor of Wolf Leslau on the Occasion of His Eighty-Fifth Birthday, November 14th, 1991*. Edited by Alan S. Kaye. Wiesbaden: Harrassowitz, 1991.

———. *The Case for Fricative-Laterals in Proto-Semitic*. AOS 59. New Haven: American Oriental Society, 1977.

———. *Early Northwest Semitic Serpent Spells in the Pyramid Texts*. HSS 61. Winona Lake, IN: Eisenbrauns, 2011.

———. "On the Dating of Hebrew Sound Changes (*Ḫ > Ḥ and *Ġ > ʿ) and Greek Translations (2 Esdras and Judith)." *JBL* 124 (2005): 229–67.

———. "On the Monophthongization of *ay to ī in Phoenician and Northern Hebrew and the Preservation of Arachaic / Dialectal Forms in the Masoretic Vocalization." *Orientalia* 76 (2007): 73–83.

———. "On the Origin of the *Ḥéðɛr* ~ *Ḥăðár* Alternation in Hebrew." *AfAsL* 3 (1976): 1–18.

———. "Variation, Simplifying Assumptions, and the History of Spirantization in Aramaic and Hebrew." Pages *52–*65 in *Shaʿarei Lashon: Studies in Hebrew, Aramaic, and Jewish Languages Presented to Moshe Bar-Asher; Vol I: Biblical Hebrew, Masorah, and Medieval Hebrew.* Edited by A. Maman, S. E. Fassberg, and Y. Breuer. Jerusalem: Bialik Institute, 2007.

Streck, Michael P. "Akkadian and Aramaic Language Contact." *SLIH*, 416–24.

Taylor, C. *Hebrew-Greek Cairo Genizah Palimpsests from the Taylor-Schechter Collections, Including a Fragment of the Twenty-Second Psalm according to Origen's Hexapla*. Cambridge: Cambridge University Press, 1900.

Testen, David. *Parallels in Semitic Linguistics: The Development of Arabic la- and Related Semitic Particles*. SSLL 26. Leiden: Brill, 1998.

———. "The Significance of Aramaic r < *n." *JNES* 44 (1985): 143–46.

Tov, Emanuel. *Textual Criticism of the Hebrew Bible*. 3rd rev. ed. Minneapolis: Fortress, 2012.

Tropper, Josef. "Akkadisch *nuḫḫutu* und die Repräsentation des Phonems /ḥ/ im Akkadischen." *ZA* 85 (1995): 58–66.

———. *Ugaritische Grammatik*. AOAT 273. Münster: Ugarit-Verlag, 2000.

Van Pelt, Miles V., and Gary D. Pratico. *The Vocabulary Guide to Biblical Hebrew*. Grand Rapids: Zondervan, 2003.

Yahalom, Joseph. "Palestinian Tradition." *HBH* 1:161–73.

Yuditsky, Alexey (Eliyahu). "דְּבַשׁ and Similar Forms" [Hebrew]. *Leshonenu* 71 (2009): 281–86.

———. "Hebrew in Greek and Latin Transcriptions." *HBH* 1:99–116; 2:62–70.

———. "New Readings of MS O39 from the Ambrosian Library" [Hebrew]. *Leshonenu* 68 (2008): 63–71.

———. "On Origen's Transliterations as Preserved in the Works of the Church Fathers" [Hebrew]. *Leshonenu* 69 (2007): 301–10.

———. "Reduced Vowels in the Transcriptions from Hebrew in the Hexapla" [Hebrew]. *Leshonenu* 67 (2005): 121–41.

———. "Transcription into Greek and Latin Script: Pre-masoretic Period." *EHLL* 3:803–22.

Wagner, Max. *Die lexikalischen und grammatikalischen Aramaismen im alttestamentlichen Hebräisch*. BZAW 96. Berlin: Töpelmann, 1966.

Webster, B. "Chronological Index of the Texts from the Judaean Desert." Pages 351–446 in *The Texts from the Judaean Desert: Indices and an Introduction to Discoveries in the Judaean Desert Series*. Edited by E. Tov et al. DJD 39. Oxford: Clarendon, 2002.

Wright, W., et al. *A Grammar of the Arabic Language*. 3rd ed. 2 vols. Cambridge: Cambridge University Press, 1896–1898.

Zewi, Tamar. *A Syntactical Study of Verbal Forms Affixed by -n(n) Endings in Classical Arabic, Biblical Hebrew, El-Amarna Akkadian and Ugaritic*. AOAT 260. Münster: Ugarit-Verlag, 1999.

Ancient Sources Index

Author Index

Rubin, Aaron D. 137 n. 46
Schott, Ben 26 n. 30
Segert, Stanislav 77 n. 45,
Seow, Choon-Leong 10 n. 3, 165 n. 8
Shatil, Nimrod 9 n. 2
Sivan, Daniel 23 n. 17, 30 n. 44, 96 n. 107, 100 n. 122, 104 n. 132, 153 n. 81
Sokoloff, Michael 27 nn. 32 and 34, 172 n. 29
Sperber , Alexander 9 n. 1, 105 n. 135, 116 n. 4, 140 n. 56, 166 n. 9
Stadel, Christian 33 n. 55, 97 n. 110, 98 nn. 111–12, 138 n. 48, 158 n. 101
Steiner, Richard C. 22, 22 nn. 13 and 15, 23 n. 18, 24, 24 nn. 21–22 and 24, 25, 25 nn. 25–26, 27, 27 n. 33, 44 nn. 91 and 93, 96 n. 107, 103 n. 131, 158 n. 99, 228 n. 15
Streck, Michael P. 28 n. 34
Taylor, C. 64 n. 5
Taylor, Michael 18 n. 1
Testen, David 47 n. 102, 130 n. 29, 168 n. 16
Tov, Emanuel 57 n. 140
Tropper, Josef 19 n. 3, 28, 28 n. 35
Van Pelt, Miles V. 42 n. 87
Yahalom, Joseph 16 n. 25, 69 n. 28
Yuditsky, Alexey (Eliyahu) 29 n. 38, 64 nn. 4–5, 65 n. 12, 69 n. 26, 70 n. 31, 84 n. 68, 89 nn. 79–80, 90 nn. 81 and 83, 91 n. 85, 92 n. 92, 93 n. 94, 96 n. 104, 106 n. 142, 152 n. 77, 231 n. 21
Wagner, Max 44 n. 93, 47 n. 102
Webster, B. 22 n. 16
Wilson-Wright, Aren 14 n. 12
Woods, Christopher 167 n. 13
Wright, W. 19 n. 5
Zewi, Tamar 172 nn. 28–29, 173 nn. 30–31 and 33, 174 n. 36, 175 n. 40

Word Index

Printed in the USA
CPSIA information can be obtained
at www.ICGtesting.com
LVHW051820131123
763817LV00004B/555

9 781628 371895